Law and Philosophy Library

Volume 128

The Law and Philosophy Library, which has been in existence since 1985, aims to publish cutting edge works in the philosophy of law, and has a special history of publishing books that focus on legal reasoning and argumentation, including those that may involve somewhat formal methodologies. The series has published numerous important books on law and logic, law and artificial intelligence, law and language, and law and rhetoric. While continuing to stress these areas, the series has more recently expanded to include books on the intersection between law and the Continental philosophical tradition, consistent with the traditional openness of the series to books in the Continental jurisprudential tradition. The series is proud of the geographic diversity of its authors, and many have come from Latin America, Spain, Italy, the Netherlands, Germany, and Eastern Europe, as well, more obviously for an English-language series, from the United Kingdom, the United States, Australia and Canada.

More information about this series at http://www.springer.com/series/6210

Pierluigi Chiassoni

Interpretation without Truth

A Realistic Enquiry

Springer

Pierluigi Chiassoni
Dipartimento di Giurisprudenza
Università di Genova
Genova, Italy

ISSN 1572-4395 ISSN 2215-0315 (electronic)
Law and Philosophy Library
ISBN 978-3-030-15588-9 ISBN 978-3-030-15590-2 (eBook)
https://doi.org/10.1007/978-3-030-15590-2

Cover design: eStudio Calamar, Berlin/Figueres

This Springer imprint is published by the registered company Springer Nature Switzerland AG.
The registered company address is: Gewerbestrasse 11, 6330 Cham, Switzerland

Contents

Chapter 1
Introduction: The Path of Analytical Realism

El hoy fugaz es tenue y es eterno; otro Cielo no esperes, ni otro Infierno

—J. L. Borges (1964)

1.1 On "Realism" and "Scepticism" in Jurisprudence

Scepticism is not a flourishing stance in contemporary jurisprudence. Hart's criticism of "rule-scepticism" in the seventh chapter of *The Concept of Law*, and the "middle path" about adjudication, the path of "vigil orthodoxy", he and fellow theorists vindicated, since the 1960s, in between the "nightmare" of (extreme) realism and formalism's "noble dream", still hold sway in legal theory, Common Law and Civil Law alike.[1] As a consequence, scepticism stands to many jurisprudes for picturesque bad view: an exaggeration from a by-gone province of learning, still unreasonably endorsed by a handful of nostalgic casts of mind.

This is unfortunate. Influential criticisms notwithstanding, scepticism (and its embedding outlook, realism) represents the good theory in town. A few terminological clarifications are worth the making, if only to prevent misunderstandings.

The expression "(legal) scepticism" is sometimes used as interchangeable with "(legal) realism" in jurisprudential discourse. This is misleading. To put it bluntly, realist theories of law—namely, as I understand them, hard-boiled empiricist and analytical legal theories—qualify as "sceptical" in the eye of friends and foes, for, in the criticism they rise against "formalism", "conceptualism" and, generally, any sort of naïf or pretended "objectivism" and "cognitivism" concerning law, they cast the light of doubt upon those rosy views, making appeal to the tribunal of facts. "Scepticism" about legal rules, legal concepts, legal interpretation, adjudication and

[1] Hart (1961), pp. 124–154; see also Hart (1977), pp. 123–143. Among the theorists who adopt the same, or a similar view, see, e.g., Carrió (1965), part II, Bulygin (1991), Marmor (2005), Moreso (1997a, b).

P. Chiassoni, *Interpretation without Truth*, Law and Philosophy Library 128,
https://doi.org/10.1007/978-3-030-15590-2_1

legal science is, accordingly, not tantamount to "realism", but, rather, a characteristic note of realist theories of law.[2]

To readers' benefit, it may be useful anticipating, in a very rough and apodictic, way, what I consider to be the central tenets of a realist, sceptical, outlook about the subjects the present book is primarily concerned with, namely, legal interpretation and adjudication.

1. Authoritative texts—source-sentences or legal provisions like, e.g., constitutional clauses, statutory provisions, regulatory provisions, etc.—are not self-interpreting entities. There must always be some interpreter to associate meaning to the otherwise dead letter of their words and phrases.
2. Authoritative texts and the previous juristic and judicial interpretations and integrations (supplements, gap-fillings) thereof, are not self-applying entities. There must always be some interpreter who takes into account the texts, together with the previous interpretations and integrations provided for them in the legal culture, and, upon a judgment that may involve selecting, modifying, or refining such previous interpretations and integrations, applies them to the individual cases at hand.
3. Authoritative texts are methodologically ambiguous. From a strictly methodological standpoint, that is to say, from the vantage point of the interpretive techniques (canons, directives, maxims, rules, principles) available in our legal cultures "here and now", authoritative texts are always capable of a plurality of alternative meanings. Indeed, any authoritative sentence whatsoever is open, technically speaking, to three alternative sorts of reading: a literal reading, an extended reading, or a restricted reading. For lovers of clear and distinct ideas,

[2] The literature on legal realism (rule-scepticism, realistic jurisprudence, etc.) is immense. Concerning contemporary reflection on legal realism, the reader may profit, to begin with, from essays by Brian Leiter (2007, 2012, 2013), Schauer (2013, 2018), Torben Spaak (2015), Dagan (2013, 2017, 2018), and the law-and-society jurists rallying under the banner of "New Legal Realism"—see, e.g., the papers collected for the Symposium "Is It Time for a New Legal Realism?" ("Wisconsin Law Review", 2005), the Symposium "The New Legal Realism" ("Law & Social Inquiry", 2006), and the two recent volumes edited by Elizabeth Mertz, Stewart Macaulay, and Thomas W. Mitchell: Mertz, Macaulay, Mitchell (2016). As it is well known, Leiter vindicates American Legal Realism against Hart's criticism and presents it as a prototype of a naturalized jurisprudence purporting to "describe legal phenomena" as they in fact are (Leiter 2007, 2012). On the same path, the New Legal Realists advocate a genuine and thorough interdisciplinary, not imperialistic, and methodologically pluralist approach to legal knowledge, combining traditional legal scholarship's doctrinal analysis with advanced social theory, the study of the "law in books" with the study of the "law in action" ("theory-driven empirical research about law in action that values qualitative as well quantitative and experimental research": McCann (2016), p. xiv; Mertz (2016), p. 3: "getting formal law and the "real world" (and in particular, the reality of the law in action as it has been revealed by decades of social science) into conversation with one another"). On the Continent, realism is presently the livery of several legal theorists, some of which belonging to the "Genoa School" (see Chiassoni 1998; Ferrer and Ratti 2010; Guastini 2015, pp. 45–54; Barberis 2016, pp. 1–8).

realism characterizes here for making an empirical claim about the universal methodological ambiguity of legal provisions.[3]

4. Authoritative texts are ideologically ambiguous. Legal cultures are typically characterized by ethical pluralism. Judges, jurists and people-at-large—even in apparently monolithic societies—typically entertain different views about the "proper" way to see the constitution, judicial review, the role of parliament, judicial interpretation, etc. As a consequence, the same legal provisions are likely to receive competing, mutually exclusive, interpretations, when they turn out as battlefields for ideological warfare. To be sure, they can also be the points where an overlapping consensus about their "proper meaning" obtains. In such an event, they are, so to speak, the "parts of the (positive law) boat" nobody (no reasonable jurist), at least during a certain time-span, would wish or dare fighting upon[4]; and the cases they regulate turn out to be (inter-ideological) easy cases.[5]
5. Judicial and juristic interpretation of authoritative texts are reflective undertakings. From a psychological point of view, they typically belong to the reflective working of the mind, not to its automatic working. They are the outputs of so-called "System 2", not of so-called "System 1".[6] Accordingly, so far as judicial interpretation of legal provisions is concerned, any view purporting to draw a line between mere understanding, which would be immediate, unreflective, and afoot in "easy cases", and interpretation proper, which would take place, instead, in case of doubt ("hard cases"), provides a misleading, impoverished, picture of the phenomenon.[7]
6. Judicial and juristic interpretation of authoritative texts are holistic undertakings. No authoritative clause, even when a judge applies it in its clear literal or conventional meaning, is ever interpreted "by itself": i.e., as an isolated legal sentence that emits a linguistic stimulus perceived by automatically reacting judicial readers. Rather, it is always interpreted within the background, and as a particle, of a larger set of rules and principles, which, for example, justify its literal interpretation and application as systemically correct.[8]
7. Judicial interpretation of authoritative texts never is a purely cognitive undertaking: never is, in Kelsenian terms,[9] a pure "act of cognition". Rather, it always

---

[3] I will come back on this thesis in chapter and Chap. 4 below.

[4] From a conceptual standpoint, I will account for this phenomenon by means of the notion of conjectural ideological interpretation. See Chap. 2, Sect. 2.2.1.2, below.

[5] On this subject, I will come back in Chap. 6, Sect. 6.5.4, below.

[6] For this distinction, see Kahneman (2011), pp. 20–24. The reflective character of juristic interpretation will be argued for in this chapter, under the headings of juristic textual, meta-textual and conjectural interpretation. The reflective character of judicial interpretation will be argued for in several parts of the book (Chaps. 2–6).

[7] See Chap. 6 below.

[8] See Chap. 6 below.

[9] Kelsen (1960), ch. VIII.

involves some piece of practical commitment.[10] To begin with, any interpretation whatsoever necessarily depends on the previous selection of interpretive criteria (rules) and interpretive resources by the acting interpreter, and this involves volition and decision-making. Furthermore, interpretive criteria and interpretive resources are usually selected out of allegiance to some legal ideology (some normative vision of positive law), which sets the "proper" goals interpretation must realize. As a consequence, any view purporting to present judicial interpretation as a cognitive enterprise, either universally, or in some sort of situations (the notorious "easy cases"), provides an impoverished, false picture of the phenomenon. To be sure, interpretive volition may sometimes be of a purely conformist sort: the interpreter decides to follow the herd, i.e., an established, majoritarian, interpretive practice, considering it to be the only course of action in fact viable to her; though, while doing so, she may deem such a way of proceeding to be unreasonable, unjust, or seriously inconvenient. A conformist decision, however, is still a decision.[11]

8. Judicial interpretation of authoritative texts is a discretionary enterprise. Judges are expressly or tacitly endowed with two basic discretionary powers, which are both required in order for them to decide individual cases. To begin with, there is the power of making decisions concerning the "correct" set of interpretation rules to be used for identifying the "correct" interpretive output and justifying it (methodological discretion).[12] Furthermore, there is the power of making decisions concerning the "correct" set of interpretive resources to be used in applying the interpretive rules that have been previously selected (resources discretion).[13]

[10] Guastini (2015, pp. 45–54) claims that judicial and most of juristic interpretation is never purely cognitive in character (never purely a matter of "knowledge"), but always involves some decision (always a matter of "will"), because legal texts, or rule-formulations (like, e.g., a constitutional provision), are indeterminate, and they are indeterminate both at the level of "abstract interpretation", due to the ambiguity of rule-formulations, and at the level of "concrete interpretation", due to the vagueness of the predicate terms used in rule-formulations. In other words, Guastini grounds (what we may call) his "universal decisional character" thesis about the nature of legal interpretation on a "universal indeterminacy thesis": universal indeterminacy makes decision-making necessary, when interpreting a rule-formulation to any practical purpose. Guastini, however, affirms that rule-formulations are "often ambiguous"; furthermore, as we all know, vagueness is an intermittent phenomenon: any predicate term can be vague, but is never vague all the time, as regards to any individual case whatsoever. Such points, clearly, are to the effect of undermining the universal decisional character thesis. Accordingly, if we want to rescue it, the universal indeterminacy thesis must be rephrased, in terms of a universal methodological indeterminacy, and supplemented with further argument, coping with situations where methodological indeterminacy is reduced (overcome) by an on-going cultural (and ideological) convergence upon "one" reasonable method and result. This is what I am going to do in this book, both in the present anticipation of the basic claims of realism, and in the following chapters.

[11] See Chap. 6, Sect. 6.3.2, below.

[12] In turn, methodological discretion comes in two varieties: selection discretion and application discretion (see Chap. 6, Sect. 6.2, below).

[13] See Chap. 6, Sect. 6.6, below.

Upon consideration, as we shall see with more detail in Chap. 5, there would be no room, in a legal culture, for conferring interpretive discretion, if the legal culture were characterized by the existence of an ideally-working interpretive code: namely, by the presence of an interpretive code characterized by the joint properties of being (a) objective, (b) intrinsically endowed with strict normativity, (c) exclusive, and (d) efficient. Where, saying it in passing, a code is *objective*, when it is an evident datum to every judge and jurist: something "out there", which can just be known by any competent lawyer. It is *intrinsically endowed with strict normativity*, when, to any competent lawyer, it is in itself binding, and undefeasibly so, on interpretation. It is *exclusive*, when no alternative objective code exists. And, finally, it is *efficient*, when the rules of the objective code (in particular, as we shall see, its translation rules) always point to definite sets of interpretive resources (which are, as we have said, the data necessary to apply them), and, in relation to such sets of resources, always point to (just) *one* definite interpretive conclusion for any case at hand.[14]

Unfortunately, such an objective, intrinsically and strictly normative, exclusive, and efficient code was never seen in our legal experiences[15]; and, due to the set of properties that characterizes it, it is very unlikely it can ever be seen. Furthermore, even if it existed, being a set of directives in a natural language, it would be neither self-interpreting, nor self-applying: How should interpreters proceed in interpreting the objective interpretive code? Perhaps, only a comprehensive, and successful, training process of psychological internalization—one that would turn the use of the code into a set of "quasi-natural" behaviours, one that would make the use of its rules something like a "second nature" for interpreters—would do.[16] A legal experience endowed with an interpretive code working in that naturalized mood, however, would be a reality very far away from our legal experiences. It would be something extremely weird. At the point that we could even doubt whether, in such situation, there would be law, at least of the variety we are acquainted to.

It may happen, to be sure, that, in a given legal culture, in relation to a certain kind of legal provisions (say, criminal or property law statutes), a certain interpretive code comes to be widely regarded by judges and jurists as the only "correct" interpretive code, and acquires in that way a (contingent) social objectivity and (something very close to) intrinsic and strict normativity. Also in those situations, however, interpreters will typically have occasions for exercising methodological discretion. They will fatally be called to making reasoned choices about precisifying, putting into hierarchical order, and enriching the directives of the "objective" code.

---

[14] On interpretive codes, see Chap. 3, Sects. 3.4, 3.5, 3.6, and Chap. 6, Sect. 6.3.2, below. In the text, I consider *interpretive* discretion only. Like conclusions hold for the twin activity of filling up gaps and identifying law's "implicit" norms. On this issue, see Chap. 2, Sect. 2.2.1.2, and Chap. 7, below.

[15] Think, for a telling instance, at the French Exegetical School (Chiassoni 2016a, ch. IV).

[16] On these phenomena, see e.g. Celano (2016), pp. 2–16.

9. Judicial interpretation of authoritative texts is a creative enterprise. It does "create law", it does "make law", in view of the decision of the individual cases at hand. How can that be? How can we make sense of this "creation" metaphor? From a realist vantage point, there are apparently (not fewer than) five different ways for judicial interpretation to be a "creative" undertaking: namely, by selection, repair, correction, methodological innovation, and enrichment.[17]

To begin with, judicial interpretation can "create law" by selection. This occurs when judges choose one meaning out of the several, alternative, determinate meanings that, for one and the same authoritative text (say, a given constitutional provision), can be justified on the basis either of current interpretive methods as a whole, or of those methods that are in tune with the several legal ideologies actually competing inside of the legal culture. The creative import of judicial interpretation consists, here, in overcoming the methodological and ideological ambiguity of authoritative texts, if only for the individual case at hand, by an act of semantic reduction that constitutively establishes a one-to-one relationship between the text, on the one hand, and one determinate meaning, on the other. Such a reduction presupposes a methodological choice in favour of some set of interpretive rules and interpretive resources, which sets are being treated as paramount as to the individual piece of interpretation to be performed.

Second, judicial interpretation can "create law" by repair. This occurs when judges fix up the defective objective meaning of the relevant legal provision at hand. The objective meaning of an authoritative text—usually, the literal, or customary, or established case-law meaning—can be defective in different ways: either by syntactic, semantic, or (illocutionary) pragmatic ambiguity, or by vagueness. In all these cases, it reveals loose ends that need repairing. The creative import of judicial interpretation consists, here, in the "sewing up" of such loose ends by means of disambiguation and precisification.

Third, judicial interpretation can "create law" by correction. This occurs when judges regard the objective meaning of the relevant provisions at hand as substantially un-correct (wrong, unlawful, illegitimate, un-constitutional): usually, by being either "over"-inclusive, or "under"-inclusive, as to the individual case at hand. The creative import of judicial interpretation consists, here, in rectifying the un-correct objective meaning: that is to say, in replacing it with a different meaning that judges consider as the proper and legally correct one for the case at hand.

Fourth, judicial interpretation can "create law" by methodological innovation. This occurs when judges provide a new meaning for the relevant legal provision at hand, on the basis of some new, so far never employed, interpretive method, that either exploits some new set of interpretive resources, or permits to use old sets of resources differently. The creative import of judicial interpre-

[17] On judicial creation of law, the most illuminating essays are, to my knowledge, Carrió (1965), Bulygin (1966), Wróblewski (1992). The account I provide in the text takes a different stance, though. I will come back to this issue in Chap. 4 below.

tation consists, here, in deciding a case at hand on the basis of a norm, presented as the meaning of an authoritative text, which is different from the ones previously "in stock".

Fifth, and finally, judicial interpretation can "create law" by enrichment. This occurs when judges add to the set of previously identified norms of the system some new, explicit or implicit, norm. These represent usually the conclusions of rhetorical forms of reasoning (by analogy, *a contrario*, *a fortiori*, from the nature of things, from principles, from juristic concepts, from juristic theories of legal institutes, etc.) from previously identified norms (usually, from norms which are the meanings of authoritative texts), and are typically added in order to fill up gaps, overcoming antinomies, concretizing legal principles, or bringing to the light the full micro normative system concerning a certain topic.[18] Here, when new implicit norms are at stake, we are by definition using an expanded meaning of "judicial interpretation", one that encompasses but goes beyond the translation of authoritative texts into (explicit) norms and consists in some piece of integration or "construction".[19]

I am conscious that the above theory of judicial creation of law may look puzzling. We may wonder about the actual occurrence and the degrees of creative intensity that characterize the five forms of interpretive creation above. Let me make a few remarks. The selection variety of interpretive creation becomes apparent whenever the interpretation of a legal text—say, some constitutional clause—is a disputed matter in the legal culture, and different methods, leading to different results, are at stake. In these situations, selection determines, for instance, which constitution the parties to a lawsuit (and, eventually, people at large) are going to live by. However, due to the fact that authoritative texts are not self-interpreting entities, and are methodologically ambiguous, creation by selection is a "global" phenomenon. It goes undercover, though, when interpreters are conformist in applying one and the same method, to one and the same result. In such an event, the degree of creative intensity connected to selection is very low. Contrariwise, the repair, correction, methodological innovation and enrichment varieties of interpretive creation are "local" phenomena. They show up in some cases only, and their degree of creative intensity is usually high, and sometimes very high.

[18] When I talk of explicit norms being created by enrichment, I have in mind the situations where a given legal provision, say LP_1, which is usually taken to express a certain norm, N_1, is made to express also a further norm, N_2 ($LP_1 = N_1$ & N_2, where "=" stands for "means" or "expresses"). On the phenomenon of "complexity" in the meaning of legal provisions, see Guastini (2011a), pp. 41–42. According to Eugenio Bulygin, judges make law whenever the general norm they apply to an individual case at hand is neither identical to any already existing norm, nor a logical derivation from already existing norms (Bulygin 1966, pp. 75–87). This is a normativist approach, deliberately opaque to interpretation. Contrariwise, the five notions of judicial lawmaking I consider in the text are interpretation-transparent. These two theoretical standpoints will be considered with more detail in Chap. 7.

[19] On this point, see Chap. 2 below.

10. When the desired result—what the judge regards as the legally just or legally correct solution to the case at hand—cannot be reached by ordinary interpretive techniques, judges can, and do usually, proceed by playing with the facts of the case (what has also been called "equitable understanding of facts", or "equitable balancing of facts"[20]). Traditionally, up to the point of resorting, in favourable cultural circumstances, to judicial fiction.[21]
11. From the standpoint of the practice of interpretation, the whole process of law-making appears a complex collective venture, where the legislature provides authoritative texts (legal provisions) and the interpreters—judges and jurists—provide the explicit and implicit meaning-contents of those texts. They both "make law", though in different guises and at different stages of the law-making process. The legislature "makes law" as a set of authoritative words and sentences. Judges (and, by way of proposal, jurists) "make law" as a set of rules and principles that are the interpretive, rhetorical "consequences" of those authoritative words and sentences.[22]
12. Judicial and juristic interpretation represent a pervasive phenomenon in any mature legal experience, like current Civil Law and Common Law legal systems. Legal theory must adjust its terminology and conceptual apparatus to the pervasive phenomenon of interpretation. It must consciously set apart interpretation-opaque from interpretation-transparent theoretical concepts.[23]

1.2 Overview

My aim, in this book, is elucidating and providing support for the realistic, sceptical claims above, as they bear on the theory of legal interpretation and a few related matters including adjudication, legal gaps, judicial precedent, judicial fictions, defeasibility, and legislation.

Chapter 2, "Interpretation, Truth, and the Logical Forms of Interpretive Discourse", sets the stage. It purports to outline a hopefully full-fledged, realistic conceptual apparatus, capable of capturing (most of) the relevant features of the phenomenon of legal interpretation, as we may perceive it in our legal cultures. In so doing, it might be regarded, to put it in immodest terms, as providing a fragment of a revisionary metaphysics concerning that peculiar corner of the social world

[20] Ferrajoli (1989), pp. 135–156; Ferrajoli (2012), pp. 216–221. The obvious reference here is also, of course, the work of Jerome Frank: see, e.g., Frank (1930), pp. 170–185, and Frank (1949a), pp. 14–36.

[21] On judicial fiction, see Chap. 8 below.

[22] On norms as "rhetorical consequences" of source-sentences, see Chap. 2, Sect. 2.3.3.2 below; on legislation from a realistic viewpoint, see Chap. 5, Sect. 5.2, and Chap. 11 below.

[23] On this distinction I will come back in Chap. 7 below.

corresponding to the activities, practices, and outputs of "legal interpretation" broadly conceived.[24]

It also puts to work the basic principles of an analytic approach to legal philosophy: of course, as I see them. Five such principles are worthwhile mentioning. The *principle of methodical ignorance* requires being distrustful about what one assumes to know, above all when it sounds familiar. The *principle of conversion*, a variety of Quine's idea of semantic ascent,[25] suggests converting metaphysical (or "ontological") issues into conceptual issues, at least as a preliminary step of the inquiry. The *principle of empirical support* requires conceptual frameworks to be worked out and evaluated in relation to empirical (social) reality. The *principle of clarification* requires a never-ending, Sisyphean, strife from (fatally) worse to (ever) better conceptual and terminological apparatuses. The *capture principle*, finally, requires designing conceptual nets capable to capture all the good fishes in the examined pond. The chapter, as readers will see, is also meant to bringing to the fore one *Leitmotiv* of the whole book: namely, the idea of the limited space legal interpretation, broadly conceived, affords for empirical truth.

Chapters 3 to 6 are devoted to arguing for what I shall call a "construction conception" of legal meaning. The basic claim I wish to make may be phrased as follows: the meaning of legal provisions—what they communicate in particular contexts of use—neither is simply discovered, nor is a matter of wholesale creation, though it may involve significant pieces of interpretive creativity. Rather, it is constructed out of pre-existing materials through a typically reflexive, multiple-stage and holistic process. In support of the construction conception, four different, mutually conspiring, lines of argument will be considered in turn. The first to come is an argument from a theory of interpretive games and Gricean pragmatics, which will be outlined in Chap. 3 ("Interpretive Games"). Second, an argument from the dispute between literalism and contextualism in contemporary philosophy of language will be outlined in Chap. 4 ("Taking Context Seriously"). Third, an argument from the failures of the container-retrieval view will be outlined in Chap. 5 ("Frames v. Containers"). Finally, an argument from the failure of pragmatic formalism, a semantics-driven pragmatic theory of legal meaning and interpretation, will be outlined in Chap. 6 ("Towards Pragmatic Realism").

The remaining chapters purport to cast the light of an analytical and realistic enquiry on a variety of interpretation-related subjects, ranging from gaps to legislation.

Chapter 7, "Legal Gaps", contains an exercise in comparative analytical jurisprudence. A sample of theories of gaps from both sides of the Atlantic is analysed and evaluated from the vantage point of an interpretation-dependent and interpretation-transparent conceptual apparatus, in tune with the realistic theory I advocate.

---

[24] According to P. F. Strawson, who coined the expression, "revisionary metaphysics" is to be contrasted with "descriptive metaphysics". The latter "is content to describe the actual structure of our thought about the world", it aims "to lay bare the most general features of our conceptual structure"; the former, contrariwise, "is concerned to produce a better structure" (Strawson 1959, p. 9).

[25] Quine (1960), pp. 271–276.

Chapter 8, "Judicial Fictions", moves from a conceptual analysis of a few theories of judicial fiction (namely, by Hans Kelsen, Alf Ross, Gidon Gottlieb, Frederick Schauer, and Sebastian Del Mar, respectively), and uses it as the basis for conceptual reconstruction. It advances the explanatory claim that the technique of fiction, in those legal cultures and orders that allow it, is typically resorted to in situations where judges (assume to) face an axiological gap, and the "bad rule" (the existing rule that stands in the way of a "satisfactory", "proper", "correct" legal solution to a case at hand) cannot be set aside by means of ordinary interpretive techniques.

Chapter 9, "Precedent", is dedicated to a realistic and analytical exploration of three basic issues in the theory of precedent. These are: (a) the notion of a *ratio decidendi*; (b) the interpretation of precedents; (c) the practical relevance of precedents. Dealing with the first issue, three notions of a *ratio decidendi* are proposed by way of a rational reconstruction of on-going concepts. Dealing with the second issue, the whole set of common law techniques for coping with precedents is considered through the spectacles of the distinction between textual interpretation of judicial decisions (the whole documents containing opinions plus normative conclusions), textual interpretation of a previously identified *ratio decidendi*, and metatextual interpretation of a previously identified *ratio decidendi*. Finally, dealing with the third issue, a few basic conceptual distinctions will be introduced, the influential proposal by the legal theorists of the *Bielefelder Kreis* will be analysed, and, thereafter, a purportedly comprehensive typology of eight ideal-type systems concerning the *formal* or *de iure* relevance of judicial precedents will be outlined, to be used as an analytical device for understanding and classifying actual legal systems.

Chapter 10, "Defeasibility and Legal Indeterminacy", concerns what was perhaps one of the hottest subjects in recent jurisprudential fads. Considering linguistic therapy as valuable on its own, it proceeds to the analysis of the structure of actual philosophical thought on the matter, and proposes a rational reconstruction thereof. The ultimate goal is contributing to the laying down of a sound, realistic, theory of defeasible norms.

Chapter 11, "Legislation", finally, casts some light (indeed, no more than a few flashes into the darkness) on the basic ideas of the realist theory of legislation. In so doing, it will be the place for rehearsing many of the theoretical theses advanced and argued for in the previous chapters.

1.3 Conceptual Analysis

As the preceding overview of the book makes clear, and it will become even clearer as the reader proceeds in her browsing through it, conceptual analysis (as I see it) has pride of place in the box of tools I have made use of in my enquiries. This requires a bit of methodological detour: if only, again, for the sake of countering misunderstandings.

In a well-known collection of essays, Brian Leiter makes a pressing call for a "naturalized jurisprudence". This aims "to describe the reality of legal phenomena", and poses as the heiress to American Legal Realism and Quine's empiricist philosophy of science.[26] In so doing, what is more relevant to the present purpose, Leiter urges the abandonment of the "method of conceptual analysis via appeal to folk intuitions".[27] He claims such a method to be doomed to failure, if one is looking for a philosophically valuable explanation of the "nature" or "essence" of law: that is to say, if one wishes to get at "necessary truths" about the law, as many *soi-disants* analytical jurisprudents, in recent times, seem fond to do.[28]

Apparently, Leiter's case for a naturalized jurisprudence, and against conceptual analysis, casts a sinister light on the possibility of fruitfully combining realism, which, with hindsight, can indeed be read as a variety of naturalized jurisprudence, on the one side, and conceptual analysis, on the other.

Upon consideration, however, Leiter's darts—assuming, for the sake of argument, his picture of "conceptual analysis" to be reliable—aim apparently at a different target. In fact, distinct forms of conceptual analysis are conceivable. To the

---

[26] Leiter (2007), p. 183 ff.; Leiter (2012). On conceptual analysis in (and) jurisprudence, see also Endicott (2002), § 3.1, Bix (2007), pp. 1–7, Marmor (2012), pp. 1–26.

[27] Leiter (2007), pp. 1–2: "the method of conceptual analysis via appeal to folk intuitions (as manifest, for example, in ordinary language), a method that was itself at risk of becoming an item of antiquarian interest in the context of the naturalistic revolution of late 20th century philosophy"; Leiter (2012), § 2: "The question that plagues conceptual analysis, post-Quine, is what kind of knowledge such a procedure actually yields? Why should ordinary intuitions about the extension of a concept be deemed reliable or informative? Why think the "folk" are right?".

[28] Leiter (2007), pp. 177–178, 196–197, where, discussing Ian P. Farrell's defence of the Hartian search for "the concept of law" as a worthwhile piece of "modest conceptual analysis", retorts: "But on Farrell's (more plausible) rendering of conceptual analysis, we do not illuminate the reality, i.e., the nature of law, we illuminate, rather, the nature of our "talk" about law [...] *Modest* conceptual analysis illuminates our concepts – our *talk*, as it were – not the referent we might have intended to understand" (italics in the text, ndr). See also Leiter (2012), § 2. Leiter's criticism is in order, when, by "modest conceptual analysis", necessary truths about aspects of reality are looked for. It does not do, contrariwise, when, following J. L. Austin's suggestion (Austin 1956–1957, pp. 129–130), such an ambitious, and mysterious, task is put down, and a "sharpened awareness of words" is looked for in order to "sharpen our perception of the phenomena", though "*not as the final arbiter of*" (italics added; the passage, without this last, quite relevant, qualification, is quoted by Hart in the opening page of the "Preface" to *The Concept of Law*: Hart 1961, vii). For a defence of "traditional conceptual analysis" in jurisprudence, like the one performed by Hart (1961), against Leiter's naturalistic attack, see Himma (2007), pp. 1–23; Himma (2015), pp. 65–92. Himma's defence, however, looks troublesome. It sets forth an apparently inconsistent view of "traditional conceptual analysis": on the one hand, it would be just about "our" concept of law, and hence would be tied, and limited, to a contingent, changeable, local, experience. On the other hand, it would lead, mysteriously, to making metaphysical claims about the nature or essence of law in general, telling us metaphysical, necessary, truths "about not just all *existing* legal systems, but all *conceptually possible* legal systems. Thus conceived, a conceptual analysis of law consists in a set of conceptually (or metaphysically) necessary truths and thus constitutes a piece of metaphysical theorizing – just as an analysis of the concept of free will is a piece of metaphysics" (Himma 2015, § 5). In the same passage, Himma also presents Hart as a torchbearer of such a metaphysical conceptual analysis. This view, nowadays common among jurisprudents, is nonetheless disputable. See, for instance, Marmor (2012), who advocates that the basic thrust of Hart's jurisprudence was not conceptual analysis, but reductionism. I have argued against the "essentialist" reading of Hart's conception of conceptual analysis in Chiassoni (2012), § 2.2, and Chiassoni (2016b), pp. 61–71.

present purpose, two pairs of opposite varieties seem worthwhile considering. Very roughly speaking, we can draw a line between conceptual analysis of a descriptive or a reconstructive character, on the one hand, and conceptual analysis of grand or modest ambition, on the other.

Descriptive conceptual analysis inquires on current conceptual and terminological apparatuses with the aim of clarifying and precisifying their scope in the light of the "intuitions" of those who make a daily use of them ("the (mythical) folks"), whatever such intuitions may be.[29] Folks' intuitions (their methodologically unaccountable "sense" about objects and concepts) are paramount: they both delimitate the ground, and determine the output, of the inquiry.[30] By contrast, *reconstructive conceptual analysis* investigates current conceptual and terminological apparatuses with the aim of eventually and ultimately replacing them with "better" ones, from the standpoint of the rational values of simplicity, clarity, precision, empirical adequacy, consistency, coherence, comprehensiveness, explanatory force, and adequacy to the (presumed) purposes of the "game(s)" they are played in. Reconstructive conceptual analysis takes into account folks' intuitions, as they are fatally embodied in, and mirrored by, linguistic practices. In doing so, however, it assumes such intuitions may back a conceptual and terminological apparatus in need of rational repair (rational reconstruction, rational revision).

Grand conceptual analysis is a Platonist-flavoured enterprise; by way of linguistic-conceptual enquiries, it presumes to be capable to "reveal" the "a priori", "necessary", "conceptual truths" about "the way things are and the way the mind works".[31] By contrast, *modest conceptual analysis*: (i) conceives of linguistic-conceptual enquiries mainly as a way to know the ways of thinking, and the sets of beliefs and attitudes, that are embodied in on-going conceptual and terminological apparatuses; (ii) grants to on-going apparatuses only a presumptive epistemic value, since it assumes that the intuitions (beliefs, attitudes) they mirror may be inchoate, confused, contradictory, idle, superstition-laden, wrong as a matter of fact, so that

[29] See Leiter (2007), pp. 1–2, 183–199; the basic source for intuitionist conceptual analysis is Jackson (1998), especially ch. 2.

[30] According to Jackson, (intuitionist) "conceptual analysis" is needed, if we want to "have much of an audience", and do not want turning "interesting philosophical debates into easy exercises in deduction from stipulative definitions together with accepted facts". If, for instance, our problem is about free action and determinism, the only fruitful way to proceed is by asking "whether free action *according to our ordinary conception*, or something suitably close to our ordinary conception, exists and is compatible with determinism" (Jackson 1998, pp. 30–31, italics in the text). The ascertainment of our (or folk's) conception of free action, in turn, requires appealing to ordinary, shared, intuitions, which reveal "our shared theory" (Jackson 1998, pp. 31–32, 46 ff.). This can be carried out by means of introspection and, above all, socio-psychological enquiries. It is worthwhile stressing that, according to Jackson, "in practice", "the role" he is "recommending for conceptual analysis will often be *very* like the role Quine gives to the [Benthamite] notion of paraphrase" (Jackson 1998, p. 46). In the light of such remark, the case against "conceptual analysis" *à la* Jackson from Quinean perspectives seems, at least partly, the fruit of an uncharitable exaggeration.

[31] These words, by which I characterize what I call "grand conceptual analysis", are from Smith Churchland (2013), pp. xi–xii.

such apparatuses may provide a misleading way to look at natural or social phenomena; (iii) adopts a conventionalist and pragmatist conception of conceptual sets[32]; (iv) does not look for "necessary", "a priori", "conceptual truths" about reality, but for the innocent, tautological ones that, to be sure, are relative to contingent, on-going, sets of concepts.[33] Nonetheless, modest conceptual analysis is more than a "glorification" of lexicography, though it may walk some way along with it. It does not aim at "teaching the use of sentences"; it does not wish making its readers "profit by the sentences" that they "see or hear", or helping them ""react to" sentences "in expected ways" and "emit sentences usefully".[34] Rather, it aims at providing its readers with improved, better, ways of thinking at some natural phenomenon or human undertaking, as observers and participants alike.

By way of combination, four complex forms of conceptual analysis result, namely: grand-descriptive and grand-reconstructive conceptual analysis (which ascribe to conceptual description or reconstruction the mysterious virtue of being capable to get at "conceptual truth about reality"); modest-descriptive conceptual analysis (which amounts to something very close to lexicography); and, finally, modest-reconstructive conceptual analysis.[35]

In the present book, I will stand for a modest and reconstructive variety. This variety, as I see it, proceeds by means of enquiries that typically encompass three stages: conceptual detection, conceptual reconstruction and conceptual therapy.

First, there comes the stage of *conceptual detection*, or conceptual analysis in a narrow sense—what J. L. Austin proposes to call "linguistic phenomenology".[36] Here, the on-going terminological and conceptual apparatus that is the subject mat-

---

[32] Such a conception of "linguistic frameworks" is defended, for instance, by Rudolf Carnap. In his view, many questions which are presented as "*theoretical* questions" (like, e.g., the question "are there natural numbers?"), should be interpreted as "*practical* questions, i.e., as questions about the *decision* whether or not *to accept a language* containing expressions for the particular kind of entities" at stake (italics added, ndr). In his view, "whether or not" a "linguistic framework" should be introduced depends on the purposes one is aiming at, and "is a practical question of language engineering, to be decided on the basis of convenience, fruitfulness, simplicity, and the like" (Carnap 1963, p. 66; see also Carnap 1950, pp. 205–221).

[33] Smith Churchland (2013), pp. xi–xiv; "So what is a philosopher to do, if not troll his mind for conceptual truths? The Quinean answer is this: *many* things, including synthesizing across various subfields and theorizing while immersed in and constrained by available facts. Despite much hand-wringing by overwrought philosophers, Quine did not aim to put an end to philosophy, but to remind us of what the older philosophical tradition had always been: broad, encompassing, knowledgeable of everything relevant, and imaginative" (xiv, italics in the text). For a condensed account by Quine himself, see e.g. Quine (1960), pp. 275–276.

[34] See Quine (1992), pp. 56–57.

[35] Ian P. Farrell apparently advocates the third variety. Leiter criticizes both forms of (what I call) descriptive conceptual analysis, i.e., the grand and the modest one, while recognizing, following Larry Laudan, the usefulness of something like the modest and reconstructive variety I stand for here (see Leiter 2007, p. 183 footnote 3; see also Leiter (2007), p. 133 footnote 45, 168 ff., 179–181, where, in line with a central, though apparently overlooked, tenet of Logical Positivism, he regards philosophy as "the abstract branch of successful scientific theory […] the abstract and reflective part of empirical science"; Leiter 2008).

[36] Austin (1956–1957), p. 130.

ter of the enquiry is identified, analysed, and its rational virtues and flaws dispassionately brought to the fore.

Second, there comes the stage of *conceptual reconstruction* or rational reconstruction. Here, the on-going terminological and conceptual apparatus is modified into a new one, that is capable of replacing it, but does, and should do, roughly the same job of the on-going one, though in a better, more rational way—for instance, due to its finer articulation in a larger, more comprehensive, set of terminologically distinct and semantically clearer and more exact concepts.

Third, and finally, there comes the stage of *conceptual therapy*. Here, the use of the reconstructed and replacing conceptual and terminological apparatus set forth in the second stage is recommended, and carried out, as a way-out from the (supposed) rational flaws of the on-going one.[37]

Conceptual analysis—in the modest and reconstructive, three-stages, variety above—should count as a fundamental instrument in the toolbox of any empirical enquiry on legal phenomena. Sociological inquiries about legal practice, even the armchair ones so typical in jurisprudential literature, bring to the fore and isolate terminologies, linguistic uses, working conceptual apparatuses, and "theories" behind them, that are fatally in need of clarification, rational reconstruction, and therapy.[38] It must be considered, furthermore, that the reality of legal interpretation and adjudication (indeed, legal reality) is largely a linguistic reality. Accordingly, a sharpened awareness of the structure of "our" talking and thinking, both as interpreters of legal texts, and as interpreters and commentators of professional interpreters' interpretations, carries with it, at the same time, a sharpened awareness of the world, which is a world made of words and pieces of linguistic communications. In fact, what is an interpretive reasoning unless a string of sentences in a natural language? What are interpretive rules and interpretive codes unless linguistic entities? If we pursue the naturalistic ideal of a genuine empirical knowledge about law and legal interpretation and adjudication, conceptual analysis—in the modest and reconstructive, three-stages, variety—appears to be a tool of enquiry that cannot be dispensed with.

---

[37] A more encompassing view of reconstructive conceptual analysis is propounded by Strawson (1962), pp. 112–118, who identifies five intertwining ways ("strands") of philosophical analysis: (1) conceptual therapy, to be used for solving paradoxes and perplexities; (2) descriptive analysis, which is about the actual working of "our" conceptual and logical apparatus; (3) explanatory analysis, which puts to work philosophical imagination in order to bring to the fore the "natural foundations" of our conceptual and logical apparatus; (4) reformist metaphysics, which puts to work philosophical imagination in view of providing a new and different conceptual framework for "our" same old world; and, finally, (5) descriptive metaphysics, which purports to clarify the "general structure" of "our" conceptual apparatus. My view of conceptual analysis may look a piece of eclecticism, where suggestions from Bentham, Russell, Carnap, Quine and Strawson, among others, are put together in a sort of mental patchwork. It is indeed. In fact, I do not care for strict philosophical allegiance. I care for (hopefully) smoothly working tools for (hopefully) fruitful jurisprudential investigations.

[38] A still valuable overview of the several, often intertwining, forms of philosophical analysis is offered by Urmson (1962), pp. 294–301; see also Strawson (1962), pp. 105–118; Strawson (1985), pp. 7–60.

Willard Quine depicts the naturalization of epistemology as a course of action that transforms "theoretical epistemology", which is a philosophical enterprise above, and outside, of science, into "a chapter of theoretical science".[39] Rejecting any "a priori" conception of philosophizing, he sees the "naturalistic philosopher" as an inquirer who:

> begins his reasoning within the inherited *world theory* as a going concern. He tentatively believes all of it, but believes also that some unidentified portions are wrong. He tries to *improve*, *clarify*, and *understand* the system *from within*. He is the busy sailor adrift on Neurath's boat.[40]

Likewise, I see the realistic jurisprudent, the sceptical legal theorist, as the busy sailor adrift on the norm-hulled, material-and-immaterial-interests propelled, juristic constructions-laden, boat of legal thinking. As an enterprise that is different from, though tightly related to, historical, sociological and psychological inquiries on legal phenomena, realist jurisprudence can be conceived as the theoretical, or philosophical, chapter of legal studies: a chapter that is largely devoted to the rationalist, modest tasks of conceptual detection, reconstruction, and therapy. Empirical legal science, legal dogmatics (the doctrinal study of law), and legal politics (as normative ethics applied to law), all are likely to earn great advantage from properly performed conceptual enquiries.[41]

The original manuscript has benefited from the thoughtful comments and helpful suggestions of two anonymous referees. I wish to express my warmest gratitude for their generous attention. I wish also to express my gratitude to Francisco J. Laporta who, many many years ago, suggested to me the writing of a book that finally turned out to be the present one, and to Riccardo Guastini, my life-long Maestro. The book is dedicated to three wonderful girls: Elmina, Josy, and Mik.

---

[39] Quine (1992), p. 19, italics added. See also Quine (1969), pp. 69–90, where epistemology, as an enquiry on the way empirical knowledge is acquired and processed, is presented as merging "with psychology, as well as with linguistics".

[40] Quine (1975), p. 72, italics added.

[41] For an archetype of such a view, see Ross (1958), ch. 1.

Chapter 2
Interpretation, Truth, and the Logical Forms of Interpretive Discourse

If we want to study the problems of truth and falsehood, of the agreement or disagreement of propositions with reality, of the nature of assertion, assumption and question, we shall with great advantage look at primitive forms of language in which these forms of thinking appear without the confusing background of highly complicated processes of thought

—L. Wittgenstein (1958)

The reconstructive attitude demands that we describe the world in a way that does not impoverish it by artificial reductions, and it thus requires that we make important distinctions wherever there is an objective need for them

—H. Feigl (1949)

2.1 A Haunting Problem

This chapter purports to provide an exploration of the connections between legal interpretation and truth.[1] The problem that will be coped with, which haunts so much work in the field, sounds roughly as follows: Has truth anything to do with legal interpretation? Is there any room for truth in the province of legal interpretation? And if there is, where is it?

Any (un-otiose) attempt to deal with this problem requires a careful elucidation of the key terms at stake. The chapter contains, accordingly, three parts. The first part is devoted to working out a net of terms and concepts that aims at capturing the several aspects of the complex social phenomenon we are used to refer to by the phrase "legal interpretation" in its widest meaning (Sect. 2.2). The second part identifies a few notions of truth that seem apt to be employed in relation to legal interpretation (Sect. 2.3). The third and last part, putting to work the conceptual frames laid down in the two preceding ones, comes to a few conclusions about the problem

[1]On the law & truth issue, see, e.g.: Patterson (1996), Pintore (1996), Diciotti (1999), Moore (2003), Sucar (2008), Bix (2009), Marmor (2011b), and Sucar and Cerdio Herrán (2017).

P. Chiassoni, *Interpretation without Truth*, Law and Philosophy Library 128,
https://doi.org/10.1007/978-3-030-15590-2_2

of truth in legal interpretation that seem not totally devoid of interest, if only for clarification's sake (Sect. 2.4). A final section connects the present chapter with the main theme of the book: the refutation of interpretive cognitivism and the defence of a non-cognitivist outlook (Sect. 2.5).

2.2 Legal Interpretation

Whatever we take the phrase "legal interpretation" to mean, the process-outcome ambiguity of the word "interpretation" makes a preliminary distinction necessary. It requires sorting out "legal interpretation" as referring to an activity performed by an individual interpreter at a certain time and place (*interpretation-activity*), on the one side, and "legal interpretation" as referring instead to the outcome, product or output of a corresponding interpretation-activity (*interpretation-outcome*), on the other.[2] "This is a piece of legal interpretation" may refer, for instance, either to the activity of a law professor who, during a class, interprets a provision of the criminal code, or to the output of such an activity, i.e., to the sentence(s) she sets forth as corresponding to the (correct) legal meaning of that provision.

The distinction between interpretation-activity and interpretation-output may look a piece of pointless triviality. It suggests, however, a few, not wholly idle, considerations.

1. Whenever we enquire upon the place of truth in the field of legal interpretation, it is apparent that the adjective "true" can be used either as a classification device (in sentences like, e.g., "X is true interpretation", "X is a true piece of interpretation", "X is truly interpretation"), or as a qualification device (in sentences like, e.g., "The interpretation X of Y is true").

   In its classificatory use, "true" is tantamount to "genuine", "authentic", "real"; it helps marking what is (really) interpretation, from what is not.

   Contrariwise, in its qualificatory use, "true" serves to mark those interpretations that have the property of being true, according to some presupposed notion of truth. In its qualificatory use, "true" can properly be applied ("fits") only to interpretation-outputs: to wit, it is a predicate convenient to interpretation-outputs conceived as *discourse entities*, namely, as sentences that are typically written in legal documents such as juristic essays, judicial opinions or forensic acts.
2. Provided the "true" predicate, as a qualificatory device, applies to interpretation-outputs as discourse entities (sentences), it is to be noticed that, from the standpoint of actual linguistic uses among jurists and legal philosophers, there are different and even heterogeneous kinds of "interpretation"-activity, and, accordingly, different and even heterogeneous kinds of "interpretation"-outputs.

---

[2] This distinction is a key point of Giovanni Tarello's theory of legal interpretation: see Tarello (1980), pp. 39–42. See also Guastini (2011b), p. 149 ff.

3. That being the case, a fair way of clarifying and capturing juristic usages of "interpretation" consists in singling out three different kinds of interpretation-activities, namely: (*a*) interpretation-activities *in a proper sense* and of a *practical* character or to a *practical* purpose; (*b*) interpretation-activities *in a proper sense* and of a *cognitive* character or to a *cognitive* purpose; and (*c*) interpretation-activities *in an improper sense.*

2.2.1 Interpretation Proper to a Practical Purpose

The activities of the first kind are interpretive *in a proper sense* for, as we shall see in a moment, the agents who perform them are in fact "interpreting the law". Furthermore, they are interpretive activities that are *practical* in character: judges and jurists perform them to purposes like deciding a lawsuit, establishing who is legally entitled to what, providing the "right" answer to a question of law, making proposals as to the foregoing sorts of decisions, etc.

The central case of interpretation proper to practical purpose (practical interpretation) is (what I shall refer to as) *textual interpretation.* Textual interpretation typically takes place in contexts where jurists and judges also perform some further activities, which are different from, but related to, textual interpretation, and are also considered to be pieces of "interpretation", though in a broad and loose sense of the word. In the following, I will refer to these further activities by the comprehensive label of *meta-textual interpretation.*

2.2.1.1 Textual Interpretation

Textual interpretation consists in determining (establishing) the legally correct meaning of authoritative legal texts to some practical purpose. Authoritative legal texts are "legal provisions", "source-sentences", "legal norms in a pre-interpretive sense", or even "rule-" or "norm-formulations", like, e.g., constitutional or statutory clauses. The practical purpose to which textual interpretation is being performed typically consists either in correctly deciding a lawsuit, as it is the case with judges, or in proposing a right answer to an abstract question of law, as it is the case with jurists. Textual interpretation can also be seen as the intra-linguistic translation of legal provisions into one or more norms ("explicit norms", as we shall see in a moment) that are (presented and usually argued for as) the legally correct meaning thereof.[3]

We may conceive the linguistic output of textual interpretation in a narrow or a broad way.

[3] On translation see, e.g.: Haas (1962), pp. 86–108; Eco (2012). On translation and legal interpretation, see the accurate review essay Mazzarese (1998), pp. 73–102.

Narrowly conceived, the output of textual interpretation just consists in one or more *explicit* norms: namely, in one or more norms that, according to the interpreter, represent the *explicit meaning* of a given legal provision, what that source-sentence is properly to be taken to *express* or *say*.[4] For instance, if the legal provision being interpreted is:

(LP_i) "No cruel punishments shall be inflicted",

and the interpreter translates it into the explicit norm:

(EN_i) "No punishments that are cruel according to the Framers' intent shall be inflicted",

the sentence EN_i, which by hypothesis represents an explicit norm, is tantamount to the linguistic output, in a narrow sense, of the textual interpretation of legal provision LP_i.

Contrariwise, if we adopt a broader view, the output of textual interpretation may be conceived as consisting in an *interpretive sentence*. Interpretive sentences are usually represented by means of logical forms like:

(*IS1*) "Legal provision LP_i ("No cruel punishments shall be inflicted") expresses the norm EN_i ("No punishments that are cruel according to the Framers' intent shall be inflicted")"
(*IS2*) "Legal provision LP_i means EN_i"
(*IS3*) "The meaning-content of provision LP_i is EN_i".

It must be noticed, however, that these forms are elliptical to the point of allowing for pragmatic ambiguity. Indeed, they do not make clear whether they are *descriptive* sentences just *reporting* that legal provision LP_i is taken—generally, or by some individual jurist or judge—to mean the explicit norm EN_i, or, contrariwise, they are rather *verdictive* sentences *putting forth* EN_i as the proper, legally correct, meaning of LP_i.[5] Accordingly, we need apparently less elliptical logical forms for interpretive sentences.

To be sure, no proposed logical form can claim absolute theoretical adequacy.[6] Considering the definition of textual interpretation above, and taking into account

[4] The distinction between legal provision, explicit norm and implicit norm (on which I will come back in a moment) is paramount to Genoese realistic theory of law and legal interpretation. See Guastini (2011a), pp. 63–74; Guastini (2011b), pp. 138–161. From a pragmatic vantage point, the explicit norm corresponds to what the sentence-in-context is taken to express (the full expressed communication); this may be different from what the sentence (the word of the law) "says", and should not be confused with what the sentence "implies". On this issue I will come back in Chaps. 4 and 5 below.

[5] It is worthwhile quoting a few lines from J. L. Austin: "Verdictives consist in the delivering of a finding, official or unofficial, upon evidence or reasons as to value or fact, so far as these are distinguishable [...] a judge's ruling makes law [...] but it still purports to be correct or incorrect, right or wrong, justifiable or unjustifiable on the evidence" (Austin 1962, pp. 153–154).

[6] In an old paper, I maintained that interpretive sentences "ascribe *one* meaning to legal provisions, ruling out other meanings that could eventually be ascribed to them" (Chiassoni 1999a, p. 27,

the rules of the interpretive games concerning legal provisions ("written law"),[7] the following logical forms—*IS4* and *IS5*—seem closer to theoretical adequacy:

(*IS4*) "The legally correct meaning of legal provision LP_i ("No cruel punishments shall be inflicted") is the norm EN_i ("No punishments that are cruel according to the Framers' intent shall be inflicted")"

(*IS5*) "The norm EN_i is (counts as) the legally correct meaning of legal provision LP_i".

They purport to bring to the fore that the interpreter *stands for* EN_i as the legally correct meaning of LP_i; that she is committed to (evaluating) that meaning as the legally correct meaning of LP_i. They also purport to emphasize that interpretive sentences are the outputs of interpretive decisions. In our legal cultures, we expect such decisions to be justified, or, at least, justifiable: we expect reasons and criteria to be offered (or be available) for them. This suggests a further, enlarged logical form for interpretive sentences (*IS6*), where the core of the justification of *IS4-IS5* type interpretive sentences is made explicit:

(*IS6*) "The norm EN_i is (counts as) the legally correct meaning of legal provision LP_i, EN_i being the meaning of legal provision LP_i according to (what should be taken as) the all-things considered correct interpretive code IC_j and the all-things considered correct set of interpretive resources IR_j".[8]

In the form *IS6*, EN_i—that is, the explicit norm the interpreter presents and defends as the legally correct translation of legal provision LP_i—is contextually justified, notice, on two conspiring grounds: on the basis of (what the interpreter considers should be taken as) "the" correct *interpretive code* IC_j, and on the basis of "the" correct set, or combination, of *interpretive resources*.

The notions of *interpretive code* and *interpretive resource* must be briefly explicated, since they will be used over and over again in this book.

36–37, 40). Likewise, Diciotti (1999, pp. 152–157, 284 ff.), on the basis of a non-cognivist theory of interpretation, comes to the conclusion that "interpretive propositions" are "evaluative propositions", the logical form of which is: "*S* is *the only* meaning that it is good to ascribe to the statutory sentence *F*, or to the term *E* contained in the statutory sentence *F*". He also claims that "the foundation" of such propositions consists "(also) in methodological principles of interpretation, that is to say, in evaluative propositions that establish the methods and arguments that it is good employing in order to ascribe a meaning to statutory texts" (like, e.g., "it is good that interpreters, and first of all the judges, ascribe to statutory texts the meaning which corresponds to the intention of the legislator"). From the standpoint of the rules of interpretive games, however, such ways of conceiving the logical form of interpretive sentences (interpretive propositions, or interpretive judgments) do not seem to be adequate. These rules require a stronger commitment. They require the meaning that an interpreter ascribes to a legal provision to be ascribed not just as the "only good" one (which conveys the idea of a partisan evaluation), but, rather, as "the legally correct meaning" of the provision (which conveys the idea of an evaluation from the standpoint of "the law").

[7] See Chap. 3 below, which revises and updates Chiassoni (1999a), pp. 72–73.

[8] On the need for a less elliptical form for (what are here) interpretive sentences, some essays by Jerzy Wróblewski have a path-breaking import: see, e.g., Wróblewski (1992), p. 93.

An *interpretive code* is a discrete set of interpretive prescriptions, including, among others, method rules and translation rules.[9] Translation rules are instructions about how the translation of a legal provision into one or more explicit norms should be carried out. For instance, the plain meaning rule (in a very broad and indeterminate version) instructs translating legal provisions into the explicit norm(s) that correspond to the ordinary meaning of the words used in the provision; the legislative intent rule (again, in one possible variety) instructs translating legal provisions into the explicit norm(s) that correspond to the semantic meaning that the legislature wished them to have; the teleological rule (again, in one possible variety) instructs translating legal provisions into the explicit norm(s) that correspond to the purpose of the provisions selves; the principles rule (as a translation rule) instructs translating legal provisions into the explicit norm(s) that correspond to the meaning suggested for them by some relevant set of ("constitutional", "fundamental", "general") principles, etc.[10] Method rules include selection rules (which identify the translation rules to be used), procedure rules (which establish the sequence in the use of the previously selected translation rules), and preference rules (which provide instructions for preferring one interpretive output among several competing ones).[11]

Interpretive resources are, instead, the data necessary to put interpretive prescriptions to work. They consist, e.g., in linguistic conventions, parliamentary reports, juristic theories about legal concepts and institutions, judicial opinions, legal principles, selected sets of norms and principles out of the macro-system of existing positive law, moral, political and legal philosophies, etc.[12]

---

[9] For a more detailed account of the rules of interpretive codes, concerning interpretive games in general and the statutory interpretation game in particular, see Chap. 3, Sects. 3.4 and 3.6, below.

[10] Six kinds of translation rules can be singled out. *Linguistic rules* make appeal to the conventions of the language by which legal provisions have been formulated. *Intentional rules* make appeal to "the intention of the author" of legal provisions, a phrase that, as it is well known, can be understood in many different ways (for instance, the "author" can be identified with the historical legislature, the present legislature, the rational or ideal legislature, etc.). *Teleological rules* make appeal to the purpose of the law, i.e., of the legal provision self, of the statute in which it is included, of the laws of the sector of positive law to which the provision belongs, etc. *Authoritative rules* make appeal to the way the legal provision has been interpreted by judicial or juristic "authorities". *Systemic rules* (like, e.g., the principles rule I have mentioned in the text) make appeal to other norms of the legal system as data from which the proper meaning of legal provisions can be gathered. *Heteronomous rules*, finally, make appeal to data like the nature of things or the norms of positive or critical moralities (Chiassoni 2011, ch. 2, where translation rules are referred to as "primary directives"). Systemic concerns can also be at work when method rules are at stake: they typically show up, in particular, in preference rules. This function is typically performed by the interpretive rules known to jurists as "the argument from coherence", "the argument from consistency", "the argument from completeness", "the argument from absurdity or reasonableness", etc.

[11] See Chap. 3, Sects. 3.4 and 3.6, below.

[12] Suppose the interpretive code encompasses an originalist literal meaning rule ("Provisions should be interpreted according to their original literal meaning"). In such a case, the correct combination of interpretive resources will encompass, for instance, what the interpreter considers as the most reliable dictionaries of the relevant natural and/or legal language at the time the provision was enacted.

One further remark is in order, before proceeding. I have defined textual interpretation as consisting in the determination (or establishing) of the legally correct meaning of legal provisions. As the logical forms above make clear, the legally correct meaning is always *relative to* an interpretive code *and* to a set of interpretive resources. The very idea of an "absolutely" legally correct meaning is a conceptual blunder. You cannot "interpret" a text without (tacitly) selecting a code and a set of resources. Nothing prevents, consequently, that one and the same legal provision be given different, mutually excluding, legally correct meanings, by interpreters who, adopting different ideological standpoints (on this point, see Sect. 2.2.2.2 below), use different interpretive codes or appeal to different sets of interpretive resources. The written law interpretive game requires interpreters to provide the legally correct meaning of the legal provisions they are going to use to some practical purpose. The structure of the game, however, allows both for a plurality of alternative legally correct meanings for one and the same legal provision, and for interpretive disagreements. The lot of legal interpreters is arguing their case in the strongest possible way. And hope for the endorsement by as many fellow judges and jurists as possible.

2.2.1.2 Meta-Textual Interpretation

"Meta-textual interpretation" refers—as I said, by way of sheer stipulation—to a set of heterogeneous activities. These activities are *meta-textual interpretation*, since they either *precede* or (usually) *presuppose* textual interpretation. Furthermore, as we shall see in a moment, some of them are pieces of "interpretation" in a proper sense of the word.

Among the several sorts of activities of meta-textual interpretation, to the present purpose I will consider five, leading to outputs that consist, respectively, in *institutional-status* sentences, *integration* sentences, *gap-identification* sentences, *antinomy-identification* sentences, and, finally, *hierarchy-identification* sentences.

Institutional-status sentences are classificatory sentences that establish the institutional value, position, or function of some previously identified object (consisting in a legal provision, an explicit norm, or an implicit norm), in relation to a previously identified or presupposed normative set (which, to the present purpose, may be tentatively characterized as a set of legal provisions and/or legal norms).

Institutional-status sentences are quite common in legal discourse, where they come, roughly, in the following forms:

(*ISS1*) "Legal provision LP_i is (counts as) a principle-provision (i.e., is capable of expressing legal principles), in relation to normative set LS_i"

(*ISS2*) "Norm *N1* is (counts as) a supreme constitutional principle, in relation to normative set LS_i"

(*ISS3*) "Norm *N2* is (counts as) a defeasible rule of conduct, in relation to normative set LS_i"

(*ISS4*) "Norm *N3* is (counts as) *lex specialis*, in relation to normative set LS_i".

Institutional-status sentences are typically used inside of reasonings devoted either to providing a systematic presentation of some sector of positive law, or to solving some previously identified antinomy. They are *interpretive* sentences, according to the notion of *interpretation* as *ascription of sense or value* to some previously identified object. They belong, furthermore, to the realm of *systemic interpretation*, for they establish the (correct) value (status, position, "sense") of something in relation to, and within, a given normative set (normative system).

In the normal course of affairs, due to the fact that the legal interpretation game (see Chap. 3 below) is a justificatory game, they ascribe sense or value to some legal item according to some presupposed juristic doctrine ("theory"), which the legal interpreter has previously selected since she considers it to be correct. Accordingly, less elliptical, pragmatically more adequate, logical forms for institutional-status sentences can be conceived as follows:

(*ISS5*) "The legally correct institutional status of *X* (provision LP_i, explicit norm N_j, implicit norm N_p), in relation to normative set LS_i, is *Y*"

(*ISS6*) "*Y* is (counts as) the legally correct institutional status of *X* (provision LP_i, explicit norm N_j, implicit norm N_p), in relation to normative set LS_i"

(*ISS7*) "*Y* is (counts as) the legally correct institutional status of *X* (provision LP_i, explicit norm N_j, implicit norm N_p), in relation to normative set LS_i, *Y* being the institutional status of *X* according to (what should be taken as) the all-things considered correct juristic theory JT_j".

Integration sentences establish that a certain norm is to be added to a given normative set, as a further, implicit, component thereof, being the output of a legally correct integration reasoning: i.e., of a reasoning that, according to the interpreter, employs the legally right set of integration directives (the legally right "integration code": IGC) in the right way.[13]

In their simplest forms, integration sentences look as follows:

(*IGS1*) "The norm N_j is an implicit component of the normative set LS_i ($N_1, N_2 \ldots N_n$)"

(*IGS2*) "Implicit norm N_j (also) belongs to the normative set LS_i"

(*IGS3*) "The normative set LS_i (also) includes the implicit norm N_j".

Such forms, however, are not wholly satisfactory. Less elliptical, pragmatically more adequate logical forms seem preferable:

(*IGS4*) "The normative set LS_i (also) includes the implicit norm N_j, N_j being an implicit component of LS_i according to (what should be taken as) the all-things considered legally correct use of the legally correct integration code IGC_j"

[13] As an instance of integration reasoning, consider the following: "The norm N_j is an implicit component of the normative set LS_i since it can be derived from N_i, which belongs to LS_i, by means of the proper integration rule IGR_o".

(*IGS5*) "The norm N_j is (counts as) a legally correct implicit component of the normative set LS_i, N_j being an implicit norm that can be added to LS_i according to (what should be taken as) the all-things considered legally correct use of the legally correct integration code IGC_j".

N_j represents, notice, a norm that is *implicit*. This means, on the one hand, that it is *not* explicit, i.e., it is not presented, nor defended, as the meaning expressed by any individual legal provision (negative condition); on the other hand, that it is the outcome of applying some integration technique (like, for instance, analogical reasoning, reasoning *a contrario*, reasoning *a fortiori*, reasoning from the nature of things, reasoning from general or fundamental principles), that the interpreter presents as all-things considered correct, to a previously identified set of explicit and/or implicit norms (positive condition).

Integration sentences typically show up in two sorts of reasoning. To begin with, they appear inside of juristic "systematic" reasonings, meant to "bringing to the light", or "digging out", the full components of a given normative set: for instance, "the whole system" of the constitutional laws concerning freedom of expression. Furthermore, they also appear inside of juristic or judicial reasonings meant to fill up some previously identified gap in the law.

As the logical form (*IGS5*) makes clear, integration sentences may also be considered as a variety of institutional-status sentences.

Gap-identification sentences establish the existence of normative gaps in the law. They state that there is a gap in the law, usually amounting to the absence of any explicit norm whatsoever for a case at hand. Their simpler form is:

(*GIS1*) "The case C_j (say, the opening of wine-bars within two-hundred meters from high school buildings) is not regulated by any explicit norm of the relevant legal set LS_i".

Less elliptical, pragmatically more adequate, logical forms may be conceived:

(*GIS2*) "The case C_j is not regulated by any explicit norm, there being no explicit norm regulating C_j that can be identified according to (what should be taken as) the all-things considered correct textual interpretation of the relevant set of legal provisions RLP_j"

(*GIS3*) "The legally correct institutional status of case C_j amounts to its being not regulated by any explicit norm, there being no explicit norm regulating C_j that can be identified according to (what should be taken as) the all-things considered correct textual interpretation of the relevant set of legal provisions RLP_j".

GIS2 and *GIS3* concern, more precisely, the identification of explicit gaps. They presuppose some piece of textual interpretation and build on its outputs.[14]

Antinomy-identification sentences establish the existence of antinomies (normative conflicts) in the law. They state that an incompatibility obtains between two

[14] On explicit gaps, see Chap. 7, Sect. 7.2 below.

norms that, by hypothesis, are both *prima facie* relevant to regulate a case at hand. Their simpler form is:

(*AIS1*) "Norm *N1* is incompatible with norm *N2* in relation to the case C_j".

Given a previously identified normative set, the identification of relations of logical incompatibility between norms is a matter of logic.[15] Two remarks are in order, though.

To begin with, the identification of logical antinomies presupposes that a normative set has already been identified. This is the output of activities of textual and meta-textual interpretation. Accordingly, the identification of logical antinomies depends, though indirectly, on previous interpretive decisions concerning the legally correct way of identifying the norms of the relevant normative set.

Furthermore, logical incompatibility does not exhaust the set of normative conflicts: there are, indeed, non-logical incompatibilities between norms, corresponding to the varieties of pragmatic, instrumental, teleological and ideological antinomies.[16] The identification of non-logical antinomies is not just a matter of logic, but requires, rather, operations consisting, for instance, in making means-to-ends judgements, drawing specific rules out of broad principles, identifying the scale of ethical values "staying in the background" of some set of positive norms.

This suggests that the simple form above (*AIS1*) is not adequate to the complexity of antinomy identification. Better logical forms may be conceived; like, e.g.:

(*AIS2*) "According to (what should be taken) as the all-things considered correct way of identifying the relevant normative set NS_i, NS_i contains the norms *N1* and *N2*, and these are (logically/non-logically) incompatible in relation to the case C_j"

(*AIS3*) "The legally correct relation between the norms *N1* and *N2* of the properly identified normative set NS_i, in relation to the case C_j, is (counts as) a relation of (logical/non-logical) incompatibility".

Hierarchy-identification sentences, finally, establish the ranking order between two previously identified norms, stating which of the two norms, if any, is superior to the other. In their simplest form, hierarchy-identification sentences run as follows:

(*HIS1*) "Norm *N1* is superior to (inferior to/on a par with) norm *N2*".

Less elliptical, pragmatically more adequate, logical forms may also be conceived:

---

[15] See Alchourrón and Bulygin (1971). For instance, given a normative set composed of two norms, N1 ("Citizens ought to pay taxes", "C –> OT") and N2 ("Farmers may not pay taxes", "F –> P¬T"), the set contains an antinomy for the case of citizens being also farmers (or farmers being also citizens) C & F –> OT & P ¬T.

[16] On non-logical antinomies see e.g. Chiassoni (2011), ch. IV. I will provide some clues on these notions in Sect. 2.3.3 below, while dealing with rhetorical normative systems and the variety of compatibility criteria that they may adopt.

(*HIS2*) "Norm *N1* is (counts as) superior to/inferior to/on a par with norm *N2*, being such a relation according to (what should be taken as) the all-things considered correct hierarchy criterion HC_j"

(*HIS3*) "The legally correct hierarchical relation between the norm *N1* and the norm *N2* is H_i (i.e., *N1* is superior to *N2*), being H_i the relation between *N1* and *N2* according to (what should be taken as) the all-things considered correct hierarchy criterion HC_j".[17]

As (*HIS2*) and (*HIS3*) forms show, also hierarchy-identification sentences are a variety—in fact, a very important one—of institutional status sentences. The correctness of the hierarchy criterion employed depends on the theory of the legal order the jurists adopt. Sometimes, hierarchies depend on established undisputable principles corresponding to the "objective architecture" of the legal system, and on easily ascertainable empirical data. For instance, in a constitutional state, any norm (which the interpreter has previously decided) that is a constitutional norm is ("formally") superior to any norm (which the interpreter has previously decided) that belongs to "ordinary legislation". Other times, however, hierarchies depend more heavily on juristic theories. For instance, in a constitutional state, some constitutional norms are (regarded as) superior to other constitutional norms in virtue of their being (classifiable as) the "supreme" or "fundamental" principles of the constitution.[18]

2.2.2 *Interpretation Proper to a Cognitive Purpose*

There are activities of interpretation *in a proper sense*—since their performance by an agent properly amounts to "interpreting the law"—that are, however, *cognitive* in character. They are not performed to the immediate purpose either of deciding some controversy at hand, as it betakes to judges, or of suggesting how it should be decided, to decide it correctly, as it betakes to jurists and lawyers. Rather, these activities aim at providing information about the *hermeneutic capacity* of legal provisions: they are about the meanings legal provisions *can* (be read to) bear. They are not, accordingly, of a practical, decision-making, ethical commitment character.

The outputs of cognitive interpretation can be conceived as *conjectural sentences*. In fact, as we shall see in a moment, they purport to express informed interpretive guesses about a legal provision at hand.

Three varieties of conjectural sentences are worthwhile distinguishing, which correspond to as many varieties of conjectural interpretation-activity. These are: sentences of methodological conjecture (*methodological-conjecture sentences*),

[17] For instance, "According to what should be regarded as the all things considered correct hierarchy criterion of ideological value (AV), norm P1, being a supreme fundamental principle, is superior to norm P2, which is an ordinary constitutional principle".

[18] On the juristic doctrine of "supreme constitutional principles", see e.g. Guastini (2011a), pp. 182–186.

which are the outputs of *methodological conjectural interpretation*; sentences of ideological conjecture (*ideological-conjecture sentences*), which are the outputs of *ideological conjectural interpretation*; and finally *creative sentences*, which are the outputs of *creative conjectural interpretation.*[19] The sentences of the first kind purport to work out the *methodological set ("frame")* of meaning of a given provision; those of the second kind the *ideological set ("frame")*; those of the third kind the *methodological innovation set ("frame").*

2.2.2.1 Methodological Conjectures

Methodological-conjecture sentences outline the methodological set ("frame") of the meanings of a given legal provision. They identify the set of alternative meanings into which one and the same legal provision can be translated, on the basis of the different interpretive rules (directives, methods, techniques, canons) that, by hypothesis, actually belong to the methodological box of the relevant legal culture of the time and are accordingly available to any "player".[20]

Methodological-conjecture sentences are the output of a complex activity having the character of a hermeneutical experiment.[21] On the basis of data gathered from legal experience, the experiment purports to investigate the hermeneutical capacity of an individual provision.[22] This occurs by means of an experimental machine that consists in a three-steps process.

The first step concerns the identification of the translation rules ("directives", "methods", "techniques", "canons") belonging to the methodological box of the legal culture of the time. This task requires, to begin with, the carrying out of a sociological inquiry detecting which methods judges and jurists employ, or regard as viable, in their writings and opinions. It may also require to provide a precisifying reconstruction of the available methods, turning the broad translation rules of ordinary juristic discourse (e.g.: "Interpret statutory provisions according to the ordinary meaning of their words") into the more precise ones that are in fact regarded

[19] "Creative interpretation" is sometimes used to refer to a radical instance of (in my terminology) textual interpretation, where the interpreter translates a legal provision into a norm that does not belong to its methodological frame of meanings (see, e.g., Guastini 2011a, pp. 141–142). In my view, one thing is "inventing" a new meaning for a legal provision; another thing is translating that provision by *that* new meaning to the practical purpose of deciding a case at hand. This is the reason why I present creative interpretation as a form of conjectural, theoretical, interpretation in the proper sense, and not as an extreme variety of textual, practical, interpretation.

[20] Clearly, the present notion of methodological conjectural interpretation represents an attempt to take seriously, and consider the theoretical potentialities of, Kelsen's idea of "scientific interpretation". See Kelsen (1960), chap. VIII. I will come back to interpretation frames in Chap. 5, Sect. 5.2 below.

[21] A hermeneutical experiment can be regarded as a variety of mental experiment. On mental experiments, see e.g. Buzzoni (2004), pp. 124–126, 265 ss. See also Brown and Fehige (2011).

[22] Like, e.g., article 3, paragraph 2, of the Italian Constitution, art. 3 of the European Convention of Human Rights, the "no establishment clause" of the American Constitution, etc.

as applicable (e.g.: "Interpret statutory provisions according to the literal meaning of their words and phrases, as it would have been understood by an ordinary reader of the time the law was enacted, considering each word and phrase in its immediate linguistic context").

In the second step, the interpreter applies in turn, to the legal provision at hand, each of the several translation rules identified and precisified in the first step. This requires the identification of the set (or sets) of interpretive resources related to each translation rule. In proceeding to the conjectural interpretation of the legal provision, the interpreter must assume, for the experiment's sake, that each of the several translation rules available, when applied, takes precedence over any other one. To the purpose of methodological conjecture, interpretive codes—which, in textual interpretation, are sets encompassing a variety of method and translation rules—boil down to a single, properly precisified translation rule.

The third step consists, finally, in the formulation of the methodological-conjecture sentence expressing the final result of the preceding operations. A viable logical form looks like a disjunctive set of conditional sentences:

(*MCS*) "Legal provision LP_i expresses either the norm *N1*, if it is being interpreted according to translation rule *TR1* and the set of interpretive resources *IR1*, or, rather, the norm *N2*, if it is being interpreted according to translation rule *TR2* and the set of interpretive resources *IR2*, or, rather, the norm …".[23]

2.2.2.2 Ideological Conjectures

Ideological-conjecture sentences outline the ideological set ("frame") of meanings of legal provisions. They identify the set of alternative meanings into which one and the same legal provision can be translated on the basis of the ideological views about the law and legal interpretation (philosophies of justice, normative theories of the state and legal order, normative theories about the "proper" role of judges, etc.), which, by hypothesis, are present in the legal culture of the time. Of course, some of these ideological outlooks will be, as a matter of social fact, dominant or highly influential. These will represent the more relevant and interesting subject of enquiry.

Methodological conjectural interpretation, as we have seen, simply pays attention to methodological devices, without considering the substantial correctness, and cultural acceptability, of the interpretive outcomes they produce. Conversely, ideological conjectural interpretation also takes into account this further aspect, giving it pride of place in the enquiry. Indeed, the idea of an ideological conjectural interpretation mirrors the—quite sensible—view according to which textual interpretation involves two further basic ingredients, besides legal texts and logical forms of reasoning: namely, ethical values and rhetorical techniques. Values, as components of ideological outlooks, intervene both in the selection of the proper (legally cor-

[23] On methodological conjectural interpretation, see also Chap. 5, Sect. 5.2., below.

rect) set of interpretive rules and in the selection of the proper (legally correct) arrangement of interpretive resources.

The experimental machine of interpretive ideological conjecture consists in a four-steps process.

The first step is devoted to identifying the ideological views that are present in the legal culture of the time, or, at least, the most influential ones (be it even by a *succès de scandale*).

The second step concerns the identification of ideologically correct interpretive codes: that is to say, of the codes that, according to each of the several ideological outlooks previously identified, interpreters must employ in order to interpret the law correctly.

The third step is devoted to the conjectural interpretation of an individual legal provision on the basis of the several ideologically correct codes. This involves the identification, for each of the codes to be applied, of the related set(s) of interpretive resources.

The fourth, and last, step is devoted to the formulation of the ideological conjecture sentence that constitutes the final result of the previous operations. This can be represented, as for methodological sentences, with the aid of a disjunctive set of conditional sentences:

(*ACS*) "Legal provision LP_i expresses either the norm *N1*, if it is being interpreted according to the ideologically correct interpretive code *IC1* and the related set of interpretive resources *IR1*, or, rather, the norm *N2*, if it is being interpreted according to the ideologically correct interpretive code *IC2* and the related set of interpretive resources *IR2*, or, rather, the norm …".

Suppose an interpreter finds that there are two influential ideological outlooks in her society (*S*): say, a majoritarian ("populist") conception and a liberal ("individualist") conception of constitutional democracy. She may also detect the commitment of each of the two outlooks to a certain interpretive code: say, a literal-intentional code and a literal-coherence code, respectively. On this basis, she will proceed to conjecturing: first, a more precise and complete interpretive code corresponding to each of the two outlooks, if necessary; second, the ideological frame of meanings corresponding to each of the several constitutional provisions, according to the two previously identified ideological codes.[24] If ideological codes contain more then one translation rules (as it is the case in the imaginary example I am presently considering), our conjectural interpreter will proceed by interpreting each provision, in turn, according to each of the translation rules of each code. If ideological codes contain translation rules already making part of the on-going methodological box, the output of ideological conjectural interpretation will be a sub-set of the output of methodological conjectural interpretation. In such a case, it will provide information about the interpretive outputs that "society" ("the legal culture", "the legal profession", etc., or some part thereof) is likely to consider not only methodologically, but also substantially (ideologically), viable.

---

[24] On ideological conjectural interpretation, see also Chap. 5, Sect. 5.2, below.

2.2.2.3 Methodological Innovation

Finally, *creative sentences* purport to identify new possible meanings for legal provisions. These meanings are new, since, by hypothesis: they do not belong to the methodological or ideological frame of meanings of the legal provision at stake; they can be identified and argued for by appealing to some new interpretive method and a related set of interpretive resources. For this reason, we can understand creative sentences as accounting for a frame of meanings depending on methodological innovation, or, in other terms, a creative conjecture. The logical form of a creative sentence may conceived as follows:

(*CCS*) "If legal provision LP_i is interpreted according to the new method M_j and the related set of interpretive resources R_j, it will express the norm N_j, which represents a new meaning for LP_i".

Suppose, for instance, an interpreter making conjectures about which new meanings could constitutional provisions be translated into, if, instead of using the traditional, ideologically approved, methods of literal and intentional interpretation, they were interpreted according to a "moral reading" or a "jurisprudence of values" method.

Clearly, here I am interested in a rational notion of creative interpretation: one that is related to the possibility of *arguing* for the new meanings that have been set forth. Whimsical creations are, at least in principle, outside of the scope of the legal interpretation game, as we know it.[25]

2.2.3 *Interpretation Improper*

The activities of interpretation *in an improper sense*, finally, are such that an agent who performs them, properly speaking, does not really "interpret the law". In fact, these are activities by which somebody either describes how other agents have interpreted a certain piece of law, or makes predictions about how other agents will interpret it, or, else, formulate prescriptions about how other agents should interpret it. Following Giovanni Tarello, I will call these activities *interpretation-detection*, *interpretation-prediction*, and *interpretation-prescription*, respectively.[26]

2.2.3.1 Interpretation-Detection

Interpretation-detection ends up in *detection sentences*.

Singular detection sentences describe individual acts of textual interpretation of legal provisions:

[25] On creative interpretation, see also Chap. 5, Sect. 5.2, below.

[26] Tarello (1980), ch. 2.

(*SDS*) "Legal provision LP_i was interpreted by judge J_i (e.g.: the Court of appeals of Yellow Falls), in judicial decision JD_i, as expressing the norm *N1*".

General detection sentences, on the contrary, are the output of generalizations from singular detection sentences, and purport to describe past interpretive trends:

(*GDS*) "During the past time-span T_i (e.g.: from 1980 to present), judges J_o (e.g.: the appeal judges of the country, the county courts, the judges of the highest court) always have interpreted provision LP_i to mean norm *N1*".

2.2.3.2 Interpretation-Prediction

Interpretation-prediction ends up in *prediction sentences*.

Singular prediction sentences predict individual acts of textual interpretation of legal provisions:

(*SPS*) "Provision LP_i will *n*-probably (e.g.: with a more than 60% likelihood) be interpreted by judge J_i (e.g.: the Court of appeals of Yellow Falls), in its decision of the case C_i, as expressing the norm *N1*".

General prediction sentences, contrariwise, purport to predict future interpretive trends:

(*GPS*) "Concerning the future time-span F_o (e.g.: during the next two years), there is a *n*-probably (e.g.: more than 60%) that judges J_o (e.g.: the appeal judges of the country) will interpret provision LP_i as expressing the norm *N1* in cases *C*".

2.2.3.3 Interpretation-Prescription

Finally, *interpretation-prescription* ends up in *prescription sentences.*

Singular prescription sentences concern individual acts of textual interpretation:

(*SPRS*) "Provision LP_i ought to be interpreted by judge J_i (e.g.: the Court of appeals of Yellow Falls) as expressing the norm *N1* in deciding case C_i".

General prescription sentences concern, instead, classes of interpretation acts:

(*GPRS*) "Provision LP_i ought to be interpreted by the judges J_o (e.g.: the appeal judges of the country) as expressing the norm *N1* in every type C case".

According to the institutional role of the interpreter, prescription sentences may have an imperative or normative character (think at the highest court issuing any such prescription to a lower court), or, else, the character of an advice or a recommendation, as it is the case with juristic prescription sentences (where juristic opinions are no part of the formal sources of law, and, hence, are not legally binding on judges and people at large).[27]

Armed with the foregoing reconstruction of interpretive discourse, very broadly conceived, as we have seen, we can finally start putting our teeth on the haunting problem I mentioned at the beginning.

When jurists and legal philosophers claim that there are, or there can be, "interpretations" that are "true" (or "false"), they usually refer to such things as "propositions of law",[28] "interpretative statements",[29] "interpretive judgements", "interpretive propositions", or "interpretive theses"[30] as being truth-apt entities. These entities correspond, roughly, to what I have here presented as the outputs of the activities of textual or meta-textual interpretation (Sects. 2.2.1.1 and 2.2.1.2 above). Indeed, they are "propositions" ("statements", "judgements", "theses", etc.) that judges and jurists formulate whenever, in view of fulfilling their professional tasks, they have come to "ascertain" what the law requires as to a certain issue at hand by interpreting constitutional, statutory, or regulatory provisions—also in the light, to be sure, of customary practices, judicial opinions, and juristic writings. In the views of some jurists and legal philosophers, (what I here call) interpretive sentences and integration sentences are, therefore, truth-apt entities. Such a view elicits a few questions: Are they right? Which truth do they have in mind when they claim "interpretive propositions" to be apt for truth? Which truth may be suitable to such entities? Which truth-conditions can make them *true*? In order to provide an answer to these questions, a very brief incursion into the (awesome) territory of truth is in order.

---

[27] The set of notions in the text represents a radical re-visitation of Chiassoni (1999a), p. 21 ff.; Chiassoni (2011), ch. II.

[28] Ronald Dworkin sees "propositions of law"—like, e.g., that "the law forbids states to deny anyone equal protection within the meaning of the Fourteenth Amendment", "the law does not provide compensation for fellow-servants injuries", "the law requires Acme Corporation to compensate John Smith for the injury he suffered in its employ last February"—as entities apt for being either true or false. Dworkin's "propositions of law" are, however, not genuine normative propositions, i.e., empirically true or false statements *about* existing norms (von Wright 1963, pp. 105–106); they are, rather, sentences *that express norms* ("normative claims"): individual or general norms, explicit or implicit norms, proposed, invoked, used, applied as "true" in connection with a legal system. The nature of such "propositions" is, more precisely, that of general or individual norms identified by means of constructive interpretation. Indeed, Dworkin makes clear that: "According to law as integrity, propositions of law are true if they *figure* or *follow from* the *principles of justice, fairness, and procedural due process that provide the best constructive interpretation of the community's legal practice*" (Dworkin 1986, pp. 4–5, 225, italic added; see also Dworkin 2006, pp. 14–15). Like positions are entertained by Patterson (1996), and, concerning law's "objectivity", Stavropoulos (1996).

[29] See, e.g., Aarnio (1981), pp. 423–448, dealing with the "truth" of "interpretative statements in legal dogmatics". According to Aarnio, interpretative statements are the outputs of the interpretation of legal texts (which Aarnio characterizes as the activity consisting in "grasping the meaning-content of the text"), and have the form "the content of the legal text is such-and-such". Clearly, the jurist making such an interpretative statement is claiming that "such-and-such" is *the* legally correct meaning of the legal text. Accordingly, when Aarnio speaks of juristic "interpretative statements" he is referring to what I here call "interpretive sentences".

[30] See Diciotti (1999), p. 91 ff., 103 ff., 152 ff., 185 ff., 283 ff.

2.3 Truth

In the opening passage of his farewell lecture, *What is Justice?*, Hans Kelsen recalls a scene from John's *Gospel* (18:38):

> When Jesus of Nazareth was brought before Pilate and admitted that he was a king, he said: "It was for this that I was born, and for this that I came to the world, to give testimony for truth". Whereupon Pilate asked: "What is truth?" The Roman Procurator did not expect, and Jesus did not give, an answer to this question; for to give testimony for truth was not the essence of his divine mission as the Messianic King. He was born to give testimony for justice, the justice to be realized in the Kingdom of God, and for this justice he died on the cross.[31]

In his report of the evangelic scene, Kelsen reminds us that the word "truth" can be used in many different ways: virtually, to refer to whatever worthwhile stuff there is on earth, or in heaven.[32] He also suggests that it would be possible adopting, to begin with, a reductionist strategy as to the problem about "truth and legal interpretation". If we understand "truth" just as one of the names for justice, the problem about whether interpretations can be "true" becomes the problem of whether interpretations are, or can be, justice-apt entities: i.e., whether they can be "just", or "in accordance with justice". Furthermore, if, following Kelsen, we also endorse non-objectivism and non-cognitivism as our meta-ethical stance (which, though being utterly reasonable, are still anathema to many scholars and people-at-large), the problem of truth in legal interpretation totally changes in character. From being, at least prima facie, an epistemic problem, i.e., a problem about the scope of objective knowledge in legal interpretation, it turns into a practical issue. It becomes, to wit, the problem of taking side within a field characterized by a plurality of competing political, legal, and moral views, and typically saddled with conflicts of material and spiritual interests between individuals and groups engaged in a never-ending search for their own social happiness under conditions of scarcity.

Suppose however we opt for not embracing the reductionist strategy suggested by Kelsen. If we do so, a further option immediately pops out. This is the option between two varieties of alethic pluralism: austere alethic pluralism and broad alethic pluralism, as we may call them. Austere alethic pluralism contemplates two notions of truth: empirical truth and formal truth. Broad alethic pluralism, contrariwise, contemplates (in the reconstruction I will adopt to the present purpose) four notions of truth: besides empirical and formal truth, it also encompasses pragmatic truth and systemic truth. If, out of an experimental and tentative mood, we decide to adopt a position of broad alethic pluralism, and leave aside formal truth, we may contemplate three notions of truth that, at least prima facie, are available to be con-

[31] Kelsen (1957), p. 1. The scene is something of a success in the truth-literature. See, e.g., Austin (1950), p. 85.

[32] This is also what John Keats's Greek Urn tells us: "When old age shall this generation waste, / Thou shalt remain, in midst of other woe/ Than ours, a friend to man, to whom thou say'st, / "Beauty is truth, truth beauty, —that is all / Ye know on earth, and all ye need to know."".

sidered fit for being applied in the field of legal interpretation. These are empirical truth, pragmatic truth and systemic truth.[33]

2.3.1 Empirical Truth

Empirical truth is informational correctness in relation to experience. Three kinds of discourse-entities are usually considered as being apt for empirical truth. These are singular descriptive sentences, singular predictive sentences, and theoretical sentences.

Singular descriptive sentences are the outcome either of observing or experiencing some actual individual event, fact, thing, state of affairs, behaviour, etc., or of remembering some individual event, fact, thing, state of affairs, behaviour, etc., that has been observed or experienced in the past. Singular descriptive sentences have, accordingly, a direct link with experience: they refer to singular facts or events in

[33] I take formal truth to encompass analytic truth and logical truth. The former depends on the meaning of the descriptive words composing a sentence. For instance, the sentence "All bachelors are unmarried men" is analytically true in the English language, because "bachelor" means "unmarried man". The latter depends on the meaning of logical terms ("and", "or", "not", etc.) and on the structure of the sentence. For instance, any complex sentence of the form "A v ¬A" ("It rains or it does not rain") is logically true, while any sentence of the form "A & ¬A" ("It rains and it does not rain") is logically false. Interpretation-outputs, as discourse entities, are apt for formal truth and falsity, for they can be tautological or self-contradictory. Austere alethic pluralism is the mark of logical positivism and empiricist epistemology. See e.g. Ayer (1952), von Wright (1951). On (broad) alethic pluralism, see, e.g.: Pedersen and Wright (2012): "'Pluralism about truth' names the thesis that there is more then one way of being true"; Pedersen and Wright (2013), ch. 1; Wright (2013), ch. 7; Wright (2001), pp. 751–787; Lynch (2001), pp. 723–749; Lynch (2009), pp. 1–6, 159 ff. By focussing on empirical, pragmatic and systemic truth, I leave out at least a fourth candidate: namely, the so-called consensus theory of truth. This holds, very roughly speaking, that a theoretical or practical claim is true, whenever it commands the universal assent of rational agents in an ideal reflexive context. It must be noticed, however, that Jürgen Habermas, perhaps the most prominent supporter of consensus theory in contemporary philosophy, from the late 1990s has come to distinguish between the "truth" of descriptive sentences, which depends on the objective world, on the one hand, and the "normative correctness" or "deontological validity" of moral judgements and moral norms, which depends, contrariwise, on their justifiability according to the "discourse principle", on the other ("A rule of action or choice is justified, and thus valid, only if all those affected by the rule or choice could accept it in a reasonable discourse": Bohman and Rehg 2014, § 3.4; see Habermas 1999, ch. 6). By the way, if we stop to reflect upon the reason which a rational agent may have to accept a rule of action or a choice as "normatively correct" or "deontologically valid", this has likely to do with the rule or choice being in tune with her ultimate practical principles and/or her preferred goals. In this way, consensus theory of normative correctness or deontological validity seems to boil down to a variety of pragmatic or systemic correctness. In order to "set the tone" concerning broad alethic pluralism, it may perhaps be worthwhile quoting a remark by Alfred Tarski: "In modern philosophical literature some other conceptions and theories of truth are also discussed [besides the classic, semantic or correspondence theory, ndr], such as the pragmatic conception and the coherence theory. These conceptions seem to be of an exclusively normative character and have little connection with the actual usage of the term "true"" (Tarski 1969, p. 64; Tarski 1944, pp. 348–349).

time and space, which have been observed or experienced by the agent who articulates them. For instance: the number of participants to the meeting *C* ("The Glorious Friends of Pink Whales") in T_i (January 2, 2017) and L_i (Winter Springs); the behaviour of Mrs. *Y* in T_j, and L_j; the colour of Mr. *X*'s robe in T_o, L_o; the organoleptic properties of the wine *W* in bottle *B* in T_p, L_p; the 1944 eruption of Vesuvius, etc. As Aristotle put it, they are true (E-true), if, and only if, things are (were) as they say they are (were); they are false (E-false), contrariwise, if, and only if, things are (were) not as they say they are (were).[34] Ruling out any form of scepticism, idealism and post-modernism, things—events, states of affairs, acts, etc.—are assumed to work as truth-makers that do exist independently of beliefs, preferences and interpretations of those who make descriptive sentences.

Singular predictive sentences are the outcome of anticipatory cognitive inquiries. They depend on observation of empirical phenomena, memory, and inductive reasoning. They state that, considering what was the case in the past, something will probably be the case in a certain future moment: there is *now* a certain probability (say 40%) that a certain event will occur in a future moment (e.g., that it will rain or snow tomorrow; that the volcano will erupt within fifteen days from now, etc.).[35]

Theoretical sentences, finally, include such discourse-entities as physical laws, maxims of experience, general descriptive sentences, sentences purporting to explain how complex phenomena are, etc.[36] They have no direct, immediate, relation to experience. Their truth depends directly on their agreement ("coherence", "compatibility") with other linguistic entities, and ultimately with a certain set of singular descriptive sentences, and only in a mediate way on experience.[37]

Regarding singular descriptive sentences, empirical truth consists in the agreement ("correspondence", "fit") between the sentence ("the words"), on the one hand, and experience ("the world"), on the other, in the way already made clear by Aristotle.[38] Regarding singular predictive sentences, empirical truth consists in their

[34] In the well known words of Aristotle: "Saying of what is that it is not, or of what it is not that it is, is false […] saying of what is that it is, or of what is not that it is not, is true" (Aristotle, *Metaphysics*, 1011b, 25–26). Aristotle's passage is commonly regarded as one of the oldest and clearest formulations of the ordinary or classic conception of truth. Tarski set forth to obtain, with the aid of the techniques of contemporary logic, a "more precise explanation of the classical conception of truth, one that could supersede the Aristotelian formulation while preserving its basic intentions"; as it is well known, Tarski's view is centred on "the equivalence of the form (T)": "(T) *X* is true if, and only if, *p*", where "p" stands for any sentence in a language and "X" stands for the name of that sentence ("The sentence "snow is white" is true if, and only if, snow is white"): Tarski (1969), p. 64 ff.; Tarski (1944), pp. 334–336; Quine (1986), pp. 35–46.

[35] See von Wright (1951), pp. 13–15.

[36] Physical law: "Water boils at 100°C"; experience rule: "Murderers always go back to the place of the crime"; general descriptive sentence: "Ravens are black"; explanatory sentence for a complex phenomenon: "Law is composed of norms".

[37] From this perspective, then, the notion of truth as coherence and the notion of truth as correspondence do not represent the core of two opposed and irreconcilable theories of truth. The opposition arises whenever the idea of coherence is part, for instance, of an idealistic conception of truth. On this point, see Quine (1987), p. 212 ff. See also Carnap (1936), pp. 119–127.

[38] Russell (1912), ch. 12; Russell (1940), ch. 21; Tarski (1944), pp. 333–334.

being justified, at the moment of their formulation, by (an adequate set of) true descriptive and theoretical sentences.[39] Regarding theoretical sentences, finally, empirical truth depends on their agreement ("coherence", "compatibility") with other sentences: on the "fit" between the sentences expressing them ("their words") and other sentences ("other words"), which include empirically true singular descriptive sentences.[40]

2.3.2 *Pragmatic Truth*

Pragmatic truth is utility in practice: instrumental, means-to-end, adequacy in relation to a previously defined set of goals.[41]

Two heterogeneous sets of discourse entities can be singled out as being apt for pragmatic truth: *theoretical sentences*, which belong to the realm of empirical knowledge and scientific research; *practical sentences*, which, contrariwise, belong to the realm of normative ethics.

Theoretical sentences—empirical theses ("claims") and (pieces of) scientific theories—are pragmatically true (P-true), if, and only if, they work successfully as tools for improving the human condition: if they provide pieces of information that help humans in bettering situations, removing obstacles, dissipating uncertainties. The success of an empirical claim or a scientific theory is measured on the reliability of the forecasts that it is capable of suggesting to the agents in connection with their existential goals.[42]

---

[39] In the text, I understand singular predictive sentences as sentences of the form "It is (now) probable that *f* will occur at time *t*", or, less precisely, "*f* will probably occur at time *t*". This is the logical form suggested by von Wright (1951), pp. 13–31; von Wright (1984b), pp. 1–13. Predictive sentences as they occur in ordinary language, however, can also be understood as propositions about contingent future events, of the form "*f* will occur at time *t*" ("Tomorrow there will be a sea battle"). In such a case, they can be considered as liable to a double check: an *ex ante* assessment in terms of adequate empirical and theoretical support, and, furthermore, an *ex post* assessment in terms of empirical fulfilment. See, e.g., MacFarlane (2003), pp. 321–336.

[40] Quine (1987), p. 212 ff.; Quine (1986), pp. 5–6.

[41] On pragmatic theories of truth see e.g. Lynch (2001), Part III.

[42] According to a passage of John Dewey, ideas and theories are true if they are "instrumental to an active reorganization of the given environment, to a removal of some specific trouble and perplexity [...] The hypothesis that works is the *true* one" (J. Dewey, *Reconstruction in Philosophy*, 1920, 156, quoted by Davidson 2005, 8, note 3). Burgess and Burgess (2011), p. 3, characterize the "Pragmatist or utility theory" of truth, among the "traditional theories", as claiming that "A belief is true iff it is useful in practice". Dewey, however, also conceived of "truths" as being "in the keeping of the best available methods of inquiry and testing as to matters-of-fact; methods, which are, when collected under a single name, science" (J. Dewey, *Experience and Nature*, 1958, 410, quoted by Davidson 2005, 7, note 1). Furthermore, he also manifested his assent to Peirce's ideal and universal agreement criterion of truth: "The best definition of *truth* from a logical standpoint which is known to me is that of Peirce: "The opinion which is fated to be ultimately agreed to by all who investigate is what we mean by the truth"" (J. Dewey, *Logic: The Theory of Inquiry*, 1938, 58, quoted by Davidson 2005, 8, note 3).

Practical sentences—moral judgements, judicial rulings, general norms of positive morality, legal principles, etc.—are pragmatically true (P-true), if, and only if, they are instrumentally adequate to furthering or achieving some set of goals which has been previously identified as ethically valuable. For instance, the singular moral judgement "It is fair to overthrow the tyrant Titus" is pragmatically true (P-true), if, and only if, by hypothesis, the overthrowing of Titus will most likely produce consequences that are ethically more favourable (valuable) than unfavourable (non-valuable): say, it will maximize people's political freedom, and that goal is, by hypothesis, our selected, privileged, goal. Likewise, the general norm of political morality "Tyrants ought to be overthrown" is pragmatically true (P-true), if, and only if, for instance: it is a reliable prediction that, from the adoption and constant enforcement of such a norm, situations will follow that will ensure the widest political freedom for the largest number of people in the world; such an outcome is assumed to be morally valuable and deserving to be achieved. When used in connection with practical sentences like the ones I have just considered, the pragmatist notion of truth (P-truth) promotes the rational evaluation of norms and ethical value-judgements: their evaluation from the standpoint of instrumental, means-to-ends, rationality.

2.3.3 Systemic Truth

Systemic truth is part-to-whole adequacy: compatibility of some previously identified "part" to some previously identified "whole" or "system".

Systems are sets of entities (ideas, beliefs, sentences, propositions, norms, etc.) identified ("kept together", "unified") by some common property: like, e.g., the common reference to a certain subject matter (freedom of expression, bonobos in their social behaviour, poisonous mushrooms, tea parties, etc.), or the common derivation from the same set of primitive sentences (the axioms of Euclidean geometry, the independent norms of a normative system, a set of observation sentences, etc.).

Systemic truth, if understood as (systemic) compatibility, can be conceived in different ways. Three notions are worthwhile mentioning: compatibility as logical derivation, compatibility as logical consistency, and, finally, compatibility as coherence (non-logical consistency).[43]

According to the first notion of compatibility, a sentence is systemically true (S-true)—i.e., it has the property of part-to-whole adequacy—if, and only if, it is logically derived, or derivable, from the primitive sentences of the system, by means of the system's own rules of inference.

---

[43] As we shall see in a moment, coherence (non-logical compatibility) comes in several varieties including instrumental compatibility, teleological compatibility and ideological compatibility.

According to the second notion of compatibility, a sentence is systemically true (S-true)—i.e., it has the property of part-to-whole adequacy—if, and only if, it is logically consistent with the other sentences belonging to the system.

Finally, according to the third notion of compatibility, a sentence is systemically true (S-true)—i.e., it has the property of part-to-whole adequacy—if, and only if, it is coherent (non-logically consistent) with the other sentences belonging to the system.[44]

To the present purpose, it seems worthwhile casting a glance on how the notion of systemic truth may work in relation to *normative systems*: i.e., to systems that include norms of behaviour. I will consider in turn two varieties: deductive normative systems and rhetorical normative systems.

2.3.3.1 Deductive Normative Systems

In very rough terms, a deductive normative system presents the following main features.[45]

1. It is made of three sets of sentences: primitive norms, transformation rules, and derivative norms.

---

[44] As it appears in the text, the notion of systemic truth I am using here is parasitic to the notion of "truth as coherence". It is meant to be wider, and more precise, than it, though. A system may consist, for instance, in the totality of the logical consequences of a certain finite set of axioms (on this point, concerning normative systems, see Alchourrón and Bulygin 1975, pp. 85–86). In such a case, if the axiomatic basis of the system contains logically inconsistent sentences, a derived sentence can be "true" from the standpoint of its logical derivation from one of the system's axioms, and at the same time be inconsistent with some other element of the system (concerning normative system, Caracciolo 1988, p. 59). A coherence theory of truth claims that "A belief is true iff it coheres with other ideas" (Burgess and Burgess 2011, p. 3). According to Otto Neurath and Carl G. Hempel, "a proposition is "true" within a given system if it is consistent with the rest of the system, but there may be other systems, inconsistent with the first, in which the proposition in question will be false" (see Russell 1940, p. 140, where he also makes clear that the "Hegelian" variety of the coherence theory of truth claims, contrariwise, that "only one body of mutually coherent propositions is possible"). On coherence theories of truth see e.g. Lynch (2001), Part II; Young (2008).

[45] For this notion of a deductive normative system I have got inspiration from the idea of axiomatic deductive system set forth in Alchourrón and Bulygin (1975), ch. IV. Talking of the basis of a normative system, Alchourrón and Bulygin say that it can be made of sentences "contained" in a code or in a statute, or "extracted" from judicial decisions, or even "coming from Natural Law" (Alchourrón and Bulygin 1975, p. 98). Furthermore, they claim they are not suggesting norms to be tantamount to normative sentences, that is, to "linguistic entities", but only that "norms", whatever their ontological status, "*can be expressed* by means of language" (Alchourrón and Bulygin 1975, p. 99, italics in the text). In the quoted passages, they do not seem to draw a sharp line between norms and normative provisions. As we shall see in a moment, the distinction I outline between deductive and rhetorical normative systems turns, contrariwise, on drawing a sharp distinction between sentences that are norms and sentences that are normative provisions, i.e., texts apt to express norms by means of interpretation. On this distinction, see Conte (1957), p. 10; von Wright (1963), p. 93, who distinguishes between "norms" and "norm-formulations".

2. Primitive norms are norms of behaviour that constitute the *axiomatic basis* of the system. Think, for instance, at an axiomatic basis composed by the Ten Commandments—"You shall not kill", "You shall not commit adultery", "You shall not steal", "You shall not bear false witness against your neighbour", etc.—conceiving them, notice, *not* as a set of *normative provisions* waiting for textual interpretation (Sect. 2.2.1.1 above), but as a set of *norms* (meaningful normative sentences). Primitive norms are identified by an act of stipulation (e.g., an act of will of the supreme moral, religious, or legal legislator), and are apt for pragmatic truth (P-true entities) (see Sect. 2.3.2 above).
3. Transformation rules are rules of deductive inference. They are, again, the output of stipulations (e.g., by the supreme moral, religious or legal legislator), and are, again, apt for pragmatic truth (P-true entities).[46]
4. Derivative norms are norms that, being different from primitive norms, are the logical consequences of primitive norms. They are systemically true (S-true), if, and only if, they derive from the primitive norms of the system in accordance with the transformation rules of the system.[47]

2.3.3.2 Rhetorical Normative Systems

Rhetorical normative systems consist of two sets of sentences: normative provisions and norms.[48]

Normative provisions are a finite set of sentences issued by some ethical authority. Think, for instance, at the sentences making up an enacted moral, religious or legal code.

Normative provisions are, furthermore, the *primitive sentences* of a rhetorical system. Contrariwise, norms are *derivative sentences*. They are, in particular, sentences that consist in the *rhetorical consequences* of normative provisions. Their derivation from normative provisions is not a matter of demonstration, though it can assume the form of a deductive inference; it depends, rather, on forms of reasoning that are meant to persuade of their correctness, usually by appealing to evident, common, or reasonable rules of transformation that are, in turn, directly or indi-

[46] Of course, those who think the rules of logical inference to be a "necessary" part of any normative system would contest this assertion of mine (see, e.g., Kalinowski 1978). I will not consider their claim here.

[47] Assume, for instance, that among the axioms of the system there is the rule "All thefts worth up to 39 schillings shall be punished with a two-months period of socially useful work"; assume, furthermore, that among the transformation rules feature syllogisms and the possibility of introducing any assumption necessary to make those inferential schemes work. If an authorized player (say, a judge) assumes that "All thefts worth £ 10 are thefts worth up to 39 schillings", then the new rule follows, according to which, "All thefts worth £ 10 shall be punished with a two-months period of socially useful work". The fact that, according to common sense, a £ 10 theft is *not* worth "up to 39 schillings", but much more, is totally irrelevant to the systemic correctness of the derivative norm.

[48] Throughout the book, I assume norms to be linguistic entities.

rectly amenable to what is traditionally considered as the "realm of rhetorics" or "rhetorical argumentation".[49]

A rhetorical normative system can be characterized, therefore, as the combination of a finite set of normative provisions plus the totality of the norms that represent the actual or potential rhetorical consequences of that finite set of provisions. Some further explanation is in order.

1. The primitive sentences of a rhetorical system, as I have just said, are not norms, but (a finite set of) normative provisions. These, very roughly speaking, may be of two different sorts: *substantive provisions* and *methodological provisions*.

   Substantive provisions are sentences apt to express norms concerning the duties, rights, powers, privileges, etc., of their addressees. Think, again, at the Ten Commandments—"You shall not kill", "You shall not commit adultery", "You shall not steal", "You shall not bear false witness against your neighbour", etc.—conceiving them, now, *not* as a set of *norms*, *but* rather as a set of *normative provisions* waiting for textual interpretation by theologians, moralists, jurists or people at large.

   Methodological provisions are sentences apt to express the transformation rules of the rhetorical system: namely, the rules that intervene in the identification of the rhetorical consequences of the normative provisions of the system.

   Notice that the identification of transformation rules from methodological provisions is necessarily entrusted to the interpreters of the system. No provision is self-interpreting; not even those that purport to regulate interpretation. As a consequence, the transformation of methodological provisions into transformation rules—which is tantamount to a piece of intra-linguistic translation—ultimately depends on discretionary, though not necessarily arbitrary, choices by the interpreters, which are fatally affected by practical considerations (ethical principles, concern for values and outcomes, sensibility to material interests, etc.).
2. Two basic kinds of transformation rules are typically at work, when an agent acts as a player in relation to a rhetorical system. I shall refer to them, respectively, as *interpretation rules* and *integration rules*.

   Interpretation rules are instructions about the proper ways of translating normative provisions into (what will be taken as) the *explicit norms* of the system (see Sect. 2.2.1.1) above). They prescribe, e.g., that "Normative provisions shall be interpreted in accordance with the conventional meaning of their words", "Normative provisions shall be interpreted in accordance with their authors' original intent", "Normative provisions shall be interpreted in accordance with the nature of things", "Normative provisions shall be interpreted as expressing a coherent set of supreme principles", "Normative provisions shall be interpreted as expressing a set of efficient, wealth-maximizing, supreme principles", etc.

---

[49] On law and rhetorics, see Perelman (1979), Perelman (1982), pp. 661–667; Tarello (1980), pp. 85–99, 341–396; Gianformaggio (1983), pp. 101–107; Chiassoni (1999a, b), ch. V; Diciotti (2007), pp. 28–42.

Integration rules, by contrast, are instructions about the proper ways of enriching a rhetorical system by identifying the norms that make up (what will be taken as) its *implicit components* (see Sect. 2.2.1.2 above). They typically include rules like, for instance, "Like cases ought to be treated alike", "Different cases ought to be treated differently", "Norms of detail should be considered as instances of wider, background, implicit principles", "*Expressio unius est exclusio alterius*", "In case of a normative conflict, a priority rule should be established according to which the more valuable norm prevails over the less valuable one", etc.

3. Transformation rules—i.e., interpretation and integration rules—set the criteria of systemic truth for the norms of a rhetorical system. They may prescribe, for instance, that the outputs of rhetorical transformations of normative provisions should abide by logical consistency, instrumental coherence, teleological coherence and ideological coherence.[50] A norm satisfies the requirement of systemic compatibility as logical consistency, if, and only if, it is not logically incompatible, either by contradiction or contrariety, with some other norm, contextually considered as superior. A norm satisfies the requirement of systemic compatibility as instrumental coherence, if, and only if, the behaviour it prescribes or the state of affairs it constitutes or promotes are (the most) efficient means for achieving the goals set by other norms of the system. Of course, the same norm *N* may be instrumentally compatible in respect to, say, norm *N1*, and, at the same time, incompatible in respect to, say, norm *N2*. In such a case, compatibility can only be gained by establishing the priority of *N1* over *N2*.[51] A norm satisfies the requirement of systemic compatibility as teleological coherence, if, and only if,

[50] By the way, the compatibility test is likely to be applied in relation, not to the rhetorical system of norms as a whole, but, rather, to just one definite subset of the whole norms of the system, which interpreters and users consider more valuable, or of a higher standing, than the norm to be assessed. Going roughly down the same path as Dworkin's, Michael Lynch characterizes the truth of "propositions of law" not in terms of correspondence with an independent, objective, reality ("it is unlikely that they are true in virtue of referential relations with mind-independent objects and properties"), but in terms of coherence ("we think that a proposition of law is true when it coheres with its immediate grounds and with the grounds of propositions inferentially connected to it. In short, legal truth consists in coherence with the body of law"), and, more precisely, following Crispin Wright's idea of "superassertibility", in terms of "supercoherence" ("Thus perhaps what makes a proposition of law true is that it durably or continually coheres with the body of law [...] In short, juridical truth might turn out to be realized by "supercoherence" with the body of law, where a proposition can fail to have this property even if it coheres with the law in the short run, or coheres with judicial decisions that are later overturned"): Lynch (2001), p. 736, 737, 738. The idea that truth, in the realm of ethics, is truth "as coherence" is endorsed by Quine (Quine 1978, p. 63: "Science, thanks to its links with observation, retains some title to a correspondence theory of truth; but a coherence theory is evidently the lot ethics") and adopted by Dorsey (2006), pp. 493–523.

[51] It is noteworthy, in passing, that instrumental coherence can also be used as a criterion for that sort of "material derivation" of a norm from another norm that goes under the name of "concretization". Concretization consists in "deriving" fairly precise rules of conduct from broad principles. How can such a "derivation" be rationally performed? One possibility is, precisely, that the concretizing norm bears an instrumental coherence relationship to the concretized norm.

it promotes a goal that can be pursued without impairing the goals fostered by other norms of the system. Finally, a norm satisfies the requirement of systemic compatibility as ideological coherence, if, and only if, it respects the same scale of values that is endorsed by the other norms of the system.

One remark is in order before concluding the present (de) tour on normative systems. "Our" legal systems are mixed systems. Their structure exhibits the traits of both rhetorical and deductive systems. On the one end, normative provisions are transformed into norms in ways susceptible of rhetorical argument. On the other end, forms of logical inference are typically used: to represent or reconstruct the logical structure of an interpretive or integration reasoning; to infer general norms from other general norms, e.g., by strengthening their antecedents or by way of hypothetical syllogism; to infer individual norms from general norms, typically, by way of categorical judicial syllogism or *modus ponens*.[52]

2.3.4 *Taking Stock*

Having so travelled through the province of truth along broad alethic pluralism, it is time to consider briefly what we have seen.

Empirical truth, pragmatic truth and systemic truth represent heterogeneous criteria of evaluation, which are fit for heterogeneous entities. Empirical truth is tantamount to the notion of truth that is operative both in ordinary, common sense, linguistic transactions concerning the description of facts (situations, states-of-affairs, aspects of the world, etc.), and in the natural and social sciences. Pragmatic truth is, contrariwise, a notion belonging to the realm of instrumental, means-to-ends, rationality. Systemic truth, so far as rhetorical normative systems are concerned, can be tantamount to logical consistency, instrumental coherence, teleological coherence and ideological coherence.

These trivial remarks suggest that broad alethic pluralism endorses an unnecessarily inflationist account of truth, which goes along with an inflated use of the "truth" vocabulary. An austere pluralist, who would only accept empirical truth and formal truth, may query why should we talk of "pragmatic truth" and "systemic truth", provided we may resort, instead, to more straightforward, and less inappropriate, expressions like "utility in practice", "instrumental adequacy", "systemic compatibility", "logical consistency", "instrumental coherence", "teleological coherence", etc.

I will not adjudicate who is right—though, from an analytical perspective, the case of the austere pluralist looks preferable.[53] In fact, any adjudication would be

---

[52] The idea of a deductive normative system presupposes a positive answer to the overwhelming question about the possibility of a logic for norms. I will content myself with such presupposition, avoiding any attempt to deal, here, with that thorny issue.

[53] For a defence of "broad pluralism" concerning truth, on the basis of a property or function shared by the different notions, see for instance Lynch (2001), p. 723 ff.; Pedersen and Wright (2012), § 4.1.

idle. Whatever view we accept about truth, one truth about the matter seems unassailable: there are clear and relevant differences between the notions of empirical truth (informational correctness in relation to experience), pragmatic truth (practical utility, instrumental adequacy in relation to a previously defined set of valuable goals), and systemic truth (part-to-whole compatibility in relation to a previously identified system). Keeping these differences in mind we can, at last, move back to the haunting problem from which we started (see Sect. 2.1 above).

2.4 The Problem Unravelled

Let us recall the problem: Has truth anything to do with legal interpretation? Is there any room for truth in legal interpretation? And if there is, where is it?

We are now in the position of outlining a solution. The preceding analysis seems to have deprived the problem "truth in legal interpretation" of any biting momentousness. Now, the issue lays bare as a dissected flower on a botanist's table, and stripped out of beauty and mystery. Let's take advantage of this painful dissection to fix a few points.

Empirical truth is suitable to the outputs of interpretation-detection: detection sentences, whether singular o general, being genuinely descriptive sentences, are apt to be empirically true or false.

Interpretation-prediction leads to outputs—prediction-sentences—that are apt for being assessed in terms both of empirical and pragmatic truth. A prediction sentence is empirically true, if it is adequately justified on the basis of the information and theories available at the time of its making (see Sect. 2.3.1 above). It is also pragmatically true insofar as, by virtue of its presumable empirical truth, it is useful to get to (what are regarded as) valuable results: like, for instance, preventing lawsuits that are doomed to failure, preventing unnecessary waste of public or private resources, suggesting reasonable compromises, suggesting successful judicial strategies, etc.

Interpretation-prescription leads to outputs—prescription-sentences—that, being normative entities (and precisely, interpretive prescriptions), are not apt for empirical truth. Instead, they are apt both for pragmatic truth (instrumental adequacy in relation to valuable ethical-normative goals), and systemic truth (compatibility to a legal system).

Conjectural interpretation, in the two varieties of methodological and ideological conjecture, leads to outputs—methodological and ideological conjectural sentences—that are apt for pragmatic truth. Conjectural sentences can be P-true sentences, insofar as the information they provide about the hermeneutic scope ("frame") of a legal provision proves useful to get to (what are being regarded as) valuable results: like, for instance, advantageous amendments to a legal text, a successful piece of legal argumentation, a fairness-promoting judicial overruling, etc.

Are conjectural sentences also apt for empirical truth? The answer cannot be straightforward. It seems safer to say that conjectural sentences are discourse entities apt for experimental truth. They are the outputs of hermeneutical experiments, which, as I said, are a species of thought experiments. Now, the truth of a sentence that represents the result of a thought experiment depends on two conditions: the data the experiment was built on must be empirically true; furthermore, the calculations the inquirer performed on the basis of those data must be correct. Accordingly, experimental truth is both a matter of agreement to experience, and a matter of reason, for calculation betakes to reason. If we understand experimental truth in this way, conjectural sentences are to be sure apt for it. On the one hand, conjectural sentences are apt for satisfying the empirical truth requirement. The data about the methodological box, the ideological outlooks and the several sets of interpretive resources that conjectural interpreters make use of in their experiments are gathered by empirical investigations resulting in descriptive sentences that can be assessed in terms of empirical truth or falsity. On the other hand, conjectural sentences are also apt for satisfying the correct calculation requirement. The use of translation rules is not an interpreter's absolute discretion game. On the contrary, translation rules—once they have been duly precisified—call for methodical application, and this, from a structural point of view, is like a calculus. Conjectural interpreters can go wrong. Furthermore, they are playing a public game. Other jurists in the legal culture are in a position to control whether they have used the translation rules and related sets of interpretive resources available in a technically proper way: namely, whether they did, or did not, do any mistake in their hermeneutical calculus.

Creative interpretation leads to outputs—creative sentences—that are apt both for experimental truth (where the calculation component is structurally preponderant), and for pragmatic truth. In particular, they are P-true whenever the new understanding that they supply, on the basis of some new interpretive method, appears to be useful for obtaining (what are being regarded as) valuable results: like, for instance, obtaining a momentous change in the law in force without changing the wording of its authoritative sources (the legal provisions). Insofar as creative interpretation can be regarded as a mental experiment, creative sentences are also apt for experimental truth.

Textual and meta-textual interpretation, finally, lead to outputs—as we have seen, interpretive sentences, institutional status-sentences, integration sentences, etc.—that are apt neither for empirical truth, nor for experimental truth. This is so, because they are linguistic entities belonging to practical discourse, which either establish what the legally correct meaning of a provision is, or point at the legally correct place for a principle within the system, set the legally proper way of filling up a gap, etc., in view of solving some practical problem. Accordingly, they are apt for pragmatic and systemic truth.

On the problem about the scope of truth in the domain of legal interpretation, a few, not clearly unreasonable, conclusions seem, therefore, in order.

1. If we adopt the vantage point of broad alethic pluralism, the entire province of "legal interpretation", in the broadest sense of the phrase, turns out to be a truth-apt province. It must be emphasized, however, that such a province is not apt just for one, and the same, kind of truth. On the contrary, different truth-apt entities

are apt for different kinds of truth, depending on whether they are detection-sentences, prediction-sentences, conjectural-sentences, prescription-sentences, interpretive-sentences, integration-sentences, institutional status-sentences, gap-identification sentences, antinomy-identification sentences, or hierarchy-identification sentences.

2. If, contrariwise, we opt for a position of austere alethic pluralism, centred on the dualism of empirical and formal truth, the room that remains for truth in the realm of legal interpretation is tantamount to the room for empirical truth. It concerns detection- and prediction- sentences, on the one side, and conjectural (methodological- or ideological-) sentences, on the other—the latter with the qualifications I mentioned a moment ago concerning experimental truth.
3. All these sentences, however, as we have seen, are either the outcomes of interpretation activities in an improper sense (Sect. 2.2.2 above), or, else, of interpretation activities in the proper sense, but of a cognitive character (see Sect. 2.2.1.1 above). From the standpoint of austere alethic pluralism, this suggests a quite dim conclusion: there is no room for truth when proper, practical interpretation is at stake. The outputs of textual and meta-textual interpretation are not entities apt for empirical truth. The province of proper and practical legal interpretation—the province of judicial and juristic interpretation—is, properly speaking, a province without truth.
4. There seems to be no mystery as to the proper theoretical way of understanding and settling the problem of truth in legal interpretation, once the several possible vantage points that may be taken as to the issue are clearly brought to the fore and dispassionately played out. In particular, once we approach the issue through the spectacles of broad and austere alethic pluralism.

2.5 Truth and the Nature of Judicial Interpretation

One issue must be considered, though in passing, before concluding. Which outputs of which activities of legal interpretation (broadly conceived) are apt for which kind of truth is a disputed issue. There is a debate in jurisprudence, going along roughly since the 1960s, about the proper way of understanding the "nature" of legal interpretation: and, more precisely, in the terminology I have set forth here, the nature of textual interpretation as it is ordinarily performed by judges. It is commonplace distinguishing three groups of competitors: the integral cognitivists ("formalists", "noble dreamers"), the non-cognitivists ("sceptics", "realists", "nightmare evokers"), and the middlemen represented by moderate cognitivists ("awakes").[54]

[54] See, e.g., Carrió (1965), Part II; Hart (1977), pp. 123–143; Moreso (1997a), Guastini (2011b), pp. 138–161. I will come back on this debate, under more precisified guises, in Chaps 3 to 6 below.

Integral cognitivists claim textual interpretation, as performed by judges, always to be a matter of objective knowledge: interpreting, they say, is tantamount to grasping the true meaning of the laws as to their application to individual cases.[55]

Non-cognitivists claim textual interpretation, as performed by judges, never to be just a pure matter of objective knowledge, provided it would always involve some piece of practical evaluation and decision-making.

Moderate cognitivists, finally, claim that there exist cases where judicial interpretation of legal provisions is, and can be, in fact a matter of objective knowledge ("easy cases"); but, they add, there also exist cases where such an activity cannot be a matter of objective knowledge, and must instead be a matter of decision and evaluation ("hard cases"). This would be so, they claim, for the following reasons. Legal provisions are sentences in a natural language. Sentences in a natural language are endowed with an objective meaning, which is provided to them by linguistic conventions. It can happen that linguistic conventions run out under the pressure of individual cases. In such situations, linguistic indeterminacy, in the forms of linguistic ambiguity and vagueness, pops out, and it can be cured only by means of judicial discretion. The indeterminacy of law, however, is moderate, not radical: it is not the case that legal provisions, being sentences in a natural language, prove indeterminate at any time and in every possible situation. There are situations where they prove determinate. Indeed, if that were not the case, natural languages would be utterly useless as means for making human communication possible. Therefore—so they conclude—the non-cognitivists, who claim legal provisions to be radically indeterminate, are wrong.[56]

In this chapter I have taken side with non-cognitivism, and argued against cognitivism. I have claimed that interpretive sentences, being the outputs of textual interpretation of legal provisions, are never apt for empirical truth. I have suggested that pragmatic truth and systemic truth, so far as a practical enterprise as law is concerned, are dependent on fundamental practical options about the goals to be pursued and the standards of systemic correctness. My arguments have been mostly undercover, though. It is time briefly to bring them to the fore and put them in a clearer form.

1. Textual interpretation is, and cannot be but, a decision-making, practical, value-laden, ideologically compromised, activity. Otherwise, it would be tantamount to interpretation-detection or to conjectural interpretation. However, when judges, in their opinions, say, e.g., that legal provision LP_i means $N1$ as to the regulation of case C_i, neither do they simply *detect* that LP_i has in fact been given such a meaning, nor do they simply *conjecture* that LP_i can bear such a meaning on the basis of extant linguistic conventions. Rather, they establish—select, adopt, stand for, decide—*that* meaning as the legally correct meaning of LP_i to the purpose of deciding the case C_i.

[55] On interpretive cognitivism in Western legal thought, see e.g. Chiassoni (2016a), pp. 565–600.

[56] For an accurate defence of moderate cognitivism, see Sucar (2008), ch. 1, § 2, and pp. 362–375.

2. Textual interpretation takes place, and is in fact a key practice, within those very sophisticated and complex instances of rhetorical normative systems that are "our" legal systems.[57] In this kind of systems, the gist of the game consists in "drawing" the correct rhetorical consequences out of a set of authoritative norm-formulations (legal provisions). Such an activity, however, is far from being a matter of logical deduction from self-evident premises. A simple, but overwhelming, explanation for this conclusion (which I have already mentioned) is available: legal provisions are not self-interpreting entities. They need (authorized) interpreters to transform them into norms to be applied to individual cases, on the basis of some discrete set of interpretive rules interpreters have to choose and side for.
3. The fact that legal provisions are sentences in a natural language does not prove, by itself, that their legally correct meaning is tantamount to their conventional linguistic meaning. Moderate cognitivists, in so far as they make such a claim, incur into a logical fallacy. From the fact that the legally correct meaning of legal provisions *could* be tantamount to their conventional, ordinary, meaning, it does not necessarily follows that it *is* so (*a posse ad esse non valet consequentia*).[58]
4. Within sophisticated rhetorical systems like our own legal systems, legal indeterminacy is not tantamount to linguistic indeterminacy. It is methodological and ideological indeterminacy, going beyond the borders of linguistic indeterminacy.[59] Therefore, moderate cognitivists, in their philosophical-linguistic argument for the moderate indeterminacy of legal provisions, provide an account of judicial interpretation that is misleading and, all things considered, wrong.

As I said in the "Introduction" (Chap. 1 above), the defence of non-cognitivism against both forms of cognitivism is one of the main tasks I wish to pursue in this book. The issue will be considered, again and again, in the following chapters, from different standpoints.

[57] Properly speaking, our legal orders have a complex structure. They are dynamic-formal systems, so far as the production of authoritative legal texts—at the several levels (constitutions, statutes, judicial decisions)—is concerned. They are static-rhetorical systems, so far as the identification of explicit and implicit norms, together with their relative institutional value, is concerned. As I said (Sect. 2.3.3.2 above), they can also be conceived as deductive-rhetorical systems: either from the standpoint of law-applying organs, or from the standpoint of juristic systematization of previously identified norms, along the lines suggested, by way of rational reconstruction, by Alchourrón and Bulygin (1971, chs. I–IV).

[58] See also Chap. 5, Sect. 5.4, below.

[59] On legal indeterminacy, see also Chap. 4, Sects. 4.2, 4.4, Chap. 10, Sect. 10.2, below.

Chapter 3
Interpretive Games

Playing a game is a human activity. It is performed according to standardized patterns [of behaviour], which can be called the moves in the game. The rules of the game determine [...] these moves or patterns – and thereby also the game 'itself' and the activity of playing it

—G. H. von Wright (1963)

3.1 Big and Small(er) Problems

Which theory of legal meaning (the meaning of legal provisions) is to be deemed adequate from a theoretical standpoint? This is, perhaps, one of the biggest problems in the theory of legal interpretation. The present chapter will provide the beginning of an answer, on the way, as I said, of a construction conception of legal meaning.[1] It will not address that problem directly, though. Rather, it will approach it by considering two related, apparently smaller problems concerning judicial interpretation of statutory provisions.[2] First, which is the structure, if any, of statutory interpretation as judges do usually perform it? Second, supposing we consider judicial statutory interpretation as an interpretive game, which sort of game is it?

The first problem—the structure problem—leads to bringing to the fore the reflexive character of statutory interpretation as an activity of the mind typically resulting in some argumentative piece of discourse. Reflexivity reveals itself in a set of tools, which are part of the stock-and-trade of the legal profession. Corrective interpretation, systematic interpretation, constitutionally adequate interpretation, and, in general, any technique that makes the interpretation of a given legal provision to depend on other (presumed) components of the law (like, e.g., authoritative

[1] See "Introduction", Sect. 1.2, above.

[2] Throughout the present chapter, I will usually refer to statutory interpretation (or statutory construction), and statutory provisions. I take the same problems and conclusions to hold, roughly, for the interpretation of any sort of legal provisions (constitutional provisions, executive branch provisions, etc.).

P. Chiassoni, *Interpretation without Truth*, Law and Philosophy Library 128,
https://doi.org/10.1007/978-3-030-15590-2_3

intentions and authoritative goals) suggest a reflexive, retro-active, back-and-forth-going way of proceeding: one where the interpreter consciously advances by tentative outputs, which she eventually modifies, up to the final output she definitely stands for. Dealing with the structure problem requires, accordingly, a bit of armchair psychological guesswork grounded on linguistic analysis of the structure of extant interpretive reasonings.

The second problem—the kind of interpretive game problem—is a problem of demarcation. Statutory interpretation and ordinary conversational interpretation look like different enterprises: or, as I put it, following a Wittgensteinian suggestion, appear to be different "interpretive games". However: where does the difference stay? How can we figure it out in theoretically clear and convincing terms?

Both problems require entering into the province of revisionary conceptual investigation. They suggest that some new piece of conceptual apparatus is needed in view of getting a (perhaps) better understanding, better capturing, and better explication of the time worn phenomenon of statutory interpretation and the interpretation of legal provisions in general.

I shall provide a tentative solution to these problems by means of a three steps approach. First, I will outline a theory of interpretive games (Sect. 3.4). Second, I will bring to the fore the main features and rules of the conversational interpretation game, taking into account Grice's principle and maxims of conversation (Sect. 3.5). Third, and finally, I will bring to the fore the main features and rules of the statutory interpretation game, by means of a comparison with the game of conversational interpretation (Sect. 3.6). There is also a criticism side to the chapter, though. The whole machinery of interpretive games is meant to support the refutation of a pair of linguistic theories of statutory interpretation, which maintain that such an enterprise is, and can be, at least in certain widespread situations (the so called "easy cases"), just a matter of pure cognition ("discovery"). Their challenge will be considered as the starting point (Sects. 3.2 and 3.3).

3.2 The Challenge of Linguistic Theories

On both sides of the Atlantic, legal theorists presume to know a lot about interpretation. They so presume, because they belong to, and are the chartered representatives of, an enduring tradition of inquiries on that subject. The tradition, in turn, mirrors deeply felt exigencies of past and present times. Interpretation is, and has always been, a basic feature in the everyday working of any legal system where written legal sources ("written law", "statutory law") exist.[3] As a consequence, legal theo-

[3] Of course, the interpretation of written law (statutes, constitutional amendments, executive orders, etc.) is not the only variety of interpretation in legal systems. Customs and judicial opinions ("unwritten law") too are the matter of interpretation, especially, so far as the latter are concerned, when they may have precedential value. On the interpretation of judicial precedents, see Chap. 9, below.

rists do not only presume to know a lot about interpretation; they have in fact to know it, in order to comply with one of their central professional duties.

Provided that is the case, what do legal theorists actually *know* about statutory construction? A cursory look at some piece of an awesome and overwhelming literature suggests that there is no general agreement about how it "really" works. On the contrary, several (purportedly) descriptive theories of statutory interpretation did, and do currently, compete for the palm of epistemic correctness.

To the purpose of the present enquiry, these theories can be regarded as belonging either to one, or the other, of two different sets.

On the one side, there are specificity theories, which openly or tacitly claim statutory interpretation (and the interpretation of legal provisions in general) to be a peculiar kind of enterprise, not reducible to other kinds of interpretation, like, e.g., ordinary language interpretation, any analogy between them notwithstanding.

On the other side, there are no-specificity theories, which purport to deny, or, at least, downsize, the specificity of statutory interpretation (and of the interpretation of legal provisions in general).

Among the no-specificity theories, two have borrowed from philosophy of language and linguistics in order to get knockdown support for their claim. I will refer to them as the word-meaning theory and the sentence-meaning theory, respectively.

3.2.1 The Word-Meaning Theory

The tenets of the word-meaning theory of statutory interpretation can be recounted as follows:

1. Statutes are made of sentences in a natural language. Sentences are made of words. Words come in two basic varieties: *logical terms* ("and", "or", "not", "if … then", and other syntactic connectives) and *descriptive terms* (names, verbs, adjectives), working as subjects or predicates.
2. Statutory interpretation consists in determining the meaning of the descriptive terms that appear in statutory-sentences (statutory provisions).
3. The process of statutory interpretation can take either one, or the other, of two courses. Interpreters—including judges—*either* do *discover* the meaning of the descriptive terms employed by the legislature, in the light of conventional semantic rules, *or* they do *make it up*, by stipulating semantic rules and establishing which is their proper meaning as to an individual case, or a class of cases, at hand (discovery-or-stipulation picture).
4. The stipulation of semantic rules necessarily takes place any time the descriptive terms to be interpreted prove indeterminate, because of their "fuzziness": i.e., of their vagueness, be it actual or potential ("open texture"). It occurs, in other terms, whenever conventional semantic rules run out.

5. If statutory interpretation works in that way—and it *does* in fact work in that way—there is nothing peculiar about it: nothing which makes of it a different enterprise from the interpretation of any other linguistic document by a competent speaker of the natural language by means of which the document has been formulated.[4]

3.2.2 The Sentence-Meaning Theory

The tenets of the sentence-meaning theory of statutory interpretation claim, roughly, the following:

1. Statutes are strings of sentences in a natural language purporting to express legal norms: rules and principles establishing the way people are legally required or permitted to behave.
2. Sentences are the minimal units of linguistic communication. They are the subject-matter of interpretation, which is the process by means of which the meaning of statutory sentences is identified.
3. How do we identify the meaning of legislative sentences? Is there anything that makes of such an interpretive process something different from the way we identify the meaning of ordinary descriptive sentences in a natural language? To be sure, some jurists and legal theorists claim interpreting legislative sentences to be a different enterprise from interpreting ordinary descriptive sentences. But they are wrong. Ordinary descriptive sentences purport to convey true or false pieces of information about the world. Legislative sentences purport to direct human behaviour. In order for them to do so, however, they must convey to their addressees some piece of information about the way they are required, or allowed, to behave. Accordingly, in order to identify the meaning of a legislative sentence like, say, "The landing of planes in National airports between 8.00 p.m. and 6.00 a.m. is hereby prohibited", it is necessary to grasp *beforehand* the meaning, either of the corresponding descriptive sentence ("No planes land in National airports between 8.00 p.m. and 6.00 a.m."), or of the corresponding propositional clause ("that no planes land in National airports between 8.00 p.m. and 6.00 a.m."). This is so, because the conditions of efficacy of the legal norm coincide, and cannot but coincide, with the truth-conditions of the corresponding descriptive sentence.[5]

---

[4] Among the representatives of the word-meaning theory, the following legal theorists can be mentioned: Hart (1958), p. 63; Hart (1961), p. 125 ff.; Carrió (1965), p. 49 ff., 70–72; Hart (1977), p. 123 ff.; Alchourrón and Bulygin (1989), pp. 306–310; Bulygin (1991), pp. 34–35; Bulygin (1991), p. 22. A stronger variety of linguistic theory of legal interpretation, where also the phenomena of syntactic and semantic ambiguity are considered, will be analysed in the next chapter, under the banner of semantic formalism (quasi-cognitivism) (see Chap. 4, Sect. 4.2.1, below).

[5] This "connection" thesis is defended, for instance, by Moreso (1997b), pp. 4–5; Moreso (1999), pp. 14–15.

4. In order to interpret the corresponding descriptive sentence, or the corresponding propositional clause, no special skills are required. It is just a matter of "mastering the language": namely, of being a competent speaker of the natural language by means of which the legislative sentence to be interpreted has been expressed—which means, among other things, knowing its semantic rules.[6]

If my account is correct, the sentence-meaning theory looks like an improved version of the word-meaning theory. From the standpoint of the sentence-meaning theory, the interpretation of the descriptive terms occurring in the sentences of legislative discourse is still, to be sure, a paramount part of the interpretation activity. However, it does not exhaust it. Two further dimensions of actual discourses are taken into account. These are the syntactic and the pragmatic dimensions. Both dimensions, by contrast, seem to be utterly overlooked if we adopt the word-meaning theory. The syntactic dimension is taken into account because, as I said in passing, the sentence-meaning theory holds that the basic units of linguistic transactions are not words, but sentences. Sentences are syntactic constructs and their syntax is necessarily to be taken into account while interpreting them. The sentence-meaning theory also takes into account the pragmatic dimension of actual discourses. Though, as I will suggest in a moment (Sect. 3.3 below), the sentence-meaning theory adheres to what looks like a semantically-biased view of the pragmatic dimension of language: that is to say, to a view that is biased towards the word-to-world direction of fit, and, accordingly, assigns semantic and pragmatic priority to a certain type of speech acts—statements or assertions—over any other type.

3.3 The Failure of Linguistic Theories

At first sight, and from the perspective of an ordinary lawyer (affected, perhaps, by sound Holmesian cynicism), the central thesis the sentence-meaning theory sets forth elicits an overall sense of oddity. The thesis, as you may remember, says that, in order to *interpret* a normative sentence—that is to say, a sentence purporting to express a norm, rule, command, order, or any other standard of behaviour—one has to take into account, and interpret, either the corresponding descriptive sentence, or the corresponding propositional clause. From this perspective, if Mrs. A, being the lawyer of Mr. B, has to interpret a normative sentence like, say:

> The door of the Old Library ought to be closed at eight o'clock,

she has first to figure out and interpret the corresponding descriptive sentence:

> The door of the Old Library is closed at eight o'clock.

[6] Moreso (1997a), pp. 218–223.

Why is that so? What theory about the meaning of linguistic expressions is presupposed by such a (weird) thesis? Is it really a useful theory of meaning in view of accounting, here and now, for the way legislative sentences are being interpreted?

As I suggested at the end of the preceding section, the theory apparently endorses an assertion centred view of sentence meaning. The view holds that, whatever their linguistic function (making questions, giving orders, laying down regulations, expressing feelings, formulating the verses of a poem, etc.), the "meaning" of non-descriptive sentences—or, more precisely, their "propositional content"—is tantamount to the meaning of their corresponding descriptive sentence: it is the propositional content of the corresponding assertion. Accordingly, one must first identify what such a propositional content is, in order to understand what the question, the order, the regulation, or the piece of expressive discourse is about.[7] Robert Brandom has expressed this view in crystal-clear terms:

> It is only because some performances function as assertions that others deserve to be distinguished as *speech* acts. The class of questions, for instance, *is recognizable* in virtue of its relation to possible answers, and offering an answer is making an assertion – not in every individual case, but the exceptions (for example, questions answered by orders or other questions) are themselves *intelligible* only in terms of assertions. Orders and commands are not just performances that alter the boundaries of what is permissible or obligatory. They are performances that do so specifically by *saying* or *describing* what is and is not appropriate, and this sort of making explicit is parasitic on claiming. Saying "Shut the door!" *counts as an order* only in the context of a practice that includes judgments, and therefore assertions, that the door is shut or that it is not shut [...] In the same way, promises are not just undertakings of responsibility to perform in a certain way. They are performances that undertake such responsibility by *saying* or *describing* explicitly what one undertakes to do. *One promises in effect to make a proposition true*, and *the propositional contents appealed to can be understood only in connection with practices of saying or describing, of ta[l]king true* – in short, of asserting what are, in virtue of the role they play in such assertions, declarative sentences.[8]

All that may be fine, as a theory of the relationships between different kinds of speech acts—though a staunch J.L. Austinian would contest it. One may wonder, however, about how it could work as a theory of *interpretation*: that is to say, as a theory that does not focus on discriminating between speech acts of different kinds, but on how meanings are being ascribed to sentences. If we read it from the latter perspective, the passage by Brandom does not make clear what the interpretive role of assertions, and of the practice of making assertions, actually is. Do they play a role *just* in *interpreting* any given speech act *as* a question, or *as* a request, or *as* a command, or *as* a piece of advice, etc., independently of its specific content (where "interpretation" is "interpretation^1", i.e., the ascription of a certain "sense", or "value", to a cultural object)? Or, rather, do they play a role *both* in interpreting speech acts *as* questions, or requests, or commands, etc. (interpretation^1), *and* in interpreting the uttered or written expressions through which they are performed

[7] See, e.g., Hare (1949), p. 10; Hare (1952), ch. II; Scarpelli (1959), chs. II–III; Brandom (1994), pp. 172–173.

[8] Brandom (1994), pp. 172–173, italics added.

("interpretation[2]": i.e., the determination of the meaning of something previously identified as a linguistic expression having such-and-such a function, by means of interpretation[1])[9]?

In the latter case, we may notice, the theory of interpretation one may derive from that standpoint is far from being satisfactory. Given a certain normative sentence—so the theory runs—its propositional content coincides with the propositional content of the corresponding descriptive sentence: the sentence expressing the assertion which is made true by a due obedience to the norm expressed by the normative sentence. But there is a problem, however: *how* do we get to such a (assumedly shared) propositional content? How do we determine the meaning of the corresponding descriptive sentence? This question—which, to our purpose, is the key question—either remains utterly unanswered, or not clearly answered (like in the passage from Brandom), or it is answered, as I suggested above (Sect. 3.2.1), by pointing out to the (current) conventional semantic (and grammar) rules of the relevant natural language. In such a case, however, the sentence-meaning theory virtually collapses into the word-meaning theory.[10] What about this latter theory? Is it really true to the facts of statutory interpretation?

I think the word-meaning theory to be wrong on three counts. First, it is wrong about the source and the kind of indeterminacy affecting legal language.[11] Second, it is wrong in considering the discovery-or-stipulation picture as endowed with explanatory power about the interpretation of sentences in general. Third, it is wrong in considering the discovery-or-stipulation picture as endowed with explanatory power in relation to legal interpretation, and, particularly, to the interpretation of legal (statutory, constitutional, etc.) provisions.

To begin with, the word-meaning theory is wrong because it equates the indeterminacy of legal language to the linguistic indeterminacy of legal provisions, and, in turn, equates such linguistic indeterminacy with linguistic fuzziness, i.e., as we have seen (Sect. 3.2.1 above), with actual or potential vagueness. In so doing, it makes a double mistake. It overlooks, first, that legal indeterminacy is not tantamount to linguistic indeterminacy; secondly, that the indeterminacy of legal language is, so to speak, not only "natural", but also "artificial".

The word-meaning theory regards legislative language as a clear instance of a "fuzzy" language. It points out that any natural, not-formalized, language is fuzzy; it recalls that legislative language is—at least, here and now—a natural, not-formalized, language, like the one we use in order to perform our everyday linguistic transactions; it emphasizes that, in fact, legislative language heavily depends on

[9] The distinction between interpretation as ascription of sense or value to a cultural object, and interpretation as determination of the meaning or content of a linguistic formula, is emphasized, e.g., in Wróblewski (1985), pp. 21–23.

[10] I say virtually, because the sentence-meaning theory, charitably understood, does not overlook the syntactic dimension of interpretation, which the word-meaning theory appears to regard as not worthwhile of theoretical consideration.

[11] I use the phrase "legal language" broadly, to refer both at the system of linguistic communication used by law, and to the legal discourses that are the outputs of using that system of communication.

some natural language, from which it borrows both the grammar and most of its words.

Now, that clearly sound theoretical claim is misleading, insofar as it overlooks that legislative language is indeterminate not only because of its being a natural, not-formalized language, but also because of the working of a further factor: the presence and working of jurists (law school professors), judges, and lawyers (attorneys at law, barristers, *abogados*, solicitors, *avocats*, *avvocati*, etc.). To explain this point in perhaps clearer terms, a little detour is necessary.

According to Aleksander Peczenik and Jerzy Wróblewski,[12] a language is "fuzzy" when its descriptive or conceptual terms work in a way that makes the two following theses to be true at once:

(FL1) There are some objects *x*, that either do [clearly, evidently] belong to the extension of a term *A*, or they do [clearly, evidently] not belong to it.
(FL2) There are some objects *x*, that neither do [clearly, evidently] belong to the extension of a term *A*, nor they do [clearly, evidently] not belong to it.

Peczenik and Wróblewski sum up the basic feature of a fuzzy language as follows:

> In a fuzzy language, a use of a name (description) occurs in three types of situations: (a) there are some *x* for which there is no doubt that they belong to *A*, i.e. the "positive core reference"; (b) there are some *x* for which there is no doubt that *x* does not belong to *A*, i.e. the "negative core reference"; (c) there are some *x* for which there is a controversy or a doubt whether *x* belongs to *A* or not, i.e. penumbra reference.[13]

By contrast, a language is "hard" when its descriptive or conceptual terms work in a way that makes the following thesis true:

(HL) For every object *x*, either *x* does [clearly, evidently] belong to the extension of a term *A*, or it does [clearly, evidently] not belong to it.

Finally, a language is "soft" when its descriptive or conceptual terms work in a way that makes the following thesis true:

(SL) For every object *x*, neither *x* does [clearly, evidently] belong to the extension of a term *A*, nor it does [clearly, evidently] not belong to it.

Hard languages are the ideal languages of scholars—logicians, mathematicians, natural scientists, etc.—advocating the working out of rigorous conceptual arrangements. By design, hard languages do not leave any room for the structural failures of natural languages, like ambiguity, vagueness, open texture, etc. Soft languages,

---

[12] See Peczenik and Wróblewski (1985), pp. 24–26, 32–34; see also Wróblewski (1983); Dascal and Wróblewski (1988), pp. 217–221. According to fuzzy thinking theorist Bart Kosko: "Law is a fuzzy labyrinth. A legal system is a pile of fuzzy rules and fuzzy principles [...] Everything is a matter of degree. Legal terms and borders are fuzzy. Try to draw a line between self-defence and not self-defence or between contract breach or not breach. The lines are curves and you have to redraw them in each new case" (Kosko 1994, p. 263).

[13] Peczenik and Wróblewski (1985), pp. 25–26; see also Hart (1961), pp. 122–132.

by contrast, are the heaven of politicians and the masters of propaganda. Unlike hard and fuzzy languages, they work in such a way as to leave no room for a settled core of positive or negative reference. Penumbra is general all over the language. And words take their meanings, ultimately, after the notorious Humpty Dumpty Rule.[14]

The distinction between hard, soft and fuzzy languages provides a useful tool for dealing with statutory interpretation, and the interpretation of legal provisions in general. From its standpoint, that practice may be conceived as follows—this is, of course, just "one view" of an immense, many-sided, cathedral.

Any actual legislative language—which is a natural, fuzzy language—is liable to designed interferences and manipulations by qualified users and interpreters, who typically pull it towards two different, incompatible, directions.

On the one hand, there is a pull towards greater hardness. This move is usually advocated by jurists and judges of a "conceptualist" cast, who pursue the goal of turning legislative language, so far as possible, into a hard ideal language, like that of the so-called "exact sciences".[15]

On the other hand, there is a pull towards greater softness. The "bad men" (i.e., every human being facing a lawsuit) and their lawyers usually advocate this move, to the extent that it furthers their momentary interests. But it may also be advocated, at least so far as some part of positive law is concerned, by jurists and judges of an "equitable", "open", or "reformist" cast, pursuing the maximum of justice for the greatest number of individual cases.

Conceptualist jurists and judges do not necessarily agree about the "proper" way of making legislative concepts hard. There can be competing, alternative proposals about the hardening of legislative language. As a consequence, the pull by conceptualist jurists and judges towards greater hardness can work to a (unintended) greater softness, by the well-known process in virtue of which the pursuit of a goal may beget contrary-to-the-goal states of affairs ("hetero-genesis of the ends").

It may also happen that hardening proposals come to compete with alternative, softening proposals by equitable jurists and judges. This will have the effect of further multiplying the meanings that can reasonably be ascribed to legislative sentences by judges in deciding cases.

Lawyers are eager, where it suits the interests of their clients, to exploit jurists' and judges' conceptual disagreements, spreading and fuelling them in the courtrooms and among the people at large.

The two opposite pulls I have just recalled—namely, towards a greater hardness and towards a greater softness—have the effect of adding to legislative language an *artificial* indeterminacy. This variety of indeterminacy, notice, does not depend on linguistic factors: on the fact that legislative language is a natural language. It

---

[14] The reference, here, is to the well known episode from L. Carroll's *Through the Looking Glass and What Alice Found There* (1896, p. 81), where Humpty Dumpty, to Alice's astonishment, claims: "When I use a word [...] it means just what I choose it to mean – neither more, nor less".

[15] See, e.g., Bobbio (1950) and Soler (1962).

depends, rather, on pragmatic factors: on the practical, conflict-ridden, argumentative character of legal practice and legal experience.

The remarks above should make clear why linguistic theories seem to provide, as a whole, an impoverished picture of statutory interpretation, and the interpretation of legal provisions in general. As I said, this is not their only flaw, though.

Coming to the second count of my criticism, the discovery-or-stipulation picture is, in general, a wrong picture that should be let down. There is something of a paradox here. The discovery-or-stipulation picture provides an adequate explanation *neither* of ordinary conversational interpretation, *nor* of the interpretation of legal (e.g., statutory) provisions. This is so because, as we have seen, linguistic theories endorse a theory of the working of natural languages that focuses on their syntactic and semantic features, and utterly overlooks their pragmatic dimension. However, as the pragmatic models concerning the interpretation of utterances in a natural language have persuasively claimed, interpretation never is just a process of conventional meaning discovery. Rather, it always involves some degree of cooperation on the part of the interpreter in co-constructing the meaning of the utterances at stake, taking into account the presumed intentions, beliefs, and needs of the speaker.[16]

Coming to the third, and last, count of my criticism, even if the discovery-or-stipulation picture would be appropriate as to interpretation in ordinary conversation (which, apparently, is not the case), it is at any rate not appropriate in relation to statutory interpretation. Indeed, statutory interpretation is an interpretive game different from conversational interpretation.

So, to sum up:

1. The sentence-meaning theory virtually collapses into the word-meaning theory.
2. The word-meaning theory is wrong, provided that:
   (a) it overlooks artificial indeterminacy and its social, pragmatic, factors, focussing on natural, linguistic, indeterminacy (fuzziness) only;
   (b) it overlooks the attitude of cooperation that is needed also for ordinary conversation to work as a rational enterprise, as it most of the times does;
   (c) it considers jurists, judges, and lawyers to be like any other "ordinary speaker" of a natural language. Jurists, judges, and lawyers, however, are not just "ordinary speakers" of a natural language, like the man on the Greenwich bus. In fact, they seldom take a bus, busy as they are, in university classrooms, courtrooms and legal offices, at working out interpretations of legal materials according to rules (canons, techniques) drawn from a long-standing argumentative tradition. Jurists, judges, and lawyers who interpret legal provisions play a different game. This is, in a sense, a very trivial statement. Linguistic theories, however, seem to overlook this plain fact, for no apparent theoretical reason.[17]

---

[16] See, e.g., Grice (1989), pp. 26–31, 368–372; Bianchi (2005), pp. 99–130; Caffi (2008), pp. 71–85. See also Sects. 3.4–3.6 and Chaps. 4 and 6 below.

[17] Obviously, they may have some good *normative* reasons to do so, like fostering some kind of "linguistic naturalism" or "linguistic legalism". In that case, however, they should avow it.

It is time to provide argument for the second and third counts of my criticism to linguistic theories. This requires casting some light on interpretive games, and the statutory interpretation game in particular.

3.4 Interpretive Games

A "game", in very broad terms, is an individual or a social activity (i.e., one involving two or more interacting individuals), which is performed in accordance with a discrete set of rules, usually but not necessarily for leisure.

A "language game"—following Wittgenstein, but in no way purporting or pretending to solve any problem of Wittgensteinian exegesis—is the operating with the words of a language to some purpose belonging to a typified linguistic activity or a typical form of linguistic social interaction (a "form of life"). Asking, thanking, cursing, greeting, praying, inventing and telling a story, describing a landscape, giving instructions for the building of a boat, giving and obeying orders, reporting an event, making and testing hypotheses, translating from one language into another, etc., all are instances of language games.[18]

An "interpretive game" is a language game, consisting in the determination of the meaning of one or more sentences, to some cognitive or practical purpose, including, of course, leisure. The sentences upon (and with) which interpretive games are played are a given for the interpreting players: usually, they come, in an oral or a written form, from another agent uttering or writing them down (daddy, the beloved sweetheart, the City Council, Jehovah on Mount Sinai, Napoleon, Edgar Allan Poe, etc.). Interpretive games can be played either by an isolated individual interpreter, to some private purpose of her own, or as a social enterprise, by a set of conspiring or competing interpreters. They display different degrees of complexity: from the relatively simple games of, say, "understanding what mom has just said while at table" or "understanding what the drill-sergeant shouts from the tower", to the more complicated games of interpreting the words of the supreme deity in chapter 6 of the Holy Book, § 201 of the *Philosophical Investigations*, the opening pages of *Du côté de chez Swann*, paragraphs 152 and 153 of the Freedonian Income Tax Code, or art. 3 of the European Convention on Human Rights.

If we pause to reflect on the rules interpretive games are played by, and focus on the most widespread variety of interpretive games, i.e., those concerning sentences in a natural language, four kinds of rules seem worthwhile distinguishing. These are: *grammar rules*, *method rules*, the *translation rules* method rules are about, and, finally, *rule-making rules*.

[18] Wittgenstein (1953), § 23. In *The Blue Book*, Wittgenstein emphasizes that "language games" are "primitive forms of language", "simple forms" of "operating with words", "the forms of language with which a child begins to make use of words", and yet ripe with instruction for understanding the working of ordinary language even in its "more complicated" forms (Wittgenstein 1958, pp. 16–17).

Grammar rules concern the basic level, the level one, in the interpretation of any sentence in a natural language. This is the level of strictly grammatical or syntactic interpretation: namely, the one which brings to the fore the logical function of words and the syntactic structure of the interpreted sentence (saying, e.g., if it is paratactic or hypotactic, and which connections obtain between principal propositions and their subordinates).[19] Grammar rules are, accordingly, instructions pointing to the grammar (broadly conceived) that should be taken into account to the purpose of grammatical or syntactic interpretation. Usually, they point to the grammar of the natural language by way of which the sentences to be interpreted are formulated. The grammar of a natural language, however, can run out, leaving the interpreter at the crossroad of grammatical indeterminacies.[20] As a consequence, the set of the grammar rules of a "well-designed" interpretive game (i.e., of a game informed to the objective of getting always to one, and only one, final and definite interpretive output for each of the sentences to be interpreted) must contain at least two items. To begin with, it must contain a *principal grammar rule*, like, e.g.:

(PGR) "In order to play at interpretive game IG_i, the grammar of natural language L_o ought to be taken into account".[21]

Furthermore, it must also contain a *default grammar rule*, like, e.g.:

(DGR) "If the grammar of natural language L_o leads to indeterminacy, interpreters ought to overcome it in the way that is arguably more in tune with the purpose of the game IG_i".

In everyday plays of interpretive games, grammar rules do usually go unnoticed, grammatical interpretation being just a part, a necessary but communicatively not autonomous part, of the overall interpretation of a sentence (be it linguistic or of other sorts).[22] They are, nonetheless, essential. Notice that the default rule DGR, in the example above, points to the purpose of the game. Grammatical indeterminacies are not self-repairing. If players wish, or have, to cure them, they must go beyond established grammar, and appeal to method rules.

Method rules are prescriptions concerning the purpose, the tools, and the permitted, mandatory, or forbidden moves of the game. We may think at method rules as coming in five main varieties: purpose rules, selection rules, procedure rules, preference rules, and default rules.

---

[19] On syntactic interpretation, see e.g. Ross (1958), ch. IV; Tarello (1980), ch. II; Chiassoni (2011), Chap. 2, Sect. 2.1.

[20] See Ross (1958), pp. 123–128, concerning the interpretation of legal provisions.

[21] Principal grammar rules may also be considered as a variety of technical norms, i.e., as norms presupposing an anankastic statement like: "Unless an interpreter takes into account the grammar of the language L_o, she will not be able to play the interpretive game IG_i". On technical norms, see von Wright (1963), pp. 9–11.

[22] A principal grammar rule can also be considered as a component of translation rules, and, in particular, of the rules of linguistic interpretation. Here, I consider them as a kind apart, just to emphasize that they are a necessary component of interpretive games.

1. *Purpose rules* establish the purpose of an interpretive game: i.e., the goal players ought to aim at. This may consist, for instance, in ascribing the meaning that is morally correct, respectful for the author's communicative intention, conducive to deeper understanding, knowledge enhancing, promoting the general welfare, suitable to the interpreter's own interests, or showing the sentences to be interpreted in their best light, etc. The purpose of the game affects the interpretive attitude interpreters are required, or allowed, to assume. Interpretive attitudes may range from full and unconditional cooperation with the author of the sentence(s), to mild conditioned cooperation, a charitable stance, an uncharitable stance, utter neglect, self-interest-seeking with guile, hard-line sabotage, etc.
2. *Selection rules* determine the translation rules (primary interpretive directives, canons, techniques, methods) interpreters ought to use. Translation rules, as we have seen,[23] are directives endowed with hermeneutical efficiency: they embody criteria, and point to resources, on the basis of which a sentence can be translated into one or more sentences that represent its meaning. Selection rules may point to the ordinary meaning rule ("Sentences ought to be interpreted according to their ordinary meaning"), either as the exclusive translation rule of the game, or, else, together with other rules. Selection rules may also select a different translation rule, for instance, author's intention, author's best interest, the nature of the text, the ("objective") purpose of the text, or the true principles of morality, as the exclusive translation rule of the game. In such an event, ordinary meaning will usually be employed too. That use, however, will be purely instrumental to abiding by the selection rule and the exclusive interpretive criterion it sorts out. Ordinary meaning works, here, simply as the departure point for the identification of further meanings: namely, the ones that really matter according to the rules of the game. Theorists of legal interpretation that give ordinary meaning pride of place, do not seem always to be aware of the distinction, we must draw, between ordinary meaning as a master criterion, and ordinary meaning as a servant resource.
3. *Procedure rules* come into play whenever selection rules point to two or more translation rules. Suppose, for instance, a selection rule pointing to the ordinary meaning and the author's intention directives. In such a case, an interpretive game may contain a rule that prescribes applying *all* the selected translation rules *in any case*. In that event, the game is to be played by a *pure procedure rule*. A game, however, may also contain a rule establishing an order of preference among the several translation rules and their respective outcomes. For instance, the rule may prescribe to apply the ordinary meaning rule first; and, if, but only if, the ordinary meaning of sentences is indeterminate, apply the author's intent rule.[24] In such a case, the game is to be played by a *hierarchical procedure rule*.

---

[23] See Chap. 2, Sect. 2.2.1.1, above.

[24] What if even the author's intent directive leads to indeterminacy? What if two or more alternative meanings are arguably in line with author's intent? As we shall see in a moment, a well-designed game will need to provide a default rule for coping with such occurrences.

4. *Preference rules* come into play whenever an interpretive game contains a selection rule pointing to two or more translation rules (for instance, to the ordinary meaning and the author's intention rules), and the application of those rules is regulated by a pure procedure rule. In such a case, a well-designed game must contain a preference rule, establishing an order of priority among the determinate meanings identified on the basis of each of the several translation rules at stake, in case these meanings be different—in the event, for instance, that the determinate ordinary meaning and the determinate intentional meaning of a sentence to be interpreted do not coincide. Preference rules may establish a fixed order of preference (e.g.: "When at odds, intentional meaning should be preferred to ordinary meaning"). In such event, the interpretive game is to be played by a *pure preference rule*. Preference rules, however, may be of a more complex cast. They may resort to preference criteria, working as comparison and ruling-out standards. For instance, they may prescribe to prefer the meaning that is arguably (the most) coherent with the whole text the sentence belongs to, or (the most) conducive to results in tune with the purpose of the game, or (the most) in tune with presenting the text in its best (moral, aesthetic, political, philosophical, theoretical, scientific) light, etc. In such an event, the interpretive game is to be played by a *criterial preference rule*.
5. *Default rules* establish the way of overcoming the uncertainties that may turn out in the application of the selection, procedure or preference rule of an interpretive game. In well-designed games, default rules are needed in three sorts of situations. First, the selection rule points to one, and only one, translation rule, and this leads to an indeterminate interpretive output.[25] Second, the use of a plurality of translation rules is allowed, but none of them leads to one determinate interpretive output, pushing the hierarchical procedure rule of the game into idleness. Third, the use of a plurality of translation rules is allowed according to a pure procedure rule, each directive leads to one determinate interpretive output, but the criterial preference rule runs out: i.e., its application does not lead to identifying one meaning as the all-things-considered correct one.[26] In all these cases, a default rule must step in. For instance, a rule empowering interpreters to overcome any indeterminacy concerning interpretive outputs by putting up the solution that, in their best judgement, fares best with the purpose and basic values of the game.

[25] Suppose the game is to be played just by the ordinary meaning directive. Ordinary language, as an interpretive resource, can run out: it can lead to semantic indeterminacy, in the well-known forms of vagueness, ambiguity or under-determination.

[26] Suppose the ordinary meaning and author's intent directives both point to a definite, but different, meaning for the same sentence. Suppose, furthermore, that the game is to be played by a criterial preference rule pointing to coherence (e.g.: "The interpretive output that better coheres with the spirit of the game ought to be preferred"). Suppose however the interpreter thinks both outputs to cohere in the same degree with the spirit of the game. How is one definite output to be finally singled out?

Rule-making rules, finally, establish whom, if any agent at all, is entitled to perform acts concerning the production (introduction, revision, elimination) of the grammar and method rules of the game, and how, and when, such acts are allowed. They are, accordingly, meta-rules as regards to grammar, method, and translation rules, standing apart from the rules by which sentence interpretation is actually being performed.

Grammar, method and translation rules make up the *interpretive code* an interpretive game should be played by. The interpretive code sets the standard of interpretive correctness within the game. Any interpretation-output which cannot be justified as abiding by the rules of the code is incorrect (wrong, invalid, void, voidable, unlawful).

The grammar, method, translation and rule-making rules of an interpretive game determine the identity of the game: if they change, the game changes.

From the standpoint of method and rule-making rules, different sorts of interpretive games can be singled out. I will briefly consider a few of them, which will turn out to be helpful in characterizing the statutory interpretation game. These are: simple and complex games; open and well-designed games; cognitive and practical games; privileged rule-making and universal rule-making games; external rule-making and contextual rule-making games; no-reinterpretation, unlimited reinterpretation, and limited reinterpretation games.

3.4.1 Simple v. Complex Games

An interpretive game is *simple*, if interpreters ought to use one, and only one, translation rule. The selection rule of a simple interpretive game may require, for instance, that:

(SR1) "Sentences ought to be interpreted according to the ordinary meaning of their descriptive words".[27]

Contrariwise, an interpretive game is *complex*, if interpreters ought to use more than one translation rule. The selection rule of a complex interpretive game may dictate, for instance, that:

(SR2) "Sentences ought to be interpreted according to: a. the ordinary meaning of their descriptive words; b. the purpose of their utterance; c. their author's best interest; d. their text's best interest".

[27] By definition, such a game would not be well-designed.

3.4.2 Open v. Well-Designed Games

Simple and complex games are identified from the perspective of how many translation rules the players are required to make use of. In both types of game, the application of translation rules may result either in no definite outcome at all, or in a variety of alternative definite outcomes. For instance, while playing at a simple game containing an ordinary meaning rule, the interpreter may face alternative outcomes because of linguistic ambiguity or vagueness—in the latter case, the alternative being between including or not-including a certain class of things within the extension of a relevant concept.[28]

Open games are games that, to some purpose, prescribe interpreters to leave interpretive indeterminacies as they are. When some indeterminacy has been brought to the fore in an all-things-considered way, the game just stops.

Contrariwise, *well-designed games* characterize, as we have seen, for providing rules that are aimed at curing interpretive indeterminacy, and allowing players always to arrive at one definite result. This is achieved, as we have seen, by resorting either to a hierarchical procedure rule, or to a preference rule, in combination with some default rule.

3.4.3 Cognitive v. Practical Games

Cognitive games are played by interpreters aiming at drawing as much knowledge as possible from the interpretation of a sentence or set of sentences. Such knowledge may consist in pieces of information about the hermeneutic potentiality of the sentences at stake.[29] It usually consists, however, in pieces of information concerning the matter the sentences are about, or the (presumable) mental states of the speaker in uttering or writing them. Cognitive games can also have a conversational structure: two or more people play at exchanging information on something. In such cases, following Grice, we may talk of *cognitive conversational games*, or *cognitive conversations*.

By contrast, when engaged in *practical games* interpreters entertain the purpose of getting out of the interpreted discourse the meaning(s) that better foster the interests they happen to pursue—which, by design, are different from any interest in obtaining, and forwarding, pieces of information (knowledge, instruction). These interests may consist, for instance, in pulling someone's leg or making a fool of somebody, arousing discontent and hatred among the populace ("Mischief, thou art afoot …"), promoting or hindering somebody else's political career, selling widgets

---

[28] Assume the ordinary meaning of "dog" to be vague as to stuffed dogs. In such case, an alternative exists between either including, or not including, the class of stuffed dogs within the reference of "dog".

[29] This is the case, for instance, when conjectural legal interpretation takes place (see Chap. 2, Sect. 2.2.2 above).

to reluctant customers, winning a lawsuit, getting wild animals out of zoos in the name of "Animal Liberation", jailing villains, fostering the Progress of Mankind, contributing to the establishment of the perfect Constitution, etc.

The purpose rule of cognitive games can be stated, tentatively, as follows:

(PR1) "Sentences ought to be interpreted so as to obtain as much (valuable) knowledge as possible".

On the contrary, the purpose rule of practical games may sound, for instance, like:

(PR2) "Sentences ought to be interpreted so as to secure at best the non-cognitive, practical, goal of respecting the political will of the author".

(PR3) "Sentences ought to be interpreted so as to secure at best the non-cognitive, practical, goal of cosmopolite justice".

(PR4) "Sentences ought to be interpreted so as to secure at best the non-cognitive, practical, material or spiritual interest you (or your client) happen to pursue", etc.

3.4.4 Privileged Rule-Making v. Universal Rule-Making Games

An interpretive game is a *privileged rule-making* game, if, according to the rule-making rules of the game, the production (introduction, revision, elimination) of the rules of the interpretive code of the game is allowed to certain agents only. These can be either an altogether different set of agents from the players', or a sub-set of players.

By contrast, an interpretive game is a *universal rule-making* game, if, according to the rule-making rules of the game, every player is entitled to participate in the production of the rules of the interpretive code of the game.

3.4.5 External Rule-Making v. Contextual Rule-Making Games

When *external rule-making* games are at stake, only empowered agents outside of any actual interpretive play may perform acts of production concerning the rules of the interpretive code of the game. Contrariwise, *contextual rule-making* games characterize for empowering interpreters to produce rules of the interpretive code of the game, while playing the game. This means that interpreters are empowered to make new rules *and* apply, follow, or use them in the very play in which they have made them.

3.4.6 No-Reinterpretation, Unlimited Reinterpretation, Limited Reinterpretation Games

Any instance of an activity of interpretation can be conceived, roughly, as a mental process of a discursive kind, which usually gets externalized ("published") in the form of some piece of speech or writing.

The structure of interpretive processes depends on the rules of the interpretive game at stake. It can be either a one-stage structure, or a multiple-stage structure.

An interpretive game is a multiple-stage game, whenever, according to the rules of its interpretive code, the interpretive process is articulated, contingently or necessarily, in two or more stages. A multiple-stage articulation is contingent, i.e., it may or may not occur, either in simple games containing a default rule,[30] or in complex games to be played by a hierarchical procedure rule.[31] It is, contrariwise, a necessary feature in complex games to be played by some pure procedure, preference and default rule.

Multiple-stage games are *reinterpretation games*. They instruct interpreters to carry over subsequent re-readings of the sentence(s) at stake, in view of reaching a final outcome that, from the standpoint of the rules of the game, can be deemed all-things-considered correct (viable, satisfactory, valid, reasonable, etc.). The interpretive output of a subsequent stage can be the same meaning ascribed to the sentence(s) at stake at a previous stage, but it can also be a different meaning. In the latter case, according to the rules of the game, the subsequent meaning may either add up to, or altogether replace, the former.

Two varieties of reinterpretation games are worthwhile distinguishing: unlimited reinterpretation games and limited, or bound, reinterpretation games.

Unlimited reinterpretation games allow interpreters to consider the sentences they interpret as belonging to something like a soft language. Some variety of the Humpty Dumpty Rule, which establishes the unbound supremacy ("right", "power") of the interpreter over the text, may be paramount. In general semiotics and literary criticism, unlimited reinterpretation games are those characterized by so-called "overinterpretation": either because there are no settled interpretive criteria, or because they virtually allow and legitimize whatever interpretation interpreters' imagination is capable of contriving.[32]

Limited reinterpretation games, contrariwise, are multiple-stage games where the outcome of the previous interpretation stage is open to interpreters' bound re-

[30] The interpretation process is potentially articulated in two stages: the stage corresponding to the application of the primary directive, and, if any indeterminacy pops out, the stage corresponding to the application of the default rule.

[31] The interpretation process is potentially articulated in as many stages as are the primary directives to be applied in turn according to the hierarchical procedure rule of the game.

[32] See e.g. Eco (1990), pp. 325–338; Eco (1992). According to Eco, overinterpretation typically goes along with hermetic semiosis: the style of virtually unbound interpretation of texts, grounded on similarity, universal sympathy and the idea of secret communications waiting to be brought to the fore, proper of the hermetic tradition.

considering. The bounds ultimately come from purpose rules that, for instance, impose overall respect for some ultimate institutional or moral value, like author's personality, certainty, human dignity, decency, the general welfare, etc.

A game is, instead, a *one-stage game*, whenever it is a simple game, containing no default rule. By design, one-stage games are over whatever their interpretive output is, even if it is indeterminate. They are, accordingly, *open* and *no-reinterpretation* games. One-stage games assume the exclusive translation rule they select to work efficiently towards univocal and determinate results, at least most of the time. They endorse, accordingly, a conception of interpretation as a (quasi) unreflective enterprise, where interpreters apply the rules of the game in a mechanical way, and react upon the meanings so identified by way of some immediate, (quasi) unreflective, verbal or non-verbal behaviour.

3.5 The Conversation Game

Consider the following exchange:

Boy: "Which time the train for Yuma, Ma'am?"
Lady: "Noon sharp, my Boy".
Boy: "Which platform?"
Lady: "Platform 2"
Boy: "Any fourth-class wagon?"
Lady: "Just behind the tender".

The two passengers are involved in an ordinary conversation game. This makes, in turn, that they are also playing an interpretive game. From the vantage point of the theory of interpretive games, the game can be characterized, roughly, as follows. It is a *cognitive* game, on the part of the Boy, and a *practical*, courtesy game, on the part of the Lady; it is a *simple* game; it is an *external rule-making* game; it is, very likely, a game where rule-making is *privileged*, being not allowed to players; it looks like a *one-stage*, *no-reinterpretation* game, or, at least, something very close to those varieties. In fact, the interpretive outcomes on the basis of which the Boy asks further questions to the Lady, on the one side, and the Lady utters her answers to the Boy, on the other side, are, apparently, the outcomes of a one-stage interpretive process, where ordinary meaning is taken into account as the exclusive, smoothly working, interpretive criterion.

It is worthwhile pausing to identify the interpretive rules that make of this conversation (something very close to) a no-reinterpretation game, where interpreters seem to ascribe meanings in a quasi-mechanical, apparently unreflective, way. To such purpose, some ideas of Paul H. Grice can be profitably put to work.

3.5.1 The Principle and Maxims of Conversation

From the perspective of Paul Grice's pragmatic analysis of ordinary linguistic exchanges, any conversation like the one I have just imagined can be understood as a "cooperative transaction", ruled by a "general principle" and a set of related "maxims and submaxims".[33]

The general principle is the *principle of cooperation* ("Cooperative principle"). It prescribes that "the conversational contribution" of each agent ought to be "as is required, at the stage at which it occurs, by the accepted purpose or direction of the talk exchange" in which she "is engaged".[34]

The maxims (and submaxims) are the result of specifying and concretizing the cooperative principle. Grice sorts out four basic kinds: maxims of "Quantity", maxims of "Quality", maxims of "Relation", and maxims of "Manner". As a whole, the cooperation principle and the maxims represent the standards of rational linguistic exchanges, as they usually take place, and should take place, in everyday reality.[35]

The maxims of Quantity require, we may say, the *quantitative adequacy* of conversational contributions. When the purpose of the linguistic transaction consists in the exchange, or one-sided forwarding, of pieces of information, they prescribe each participant to provide *all* the information required, and *only* the information required ("1. Make your contribution as informative as is required (for the current purpose of the exchange). 2. Do not make your contribution more informative than is required"[36]).

The maxims of Quality require the *qualitative adequacy* of conversational contributions. When the purpose of the linguistic transaction consists in the exchange, or one-sided forwarding, of pieces of information, they prescribe each participant to abstain from providing information that either they positively know to be false, or for which they do not have enough evidence ("You shall provide neither knowingly false, nor knowingly unsound, information"; "Try to make your contribution one that is true"[37]).

The maxims of Relation require the *content adequacy* of conversational contributions. They prescribe each participant to formulate pieces of discourse that can (reasonably) be considered relevant (pertinent) in relation to the stage, purpose, and direction of the linguistic exchange ("Be relevant"[38]).

Finally, the maxims of Manner require the *expressive adequacy* of conversational contributions. They prescribe each participant to be perspicuous ("avoid obscurity

---

[33] Grice (1989), pp. 22–40.

[34] Grice (1989), p. 26.

[35] Grice (1989), p. 26.

[36] Grice (1989), p. 26.

[37] Grice (1989), p. 27.

[38] Grice (1989), p. 27.

of expression"), avoid ambiguity, be brief, and be ordered ("You shall provide plain, univocal, short, tidy, and easily understandable contributions").[39]

3.5.2 *The Principle and Maxims of Conversational Interpretation*

The Gricean principle of cooperation and related maxims concern the behaviour of any participant to a linguistic exchange, who, having previously interpreted somebody else's discourse, is going to provide a reply (a conversational contribution).

Provided any linguistic exchange necessarily involves interpretation (in a broad sense of the word), it necessarily involves playing some sort of interpretive game. A relevant variety of linguistic exchange is cognitive conversation, where the accepted purpose of the game consists in exchanging or forwarding pieces of information. It is worthwhile inquiring for the principle and maxims that can reasonably be supposed to work as the *interpretive* counterparts of the Gricean conversational principle and maxims, when cognitive conversations are at stake.

To begin with, it seems reasonable to regard the cognitive conversation interpretive game (henceforth: conversational interpretation game) as ruled by a general *principle of interpretive cooperation*. The principle amounts, at least, to a *principle of charitable interpretation*. Being a cooperative interpreter means, at least, to be a charitable interpreter. Each participant to a cognitive conversation ought to interpret charitably what the other participants say: "You shall not provide knowingly uncharitable interpretations"; "You shall not interpret other players as talking nonsense, or being obscure, vague, or ambiguous in their utterances, unless sound and overwhelming evidence supports such conclusion of yours" are possible formulations. The principle of interpretive cooperation, however, may be understood as requiring more than being charitable. For instance, it may be understood to require the supplementing of defective communication, when needed.

The principle of charitable interpretation can be reasonably specified, in turn, into four maxims. These are the maxim of *exhaustive interpretation*, the maxim of *fair interpretation*, the maxim of *relevant interpretation*, and, finally, the maxim of *clear interpretation*.

The *maxim of exhaustive interpretation* represents an interpretive counterpart to a Gricean maxim of Quantity. It concerns the *quantitative adequacy* of conversational interpretation. It requires each interpreter to take into account *every part* of the discourse to be interpreted, nothing excluded ("You shall interpret the whole set of sentences to which you have to reply").

The *maxim of fair interpretation* represents an interpretive counterpart to a Gricean maxim of Quality. It concerns the *qualitative adequacy* of conversational interpretation. It prescribes each interpreter to be fair and honest to other partici-

---

[39] Grice (1989), p. 27.

pants in the conversation. This requires them to abstain from knowingly ascribing to the sentences formulated by other players any indeterminate, vague, obscure, weird or absurd meaning which they know, or have good evidence to presume, was not intended ("You shall not knowingly misunderstand what other players say").

The *maxim of relevant interpretation* represents an interpretive counterpart to a Gricean maxim of Relevance. It concerns the *content adequacy* of conversational interpretation. It requires each interpreter to abstain from "reading" into other people's sentences any unnecessary, irrelevant, not pertinent, divagating content ("You shall not overinterpret").

Finally, the *maxim of clear interpretation* represents an interpretive counterpart to a Gricean maxim of Manner. It concerns the *expressive adequacy* of conversational interpretation. It requires each interpreter to translate other players' sentences by means of clear, or even clearer, sentences of her own ("You shall provide plain, univocal, tidy, easily understandable, and ordered interpretation-outputs").

3.6 The Statutory Interpretation Game

Let us put on the glasses provided by the theory of interpretive games (Sect. 3.4) and the preceding experiment about the principle and maxims of conversational interpretation (Sect. 3.5.2).

If, with the aid of those lens, we look at the practice of judicial interpretation of statutes—that is to say, at the game that is being played by judges any time there are statutes to be applied, enforced, challenged, derogated, declared void, declared unconstitutional, eluded, violated, etc.—we get to the conclusion that the statutory interpretation game differs from the conversational interpretation game on several counts. Not least than four counts are worthwhile mentioning.

1. The statutory interpretation game is a *complex game*. At least so far as "our" legal culture and experience are concerned, judges are typically required to apply a plurality of translation rules (appealing, e.g., to ordinary meaning, legislative intent, statutory purpose, precedent, history, juristic doctrines, constitutional principles, the nature of things, natural law, etc.), according to selection rules the sources of which are usually traced to legislative enactments, judicial opinions, and the methodological thinking embodied in juristic essays.
2. The statutory interpretation game is a *privileged rule-making game*. The production (introduction, modification, elimination) of the rules of the game (in particular, grammar and method rules) is usually reserved to legislatures, judges, and jurists, according to their respective institutional roles. Apparently, the man on the Greenwich bus does not have any say in the process. Indeed, he seldom interprets any statute whatsoever, and, when he does so, he ultimately gets statutory meanings from the experts' community: from Judges & Co., as Bentham would have said.

3. The statutory interpretation game is a *contextual rule-making game*. Due to the plain, though often overlooked, fact that no text is a self-interpreting entity, judges necessarily create the rules of the game—if only by way of selection, but also by way of repair, correction, or integration[40]—and contextually apply them to the interpretation task at hand.
4. The statutory interpretation game is, finally, a *multiple-stage* and (something very close to) a *limited reinterpretation game*. The multiple-stage property comes from the complexity of the game, which is usually played according either to some hierarchical procedure rule, or to some pure procedure plus a preference rule. As a consequence, judges are typically required to reinterpret the legal provisions at stake, until they have reached an interpretive result that, by the rules of the game, is to be deemed all-things-considered correct.[41] Judicial reinterpretation is not unlimited, though. Rather, it is subject to institutional and cultural bounds. These are usually embodied in the purpose rule of the game. In very broad terms, the purpose rule of the statutory interpretation game prescribes judges to provide statutes with their legally correct meaning: judges ought to identify "the true meaning of the statute in view of its application to the individual case at hand", as some French Exegetical School jurists used to say.[42] Which meaning, however, is legally correct? Which is the "true meaning" of a statutory provision in view of deciding an individual case at hand? Here, ethical views about positive law, the nature of legislative or constitutional state, separation of powers, and the legislature-judge connexion necessarily step in. In a legislative state, for instance, the purpose rule is likely to be understood as prescribing "respect for the legislature". In a constitutional state, contrariwise, it is often understood as requiring "respect for the constitution", which requires in turn "constitution-oriented statutory interpretations". What "respect for the legislature" or "respect for the constitution" amount to is, however, an issue usually open to a variety of alternative answers.

There is a further difference between the statutory interpretation game and the conversational interpretation game that must be considered, though. Is statutory construction a *cognitive* or a *practical* game? The question requires a discriminating answer.

So far as lawyers and jurists are concerned, it seems hard denying the interpretive game they play with statutes to be a *practical* game: one where interests different from objective empirical knowledge of the law are paramount, ranging from winning the lawsuit to promoting "true justice" in individual cases. This feature—it must be noticed—has momentous effects on the principle and maxims of the statutory interpretation game, as played by lawyers and jurists.

---

[40] On these notions, see "Introduction", Sect. 1.1, and Chap. 2, Sect. 2.3.2 above, and Chap. 4, 4.4 , below.

[41] In hermeneutical theory, the phenomenon of reinterpretation is captured by the metaphor of the hermeneutical circle, in fact, the combination of three interacting circles: the pre-comprehension and text circle, the norm and system circle, the norm and fact circle.

[42] On the Exegetical School, see e.g. Chiassoni (2016d), pp. 565–581.

Concerning lawyers, the practical nature of the interpretive game they play on behalf of those (fatally) "bad men" that are their clients, suggests the principle and maxims of statutory interpretation to be different from the principles and maxims of conversational interpretation.

To begin with, the principle of interpretive cooperation appears to be turned upside down. The basic principle of the lawyers' statutory interpretation game looks, indeed, like a *principle of interpretive no-cooperation*. It prescribes that lawyers ought to *interpret statutory clauses uncharitably*, *unless* a charitable interpretation better suits to the momentary interests of their clients. The same fate betakes to the four interpretive maxims. Statutory interpretation by lawyers ought to be exhaustive, fair, relevant, and clear, *if, and only if*, and up to the point in which, such courses of action, again, suit to the best interest of their clients. The virtually undefeasible prescriptions of conversational interpretation turn, here, into as many defeasible instructions.

Like considerations hold concerning the juristic interpretation of statutes. Here, whether, when, and up to which point the principle of interpretive cooperation is an accepted and working rule ultimately depends on jurists' ethical view about the legal order they are working in. It may be the case, for instance, that, in a constitutional state, most jurists adopt a general principle of uncharitable interpretation of statutes, in view of promoting the maximum possible extent of judicial and political control upon laws that they consider to be formally or substantially at odds with the constitution. In such situation, also the maxims of exhaustive, fair, relevant, and clear interpretation can be turned into defeasible prescriptions.

What about the judges? To be sure, there is still somebody who, under the banners of some form of judicial "passivism", claims judges ought simply to "discover" the true, objective meaning of statutory provisions and be content with that. As soon as we cast a glance at the rules of the game by which such a "discovery" should be carried out, however, three facts command our attention.

First, like in the jurists' statutory interpretation game, the rules of the judicial statutory interpretation game ultimately depend on value judgements about the ethically correct way of interpreting statutes and the ethically proper role of judges *vis à vis* the legislature—where correctness and appropriateness are *ethical* properties, measured on the rod of legal, moral and political philosophy's standards. Accordingly, it may occur that (most) judges in a legal order adopt a *principle of interpretive no-cooperation*, in view of promoting judicial control on (purportedly) unconstitutional statutes.

Second, even in the event that judges endorse a principle of interpretive cooperation as paramount, such principle needs precisification. Indeed, being charitable (exhaustive, fair, relevant, clear) interpreters in relation to the statutory clauses enacted by a collective, institutional body is not the same thing as being charitable to the utterances of some flesh-and-blood individual agent with whom we are having an immediate linguistic exchange.

Third, the interpretation of statutory provisions, to be sure, can—and usually does—involve genuine acts of knowledge. However, these acts by no means exhaust it. On the contrary, genuine acts of knowledge are always performed inside of a process that both presupposes, and contains, practical evaluations, commitments, and decision-making.

It is worthwhile noticing, in passing, that the remarks above, concerning the judicial game of statutory interpretation, find evidentiary support in the "theory of legal interpretation" the philosopher of language Scott Soames has set forth in some recent essays.[43]

Soames claims that judicial interpretation of "legal texts", in the U.S. legal order, is, and ought to be, governed by a "general legal rule" he articulates as follows:

> Courts are not to legislate, but are to apply the laws adopted by legislative authorities to the facts of particular cases. When the content of the laws fails to provide reliable guidance in determining a unique acceptable legal outcome – either because it leads to inconsistent outcomes, or because it fails to lead to any outcome, or because it leads to an outcome that is both patently absurd and unforeseen (in cases in which a single, definite, and otherwise acceptable outcome is needed) – the task of the judicial authority is (i) to discern the predominant legislative rationales of the lawmaking bodies in adopting the laws or legal provisions, and (ii) to fashion the minimal modification of existing legal content that removes the deficiency and allows a decision to be reached, while maximizing the fulfillment of the discernable legislative rationales of the relevant laws or legal provisions.[44]

From the standpoint of the theory of interpretive games I have outlined here, Soames's "general rule" is tantamount, it must be noticed, to a set of method rules. It includes a purpose rule (in very rough terms: "Legal texts ought to be interpreted in such a way as to prevent, in the highest degree possible, judicial legislation"), and, furthermore, a default rule (in very rough terms: "When the content of a legal text is defective, judges ought to fix this up by the minimal modification that maximizes the furthering of the discernible and paramount legislative purpose(s)"). Besides, Soames's "general rule" presupposes a selection rule, which points to a translation rule of semantic-pragmatic interpretation of legal sentences, making appeal to such interpretive resources as the conventional or referential meaning of words, context, and the illocutionary intention of the lawgiver.[45]

Now, three points are apparent, and worthwhile emphasizing.

First, Soames has not simply *discovered* the general rule of (deferentialist) judicial interpretation he articulates. Rather, as he plainly avows, that rule is the outcome of his own reconstruction of (a "reasonable approximation" from) existing interpretive practices, in the light of a "conservative" ethical view concerning the proper role of judges *vis à vis* to law-making democratic authorities.[46]

Second, the use by any (American) judge of such general legal rule, in the way suggested by Soames, involves a practical commitment, which depends, in turn, on the acceptance of that certain "conservative" ethical view.

---

[43] Soames (2011), pp. 231–259; see also Soames (2014), pp. 101–122, where the theory gets baptized as "Deferentialism".

[44] Soames (2011), p. 233, 234.

[45] Soames (2011), p. 236 ff., 242 ff.: Soames (2007).

[46] Soames (2011), pp. 232–233, 258–259.

Third, genuine acts of knowledge are, to be sure, involved in the application of the general rule. They are, nonetheless, to take place within a process that is thoroughly biased by the practical goal of maximizing legislative authority and minimizing judicial legislation.

3.7 A Concluding Note

I have considered two linguistic theories concerning the interpretation of legal provisions—the word-meaning theory and the sentence-meaning theory (Sect. 3.2 above)—since they have been set forth by influential legal theorists aiming at providing a true, explanatory, account. Both theories, as we have seen, downsize the specificity of legal interpretation *vis à vis* to the interpretation of linguistic entities (sentences, utterances, inscriptions) in general. I have tried to show that the picture they offer of a socially paramount game like statutory interpretation (and the interpretation of legal provisions in general), though not completely incorrect, is nonetheless misleading, for it pretends to be exhaustive about the way that game is played, here and now, by judges, jurists, and lawyers. I suggested that legal theory needs an account richer in complexity and detail. I argued such an account can be provided from an interpretive game perspective: like, for instance, the one I have outlined here, which takes advantage of a philosophy of language not biased towards semantics, but giving pride of place to the pragmatic dimension of language use and interpretation.

In the opening section, I said the present enquiry is indirectly related to supporting a construction conception of legal meaning. The construction conception emphasizes that legal meaning is never a matter of pure discovery, but always the output of a complex reflexive activity, by which the meaning of legal provisions is actively built up by the interpreters. The interpretive game perspective upholds the construction picture. It brings to the fore the specificity of legal interpretation games *vis à vis* to ordinary conversational interpretation, and emphasizes their practical, complex, (potentially or actually) multi-stage, and (bound) reinterpretation character.

The virtues of a game-pragmatic approach will be put to further test in the following chapters.

Chapter 4
Taking Context Seriously

[G]etting rid of the last literalist prejudice, we must stop presupposing that there is such a thing as the minimal proposition expressed by an utterance

—F. Recanati (2003)

È il contesto che fissa il significato e quindi le condizioni di verità

—A. Varzi (2005)

4.1 A Kantian Reproach

Let me recall the basic claim I purport to defend. The legal meaning of legal provisions is a constructed item: it is the output of a typically multi-stage, reflexive, holistic and re-interpretive process; the construction involves the use of an interpretive code (a discrete normative set including grammar, method and translation rules[1]) together with a set of interpretive resources,[2] and depends ultimately on each interpreter's cooperative, or non-cooperative, attitude towards the text, the issuing authority and the legal order as a whole, where the interpreter's attitude may in turn be, and usually is, the effect of the endorsement of some (comprehensive) legal ideology.[3]

---

[1] See Chap. 2, Sect. 2.2.1.1 and Chap. 3, Sect. 3.4, above.

[2] As you may remember (Chap. 2, Sect. 2.2.1.1), these are the data, or pieces of information, needed to apply interpretive directives. For instance, if the directive to be applied prescribes to interpret statutory provisions according to constitutional principles, interpretive resources amount to the set of constitutional principles the interpreter considers relevant to that task.

[3] On the cooperation and no-cooperation principles see Chap. 3, Sects. 3.5 and 3.6, above. The idea that cooperation attitudes play a paramount role in communication by means of natural languages, besides representing a central point in Paul Grice's theory of ordinary conversation (Grice 1989), is now commonplace in contemporary pragmaticist literature. For instance, Caffi (2008), p. 85, while accounting for Grice's pragmatics, speaks of "cooperation" as "co-construction of the meaning" of an utterance. It must be noticed, however, that, from a more general pragmatic standpoint, viz. one embracing also interpretive games that are different from ordinary conversation, the

P. Chiassoni, *Interpretation without Truth*, Law and Philosophy Library 128,
https://doi.org/10.1007/978-3-030-15590-2_4

I am aware such claim may look trivial, and, therefore, not worth the making. I think nonetheless that there is some use in setting it forth, if only to cope with what I perceive as two persistent theoretical needs. On the one hand, there is the need to refute a still influent view in legal theory, which claims that legal interpretation consists, at least in certain cases, in the "discovery" or simple "understanding" of legal meaning; on the other hand, there is the need of providing a clearer account of the notion of interpretive "creation", which is commonly assumed to play a central role in sceptical, realistic theories of law.

In support of the construction conception of legal meaning, four different, interlocked and conspiring arguments seem worthwhile considering: first, an argument from interpretive games, i.e., from the structural differences between the conversational interpretation game, on the one hand, and the legal provisions interpretation game(s), on the other; second, an argument from the dispute between literalism and contextualism in philosophy of language and linguistics; third, an argument from the failure of pragmatic formalism (quasi-cognitivism), which aims at contrasting the attempt to defend interpretive cognitivism in law by means of a pragmatic approach; fourth, and, finally, an argument from the failure of the semiotic vindication of "texts' rights" and "the limits of interpretation".[4]

I have presented the first line of argument in the preceding chapter. Here, the second line will be set forth. The chapter contains three parts. In the first part, I will provide a précis of two competing jurisprudential theories about legal meaning and interpretation: semantic formalism (semantic quasi-cognitivism) and pragmatic realism (pragmatic non-cognitivism) (Sect. 4.2 below). In the second part, I will offer a bird-eye account of the dispute between literalism and contextualism in contemporary philosophy of language and linguistics (Sect. 4.3 below). In the third, and last, part, I will bring to the fore the pieces of "instruction" (as John Austin would have said) a jurist concerned with legal meaning and legal interpretation could get out of the dispute. I will argue that it provides substantive suggestions for getting rid of semantic formalism and endorsing a meaning construction version of pragmatic realism (Sect. 4.4 below).

Before proceeding, however, it seems worthwhile stopping, so to speak, at the hedge of the wood. The immense literary phenomenon represented, in our legal culture, by the writings dedicated to the subject of interpretation is likely to elicit

construction of utterance meaning can also be the output of a non-cooperative attitude, and such an attitude can be part of the stock-and-trade of the game. On this point, see e.g. Chiassoni (2000a), pp. 89–90, 94–97, which is an older version of the ideas I here convey in Chap. 3; Poggi (2011), pp. 21–40; Jori (2016), pp. 74–75.

[4] For such a vindication, see Eco (1990). The present chapter represents a thoroughly revised and expanded version of Chiassoni (2006). In recent years, a construction conception of legal meaning, as I call it, has been defended in Villa (2012), ch. V. Villa applies contextualist theory of ordinary sentences interpretation to the interpretation of legal provisions, upholding a "sameness claim": "the expressions used in legal language (in […] the language of *legal provisions*) suffer from the same kind of underdeterminacy affecting ordinary language expressions, and, therefore, need context […] in order to receive a full-fledged meaning, to be transferred to the sentence in which they are included" (Villa 2012, p. 125, italics in the text).

from an external observer, who were remindful of Immanuel Kant's sarcastic note about the poverty of jurisprudence,[5] a similar dishonourable comment. Indeed, our external observer could safely remark that: "Jurists are still searching for a theory of legal interpretation". Why? Three basic factors are to be considered by way of a tentative, and by no means exhaustive, explanation. These are the flux of experience, unawareness, and, not the least, reductionism, or the evergreen spell of theoretical Procrusteanism.

Experience in Flux Let me make another trivial point. Legal experience, legal thinking, the conceptual frameworks used by jurists, judges and lawyers at large in their everyday business, as well as people's interests, beliefs, attitudes, knowledge, philosophies, ideologies, and expectations about the law are fatally in a state of constant change. This makes the "theories of legal interpretation" likely to become obsolete, unfit, or even obnoxious constructs, as time goes by.

Unawareness Though this may sound a bit paradoxical, theorists of legal interpretation seem not to be always fully aware about what they are actually doing, when they "theorize about legal interpretation". To put it in perhaps more precise terms, they (but, of course, I put myself too into the same cage) seem not to be always fully aware about the *subject matter*, the *direction of fit*, and, given a certain direction of fit, the *perspective* a "theory of interpretation" can have by design, and, consequently, about the subject matter, the direction of fit, and the perspective of their own theory of interpretation.

Unawareness is favoured by the fact that different, even heterogeneous, enquiries can be carried out under the banner of "a theory of legal interpretation". In fact, any such theory can be either normative or descriptive as to character and function. Normative theories are about how legal interpretation—either in general, or in a definite area of some positive law—ought to be. They set out, and argue for, standards of interpretive (textual or meta-textual) correctness.[6] The direction of fit goes, in this case, from the world of interpretive practice to the several alternative normative theories, each one purporting to set the (exclusive) "proper" standards for it. Descriptive theories purport, contrariwise, to explain how legal interpretation in fact is: in general, or with regard to some particular legal order or part thereof.[7] Here, the direction of fit goes, like for any other piece of descriptive discourse, from the purportedly descriptive theories to the world of interpretive practices. Descriptive theories of textual interpretation are typically about four different though related topics. To begin with, they may concern the *nature* of textual interpretation, with particular

[5] "Jurists are still searching for a definition of their concept of law" (Kant 1787, p. B759 A731).

[6] On textual and meta-textual interpretation, see Chap. 2, Sect. 2.2.1 above. Usually, normative theories defend an interpretive code that, in their view, is conducive to "proper", "correct" interpretations, according to some paramount legal axiology.

[7] Sometimes, normative theories of legal interpretation go undercover. They pretend to be descriptive, claiming what "interpretation" has *necessarily* to be like, to be really "interpretation", or to avoid some *evidently* unwelcome consequence *z*.

attention paid to judicial interpretation (Which kind of activity is it? Is it discovery, understanding, decision, creation, or what else?). They may also concern the *structure* of textual interpretation, as an intellectual process in the mind of interpreters (How does an interpreter proceed while she is interpreting a legal text?).[8] Furthermore, they may be about the *tools* of textual interpretation, as they show up in interpretive discourses (like, e.g., the interpretive reasoning in judicial opinions and juristic writings), in order to bring to the fore "living" interpretive codes and reconstruct the logical structure of interpretive arguments (Which interpretive codes are jurists making use of? Which interpretive tools are available to the judges and jurists working in "our" legal culture? Which is their structure? How do they work? Which typical effect do they promote, if any? etc.). Finally, they may concern the *actual* or *probable social constraints* to the performance of legal interpretation and the use of the methodological tools available (Provided interpreters in legal order LO_1 are supplied—by law, legal culture and tradition—with the set of tools T_1, which may work in such-and-such a way to such-and-such an effect, would it be socially acceptable for an interpreter to use, say, tool 1, to support the interpretive output E_1, in cases C_1?). Descriptive theories of textual interpretation can take different perspectives. They can be (a) psychological theories, inquiring upon the nature and structure of interpretation as a mental process, usually through a blending of linguistic behaviourism and introspection; (b) analytical-methodological theories, inquiring upon extant interpretive "methods", "canons", "rules", "directives", or "techniques", and aiming at bringing to the fore their structure and function; (c) sociological theories, inquiring upon the connections between interpretation, as actually or predictably performed by judges and jurists, on the one side, and "social needs", "social interests", "social standards" or "social values", on the other. Furthermore, they can deal with the subject of interpretation at different levels of generality: they can be more or less local, more or less general, as to the theoretical claims they make and the sort of evidence they are grounded upon.

To sum up: the matter of "a theory of interpretation" may consist in quite different phenomena, which encompass the activities, and outputs, of textual and metatextual interpretation. The direction of fit of "a theory of interpretation" concerning textual or metatextual interpretation may be either normative (world-to-theory) or descriptive (theory-to-world). Once a descriptive direction of fit has been adopted, several perspectives—in particular, the three ones I have just considered—are available. Rational theorizing upon interpretation requires that legal theorists carefully identify—and put to the fore—the subject matter, the direction of fit, and the perspectives of their own inquiries, as a preliminary step necessary to the making of "good theory". The failure of doing so has contributed, and is likely to contribute, to confusion, misunderstanding, obscurity, pointlessness, and the rise of "theoretical" disputes that, upon consideration, may be perfect fakes.

Reductionism One last factor must be mentioned among those that contribute to the extant condition of the theory of legal interpretation. This is reductionism, or, as we

---

[8] On this problem, see Chap. 3, Sect. 3.1, above.

may also say, theoretical Procrusteanism. It consists in accounting for legal interpretation according to a three-stages pattern. In the first stage, the theorist selects some theory of interpretation that has been worked out outside of legal culture, assuming it to be capable of providing an explanation of the phenomenon of legal interpretation that is better (deeper, clearer, more illuminating, more complete, etc.) than those provided by current juristic theories. In the second stage, the theorist makes the phenomenon of legal interpretation to "lay down" on that external theoretical outlook. In the third, and last, stage, the theorist chops out from the description of legal interpretation everything that does not fit with the selected theoretical outlook.

Keeping the foregoing remarks in mind, we can finally enter the wood.

4.2 Two Theories of Legal Interpretation

Apparently, in the here and now of contemporary jurisprudence, two descriptive theories about judicial interpretation of legal provisions compete for paradigmatic supremacy. I will refer to them as semantic formalism and pragmatic realism, respectively.[9]

4.2.1 Semantic Formalism

Semantic formalism—the so-called "intermediate", "midway", or "vigil" theory, in between "the noble dream" of radical "interpretive formalism" and the "nightmare" of "interpretive scepticism"—is a *semantic* theory, since it approaches legal interpretation and legal meaning by focussing on the relationships between the words and sentences of authoritative legal discourse and the "system" of linguistic conventions of the natural language they belong to. Furthermore, it is a *formalist* theory, and more precisely, an instance of moderate or partial interpretive cognitivism ("quasi-cognitivism"), since, as we shall see in a moment, it endorses a discovery-or-stipulation model of (judicial) interpretation.

The core of semantic formalism can be recounted by way of nine claims.[10]

[9] I will analyse a third view, pragmatic formalism, which is again on the cognitivism side, in Chap. 6, Sects. 6.4 and 6.5 below. I have already considered semantic formalism, by a bird-eye view (Chap. 2, Sect. 2.5 above) and under the guises of the word-meaning theory and the sentence-meaning theory (Chap. 3, Sect. 3.2 above). The present chapter's reconstruction is meant to go deeper and wider.

[10] See, *e.g.*, Hart (1958a), p. 63; Hart (1961), p. 125 ff.; Carrió (1965), p. 49 ff., 70–72; Hart (1977), p. 123 ff.; Alchourrón and Bulygin (1971), Bulygin (1986), p. 125 ff.; Bulygin (1991), p. 257 ff.; Bulygin (1995), p. xii: "The problem of legal interpretation is dealt with [...] as a *semantic problem*" (italics added, ndr); Bulygin (1999), pp. 156–157; Moreso (1997a), p. 218 ff.; Marmor

1. Semantic Un-specificity From the vantage point of the semantic dimension of communication by means of a language, interpreting legal provisions is like interpreting any other piece of written words: it consists in reading words and sentences according to their linguistic, conventional meaning.

2. The Linguistic Nature of Interpretive Problems Problems of interpretation, both inside and outside of the law, arise out of linguistic indeterminacy.

3. Two Sources of Linguistic Indeterminacy Linguistic indeterminacy depends on two factors: namely, ambiguity and vagueness. On the one hand, legal provisions may be affected by syntactic or semantic ambiguity. On the other hand, the descriptive terms employed inside of legal provisions (or inside of the corresponding abstract norms, as we shall see in a moment) are liable to suffer from vagueness (imprecision)—which, in its potential variety ("the possibility of vagueness"), is usually known among jurisprudents, after Hart (and Friedrich Waismann), as "open texture".[11]

4. Two Stages in the Process of Interpretation Ambiguity and vagueness, the two factors of indeterminacy, show up at different stages of the interpretive process. This can be brought to the fore by means of a simple, two-stages representative model. On the one hand, ambiguity is likely to show up at the first stage of so-called *abstract* or *text-oriented interpretation*: namely, in the process of identifying the norm which represents the overall linguistic meaning of the legal provision at stake, no attention being paid to its application to individual cases. On the other hand, vagueness is likely to show up at the second stage of so-called *concrete* or *fact-oriented interpre-*

(2005), p. 9 ff., 64, 95 ff. Marmor's version is, in fact, a little bit different from most of the previous ones, being centred on the distinction between the "simple understanding" of a "legal rule" according to its linguistic meaning ("literal construction"), on the one side, and its "interpretation", on the other side. "Understanding" (is all that) takes place when the language of legal provisions works smoothly in providing judges and jurists with a clear and determinate norm for the case at hand. It is basically an act of knowledge. "Interpretation", by contrast, takes place whenever the language of legal provisions has proved indeterminate (linguistic rules have run out), and judges and jurists must make some choice to get out of the *impasse*. They must necessarily engage in the "creation" and/or "modification" of the existing law, according to their ideas about what the law *ought to be*. Furthermore, among the causes of linguistic indeterminacy, he adds family-resemblance to (ordinary) vagueness and open texture. I will analyse Marmor's more recent pragmatic turn (Marmor 2014), always in defence of a quasi-cognitivist theory of judicial interpretation, in Chap. 6 below.

[11] See Waismann (1951), p. 119, 120, where he considers "a factor which, though it is very important and really quite obvious, has to my knowledge never been noticed – [...] the "open texture" of most of our empirical concepts [...] the fact that most of our empirical concepts are not delimited in all possible directions. Suppose I come across a being that looks like a man, speaks like a man, behaves like a man, and is only one span tall – shall I say it *is* a man?". As Waismann acknowledges, it was William Kneale who suggested the expression "open texture" as a translation for the German *Porosität der Begriffe*. Actual or potential vagueness, as you may recall, is the main source of linguistic, and legal, indeterminacy according to the word-meaning theory (see Chap. 3, Sect. 3.2.1, above). Semantic formalism represents, accordingly, an improved variety of semantic quasi-cognitivism.

tation: namely, in the process of applying a previously identified abstract norm to the facts of an individual case. Notice that in the first stage of the interpretive process the interpreter goes, so to speak, from a norm formulation (legal provision) to its corresponding abstract norm. In the second stage, she goes from the abstract norm to the (more) concrete norm for the case at hand.[12]

5. Overcoming Ambiguity by Rational Disambiguation Decision Whenever a legal provision proves to be ambiguous, it is up to the interpreter to decide which one, out of its alternative linguistic meanings, is to be regarded as "its" proper, legally correct, meaning. Such decision is commonly affected by the (rational) goal of presenting the law as a complete and coherent system of norms. In most cases, however, there will be no need for any decision-making by the interpreter, since legal provisions prove univocal.

6. Overcoming Vagueness by Rational Precisification Decision Likewise, whenever an abstract norm appears to be vague in the face of some individual case waiting for legal regulation (due, as we have seen, to the vagueness of some of its descriptive terms), linguistic meaning has run out. It betakes therefore to the interpreter the fixing up of that language failure by stipulating a precise meaning for the vague expression at hand. Precisification is tantamount to ascribing to the expression a meaning that goes necessarily beyond its settled linguistic meaning. Furthermore, it represents the outcome of a discretionary—though not necessarily an arbitrary—judgement. Indeed, it is usually performed in view the rational goal of making the law work to some valuable effect, and is usually supplied with argument. Abstract norms, however, are by no means vague linguistic vessels all the time. On the contrary, in most situations they prove determinate in relation to the facts of the individual cases to be decided: that is to say, their linguistic meaning is determinate enough so as to clearly include them within the scope of the norms, or clearly exclude them from it. In most situations, the language of abstract norms works as a hard language.[13]

7. The Double Nature of Interpretation When legal provisions and the corresponding abstract norms prove determinate (neither ambiguous the former, nor vague the latter), the whole business of interpreters simply amounts to read them straightforwardly according to their linguistic meaning. In such cases, one may safely claim that interpreters have simply "found" or "discovered" the norms they have identified out of norm-formulations.[14] No stipulation, no decision-making, no exercise of

[12] On abstract text-oriented and concrete fact-oriented interpretation see also Chap. 6, Sect. 6.2 footnote 3, below.

[13] See Chap. 3, Sect. 3.3, above.

[14] As I said in footnote 10 above, Andrei Marmor emphasizes the difference between the situations of linguistic determinacy and those of linguistic indeterminacy by resorting to the distinction between "understanding" and "interpretation" (see Marmor 2005, p. 9 ff., 64, 95 ff.). I will analyse Marmor's more recent pragmatic turn (Marmor 2014), always in defence of a quasi-cognitivist theory of judicial interpretation, in Chap. 6 below.

interpretive discretion, no act of will is required there. Thus, as Hart puts it in a famous 1977 essay, "the truth, perhaps unexciting" is that interpretation, sometimes is discovery (in the "easy cases" where legal provisions prove linguistically determinate), sometimes is decision or "law-creation" (in the "hard cases" where legal provisions, or the corresponding abstract norm, prove linguistically indeterminate).[15]

8. The Discovery Side of Thick Evaluative Concepts Even in those cases where the abstract norms contain essentially vague expressions—like the phrases naming evaluative concepts in constitutional clauses ("free speech", "due process of law", "cruel and unusual punishment", "inviolable rights", etc.)—the business of interpreters may still be discovery. Indeed, it is necessary to keep carefully separate "thick" evaluative concepts, which are provided with a solid core of conventional meaning and paradigmatic references (like e.g. "cruel punishment"), on the one side, from the most airy, "thin", concepts, which perhaps have almost no core at all (like e.g. "liberty"), and are therefore the pieces of a *soft* language, on the other side.[16]

9. The Code Model of Legislation It is worthwhile noticing, to conclude, that semantic formalism adopts a view of the process of legislation that, among the philosophers of language, is known as the "code model".[17] Indeed, it suggests the following picture. A legislature, wishing to convey a certain regulation of a certain matter, codifies the intended regulation in a message made of a string of sentences in a natural language, according to the grammar and semantics of that natural language. In the form of a statute published, say, in the Official Journal, the message is sent to the interpreters (the judges). These, in turn, translate—decode—it according to the grammar and semantics of that natural language, retrieve the normative communication the legislature meant to convey—unless, of course, the message proves linguistically indeterminate—, and use it to decide individual cases.

If asked about why we should adopt the code model, semantic formalists would answer, apparently, either by pointing to the "evident" explanatory correctness of the model (the relation between legislature and judges plainly works in *that* way),[18] or by suggesting that it would be absurd denying the code model, since legal provisions are formulated in a natural language precisely to that very purpose,[19] or else by claiming that it is the only way compatible with allowing for the existence of (definite) legal norms, indeed, with our "having norms" at all.[20]

---

[15] Hart (1977), p. 144: "The truth, perhaps unexciting, is that sometimes the judges do one [make the law] and sometimes the other [find the law]".

[16] On soft language, see Chap. 3, Sect. 3.3, above.

[17] On the "code model" see e.g. Bianchi (2005), pp. 100–104; Wilson and Sperber (2012b), pp. 2–3.

[18] This seems the answer implicit, e.g., in Hart (1961), ch. VII.

[19] See, e.g., Carrió (1965), pp. 49–61.

[20] See, e.g., Bulygin (1999), pp. 156–157.

4.2.2 Pragmatic Realism

Pragmatic realism, the peculiar variety of interpretive realism I have in mind, stands in overt opposition to semantic formalism. It is a *pragmatic* variety of realism because it adopts a pragmatic approach to linguistic (and legal) interpretation: one that focuses on the relationships between natural languages and their users and interpreters. It is a *realistic* view, since it rejects the discovery-or-stipulation model in favour of a decisionist model. Assuming a pragmatic vantage point, it claims semantic formalism to be wrong: both as to the view it entertains about linguistic interpretation in general, and, more specifically, as to the view it entertains about judicial interpretation of legal provisions.[21]

The core ideas of pragmatic realism can be recounted as follows.

1. Pragmatic Un-specificity At a very high level of abstraction, the interpretation of legal provisions is indeed like the interpretation of any other sentence in a natural language. This is so, however, in virtue of a different explanatory factor than the one invoked by semantic formalism. Semantic formalism, as we have seen (Sect. 4.2.1, above), claims the interpretation of whatever sentence in a natural language, in virtue of its being a sentence in a natural language, to be a matter of putting linguistic knowledge (skill, competence, mastery, know-how) to work. In so keeping to the syntactic and semantic sides of sentences, however, it overlooks the pragmatic dimension of linguistic communication. It misses, to wit, that interpretation of legal provisions and ordinary conversational interpretation are alike because, in both cases, an attitude on the part of each interpreter, involving some (degree of) cooperation or no-cooperation to the (actual or potential) linguistic exchange, is the necessary and moving factor.[22]

As a consequence of overlooking the pragmatic dimension of interpretation, semantic formalism incurs in further mistakes. These concern both its theory of interpretation in general, and, more specifically, its theory concerning the interpretation of legal provisions.

2. Semantic Formalism Endorses a Wrong Theory of Interpretation in General Semantic formalism endorses a wrong theory of interpretation in general. Indeed, the theory misses three momentous aspects of the interpretive phenomenon.

First, any interpretation of any sentence whatsoever, whether it takes place inside of an ordinary conversation, or in relation to a legal text, always counts as a move in a game.[23]

[21] Semantic quasi-cognitivists—or their proxy defenders (see, e.g., Barberis 2001, pp. 1–36)—sometimes charge pragmatic non-cognitivists of being either hard-sceptics, or no-sceptics at all. But this is a story to be told elsewhere. I tried to do something like that in Chiassoni (2001), p. 365 ff.

[22] See Chap. 3, Sects. 3.5 and 3.6, above.

[23] On interpretive games, see above, Chap. 3, Sects. 3.4–3.6.

Second, the selection and use of translation rules—from the "literal rule", appealing to sentence meaning, to rules pointing to speaker's meaning, speaker's intention, the point of the linguistic transaction, the cherished purpose of background all-mighty Deities, the dictates of Reason, Nature's hard necessities, etc.—always depend on a range of pragmatic factors.[24]

Third, among the pragmatic factors bearing on the selection and use of translation rules three are paramount. These are: the role interpreters decide to play—a decision that is affected, in turn, by their institutional position and the ways they perceive it; their immediate, mid-term, or long-term interest(s) and goal(s); the institutional and cultural constraints they estimate to be afoot.

3. Semantic Formalism Provides a Wrong Theory of Legal Interpretation Semantic formalism provides a wrong theory about the interpretation of legal provisions. Indeed, it overlooks the following facts.

First, an array of interpretive attitudes, and corresponding roles, is available to interpreters in law, ranging from the one extreme, represented by full and intelligent cooperation with legal authorities (the norm-formulations maker, the legislature, the sovereign, etc.), to the opposite extreme represented by deep and manifest hostility, passing through qualified forms of cooperation and undercover sabotage.

Second, interpreters can select the interpretive codes they are going to use, according to the goals they have decided to pursue, out of a wide and changing set ("body") of interpretive rules handed down and developed by legal methodology.

Third, interpreters' allegiance to any definite interpretive code is not necessarily fixed once and forever; in fact, it can be wholly momentary, provided the legal culture tolerates situation-sensible shifts of codes.

4. The Embedded and Artificial Nature of Literal Interpretation Some interpretive rules instruct interpreters to read legal provisions according to their "literal" or "conventional linguistic meaning": be it the conventional meaning at the time the provisions were enacted (original conventional meaning), or the conventional meaning at the time of their use to decide a case (present, updated, evolutionary conventional meaning). Literalist translation rules, however, never walk alone. As we know, they are just a set within a larger set (or "body") of tools. Besides, they always work as parts of some interpretive code.[25] Accordingly, resorting—and, above all, sticking—to literal meaning (or better: to some variety of literal meaning[26]), when legal provisions are concerned, is by no means a pure "matter of course": it is not a spontaneous, value-free, course of action, but one saddled with ploy. Leaving aside any material (or un-avowable) interest the interpreter may happen to pursue, such an option depends, rather, on some interpretive ideology: like,

---

[24] On translation rules, which correspond to most of the items usually referred to as "canons", "rules", or "directives" of interpretation, see Chap. 2, Sect. 2.2.1.1, Chap. 3, Sect. 3.4, above.

[25] See Chap. 3, Sect. 3.4, above.

[26] A paradigmatic instance of a dispute where different notions of "literal" or "ordinary" meaning" are at stake is offered in the majority and dissenting opinions of the U.S. Supreme Court's decision *Smith v. United States*, 508 U.S. 223 (1993).

for instance, the enlightenment ideology of plain interpretation of plainly formulated statutes, liable to be understood by ordinary people at large.[27]

5. The Superior Explanatory Power of a Pragmatic Vantage Point As soon as we take into account the pragmatic dimension of linguistic communication, a few theoretical claims, quite different from those characterizing semantic formalism, must be put forth.

First, interpretive problems are not reducible to problems of linguistic indeterminacy of legal provisions. Unless, of course, interpreters decide to make use of a simple code that only encompasses a literal meaning translation rule.[28]

Second, provided any act of interpretation depends on some commitment to an interpretive code (a discrete set of interpretive rules), the interpretation of legal provisions can never amount solely to a value-free, linguistic "discovery" or "finding" of the law, not even in so-called "clear" cases.

Third, when semantic formalists (quasi-cognitivists) claim there are cases where interpretation is just a matter of discovery, they call "discovery" the practical attitude of conformism, on the part of interpreters, towards some culturally dominant interpretive doctrine or some piece of "living law" (*lebendes Recht*).

Fourth, the code model of legislation adopted by semantic formalism provides a misleading representation. The model pre-empts realizing that, as a matter of fact, legislation is the enactment of legal provisions by an authorized agency (the legislature), the meaning of which is necessarily to be provided by a set of authorized interpreters (the judges). On the sending side, there is a body of agents busy with establishing an authoritative text. On the reception side, there is no automatic decoding machine; there is, instead, a body of agents who are endowed with, and exercise, interpretive powers, according to their beliefs and attitudes concerning legislation and their own institutional role.

It is time to take stock. Semantic formalism and pragmatic realism are rival, incompatible, descriptive theories about judicial interpretation of legal provisions. Which one is right? No knockdown argument seems available; and legal theory may look as being at a deadlock. Something can be done, however, in order to get out of the apparent *impasse*. In the preceding chapter, I argued for interpretive realism, and against semantic formalism (in the forms, as you may remember, of the word-meaning and sentence-meaning theories), on the basis of a theory of interpretive games and an extension of Grice's theory of conversational maxims.[29] In the present chapter, I purport to do the same by resorting to the debate between "Literalism" and "Contextualism" in contemporary philosophy of language and linguistics.[30] The

[27] See, e.g., Carrió (1965), pp. 49–61.

[28] On simple codes, see Chap. 3, Sect. 3.4.1, above.

[29] See Chap. 3 above.

[30] Sometimes, Grice is regarded as a representative of literalism (which embraces semantic minimalism and indexicalism), sometimes as a contextualist (see, on the point, Bianchi 2009, p. 172). Be it as it may, the Gricean argument I put forth in Chap. 3 is different, and complementary, to the contextualist argument I outline in the present chapter.

contextualist critique to literalism, and some literalist adjustment to it, cast light on aspects of linguistic communication and interpretation that support a further line of argument for interpretive realism, on the one side, while turning down semantic formalism, on the other. This is what I am going to suggest in the final section of the chapter (Sect. 4.4), after providing a very swift account of the two fighting camps (Sect. 4.3).

4.3 Literalism v. Contextualism

Few words are enough for conveying the gist of the dispute between literalism and contextualism.[31]

On the one hand, contextualism stands as a critical reaction to the (pretended) failure of "the traditional semantic paradigm", the "traditional literature in philosophy of language and linguistics", Gricean pragmatics, and some more recent theories like "indexicalism" and "semantic minimalism". All these theories, contextualism claims, are guilty of the capital sin of "literalism": to wit, they would overrate the virtue and role of semantic meaning in communication by means of natural languages.[32]

On the other hand, literalists retort that "contextualism" (an expression some of them use with a derogatory tinge) would be guilty of a specular sin. That would be the sin of overrating the virtue and role of context in communication by means of natural languages.[33]

From the standpoint of an external observer, the dispute between literalism and contextualism looks, thus, as a contest between two (pretended) exaggerations. It must be emphasized, furthermore, that literalism and contextualism are far from being two monolithic outlooks, being rather the labels for a variety of positions

[31] In its more general and abstract meaning, "contextualism" refers to any intellectual position, which may be a piece of some larger view, according to which "context is relevant": whatever one may mean by "context", and whichever the enterprise it may be deemed "relevant" for. Thus, as soon as we consider the several fields of learning, we can speak of "contextualism"—and of a "contextual perspective", a "contextual turn", etc.—as regards to different subjects as artificial intelligence, epistemology, hermeneutics, linguistics, philosophy of language, theology, etc. See e.g. Penco (2002b), pp. xiii–xxxv; Stalnaker (2014). Here, as it is apparent, I will be concerned with linguistic contextualism.

[32] My sources for this presentation of literalism and linguistic contextualism have been primarily the following: Searle (1978, 1980), Bianchi (1998), Bianchi (2001), Bianchi (2002), pp. 253–265; Recanati (2004), Bianchi (2005), pp. 50–54, 99–130; Cappelen and Lepore (2005), who aim at providing a knock down defence of semantic minimalism; Bianchi (2009), pp. 171–175, 180–193, 204–213; Recanati (2010), Wilson and Sperber (2012a); Domaneschi (2014), ch. 3. The semantics/pragmatics debate is profitably rehearsed in Penco and Domaneschi (2013).

[33] See, e.g., Cappelen and Lepore (2005), p. x: contextualists "inflate the role of context in semantics".

on both sides, from more to less "extreme" or "radical" stances.[34] To the present purpose, however, my account will stay with a hopefully fair reconstruction of (what I assume to be) their respective basic claims.

4.3.1 Literalism

The core of literalism is made of a set of ideas that can be recounted as follows:

1. Three kinds, and levels, of meaning are worthwhile distinguishing in relation to any act of linguistic communication (the uttering of a sentence in a spatio-temporal frame). These are the *linguistic meaning* (sentence meaning, semantic content) of the type-sentence, the *semantic meaning* (semantically expressed proposition) of the token-sentence, and *speaker's-intended meaning*;
2. The semantic meaning (semantically expressed proposition) of a token sentence depends on linguistic rules, is determinate, and, but for the phenomenon of context-sensitivity, is constant over contexts;
3. The semantic meaning (semantically expressed proposition) of token sentences is the output either of a purely linguistic computation, or of a linguistic computation combined with a linguistically driven (grammatically triggered) contextual investigation;
4. The speaker's intended meaning is always context-dependent;
5. It is worthwhile distinguishing between pre-semantic, semantic and post-semantic use of context in the interpretation of any act of communication;
6. Semantics (the system of language) always provides a self-sufficient contribution (amounting to a truth-apt proposition) to the overall meaning of any act of communication.

1. Determinacy and Fixity of Semantic Meaning With the precision that we shall see at point 5 below, the syntactic and semantic rules of a natural language determine, in an exhaustive way, both the application conditions of (descriptive) words and the satisfaction-conditions of sentences, whichever their context of utterance. This means, in other words, that syntactic and semantic rules make possible calculating, for any token sentence whatsoever, a semantic meaning (a semantically expressed proposition) amounting to a *full-fledged proposition*: i.e., a meaning that is complete from the standpoint either of its truth-condition, in the case, usually

[34] On the varieties of literalism and contextualism see e.g. Recanati (2003, 2004), Cappelen and Lepore (2005), pp. 5–11. It is commonplace distinguishing between "radical minimalism", "moderate minimalism", "radical contextualism" and "moderate contextualism" (see, e.g., Bianchi 2001, p. 279 ff., 297 ff.). Recanati, however, claims that what a supporter of literalism regards as "moderate contextualism" may look, to a supporter of contextualism, as "moderate literalism". And what a literalist regards as "radical contextualism" looks to a contextualist just as "contextualism" in its pure (Recanati 2010, p. 5 footnote 3). Likewise, Cappelen and Lepore claim the distinction between moderate and radical contextualism is apparent, since moderate contextualism "collapses into" radical contextualism (Cappelen and Lepore 2005, p. 14).

considered by language philosophers and linguists, of declarative sentences, or of its abiding-conditions, in the case, relevant to lawyers, of normative sentences.[35] Besides being a determinate truth-apt (or abiding-apt) proposition, the semantic meaning of token sentences, but for the cases of context-sensitivity, is also constant across contexts: that is to say, it is the same, whatever the context in which the sentence is being used.

2. Purely Linguistic v. Mixed Computation of Semantic Meaning The semantic meaning (semantically expressed proposition) of token sentences is the output, either of a purely linguistic computation, or of a linguistic computation combined with a contextual investigation guided by semantic "rules of saturation".[36]

Purely linguistic computation occurs when *context-independent* (context-insensitive) *sentences* are at stake. These are sentences that contain no context-dependent (context-sensitive) expression. All their components are context-independent: being, for instance, logical terms ("and", "or", "not", "if … then", etc.) and descriptive terms like "house", "tree", "duck", "vehicle", "red", "thick", "tall", "dance", "justice", "malice", "law", etc. When a sentence is context-independent, it is endowed in itself with a complete, truth-apt (or abidance-apt) semantic meaning. This meaning can be identified by keeping within each interpreter's linguistic competence, and putting it to use according to the twin principles of compositionality and context—where the "context", here, is the whole sentence in relation to each of its single component expressions. When context-insensitive sentences are at stake, semantic meaning (proposition) and sentence meaning (linguistic meaning) coincide.

Contrariwise, the identification of the full-fledged semantic meaning of a token-sentence depends on a mixed enquiry, when context-dependent sentences are at stake. These are sentences that contain context-dependent (context-sensitive) expressions: namely, pure indexicals ("I", "now", "here", "today", "tomorrow", etc.), demonstratives, personal pronouns and adjectives ("he", "she", "this", "those books", "that cat", etc.), or other contextual phrases ("my book", "Johnny's dog", "the horse of Caravaggio", "Rebecca's masterpiece", etc.).[37] When a sentence is context-dependent, it is not endowed, by itself, with a complete, truth-apt (or abidance-apt) semantic meaning, identifiable by means of a pure linguistic calculus. In order to identify the full, truth-apt, semantic meaning of the sentence, its

---

[35] On the interpretation of non-declarative sentences, see e.g. Wilson and Sperber (2012c), pp. 210–229.

[36] The coining of the now current technical term "saturation" is due to François Recanati (see Recanati 2010, p. 4).

[37] Apparently, the line dividing the two varieties of literalism—"semantic minimalism" (defended, e.g., by Emma Borg, Ernst Cappelen, and Henry Lepore) and "indexicalism" (defended, e.g., by Jason Stanley and Zoltan Szabó)—passes here: semantic minimalists adopt a more restricted view about context-dependent expressions, limited to pure indexicals and broadly understood "demonstratives" (see Cappelen and Lepore 2005, pp. 1–4, 144; Bianchi 2009, pp. 172–176; Recanati 2010, p. 5; Domaneschi 2014, pp. 129–134).

(semantic) context of utterance must be resorted to. The data, different from those about speaker's intention, concerning the time and place in which the sentence has been uttered, the persons of the speaker and hearer(s), the subject-matter the sentence is about, etc., must be brought to bear on the semantic interpretation of the sentence.[38] The semantic spaces left empty by context-dependent expressions must be filled up ("saturated"). To this effect, the conventional literal meaning of context-dependent expressions works either as a "rule of automatic saturation", when pure indexicals are at stake,[39] or as a rule of semantic governance of saturation, when demonstratives and other contextual expressions are present[40]; it points, in both cases, to what is their reference in the world. When context-sensitive sentences are at stake, semantic meaning (proposition) and sentence meaning (linguistic meaning) do not coincide. The proposition is nonetheless determined, literalists claim, according to the rules of the language. This is why it represents, nonetheless, the semantic meaning (the semantically expressed proposition) of the token sentence.

It seems useful recapitulating briefly what the claims so far considered of literalism suggest.

Sentence meaning (conventional meaning, linguistic meaning, semantic content) can be locally underdetermined (*local underdeterminacy*). It is underdetermined, as we have seen, when, and only when, context-dependent sentences are at stake.

Semantic meaning (proposition, semantically expressed proposition) is, by contrast, always determined (*global determinacy*). Linguistic rules make it to be the

---

[38] Not all literalists would agree with the idea of a "semantic context" as reported in the text. For instance, Cappelen and Lepore maintain the notion of "semantic context" to be a trick invented by contextualists to bring literalism into disrepute. They assert that, surely, also from the standpoint of the "semantic minimalism" they defend, the saturation of (genuine) context-sensitive expressions may require appealing to speaker's intention (Cappelen and Lepore 2005, pp. 147–149). Notice, by the way, that "context" usually stands for a given set of information, or data, about time, place, persons, things, attitudes, beliefs, interpretations of previously uttered sentences, etc. Different sets of information identify different contexts. Usually, the data making up the context of an utterance are regarded as shared by the parties to a linguistic exchange. For instance, according to Robert Stalnaker, "context" is to be understood as "*common ground*", i.e., as "a body of information that is presumed to be shared by the parties to a discourse. The course of the discourse and the interpretation of what is said in it are guided by that body of information and by the way that it evolves in response to what is said" (Stalnaker 2014, pp. 2–3, 13 ff.).

[39] For instance, "I" always refers to the person who is speaking or writing; "here" always refers to the place where the person speaking or writing is supposed to be, etc.

[40] In the case of demonstratives and other contextual expressions, an appeal to the speaker's (presumed) communicative intention appears unavoidable (a point some literalists agree upon, as we have seen above, footnote 31). For instance, if Geneva says to Lancelot: "Open that window", and the room contains two closed windows, say, a double lancet window and a triple lancet window, Lancelot cannot identify which one is to be opened by the only means of the semantic rules presiding over the use of the demonstrative "that". Clearly, it is dubious where such an interpretation is still within the domain of semantics, or is, rather, pragmatic, provided the "pragmatic context" include "the set of hypotheses about the world made by the subjects [of a conversation], their beliefs, wishes, intentions, activities" (Bianchi 2005, p. 116, 52).

case: either directly, when context-independent sentences are at stake,[41] or indirectly, when context-dependent sentences are at stake.

Whenever indirect determination is necessary, the semantic meaning depends on the context of utterance of the sentence at stake. There is, in other words, a *local contextual dependence* of semantic meaning. The context at stake, however, is the so-called *semantic context*. It is, in any case, a set of data the interpretive relevance thereof is thoroughly "signal-driven": triggered, driven and controlled by semantic and syntactic rules.[42] The saturation that is needed in order to get to the semantic meaning (proposition) is, accordingly, wholly within the domain of "semantics".[43]

3. Three Varieties of Meaning It is theoretically worthwhile distinguishing between three kinds, and levels, of meaning in relation to any act of linguistic communication. These are: the linguistic or sentence meaning of the type-sentence, the semantic meaning of the token-sentence ("proposition", "semantic content", "semantically expressed proposition"), and, furthermore, the speaker's-intended meaning.

Sentence meaning is tantamount to the meaning that can be identified for a sentence by the only means of linguistic (syntactic and semantic) rules: no reference being made either to the semantic, or the pragmatic, context of utterance. It is, accordingly, the purely conventional meaning of a sentence. It corresponds to "what is proffered".[44]

Semantic meaning is the meaning the identification of which depends on linguistic rules and, in the case of context-dependent sentences, on the semantic context of utterance. In the latter event, its computation involves the (semantic) saturation of indexicals, demonstratives and other contextual expressions. It is, in any case, the truth-apt (or abiding-apt) proposition expressed by the "utterance". It corresponds to "what is said".[45] As we have seen, semantic meaning (proposition, what is said) and sentence meaning (conventional meaning, linguistic meaning, what is proffered) coincide when context-independent sentences are at stake.

Speaker's-intended meaning, finally, is the meaning, different from sentence and semantic meanings, the speaker intends to communicate by uttering a sentence in a spatio-temporal frame ("what is communicated"). It consists in a set of *implicit propositions* (implicatures) that are identified on the basis of the explicit linguistic proposition (what is said), with the aid of devices like Grice's conversational principle and maxims.[46]

It must be noticed that the tripartite typology above is proper of the so-called traditional semantic theory and Gricean ("literalist") pragmatics. In their defence of

[41] Think at sentences, which are plenty in any language, like "Italians do not like spaghetti", "No vehicle is allowed in any park", "Tyranny is ever-growing", etc.

[42] I borrow "signal-driven" from Recanati (2010), p. 4.

[43] According to the principle of "isomorph correspondence" between the (deep) syntactic structure of a sentence and its semantic interpretation (on this point, see Bianchi 2005, p. 123).

[44] Bianchi (2005), p. 120.

[45] Bianchi (2005), p. 120.

[46] Bianchi (2005), p. 116 ff.; Domaneschi (2014), pp. 56–57.

that variety of literalism known as semantic minimalism against the contextualist critique, however, Herman Cappelen and Ernie Lepore set forth a different view. By way of an overt departure from the Gricean picture, they distinguish—in the terminology I am using here—the semantic meaning ("the semantically expressed proposition"), speaker's explicit meaning, and speaker's implicit meaning. In their view, therefore, due to the phenomenon of "speech act pluralism",[47] there are two sorts of explicit meaning for any token-sentence; furthermore, the semantically expressed proposition, the "minimal semantic proposition", is not (necessarily) identical to "what is said" or "what the speaker said".[48]

4. Contextual Dependence of Speaker's Meaning Speaker's meaning, i.e., the implicit component of the overall meaning of an act of communication, is parasitic upon the semantic meaning of the token sentence at stake. The proposition expressed by the token sentence works as the starting point from which the implicit meaning of the act of communication can be identified by means of pragmatic interpretation. This takes into account, and always depends on, the pragmatic context of utterance, which, going beyond the semantic context, encompasses such things as speaker's and interpreter's (assumedly shared) encyclopaedia, intentions, beliefs, attitudes, etc.

5. Pre-semantic, Semantic and Post-semantic Use of Context Sentences in a natural language are often saddled with ambiguity or vagueness. Literalists are conscious that ambiguity and vagueness affect the determinacy of sentences in a natural language. Apparently, they follow two different strategies for coping with them.

Traditional literalists tend to push ambiguity and vagueness out of the "semantic space" delimited by semantic interpretation proper. They proceed as follows: (*i*) it is worthwhile distinguishing three uses of the context of utterance in the interpretation of an act of communication: namely, the "pre-semantic", the "semantic", and the "post-semantic" use; (*ii*) whenever a sentence in a natural language proves syntactically or semantically ambiguous, the very identification of its linguistic meaning depends on an operation of disambiguation, which involves a pre-semantic use of context, since it precedes the semantic interpretation proper of the sentence at stake[49]; (*iii*) the semantic use of context concerns the identification of the proposition expressed by a token sentence, whenever the latter is context-dependent; (*iv*) the post-semantic use of context, finally, presupposes that the full-fledged proposition has already been calculated; context is used therefore either to overcome the phenomenon of vagueness, whenever it shows up, or in view of identifying the

---

[47] "No one thing is said (or asserted, or claimed, or ...) by any utterance: rather, indefinitely many propositions are said, asserted, claimed, stated [...] an utterance can assert propositions that are not even logical implications of the proposition semantically expressed. Nothing prevents an utterance from asserting [...] propositions incompatible with the proposition semantically expressed by that utterance": Cappelen and Lepore (2005), p. 4; see also 190–208.

[48] Cappelen and Lepore (2005), pp. 150, 180–181.

[49] Bianchi (2005), p. 53; Perry (2002b), pp. 241–243.

implicit speaker's meaning, be it figurative (metaphoric, metonymical, hyperbolic, by understatement, ironic) or made of further conversational implicatures.[50]

By contrast, semantic minimalists consider ambiguity and vagueness as phenomena to be coped with, and overcome, by means of semantic interpretation: ambiguous or polysemous expressions must be disambiguated, and vague expressions must be precisified, in "order to fix or determine the proposition semantically expressed by an utterance of a sentence".[51]

6. The Self-Sufficient Contribution of Semantics to the Overall Meaning of Any Act of Communication An act of communication consists, as I have said, in uttering a sentence in a certain spatio-temporal frame. The frame identifies the semantic context of utterance, which is embedded, in turn, into a larger context or set of contexts (pragmatic context). On the basis of the previous remarks, the full meaning of any individual act of communication generally corresponds to the combination of two separate components. On the one hand, there is the full-fledged, self-sufficient semantic meaning of the token sentence, which may (or may not) coincide with the linguistic meaning of the type-sentence, and is determined by linguistic rules (the linguistic system). On the other hand, there is the speaker's intended meaning: be it regarded as being wholly implicit,[52] as by "traditional theory", or as partly explicit and partly implicit, as by semantic minimalism.[53] In any case, the "semantics" (broadly understood) of the relevant natural language provides a self-sufficient contribution to the overall meaning of any act of communication.[54]

4.3.2 Contextualism

The main ideas composing the core of contextualism can be recounted as follows:

1. Three kinds, and levels, of meaning are worthwhile distinguishing in relation to any act of linguistic communication: namely, the *linguistic meaning* of the token-sentence ("conventional meaning", "sentence meaning", "minimal proposition"), the *speaker's-intended explicit meaning* of the token-sentence ("proposition" in a pragmatic sense, pragmatic explicit meaning), and, finally, the *speaker's-intended implicit meaning* (pragmatic implicit meaning);
2. The linguistic meaning of token sentences is generally underdetermined;
3. The linguistic meaning of token sentences is liable to change according to the shifting of the contexts of utterance;

[50] According to traditional semantic theory, as complemented by Gricean pragmatics, figurative meanings are implicit and identified as a variety of conversational implicatures. See Wilson and Sperber (2012d), pp. 123–145.

[51] Cappelen and Lepore (2005), pp. 144–145.

[52] See Bianchi (2001), p. 24 ff.

[53] Cappelen and Lepore (2005), p. 150, 180–181.

[54] Cappelen and Lepore (2005), pp. 4–5, 143–189, 190–208.

4. The full-fledged, truth-apt (or abiding-apt) meaning of token sentences is generally different from their linguistic meaning;
5. The identification of the full-fledged, truth-apt (or abiding-apt) meaning of token sentences is always the output of an activity of pragmatic, context-based, interpretation;
6. The contribution of semantics (the system of language) to the overall meaning of any act of communication is generally not self-sufficient.[55]

1. General Underdeterminacy and Possible Shifting of Linguistic Meaning The linguistic meaning of token sentences is generally underdetermined: in a widespread and frequent series of cases, by itself it does not amount to a full-fledged, truth-apt (or abiding-apt) proposition. Furthermore, due to a factor that we shall consider in a moment, it can change across the contexts of utterance.

The general underdeterminacy of linguistic meaning, the fact that the linguistic meaning of a token sentence generally does not amount to a full-fledged, truth-apt (or abiding-apt) proposition depends—contextualists claim—on three main conspiring factors.

First, the meaning of descriptive terms (concept-word) is not a fixed set of necessary and sufficient conditions of application, as it is assumed by traditional semantic theories. On the contrary, it is a set of past applications of the expression, pointing to different references. These applications, which are recorded and typified in dictionaries, only provide the "semantic potential" of the expression, the application of which to further cases depends on context-dependent considerations about analogy and difference.[56]

[55] In their defence of semantic minimalism, Cappelen and Lepore identify two varieties of contextualism: radical contextualism and moderate contextualism (Cappelen and Lepore 2005, pp. 5–11). Very roughly speaking, they characterize radical contextualism as endorsing what I call a *global underdeterminacy thesis*: the linguistic meaning (the semantically expressed proposition) of *any* token sentence *whatsoever* is *always* underdetermined; it *never* expresses a full-fledged, truth-apt, proposition. Contrariwise, moderate contextualism endorses what I shall call a *widespread underdeterminacy thesis*: the linguistic meaning of token sentences is underdetermined in a much widespread series of cases than literalism concedes. Contextualists—it must be noticed—are not crystal-clear on the point. Even John R. Searle, whom Cappelen and Lepore put in the cage of radical contextualism, seems content to claim that the phenomenon of underdeterminacy of linguistic meaning is, notice, "quite general": that it obtains "for a large number of cases (perhaps not all)" (Searle 1980, p. 227). In my simplified account, considered the purpose of the present paper, I will identify contextualism *sans phrase* with upholding a *general underdeterminacy thesis*: meaning, by that, that underdeterminacy is a widespread, statistically significant phenomenon, that occurs very often, and goes well beyond the limited borders of literalism's context-sensitiveness. Furthermore, I will adopt a charitable view, purporting to present its ideas as being as much sensible as possible.

[56] This position corresponds to the variety of contextualism Recanati calls "Wrong Format View". According to it, "the sense expressed by an expression must always be contextually constructed on the basis of the (overly rich or overly abstract) meaning or semantic potential of the word type". The "Wrong Format View" has a more radical relative: "Meaning Eliminativism". According to it, "we don't need linguistic meanings even to serve as input to the construction process. The senses that are the words' contributions to contents are constructed, but the construction can proceed without the help of conventional, context-independent word meanings" (Recanati 2003, pp. 19–20).

Second, the sentences used in ordinary communication are frequently elliptical: some phrases, which are necessary in order to get out of them a full-fledged proposition, are frequently missing.[57]

Third, even when a sentence is formulated in a relatively careful way, it may nonetheless be unable to express a full-fledged proposition, unless, and until, its linguistic meaning is being complemented by some piece of background information necessary to reconstruct the full "literal meaning" of the sentence.[58]

The previous remarks suggest three conclusions.

To begin with, the area of linguistic underdeterminacy is larger than literalists seem willing to concede. Indeed, it goes well beyond the province of the context-sensitive expressions they usually contemplate (pure indexicals, demonstratives, etc.) (see Sect. 4.3.1. above).

Furthermore, and consequently, the full-fledged proposition expressed by a token sentence is different from its linguistic meaning in a much wider and frequent range of cases than literalism concedes, up to the point of representing a typical, general, feature in the use of a natural language.

---

[57] An example should convey what different contextualists have in mind when they claim sentences to be generally elliptical (as I put it), from the standpoint of their capacity of expressing a full-fledged "applicable" (truth-apt or satisfaction-apt) meaning. Suppose somebody says: "Judith is ready". Literalists claim that such a sentence clearly expresses a truth-apt proposition: namely, the proposition *that Judith is ready*, which is true if, and only if, Judith is ready—and the same applies to "Hilary is tall", "Hannibal dances", "It rains", "Al is short", etc. Contextualists reply, however, that in such cases truth-aptness is apparent. If we do not know *what is* Judith *ready for* (Beheading Holophern? Going to the Great Blue Cheese Exhibition? Becoming Governor General of the country? Marrying Tom?), we are not able to verify it; the linguistic meaning (the minimal proposition) does not amounts to a definite truth-apt proposition, but to a "frame", a "structure", a "skeleton" allowing for several different and alternative possibilities of enrichment. The sentences, notice, are elliptical for they apparently lack a necessary semantic complement: some further expression without which the linguistic meaning of the sentence appears to be floating in the air. It is elliptical, some contextualist would say, for it requires to be complemented by some "unarticulated constituents" (Perry 2002b, pp. 248–251).

[58] Suppose, to rehearse a famous example from John Searle (Searle 1978, p. 127), somebody enters a diner and says: "Give me a hamburger, medium rare, with ketchup and mustard, but easy on the relish". By staying with the sole linguistic meaning of the sentence, contextualists claim, the waiter could not satisfy the customer. That could only be done by appealing to some set of background information ("background assumptions") concerning the quantity and quality of the meat, the way of cooking it, the way of packaging and delivering it to the customer, etc. The sentence, notice, is not elliptical in the way the sentence "Judith is ready" is assumed to be. Here, in order for it to express an applicable meaning, the interpreter must refer to information from an on-going social practice, from a "background of meaning" that can never be entirely translated into additional pieces to the proffered sentence, unless at the cost of making verbal communication very burdensome, and perhaps totally impair it. See also Searle (1980), pp. 221–232; Bianchi (2002), p. 256; Recanati (2003), pp. 15–19. I have briefly outlined Searle's conception of literal meaning as a model for juristic reflection about the literal meaning of legal texts in Chiassoni (2000a), p. 20 ff.

Finally, where the linguistic meaning is elliptical, the meaning of the type sentence ("The car is red", "Judith is ready", "It rains", "Hannibal is tall", "Al is short") is not constant across contexts: rather, it changes as contexts shift.[59]

2. Context-Dependence of Full-Fledged Propositions and the Scope of Pragmatic Interpretation The identification of the full-fledged, truth-apt (or abiding-apt) meaning of token sentences always depends on an activity of pragmatic, context-based, interpretation.

Pragmatic interpretation is the interpretation of an act of communication as a whole.[60] It interacts systematically with semantic interpretation (the interpretation of token sentences according to linguistic rules) and complements it.

At a closer glance, pragmatic interpretation brings about the identification of the full-fledged, truth-apt (or abiding-apt) meaning of token sentences in six different ways: namely, by disambiguation, precisification, saturation, enrichment, substitution ("transfer"), and confirmation.[61]

Disambiguation occurs when the token sentence proves syntactically or semantically ambiguous (see Sect. 4.3.1, point 5., above).

Precisification occurs when the token sentence contains vague descriptive terms (see Sect. 4.3.1, point 5., above).

Saturation occurs when the token sentence contains context-sensitive expressions (indexicals, demonstratives, etc.: Sect. 4.3.1, point 2., above).

Enrichment (completion, expansion, free enrichment) occurs when the token sentence is elliptical, and unarticulated components must be identified and added up to it.

Substitution ("transfer", "predicate transfer") occurs when the token sentence has been used in a figurative way: to wit, when it contains a metaphor, a metonymy, a hyperbole, an understatement, a over-general or over-precise expression, or when it has been used out of irony. Pragmatic interpretation substitutes the linguistic meaning, which sounds inappropriate to the context, with the figurative meaning the speaker intended explicitly to convey.[62]

Confirmation occurs, finally, when, having paid attention to the context of utterance, the interpreter establishes that the linguistic meaning (the semantically expressed proposition, the minimal proposition) of the token sentence is tantamount to a full-fledged, truth-apt (or abiding-apt) proposition, and represents "what is (pragmatically and semantically) said" by its utterance. Confirmation, it must be

---

[59] Domaneschi (2014), pp. 134–135. For an articulated reply to this "context-shifting argument" on behalf of semantic minimalism, see Cappelen and Lepore (2005), pp. 155–175.

[60] Recanati (2008), p. 260.

[61] Bianchi (2005), pp. 121–123; Cappelen and Lepore (2005), pp. 4–5; Recanati (2010), ch. 1; Wilson and Sperber (2012b, c).

[62] Some contextualist claim, however, that when figurative uses of token sentences are afoot, pragmatic interpretation does not proceed, say, to the metaphorical meaning by passing first through the literal meaning, and replacing it, but directly jumps to the metaphorical meaning, on the wings of participants' shared intuitions. See Domaneschi (2014), pp. 136–137.

noticed, is not part of standard accounts of pragmatic interpretation. The item is, nonetheless, worthwhile adding to the list, since it seems presupposed by philosophers of language and linguists when they deal with pragmatic interpretation.[63]

The context on which the identification of full-fledged propositions depends is the full pragmatic context of utterance. Besides the data about the spatio-temporal frame of the utterance, it encompasses such things as the linguistic co-text (previous, related sentences and the interpretation thereof), on the one side, and the extra-linguistic context, where dwell the beliefs, intentions, attitudes, shared encyclopaedia, background assumptions and forms of life of the speakers, hearers and interpreters involved, on the other side.[64]

Literalists—contextualists claim—pretend to draw a line between semantic context and pragmatic context.[65] The line, however, is illusory. For instance, if Geneva says to Lancelot: "Open that window", and the room where Geneva and Lancelot stay contains two closed windows (one two-lancet window and one three-lancet window), it is not possible to establish *which* window is to be opened, unless by making reference to Geneva's intention. Indeed, Geneva may well wish to refer to a window that is in another room, or may even use the sentence in a metaphorical way. How can we tell that, without resorting to the (full) pragmatic context of utterance?

The distinction between pre-semantic, semantic, and post-semantic uses of context (see Sect. 4.3.1, point 5, above)—contextualists claim—is likewise preposterous. There is only one use of the same context: the use of the pragmatic context in order to carry out a pragmatic interpretation of the token sentence and get to the full-fledged, truth-apt (or satisfaction-apt) proposition.

It cannot be ruled out, as we have just seen, that the full-fledged, truth-apt (or satisfaction-apt) proposition may coincide with the linguistic meaning of the token sentence. In such a case too, which I have considered under the heading of *confirmation*, the proposition is not just the output of a purely semantic interpretation of the token sentence, one where only the linguistic competence of the interpreter is required. Rather, it is, again, a pragmatic, context-dependent, entity. Indeed, it is only *after* the context has been taken into account, *after* pragmatic interpretation has been performed, that the coincidence between proposition (in pragmatic sense, speaker's intended explicit meaning) and linguistic meaning (semantically expressed proposition) can be established. Thus, in any case, the full-fledged proposition is, in the sense made clear now, pragmatic and context-dependent "through and through".[66]

3. Three Varieties of Meaning A different typology must replace the tripartite typology of meanings endorsed by ("traditional") literalism (Sect. 4.3.1, point 3,

[63] Wilson and Sperber, for instance, claim: "the literal meaning of a sentence never coincides with what the speaker explicitly communicates by uttering this sentence (except in the case of genuine "eternal sentences", if such things exist or are ever used)" (Wilson and Sperber 2012c, p. 79).

[64] See Bianchi (2002), pp. 259–261, 263; Bianchi (2001), p. 279 ff.

[65] See, however, Cappelen and Lepore (2005), p. 150.

[66] Recanati (2004, 2010) and Wilson and Sperber (2012b).

above): one that is more in tune with the reality of communication through natural languages.[67] It encompasses the following three kinds, and levels, of meaning to any act of communication: the linguistic meaning of the type-sentence ("conventional meaning", "sentence meaning", "minimal proposition"), the speaker's-intended explicit meaning of the token-sentence ("proposition" in a pragmatic sense, pragmatic explicit meaning), and the speaker's-intended implicit meaning (pragmatic implicit meaning).

Linguistic meaning is identified by means of syntactic and semantic rules of the relevant natural language. It is the output of a *decoding* activity (semantic interpretation), and is, accordingly, thoroughly conventional. It is tantamount to *what is proffered*.

Pragmatic explicit meaning is identified by pragmatic interpretation (by way of disambiguation, saturation, precisification, enrichment, substitution, etc.) from linguistic meaning and context.[68] It is the output of *inferential* processes and corresponds to a truth-apt (or abiding-apt) "maximal" proposition—as opposed to the "minimal" proposition that, according to traditional semantic theory (and current semantic minimalism), would be the purely semantic, truth-apt (or abiding-apt), meaning of a sentence. It is tantamount to speaker's-intended explicit meaning or *what is said*.

Pragmatic implicit meaning, finally, is the set of implicit propositions (implicatures) that are identified by means of a pragmatic interpretation performed on the basis of hermeneutical tools like, e.g., Grice's cooperation principle and conversational maxims, or Relevance Theory principles and heuristic of relevance.[69] It is tantamount to speaker's-intended implicit meaning or *what is implied*.

4. The Generally Not-Self-Sufficient Contribution of Semantics to the Overall Meaning of an Act of Communication The previous claims (points 1. and 2. above) suggest a solution to the semantics/pragmatics puzzle that is different from the one sponsored by traditional semantic theory. Generally, semantics contributes to the overall meaning of any act of communication by way of an inchoate linguistic, conventional meaning. This needs to be supplemented by pragmatic interpretation, in order to get both to a full explicit meaning (the maximal proposition), and to the implicit meaning of the communication act. The "what is said" already situates in the province of pragmatic interpretation.

---

[67] As I have noticed (Sect. 4.3.1. above), however, semantic minimalism sets forth a typology of the meanings of an act of communication that is more on the contextualist side.

[68] Remember, however, the remark I made in footnote 61 about figurative speech.

[69] See, e.g., Wilson and Sperber (2012b), pp. 3–4, 6–7. On Gricean principle and maxims see Chap. 3, Sect. 3.5.1 above.

4.4 What a Jurist Can Learn

It is time to take stock of the preceding journey through the (impervious) regions of literalism and contextualism. A question seems in order: Is there any useful instruction that a jurist interested in legal interpretation and legal meaning could derive out of the dispute opposing literalists and contextualists?

I think the question commands a positive answer. Literalism and contextualism bring to the fore a few ideas that, though concerning ordinary sentences in a natural language and their interpretation, our jurist would surely consider as endowed with a clarifying impact on the matters of legal interpretation and legal meaning. The ideas I have in mind concern: (a) the plurality of meanings, (b) the problematic nature of the notion of explicit meaning, (c) the pervasive character of pragmatic, context-based, interpretation, and, related to the latter, (d) the priority of context over system.

Meaning Pluralism Every act of linguistic communication is apt to convey, and usually conveys, a plurality of meanings. As a consequence, in order to be able to understand how the interpretation of ordinary sentences in a natural language works, it is necessary to multiply the notions of meaning associated to any such act. To this purpose, a few distinctions seem worthwhile emphasizing.

A first distinction runs between *explicit meaning* and *implicit meaning*. Explicit meaning is any meaning that can be read in a token sentence in the light of the system of language and the context of utterance, by means of semantic and pragmatic interpretation. Implicit meaning is, contrariwise, any meaning that cannot be read in a token sentence, but is identified by way of inferences, using as starting point some previously identified explicit meaning of the sentence, with the aid of some explicitation tools (assumptions, premises, principles, etc.).

A second distinction brings to the fore the *variety of explicit meanings*. In fact, not fewer than six kinds can be singled out, from the standpoint of the way they are identified. These are compositional meaning, disambiguated meaning, precisified meaning, saturated meaning, enriched meaning, and substituted meaning. *Compositional meaning* is computed conventional meaning; it is the output of context-independent semantic interpretation. It may amount to the "what is said" meaning of the sentence, if confirmed by pragmatic interpretation. The other kinds of explicit meaning are the outputs of pragmatic interpretation. *Disambiguated meaning* is the output of context-dependent disambiguation of compositionally ambiguous token sentences. *Precisified meaning* is the output of context-dependent precisification of vague expressions contained in token sentences. *Saturated meaning* is the output of context-dependent saturation of context-sensitive expressions contained in token sentences. *Enriched meaning* is the output of context-dependent completion of elliptical token sentences. *Substituted meaning* is the output of context-dependent replacement of the linguistic meaning of a token sentence with the figurative meaning it supposedly conveys in the situation of utterance.

The Problematic Nature of the Notion of Explicit Meaning The second idea concerns the problematic nature of the notion of explicit meaning.

As you may recall, some literalists conceive the compositional or saturated meaning of a token sentence as its sole, properly explicit meaning: the one amounting to "what is said". Other literalists (the semantic minimalists), however, hold a broader notion of explicit meaning to be theoretically proper: one that also encompasses the speaker's explicit meaning, and severe the connection between semantic meaning (the semantically expressed proposition) and "what is said". Contextualists endorse a pragmatic notion of (the full) explicit meaning, corresponding to the speaker's-intended explicit meaning or "what is said".

Now, from an external point of view interested in a dispassionate understanding of the "mechanics" of ordinary sentences interpretation, extreme positions look unduly reductionist and idle. The dispute suggests, apparently, that the more reasonable stance consists in adopting a tolerant notion of explicit meaning, according to which is *explicit* any meaning that can be read into the token sentence: either by way of semantic interpretation, or by way of a pragmatic interpretation along the six forms previously mentioned (Sect. 4.2.2, point 2, above).

The Pervasive Character of Pragmatic Interpretation and the Priority of Context Over System The third idea concerns the pervasive character of pragmatic, context-based, interpretation. As we have seen, semantic minimalists endorse it, so far as the identification of explicit speaker-intended meanings is concerned.[70] Contextualists, however, combine it with a further idea, the fourth one I mentioned above. This is, in very rough terms, the priority of context over system, or, in a perhaps more obscure mood, the context self-dependence thesis. The relevance of context in the determination of the meaning of token-expressions and token-sentences, and, furthermore, the very value to be ascribed to linguistic rules ("semantic structures") in such determinations, do not depend on semantic conventions (the system of language), as the traditional semantic theory seems to claim. They depend, on the contrary, on components (normative attitudes, scientific beliefs, etc.) of the very context in which token-expressions and token-sentences are used. It is these components that establish which value the system of language, or certain contextual factors like the speaker's or hearer's intent, should have. So it is the "context", in the way I have just made clear, that rules over its own relevance, and the relevance of the system of language.

I said that the ideas above are ripe with explanatory virtue concerning legal interpretation and legal meaning. I think that property to be evident. Nonetheless, a few remarks are worthwhile making by way of conclusion.

1. From the vantage point of the dispute between literalism and contextualism, semantic formalism (Sect. 4.2.1, above) appears to have endorsed the ideas of literalism in its "traditional semantic theory" variety ("traditional literalism"). In

[70] See Sect. 4.3.1, point 3, above.

so doing, it appears to be committed to a theory of meaning and interpretation that is flawed, at least, on two related counts.

In the first place, semantic formalism provides an incomplete and misleading picture of the variety of possible explicit meanings of legal provisions. It only considers computational meaning, disambiguated meaning and precisified meaning. In this way, however, it overlooks that legal provisions can also be read to express enriched and substituted meanings. They express enriched meanings, for instance, whenever an exception or a qualifying clause is added to the text of the provision (or, better, to the corresponding isomorphic abstract norm). They express substituted meanings, for instance, when the clear literal (computational) meaning is corrected (modified) in order to make it correspond to what is considered appropriate.[71]

In the second place, semantic formalism endorses a false view about the nature of legal interpretation. It presents it as being essentially a form of semantic interpretation, which usually leads to the identification of full-fledged, abiding-apt, computational legal meanings, and has priority over pragmatic interpretation, which only intervenes in default situations, to repair ambiguous legal provisions or vague abstract norms (Sect. 4.2.1, above). In such a way, however, it misleadingly obscures the pervasive, not merely supplementary, role that pragmatic, context-based, interpretation ordinarily plays—and must play—in the construction of legal provisions.

To recapitulate: due to these flaws, from a theoretical point of view, semantic formalism appears to provide a false, impoverished and misleading theory of legal meaning and legal interpretation.

2. If we adopt the contextualist thesis of the superiority of context over system, what jurists are used to call the "literal meaning" of legal provisions is to be regarded as a *pragmatic entity*. Accordingly, literal meaning is not the white galleon of objective semantic meaning flying its unscathed hull above the muddled and mutinous waters of context-dependent, pragmatic, meanings. On the one hand, the very appeal to "literal meaning" necessarily depends on a methodological option that is not, and cannot be, dictated by words and sentences selves (Which literal meaning? Is it explicit semantic meaning or, rather, explicit pragmatic meaning?). On the other hand, the identification of "the literal meaning" of legal provisions, whichever notion has been selected, requires pragmatic considerations (Which linguistic conventions? Which background assumptions? Which unarticulated components are to be considered, if any?). Both activities clearly belong to the realm of practice: namely, to the realm of actions that must be justified by appealing to rules and principles, which are not *semantic* rules and principles.
3. By endorsing traditional literalism, semantic formalism pretends to provide a general theoretical solution to the delicate problem concerning the way of

[71] In many cases, correction proceeds by the enrichment of the text of the legal provision /isomorphic abstract norm. There may be cases, however, where correction is performed by subtracting or replacing words in the text of the legal provision/isomorphic abstract norm.

distinguishing, as regards to any positive legal order whatsoever, between "the law as it is" and "the law as it ought to be". It pretends to do so by turning the "law as it is v. law as it ought to be" problem into a problem of philosophy of language and linguistics, and claiming that such a problem admits of just *one* solution. The solution makes "the law as it is" to coincide with the clear and univocal computational meaning of legal provisions. Unfortunately, the multiplicity of explicit meanings, the pervasive character of pragmatic interpretation, and the priority of context over system suggest such a solution to be theoretically spurious. And driven, though perhaps unconsciously, by some undercover normative preoccupation: like, for instance, the preoccupation for establishing the code model of the relation between legislature and judges, or the preoccupation for "having norms at all" (see Sect. 4.2.1, point 9, above).
4. I said at the outset that one persistent issue in contemporary jurisprudence concerns the notion of "interpretive creativity". It is often claimed judicial interpretation to be a "law creating" activity. The notion and forms of "interpretive creativity", however, are far from being clear.

Now, the distinction between semantic and pragmatic interpretation, the distinction between explicit and implicit meaning, and the variety of notions of explicit meaning, seem to bring light on the issue, and provide theoretical support for a realistic theory of interpretive creativity. Let's make a very short experiment.

Suppose a realistic theory comes up that, out of a careful analysis of judicial practice, claims judicial interpretation to be a "creative undertaking" in not least than five different ways, namely: by selection, repair, correction, methodological innovation, or integration.[72]

Suppose, furthermore, that the theory makes clear that:

(a) Judicial interpretation "creates law" *by selection*, when judges choose one meaning out of the several, alternative, determinate, meanings that, for a given legal provision, can be justified on the basis of current interpretive methods and current legal ideologies;
(b) Judicial interpretation "creates law" *by repair*, when judges fix up the objective meaning of a legal provision—usually, its literal, customary, or established case-law meaning—that has proven to be defective (i.e., affected by ambiguity or vagueness);
(c) Judicial interpretation "creates law" *by correction*, when judges consider the objective meaning of a legal provision as substantially un-correct (wrong)—usually, by being either "over"-inclusive, or "under"-inclusive, as to the individual case at hand—and proceed to its modification ("modulation").
(d) Judicial interpretation "creates law" *by methodological innovation*, when judges provide a new meaning for a legal provision at hand, on the basis of some new, so far never employed, interpretive method, that either exploits some

[72] On judicial creation of law, the most illuminating essays are, to my knowledge, Carrió (1965), Bulygin (1966), Wroblewski (1992). The account I provide in the text takes a different stance, though.

new set of interpretive resources, or permits to use old sets of resources differently;

(e) Finally, judicial interpretation "creates law" *by integration*, when judges add to the set of previously identified norms of the system some new implicit norm that is the output of some form of reasoning (analogical, *a contrario*, *a fortiori*, from the nature of things, from principles, from juristic concepts, from juristic theories of legal institutes, etc.) from previously identified norms (usually, from norms which are the meanings of legal provisions).

In which way the distinction between semantic and pragmatic interpretation, the distinction between explicit and implicit meaning, and the variety of notions of explicit meaning can bring light on the notion of judicial interpretive creativity? In which way can they provide theoretical support to the realistic account of judicial interpretive creativity above?

The questions can be given a clear answer. From the a semantics-pragmatics perspective, the five judicial operations the realistic theory considers as instances of interpretive creativity lay all outside of the province of purely computational, context-independent semantic interpretation. Indeed, they all belong to the province of pragmatic interpretation, and have as outputs context-dependent, explicit or implicit meanings.

Chapter 5
Frames v. Containers

> *If "interpretation" is understood as cognitive ascertainment of the meaning of the object that is so interpreted, then the result of a legal interpretation can only be the ascertainment of the frame that the law that is to be interpreted represents, and thereby the cognition of several possibilities within the frame*
>
> —H. Kelsen (1960)

5.1 A Demarcation Problem

It is commonplace distinguishing two main varieties of legal argumentation. These are factual argumentation (argumentation "in fact" or "as to the fact" of the case) and interpretive argumentation.[1]

The former concerns the justification of factual sentences, i.e., sentences about the relevant facts to a lawsuit (like, e.g., "John Smith pushed a twenty-inches knife into Henry Doe's chest, between the third and fourth left rib, on May 5, 2019, at about 9.30 pm, in the reading room of the Union Club"), and is typically deployed for claiming such sentences to be "true", "false", "established beyond any reasonable doubt", "utterly (un)sound", etc.

The latter concerns the justification of interpretive sentences, i.e., sentences concerning the meaning of legal provisions (like, e.g., "Section Y of the Traffic Code expresses the norm N_i", "The term 'T' in section Z of the Civil Code refers to $C_1 \ldots C_n$", etc.),[2] and is typically deployed for claiming such sentences to be legally "correct", "right", "wrong", "true", "false", etc.

As soon as we move from the needs of ordinary law-jobs to the more demanding requirements of legal theory, however, the very notion and scope of interpretive

[1] Interpretive argumentation is, in turn, one variety of argumentation "in law", or "as to the law", along with argumentation concerning the filling up of gaps (integrative argumentation), the resolution of antinomies (normative conflict argumentation), etc. On these topics, see Chap. 2, Sect. 2.2.1.2 above and Chap. 7 below.

[2] On interpretive sentences, see Chap. 2, Sect. 2.2.1.1, above.

P. Chiassoni, *Interpretation without Truth*, Law and Philosophy Library 128,
https://doi.org/10.1007/978-3-030-15590-2_5

argumentation appear saddled with uncertainty: What exactly does a piece of interpretive argumentation amount to? How can we tell genuine interpretive argumentation tokens from spurious ones? When is a purported instance of interpretive argumentation really "interpretive"?

All such questions point to a demarcation problem, involving momentous jurisprudential issues like the proper concept (and theory) of legal interpretation, and the proper theory of legal norms, in so far as it intertwines with the former.

My purpose in this chapter is describing and comparing two theories, both within the province of analytical jurisprudence (they have in fact very easily recognizable "godfathers" in such a line of enquiry), which provide alternative views about legal interpretation, written-law norms and interpretive argumentation. These are the frame of interpretations theory ("frame theory"), on the one hand, and the container-retrieval theory ("retrieval theory") in the conventional linguistic meaning variety ("conventional meaning variety"), on the other.[3]

Supporters of the conventional meaning variety of the retrieval theory claim the frame theory to be indefensible.[4] By a critical survey of both theories, I will bring to the fore a few arguments for considering resistance to the retrieval theory, even in its conventional meaning variety, as a very reasonable stance: indeed, as amounting to what a clear mind should take as a theoretical must.

5.2 The Frame of Interpretations Theory

The frame theory is an interpretivist descriptive theory in the stream of analytical Kelsenian realism.[5] It considers interpretation to be a key, paramount, activity that intervenes at all crucial points in the working of "our" legal systems. It claims, accordingly, that the terminology and conceptual apparatus of a useful legal theory should accommodate to the pivotal role interpretation plays in legal experience. It suggests that theoretical concepts, to be adequate-to-facts, must be either *interpretation-dependent* (that is to say, they must, so far as possible, bear a conceptual connection to interpretation), or *salva interpretatione* (that is to say, they must avowedly rule out such a connection to some valuable theoretical purpose at hand).

[3] The idea of staging a contest between the "frames of interpretations" theory and the "container-retrieval" theory came to me from reading a discussion on Riccardo Guastini's book *Interpretare e argomentare* (Guastini 2011a), edited by Vito Velluzzi (2013b), with essays by Velluzzi (2013a, pp. 73–76), Pino (2013, pp. 77–101), Diciotti (2013, pp. 103–123; for a sequel to the discussion, see also Diciotti 2014, pp. 57–71), and Guastini (2013, pp. 125–136). There, the usual terminology is employed and old characters are around. I thought the experiment of upsetting terminology and disguising old characters useful; furthermore, the "frames of interpretations" theory does not correspond, from a strictly philological perspective, to the theory of any individual author participating in that debate. It is my own rendering and reconstruction of a set of ideas I deem worthwhile considering.

[4] Diciotti (2013), pp. 118–122; Diciotti (2014), pp. 60–70.

[5] On Kelsen's "Wiener Realism", see Chiassoni (2013).

The core of the frame theory, in view of testing it by a comparison with the retrieval view, is captured by the following ideas:

1. the distinction between legal provisions, explicit norms and implicit norms;
2. the distinction between interpretation and interpretation-outputs, on the one hand, and integration ("juristic construction", "juristic law-finding", "juristic law-making") and integration-outputs, on the other hand;
3. the argumentative side of legal interpretation and integration;
4. the conception of interpretive and integrative argumentation as institutional games;
5. the distinction between practical and cognitive interpretation;
6. the twin claims of universal methodological ambiguity and potential ideological ambiguity;
7. the idea that the general norms of written-law are frames of interpretation-outputs, and the related minimalist conception of "written law".

1. Legal Provision, Explicit Norm, Implicit Norm Naïf normativism provides theories of law describing positive legal orders as *normative orders*: namely, as discrete sets of interrelated *norms*. From its standpoint, the elementary, atomic component making up any positive law whatsoever is "the norm".

As soon as we shift to the interpretive perspective advocated by the frame theory, however, the elementary, atomic notion of the norm proves misleading, and is to be replaced by three related notions: *legal provision*, *explicit norm*, and *implicit norm*.

Legal provisions (authoritative legal sentences, authoritative norm-formulations, legal clauses) are sentences enacted by law-making authorities; they make up the elementary components of such documents as written constitutions, charters, international treaties and covenants, civil and criminal codes, statutes, executive regulations, etc.

Explicit norms are normative sentences (in the broadest sense of the phrase) that represent the explicit meaning of a legal provision (what the legal provision says).

Implicit norms are normative sentences that, by definition, are not the meaning of any legal provision, but can nonetheless be considered as components of a legal order by means of some method of integration available to legal operators (to this point I will come back in a moment).[6]

[6] On these notions, see also Chap. 2, Sect. 2.2, above. What about customary law and case law? Clearly, the apparatus I am rehearsing in the text does not apply to these forms of "unwritten law". Nonetheless, it can be used to build up conceptual structures endowed with like clarification virtue. Concerning customary law, it suggests distinguishing between custom-practice and custom-rule. Custom-practice is the set of iterated behaviours that make up the behaviouristic "text" out of which some custom-rule can be extracted, by way of an activity of custom-practice interpretation. The custom-rule is, accordingly, a rule that is the output of interpreting a custom-practice. Clearly, the whole activity is thoroughly "theory-laden". It requires the choice and mastery of some conception of customary law, providing criteria for distinguishing custom-practices from like social phenomena, and living custom-rules from dead or still-to-be-born ones. Furthermore, it requires identifying a social practice as a custom-practice, and then interpreting it. Concerning case law, it suggests, likewise, distinguishing between precedent-opinion and precedent-rule (precedent-hold-

2. Interpretation v. Integration The notions of legal provision, explicit norm and implicit norm are interpretation-dependent. They all bear a conceptual connection to interpretation. Legal provisions are authoritatively enacted sentences that represent the matter of interpretation: what is interpreted, texts waiting for interpretation. Explicit norms are the meanings of legal provisions: they are the dependent variables of interpretation, or interpretation-outputs. Implicit norms, finally, are normative sentences that cannot be identified by means of interpretation, but only by resorting to some integration technique.

The activity of interpretation—the matter of which are legal provisions and the outputs of which are explicit norms—as it is usually performed by judges, other legal officials, jurists and lawyers at large is interpretation-translation to a practical purpose. It is performed in order to replace a legal provision with one or more sentences representing its "correct" ("proper", "true", "right") legal meaning, in view either of deciding a lawsuit (judicial interpretation), or of affecting such a decision (forensic interpretation), or else of providing the "right" solution to an abstract *quaestio iuris* (juristic interpretation). It is, in any case, a will-geared, decision-making activity: it decides for a meaning as "the correct" meaning of a legal provision, at the same time tacitly or expressly ruling out alternative possible meanings as "incorrect".[7]

By contrast whenever, for instance, a judge identifies an implicit norm in view of deciding a lawsuit, by definition such an activity of hers is not interpretation: it is rather a piece of *law integration*. Indeed, she determines the "proper" ("correct", "true") implicit norm to be applied to a case at hand, presupposing explicit norms have run out.[8]

3. Interpretation and Integration Have an Argumentative Side Interpretation and integration, in their external, public, dimensions, are both—actually or at least potentially—*activities with an argumentative side*. Interpretation, according to the definition I have just offered, does not consist just in translating a legal provision into any explicit norm *whatsoever*.[9] It consists, rather, in providing "the correct" ("proper", "true", "right") translation of a legal provision: it consists, more precisely, in translating a legal provision into an explicit norm and presenting (or being willing and able to present) such a norm as "the correct" legal meaning of the provision to some practical purpose, on the ground of a (purportedly) adequate set of contextually formulated arguments. The arguments that may be used to justify such operations are *interpretive* arguments (like, e.g., the literal, legislative intent, and

ing). The former is the text out of which the latter is identified by means of interpretation. On interpretation of judicial precedent, see Chap. 9, Sect. 9.4, below.

[7] I have dealt with this notion of interpretation before, under the name of "textual interpretation". See Chap. 2, Sect. 2.2.1.1 above.

[8] See Chap. 2, Sect. 2.2.1.2 above.

[9] Of course, the outcome of practical interpretation proper can also be translating a legal provision into two or more explicit norms. In the text, I will always refer to a singular norm for simplicity's sake.

teleological arguments). The argumentative apparatus can be dispensed with any time the explicit norm at hand is such a matter of course in the legal culture that no argument is needed. This does not mean, however, that arguments could not be provided, if necessary: for instance, in order to show to an apprentice lawyer which arguments judges could deploy in favour of a usually never-argued-for explicit norm they commonly apply in their decisions. Similar remarks apply to law integration, the results of which are (liable to be) supported by some set of *integration* arguments (like, e.g., some integration use of analogical, *a contrario*, *a fortiori*, or general principle reasoning).

4. Interpretation and Integration are Argumentative Games The activities of interpretation and integration, as they are actually performed by judges, lawyers and jurists, are tantamount to the playing of law-specific *argumentative games*, where licensed agents (judges, attorney at law, legal scholars) argue for interpretive or integrative outputs by employing a discrete set of tools ("arguments") they have previously selected out of a toolbox that is usually provided by the methodological tradition, and is assumed to be expressly or tacitly "approved" by the law.

Interpretive arguments are built upon interpretive rules. For instance, any literal argument concerning any piece of legislation has its justifying starting point in a translation rule, like "Statutory provisions should be interpreted according to their literal meaning".[10]

The discrete set of interpretive rules that a licensed player selects and employs to argue that a norm is "the correct" legal meaning of a legal provision is an interpretive code. An interpretive code, as a tool for justifying interpretive outcomes, is typically made of three sorts of interpretive rules: translation rules, procedure rules, and preference rules.[11]

Translation rules contribute to justifying an interpretive output as (all-things-considered) "legally correct", by pointing to the (all-things-considered) "legally correct" resources (empirical data, actual or imaginary pieces of information, actual or conjectural ingredients of the legal order and legal experience) by means of which a legal provision should be translated into some explicit norm.[12]

---

[10]The logical structure of an interpretive argument can be reconstructed, for instance, as follows: 1. Statutory provisions should be translated into the norm(s) corresponding to their literal meaning. 2. *a* is a statutory provision. 3. *b* is the norm corresponding to the literal meaning of *a*. 4. *a* should be translated into the norm *b*. The adoption of premise 1 can also be considered as what justifies a different logical structure, like, e.g., the following.: 1'. The legally correct meaning of statutory provisions corresponds to their literal meaning. 2. *a* is a statutory provision. 3'. *b* is the literal meaning of *a*. 4'. *b* is the legally correct meaning of *a*. On translation rules, see Chap. 2, Sect. 2.2.1.1 and Chap. 3, Sect. 3.4 above.

[11]Interpretive codes may also be used as heuristic devices: as tools for *getting to* the correct meaning of legal provisions. This is how they are presented in Chap. 2, Sect. 2.2.1.1 and Chap. 3, Sect. 3.4 above.

[12]As you may remember (Chap. 2, Sect. 2.2.1.1, Chap. 3, Sects. 3.4 and 3.6 above), we may single out six different types of translation rules: (a) rules of linguistic interpretation (e.g., "Statutory provisions should be interpreted according to the ordinary linguistic meaning of their expressions at the time of their enactment"); (b) rules of intentional or genetic interpretation (e.g., "Statutory

Procedure rules contribute to justifying an interpretive output as (all-things-considered) "legally correct", by pointing to the (all-things-considered) "legally correct" order in the use of the translation rules that ought to be used.[13]

Finally, preference rules contribute to justifying an interpretive output as (all-things-considered) "legally correct", by pointing to the (all-things-considered) "legally correct" hierarchy between the outputs of the several translation rules that ought to be used.[14]

The methodological tradition usually provides lawyers with a disordered set of indeterminate interpretive rules.[15] Thus, when lawyers use interpretive codes to justify some interpretive outcome (i.e., some explicit norm), such codes are usually made of rules they themselves have somehow shaped, sharpened, precisified as to the interpretive resources to be used, and put in the "proper" order. Fatally, such a shaping, sharpening, resource selecting and ordering is likely to mirror, and be affected by, each lawyer's own methodological attitude, ideological stance and material interests. In the light of this, the basic rule of the interpretive argumentation game, as played by judges, jurists and lawyers here and now, can be formulated, roughly, as follows: "Employ the interpretive code that enables you to deploy the best set of arguments in view of presenting the interpretive output you stand for as the only correct one for the case at hand". This suggests, in turn, the following conclusion: the selection and use of an interpretive code by a lawyer interpreting a legal

---

provisions should be interpreted according to the original semantic intention of the historical legislator"; "Statutory provisions should be interpreted according to the counter-factual semantic intention of the historical legislator", etc.); (c) rules of teleological interpretation (e.g., "Statutory provisions should be given the meaning pointed out for them by the objective purpose they serve"); (d) rules of authoritative interpretation (e.g., "Statutory provisions should be given the meaning established for them by the Supreme Court in its opinions"); (e) rules of systemic interpretation (e.g., "Statutory provisions should be given the meaning pointed out for them by the relevant constitutional principles"); (f) rules of "heteronomous", substantive, normative-ethics, interpretation (e.g., "Statutory provisions should be given the meaning pointed out for them by the critical morality they refer to").

[13] For instance: "N1 is the (all-things-considered) legally correct meaning of legal provision LP1, since it corresponds to the literal meaning of LP1, amounts to a clear prescription as to the individual case at hand, and there is no room for legislative intent, or any other form of interpretation, when the literal meaning is clear". As we have seen, which translation rules should be used depends on the selection rule the interpreter stands for. See Chap. 3, Sect. 3.4, above.

[14] Preference rules typically include rules of systemic interpretation, like, e.g., the consistency and completeness rules: "Statutory provisions should not be given any meaning logically incompatible with constitutional principles", "Statutory provisions should not be given any meaning incompatible, from a teleological perspective, with the fundamental principles of the legal system", "Statutory provisions should be given the meaning, among the several ones identified by means of translation rules $TR_1 \ldots TR_n$, that is most instrumentally in tune with the requirements of fundamental principles", "Statutory provisions should not be given any meaning showing the law to be incomplete as to the case at hand", etc. On preference rules see Chap. 3, Sect. 3.4, above.

[15] The situation does not change when legal provisions concerning the "proper ways" of interpretation and integration are enacted. First, such provisions are not self-interpreting: they need to be interpreted by judges, jurists and lawyers. Second, on a literal reading, they usually provide a set of fatally indeterminate and dubiously ordered interpretation and integration rules.

provision, i.e., playing at the interpretive argumentation game, is a discretionary, value-laden, activity. This is one of the reasons—perhaps, the main reason—why, as I said before, interpretation is, according to the frame theory, a will-geared, decision-making activity. The same remarks apply to the game of law integration.[16]

5. Practical v. Cognitive Interpretation So far, interpretation has been defined as any activity that consists in translating legal provisions into explicit norms presented as the correct legal meaning thereof on the ground of some interpretive code. This notion points, accordingly, to the practical variety of interpretation-as-translation. However three further varieties of interpretation-as-translation, not to a practical but to a cognitive or theoretical purpose (cognitive interpretation proper, theoretically oriented interpretation), are also to be taken into account. These are the varieties of methodological conjectural interpretation, ideological conjectural interpretation and creative interpretation.[17]

Methodological conjectural interpretation consists in laying bare, as to a given moment *t*', the meanings that can be ascribed to a legal provision (say, LP_i), on the ground of the interpretive rules the legal culture considers as "required" or "approved" "by the law".[18] In so doing, the interpreter must avoid qualifying any of such meanings as "the only correct" ("true", "right", "just") legal meaning of the legal provision at hand. Rather, she should limit herself to working out a dispassionate inventory of conjecturable meanings. This can be a minimal or a maximal inventory: in the latter case, she will claim it to account for (almost) *all* the methodologically viable meanings of legal provision LP_i, exhausting the hermeneutical potentialities of LP_i, reaching, so to speak, the ultimate frontier of its possible meanings. As we have seen, the output of this sort of interpretation is a methodological conjectural sentence, where the several alternative meanings of the legal provision are listed.[19] The set of alternative meanings so identified for legal provision LP_i—or, in other words, the set of alternative explicit norms (EN_1 … EN_i) into which LP_i can be translated—makes up the *methodological frame* of possible interpretations of LP_i. Each of those meanings is a methodologically correct meaning: that is to say, it is correct, by hypothesis, from a purely methodological point of view.

When ideological conjectural interpretation is performed, the interpreter, as we have seen, aims at identifying, not the methodological frame of a given legal provision (say, LP_i), but its *ideological frame*. Such a frame depends, more precisely, on

---

[16] The "maxims" that rule over interpreters dealing with interpretive rules will be considered further in the next chapter (see Chap. 6 below).

[17] The original source of these remarks is obviously the Kelsenian notion of "scientific interpretation" (Kelsen 1960, ch. VIII). On cognitive interpretation proper, see above, Chap. 2, Sect. 2.2.2.

[18] There may be methodological disputes in a legal culture as to the methods to be considered as "approved" by the law. In such cases, conjectural interpreters must record and take into account them in their inquiries.

[19] (MCS) "Legal provision LP_i expresses either the norm *N1*, if it is being interpreted according to the (paramount) translation rule *TR1* and the set of interpretive resources *IR1*, or, rather, the norm *N2*, if it is being interpreted according to the (paramount) translation rule *TR2* and the set of interpretive resources *IR2*, or, rather, the norm …". See Chap. 2, Sect. 2.2.2.1, above.

the ethical views (normative theories of law, philosophies of justice, legal ideologies, constitutional theories, and similar value-laden, committed, outlooks) that, upon a sociological enquiry, are extant in the legal culture and society of the time.[20] These views may make a methodologically viable interpretive outcome unviable, for reasons having to do with the prevailing negative substantive social value of such an outcome.[21] Accordingly, the scope of the ideological frame of meanings corresponding to a legal provision can be narrower than the scope of its methodological frame.

Finally, creative interpretation consists, as we have seen,[22] in the identification of one or more meanings for a given legal provision (say LP_i) that, by hypothesis, are outside of its current methodological frame. Creative interpretation is a conjecture about *new* meanings for existing legal provisions, which can be grounded on some new interpretive rule that, by hypothesis, is not so far part of the available stock. In this case too, the interpreter does not claim the new meanings she conjectures to be the only correct ones. She just wishes to point out some way of moving forward the frontier of the hermeneutic possibilities of a legal provision.

The difference between cognitive conjectural interpretation and practical interpretation can be gathered from the logical forms of their discourses. The logical form of a discourse belonging to practical interpretation runs roughly as follows:

> To the purpose of providing a legally right answer to *quaestio iuris* QJ_i, the (all-things-considered) legally correct meaning of legal provision LP_i is explicit norm EN_i, EN_i being justified by interpretive arguments $IA_1 \ldots IA_n$, which are grounded in turn on the (all-things-considered) legally correct interpretive code IC_i and the correctly selected set of interpretive resources IR_i.

By contrast, the logical form of a discourse of conjectural interpretation, in its methodological variety, runs roughly as follows:

> By way of methodological conjecture, legal provision LP_i can be interpreted, here and now, as capable of being translated (at least) into the following explicit norms: EN_1 [f(IC_1, IR_1)], *or* EN_2 [f(IC_2, IR_2)], *or* EN_4 [f(IC_4, IR_4)], … *or* EN_m [f(IC_m, IR_m)].[23]

6. Universal Methodological Ambiguity v. Potential Ideological Ambiguity The distinction between methodological and ideological conjectural interpretation, and the related distinction between the methodological and the ideological conjectural frames of the meanings of any given legal provision, suggest two theses that are paramount to the frame theory: the universal methodological ambiguity thesis and the potential ideological ambiguity thesis.

The first thesis claims that the ambiguity of legal provisions is universal from a purely methodological standpoint. This means, in other words, that, from the stand-

---

[20] See Chap. 2, Sect. 2.2.2.1, above.

[21] For instance, a methodologically viable interpretation of a marriage provision to the effect of covering same-sex unions may be unviable—i.e., likely to be considered "wrong" and rejected—from the standpoint of prevailing social ideologies.

[22] See Chap. 2, Sect. 2.2.2.3, above.

[23] See also Chap. 2, Sect. 2.2.2.1, above.

point of the tools available in our methodological tradition, *every* legal provision is fraught with ambiguity: every legal provision is capable of different, alternative, readings, between the extremes of the broadest and the narrowest interpretations, passing through shades of ordinary meaning and degrees of defeasibility.

The second thesis claims that the ambiguity of legal provisions is, contrariwise, only potential, a contingent property, from an ideological standpoint: not all the methodologically viable readings of a legal provision are at the same time viable (acceptable, right, proper, correct) from the standpoint of the ethical outlooks extant in a society or a legal culture at a certain time. This explains why there are "easy" interpretive cases: why lawyers (jurists, judges, attorneys, etc.), at a certain moment, consider certain interpretations of certain legal provisions as "settled" or "a matter of course".[24]

7. What the Legislatures Produce We are used to think that legislatures "produce" norms. From the perspective of the frame theory, however, such a commonplace view can be accepted only upon condition of articulating a few refinements. Surely, what legislatures do produce are statutory and constitutional *texts*: they produce sets of legal provisions that are the matter of statutory and constitutional interpretation. Do legislatures also produce statutory and constitutional *norms*?

According to the frame theory, such a question is not for a simple answer. Statutory and constitutional interpretation, as you may recall, are argumentative games. Which norm(s), if any, a statutory or constitutional provision does express depends on how the interpretive argumentation game is being played in a legal order. And this depends, in turn, on contingent normative and methodological attitudes in the legal profession and the society at large. Thus, from the perspective of the frame theory, the only proper answer to that question runs as follows: legislatures surely produce authoritative texts (documents made of legal provisions); legal provisions, on the ground of the interpretive rules "approved" in a legal culture, are usually capable of expressing frames of interpretations, sets of alternative explicit norms for each legal provision. Accordingly, if we stay with the idea of legislatures that "produce norms", we need to make clear that the norms they produce are frame-norms: a text plus the set of its methodologically and/or ethically viable interpretations, as performed by licensed interpreters. These remarks hold, of course, for any other variety of so-called written law. Supporters of the frame theory maintain a minimalist, counter-intuitive, but descriptively sound, view of written law.

[24] Methodological ambiguity, it must be emphasized, is not tantamount to linguistic, semantic or syntactic, ambiguity. Not every legal provision, being methodologically ambiguous, is at the same time linguistically ambiguous. On "easy cases" see also Chap. 6, Sect. 6.5 below.

5.3 The Container-Retrieval Theory

I said at the outset that, though that may sound paradoxical, the very notion of interpretive argumentation is saddled with uncertainty. This is so because of a demarcation problem: legal theorists do not agree upon the "right" way to draw the conceptual line between legal interpretation "proper" ("properly so-called", "properly and exactly conceived", etc.), on the one hand, and what lays beyond and outside of legal interpretation "proper", being instead tantamount to "law integration", "law making proper", "juristic construction", "juristic law-making", etc., on the other hand.

We have just seen how the frame theory proposes to draw such a line.[25] That is not the only way to do so, however. Another way consists in adopting what can be regarded as a container-view of legal provisions (like, e.g., constitutional and statutory provisions). This view goes along with, and is matched by, a retrieval-view of interpretation proper. The key tenets of the retrieval theory, as we may call it for brevity sake, may be recounted as follows.

1. Each legal provision contains a set of legal norms.
2. Legal interpretation in a proper sense is, accordingly, the activity that consists in retrieving the set of legal norms contained in a legal provision, which usually amounts to a single norm.
3. The legal norms of the set contained in a legal provision are explicit legal norms: they are the norms actually expressed by that text.
4. A legal norm that is not contained in any legal provision cannot, by definition, be identified by means of interpretation proper. Its identification must instead be the output of an activity of a different kind: namely, of some piece of law integration, juristic law making, juristic construction, etc.
5. Any such legal norm is an implicit or unexpressed norm: it is a norm that is not expressed by any legal provision, but can be identified and supported only by means of some form of reasoning from previously identified norms.[26]

The retrieval theory of interpretation enjoys the favour of commonsense. Furthermore, it seems to provide a simple and working solution to the demarcation problem we are considering.

Unfortunately, the appearance of simplicity and working virtue is tricky. Legal provisions are not containers, after all: they are linguistic entities, grammatically patterned strings of written words. It must be observed, as a consequence, that the retrieval theory provides a metaphorical account of legal texts and their interpretation: one that evokes the idea of sentences as "vessels" where meaning, according to the situation, can be poured in or poured out. Metaphors are potentially misleading

[25] See Sect. 5.2 above.

[26] A container-retrieval view like the one I consider in the text is apparently endorsed, e.g., by Diciotti (2013), pp. 103–124, at pp. 105 ff. Here and in other parts of my paper I will use Diciotti's views, as I see them, as endowed with exemplary value to the purpose of my argument.

contrivances. Is there any viable way of showing the container-retrieval metaphor to be good to theoretical purpose? It is here, apparently, that comes into play the conventional linguistic meaning variety (conventional meaning variety) I mentioned at the outset (see Sect. 5.1 above).

The conventional meaning variety makes two basic claims in support of the container-retrieval metaphor.[27]

First, legal provisions are indeed like containers: they are sentences in a natural language; hence, they contain the conventional linguistic meanings pointed out by the grammatical and semantic rules of that language.

Second, the conventional linguistic meaning of legal provisions is the only meaning properly contained in legal texts: it is the exclusive sort of meaning being *in the legal texts themselves*, going along with them, being carried, expressed or conveyed by them, comes what it may.

It is worthwhile considering a few of the other key ideas of the conventional meaning variety. This will make possible appreciating how much that theory differs from the frame theory.

A. If, as it is worthwhile doing, we consider legal interpretation proper as consisting mainly (this qualification will be made clear in a moment) in the retrieval of the meanings contained in legal provisions, provided there is only one kind of meaning properly contained by legal provisions (that is, conventional linguistic meaning), legal interpretation proper is basically the retrieval of the conventional linguistic meaning of legal provisions.
B. Conventional linguistic meaning of legal provisions represents the objective meaning of legal provisions: it is *in there*. Accordingly, legal interpretation proper is basically a cognitive activity: it basically consists in coming to know the objective meaning contained in legal provisions, by means of the grammatical and semantic rules of the relevant natural language.
C. Provided explicit norms are the meanings of legal provisions, and provided legal provisions properly contain only one kind of meaning, namely, their objective linguistic meaning, explicit norms, properly considered, are tantamount to the objective, linguistic meanings of legal provisions.
D. Provided explicit norms are objective meanings contained in legal provisions, and provided they go along with legal provisions, comes what it may, the commonsense view according to which "legislatures produce norms" is by no means the result of a collective hallucination or (self-) deception. Legislatures *do in*

[27] The archetype of the container-retrieval view in contemporary jurisprudence is usually located in ch. VII of Hart (1961). For a similar view of more recent cast see Soames (2007). In his *Problems of the Philosophy of Law* (Hart 1967, pp. 105–108) and the *Introduction* (Hart 1983a, pp. 7–8) to his *Essays in Jurisprudence and Philosophy* (Hart 1983b), Hart avows his former view was an "oversimplification", and makes clear that the determinate meaning of legal rules may depend not only on linguistic conventions, but also on the "special conventions on the legal use of words" and on interpretive techniques (like, e.g., resort to "the obvious or agreed purpose of a rule"). Apparently, in his rejection of a purely "retrieval conception" of legal interpretation, J. Raz goes along the same line as the "second" Hart. See Raz (2009), part III.

fact produce norms: they produce, more precisely, the explicit norms contained in the legal provisions they enact.

E. Explicit norms, being the linguistic meaning of sentences in a natural language, may be defective. To begin with, they may prove indeterminate (ambiguous, vague, open textured). Furthermore, they may be determinate, but practically inadequate (because of the phenomena of over-inclusion and under-inclusion, or even due to flat incompatibility with superior norms).

F. Whenever an explicit norm is defective because of linguistic indeterminacy, its simple "fixing up" is still to be regarded as legal interpretation proper.[28] In such a case, notice, interpretation is not anymore just a matter of cognition; it is, rather, a matter of decision (stipulation). In order for it to stay still within the boundaries of interpretation proper, however, such an interpretive decision must consist: *either* in opting for one of the explicit norms simultaneously expressed by an ambiguous legal provision; *or* in making a vague explicit norm (more) precise, by including or excluding from its scope some class of objects dwelling in the penumbra of its reference.[29] This qualification explains why legal interpretation proper is to be conceived *mainly* as a retrieval, cognitive, job (see point A above), and why, when it is decision, it *still* amounts to interpretation proper, and not to integration.[30]

G. Whatever activity differs, either from the simple retrieval of the objective, linguistic meaning of legal provisions, or from its fixing up, along the lines previously considered (see point F above), is not, by definition, legal interpretation proper. It is rather law integration ("juristic construction"), even though it may present itself as an activity purporting to translate a legal provision into an explicit norm (into "the true", "the correct" explicit norm expressed by the provision). For instance, any activity by means of which an interpreter *corrects* (amends) some explicit norm deemed to be either under-inclusive, or over-inclusive, is not interpretation proper; it is, rather, law integration; its outcomes are not explicit norms proper, but implicit norms "read into" the legal provision.

H. The scope of interpretive argumentation proper is to be conceived in narrow terms. Actually, it basically amounts to the deployment of linguistic arguments, plus, eventually, the arguments needed to justify the disambiguation or precisification of indeterminate literal meanings. As a consequence, the bulk of what

[28] Diciotti calls it "interpretation *strictu sensu*" (in a narrow sense): Diciotti (2014), p. 62.

[29] Vagueness collapses into ambiguity, since it consists in the possibility of two alternative meanings for the same vague text: a wider meaning, including the penumbral case in the area of the "positive reference" of the vague predicate, and a narrower meaning, including the penumbral case in the area of the "negative reference" of the vague predicate. On the collapse of vagueness into a form of ambiguity insists Diciotti (2014), pp. 64–65, who talks of "potential ambiguity".

[30] The argument runs as follows. Whenever an agent (say, a judge) disambiguates or precisifies the literal meaning of an ambiguous or vague legal provision, the output is still made of literal meaning: the alternatives among which the agent makes a choice "can be considered norms that are expressed" by the legal provision at stake, since they are the output of a "simple" disambiguation or "precisification of the literal meaning of" the legal provision (Diciotti 2014, p. 64).

the frame theory considers as *interpretive* argumentation is, properly, to be regarded rather as *integrative* argumentation, by means of which lawyers amend or put aside legislatures' explicit norms.

I. Conjectural interpretation, in so far as it goes beyond identifying the conventional, linguistic meaning of a legal provision, really is conjectural *integration*: the laying down of the several possibilities of amending or putting aside the explicit norms available, from either a methodological or an ideological standpoint.

5.4 A Few Virtues of the Frame Theory

To supporters of the frame theory, the retrieval theory, even in its conventional meaning variety, appears objectionable: both as to its critique side, and as to its proposal side.

In the following, I will articulate a few reasons why it is so.

First, I will deploy a logical fallacy argument, meant to bring to the fore the normative commitments by which the conventional meaning variety is saddled (Sect. 5.4.1 below).

Second, I will turn down two critiques that, according to supporters of the conventional meaning variety, would strike a fatal blow to the frame theory: i.e., the critique pointing to the impossibility for the frame theory of distinguishing between explicit norms and implicit norms, and the critique pointing to the impossibility for the frame theory of distinguishing between legal orders where legislation is a source of law from legal orders where it is not so (Sect. 5.4.2 below).

Third, I will argue that the frame theory enjoys a competitive advantage over the conventional meaning variety from the vantage point of juristic commonsense, contemporary pragmatics, ideological neutrality (*Wertfreiheit*), and conceptual adequacy (Sect. 5.4.3 below).

5.4.1 Ab posse ad esse non valet consequentia

The conventional meaning variety insists, as we have seen, that legal provisions really are like containers. They are so, because they are sentences in a natural language; as a consequence, they have an obvious, natural, objective *legal* content, represented by their conventional linguistic meaning.

Such a line of argument, convincing as it may appear, is flawed.

Surely, legal provisions are sentences formulated by legal authorities using words and grammatical patterns borrowed from a natural language. Surely, we *can* read legal provisions as if they were just ordinary sentences in a natural language. Surely, we *can* maintain that the *legally correct* meaning of legal provisions, being sentences in a natural language, is tantamount to their conventional meaning. Surely, the conventional meaning of legal provisions *can* be their legally correct meaning, at least *prima facie* or by way of a defeasible presumption.

However, *ab posse ad esse non valet consequentia*: from the fact that all that *can* be so, it does not follow that *it is*, or *must be*, so. This further step—from the statement that legal provisions are made out of the materials of a natural language, to the conclusion that their correct *legal* meaning is their ordinary linguistic meaning—is *not* warranted, unless we add some further premise. Unless, for instance, we add the premise that the correct legal meaning of legal provisions depends on (the nature of) the language that has been used to formulate them; that whoever uses a natural language wishes his sentences to be understood according to the grammar and lexicon of that language, and has a legitimate claim to that, commanding respect; that legal authorities must be presumed to want their provisions to be interpreted according to the grammar and lexicon of the language they have chosen to employ (otherwise, why would have they used a natural language?), etc.

The need for adding such further premises is, apparently, something supporters of the conventional meaning variety seem to overlook, being somehow bewitched by a sort of "linguistic naturalism". There is indeed a further point they seem to overlook when they present the conventional linguistic reading of legal provisions as the "proper", "obvious", "natural", "evident" *legal* way of reading them. They seem to overlook that such a claim—whenever is not simply a report about somebody else's belief or attitude—actually belongs to the normative theory of interpretation and normative philosophy of law. Indeed, it is in fact a claim about the *correct*, *proper*, *natural* way of interpreting legal provisions, and, consequently, a claim concerning the *correct*, *proper*, *natural* way of establishing *what the law—what the actual content of legal systems—really amounts to*. A moment's reflection suggests that the conventional meaning variety is the (perhaps unconscious) servant to an influential practical master: the legal policy master preoccupied with such ethical goals as "making practical sense of legislation", "restoring the dignity of legislation as a veritable legal source", "establishing legal security so far as possible", "making the law, so far as possible, readable and knowable to any competent speaker of the relevant natural language", etc. Notice that all these ethical goals belong to the Enlightenment doctrine of legislation. They belong to a specific normative view of legislation and statutory construction.

It is of course understandable that supporters of the conventional meaning variety may find such a doctrine greatly appealing and commendable on practical grounds. But, in such a case, they should openly avow their ideological allegiance.[31]

[31] A further possibility of making sense of the conventional meaning theory would be reading it as an empirical claim about what is the "common way" of reading legal provisions and establishing the content of legal system. As to "our" legal systems, however, such claim would be clearly false.

5.4.2 *Two Misfired Critiques*

I have just argued that the conventional meaning variety is either logically flawed (*qua* theory), or no theory at all, being rather, for good or bad, Enlightenment propaganda in disguise.

Its supporters, however, maintain the conventional meaning variety to be theoretically warranted.

On the one hand, they claim, it lays on the solid ground of conventional linguistic meaning—of a meaning "out there"—the distinction, which otherwise would be baffling, between explicit norms and legal interpretation proper, on the one hand, and implicit norms and legal integration (juristic law making, juristic construction), on the other hand, while, contrariwise, the frame theory is not able to provide a reliable way for drawing those very distinctions.

On the other hand, they claim, it makes sense of the fact of legislation as a source of law, allowing for a clear-cut distinction between legal orders where legislation is a source of law and legal orders where it is not so, while, contrariwise, the frame theory would make such a distinction impossible.

As I said, I think both critiques fail. Let's have a closer look on them.

5.4.2.1 On the Alleged Impossibility of Distinguishing Explicit from Implicit Norms

Here you are the gist of the conventional meaning variety's argument against the frame theory on the explicit/implicit norms divide issue.

a. The legal theorists who insist on the theoretical relevance of distinguishing between explicit norms and implicit norms usually maintain that explicit norms are the norms that can be identified as meanings of a legal provision by means of the "interpretive methods" (rules, arguments, directives, canons, techniques) in use in "our" legal culture and experience.
b. Such a claim however is sound, if, and only if, it is possible to draw a clear-cut distinction between the methods and arguments which are properly and strictly *interpretive*, being apt for identifying and justifying explicit norms, on the one side, and the methods and arguments which play instead an *integration* function, being apt for identifying and justifying implicit norms, on the other side. This is so since, if such a clear-cut distinction within "interpretive methods" is not possible, "interpretive methods" cannot be used as a reliable vantage point for sorting out explicit norms from implicit ones.[32]
c. Unfortunately, the required clear-cut distinction between strictly interpretive and integration methods is not possible. As a matter of fact, the most important

[32] "If such a distinction is not possible, it is also impossible to distinguish explicit norms [norme espresse] from implicit norms [norme inespresse] by looking at the methods by means of which they are identified" (Diciotti 2013, p. 106, my translation).

methods (arguments) in "our" legal culture (like, e.g., the argument *a simili* and the so-called dissociation argument) may be used for identifying (and justifying the identification of) *both* explicit norms *and* implicit norms; they may function *both* as strictly interpretive arguments, *and* as integrative methods.

d. Interpretive methods as a whole are accordingly *not* a viable vantage point for distinguishing between explicit and implicit norms.
e. There is, to conclude, only one way to make such a distinction possible. And this way consists in resorting to the criterion of conventional linguistic meaning. A norm is an explicit norm, if, and only if, it can be identified as belonging to the set of conventional linguistic meanings of a legal provision.

The preceding line of argument is, to be sure, appealing. Unfortunately, from the standpoint of the frame theory, it does not work, for at least two reasons.

(1) In their reasoning, as we have just seen, the supporters of the conventional meaning variety of the retrieval view deal with "the argument *a simili*" as if it were just *one* and *the same* argument, from the standpoint of *function* and *structure*, both in its strictly interpretive uses, and in its integration uses. Such a claim is questionable. In fact, it is possible distinguishing two varieties of the so-called argument *a simili*: a strictly interpretive variety and an integration variety. They share the *same* function (dealing with gaps), but have a *different* structure. The analogical argument in its interpretive variety is a means of arguing for a certain ascription of meaning to words and phrases contained in a legal provision. It contributes to the process of translating a legal provision into (explicit) legal norms. It supports the performance of so-called *extensive interpretation* of legal texts, and serves to overcome ("pre-empt") the gaps "revealed" by a first, literal or usual (authoritative, traditional, historical), reading of legal provisions. By contrast, the analogical argument in its integration variety is employed whenever interpretation proper is (deemed to be) over, and there is a need to argue for the existence and applicability of a further, implicit, norm, taking as starting point some previously identified explicit norm, together with the principle of analogical integration. This variety of analogical reasoning supports the performance of overt gaps-filling operations. If we follow the suggestion of supporters of the conventional meaning variety, however, we must consider both sorts of analogical reasoning as concerning the identification of *implicit* norms; we must apply the same label ("implicit norm") to two very different kinds of "implicit" norms, losing the possibility of sorting them out by appealing to the structure of the reasoning employed to justify them.
(2) Coming to the second reason, the examples the supporters of the conventional meaning variety provide, in order to show the competitive advantage of their own view upon the frame theory, are not, after all, convincing. Here you are the examples.[33]

[33] Diciotti (2013), pp. 107–108.

Suppose that, on the main entrance to a public park, there is a legal provision (LP_i) saying: "No vehicles in the park". Suppose three problems arise: (*i*) whether roller-skates are a "vehicle" and thus should not be allowed into the park (problem of vagueness); (*ii*) whether the prohibition to enter the park does hold also for horses, assuming that horses are not "vehicles" according to the conventional linguistic meaning of "vehicle" (problem of under-inclusion); (*iii*) whether the prohibition to enter the park does hold also for an ambulance coming into the park to rescue a seriously injured man, though an ambulance is clearly a "vehicle" according to the conventional linguistic meaning of "vehicle" (problem of over-inclusion).

By means of an argument *a simili*, it is possible to solve the first problem in a way that consists in making the content of the norm expressed by LP_i more "precise". This may be done, for instance, by the following line of reasoning: (*a*) there is an explicit norm not allowing vehicles into the park; (*b*) the explicit norm clearly refers to trucks and automobiles, but it is dubious whether it also refers to roller-skates; (*c*) the purpose (the *ratio*) of the norm is protection of the physical integrity of the people in the park; (*d*) surely, trucks and automobiles are a threat to the physical integrity of the people in the park; (*e*) surely, roller-skates too are a threat to the physical integrity of the people in the park; (*f*) hence, provided trucks, automobiles, and roller-skates are similar things from the standpoint of the *ratio* of the norm, we must conclude that roller-skates too are "vehicles" to the purpose of the explicit norm "no vehicles allowed into the park", and should not enter the park. In this case, notice, the argument *a simili* functions as a way to identify and justify an *explicit norm*: the norm according to which "no vehicles (i.e., no trucks, no automobiles, *and no roller-skates*) are allowed into the park".

Reasoning by analogy also allows coping with the second problem. Here, however, according to the supporters of the conventional meaning variety, the argument *a simili* would be clearly a means for identifying and justifying an *implicit norm*: namely, the implicit norm according to which "No horses are allowed into the park". The reasoning goes as follows: (*a*) there is an explicit norm not allowing vehicles (i.e., trucks, automobiles, roller-skates, etc.) into the park; (*b*) surely, horses are *not* vehicles (according to the conventional meaning of "vehicle"); (*c*) the purpose of the explicit norm is protecting the physical integrity of the people in the park; (*d*) surely, horses too represent a threat to the physical integrity of the people in the park; (*e*) hence, we must conclude that, along with the explicit norm "no vehicles into the park" it goes by analogy the further, implicit, norm "No horses are allowed into the park".

Finally, the dissociation argument is useful for coping with the third problem, which is a problem of over-inclusion. Here again, however, according to the supporters of the conventional meaning variety, the argument would be a means to identify and justify an *implicit exception* to the explicit norm "No vehicles (i.e., no trucks, no automobiles, no roller-skates, etc.) are allowed into the park". The reasoning goes as follows: (*a*) there is an explicit norm not allowing vehicles (i.e., trucks, automobiles, roller-skates, etc.) into the park; (*b*) surely, an ambulance is a vehicle and, from the standpoint of the explicit norm considered in itself, it ought not to be allowed into the park; (*c*) the purpose of the explicit norm is protecting the physical integrity of the people in the park; (*d*) the ambulance clearly fulfils such a purpose, since it comes to rescue a seriously injured man; (*e*) hence the general prohibition of the explicit norm must be relaxed to allow into the park those vehicles performing valuable services to the people inside the park; (*f*) hence we may properly amend the explicit norm as follows: "No vehicles (i.e., no trucks, no automobiles, no roller-skates, etc.) are allowed into the park, *unless they serve a socially valuable function*".

Now, according to the supporters of the conventional meaning view, the three examples above would show that only if we adopt their view it is possible to draw a clear-cut distinction between interpretation and integration. Example (*i*) would be a (clear) case of interpretation proper, while examples (*ii*) and (*iii*) would be (clear) cases of integration. According to the frame theory, on the contrary, all the three examples would be instances of interpretation proper: in all cases, the outcome either of reasoning by analogy, or of resorting to the dissociation argument, would be explicit norms, i.e., norms capable of being presented as the (legally correct) meaning of the legal provision "No vehicles in the park"—on the basis, of course, of translation rules different from the literal meaning rule.

Are the conventional meaning variety supporters right? Is there any overwhelming reason to endorse it? I do not think so.

As we have seen (Sect. 5.3, point F above), the conventional meaning variety's notion of interpretation proper regards as genuine interpretation also the "fixing up" of vagueness in cases like example (*i*). However, vagueness is a situation where linguistic rules have run out, where they do not provide any clear guidance. So, if we use linguistic meaning as the benchmark to tell explicit norms from implicit ones, also such a fixing up should be regarded as a piece of *integration*.[34]

Some supporter of the conventional meaning variety would retort that the norm the interpreter adds to the law is nonetheless *explicit*, for it coincides with one of the possibilities pointed out by the legislature.[35]

When vagueness shows up, however, it is as if the legislature had said to the judge: "As to roller-skates, either they are vehicles, and so they are not allowed to enter into the park, or they are not vehicles, and therefore the prohibition does not apply to them. Decide for the alternative you deem to be, all-things-considered, the legally right one". Vagueness goes along with the exercise of a delegated law-making power (of course, iff judges have the duty to decide the lawsuit). Therefore, presenting such an exercise of law-making power as getting, nonetheless, to an *explicit* norm looks preposterous.

We have apparently arrived at the following conclusion. From the very standpoint of a consistent and rigorous conventional meaning variety of the retrieval theory, all the three examples above should be regarded, properly, as three instances of *integration*, where a new, implicit norm is added to the set of (properly) explicit

[34] Indeed, unlike Diciotti (2013), Hart seems to see this situation precisely as a case of gap (Hart 1961, ch. VII; Hart 1977).

[35] Diciotti (2014), pp. 63–65.

ones. If that is the case, the concept of explicit norm the conventional meaning variety presently endorses (see Sect. 5.3, point F, above) must be modified. Explicit norms must be regarded as coinciding solely with the *determinate* linguistic meaning of legal provisions.[36] From a theoretical point of view, however, for the reasons we have just seen (see Sect. 5.4.1 above), such a stipulation is questionable.

5.4.2.2 On the Alleged Impossibility of Making Sense of Legislation as a Source of Law

The frame's theory thesis about the will-geared, decisional character of judicial interpretation (as a variety of interpretation to a practical purpose) has been criticized by supporters of the conventional meaning variety of the retrieval theory, on the count that it would be at odds with legislation being a (true) "source of law".

Their argument runs as follows. If judicial interpretation always is "decision upon the meaning of a statutory text", they claim, then any difference between the legal orders where legislation is a source of law, on the one hand, and the legal orders where, contrariwise, it is not a source of law, on the other hand, just disappears: it becomes "impossible identifying the legal orders where legislation is source of law".[37] Indeed, so the argument proceeds, "the statement according to which legislation is a source of law in a certain legal order *only makes sense* if we *assume that the legislative texts have in themselves a meaning, express by themselves certain norms*".[38]

Supporters of the conventional meaning variety brandish against the frame theory an argument that seems to have all the knocking-down force of an invincible argument *ad absurdum*. If we maintain that judicial interpretation always is decisional in character, then we must give up the very idea of legislation as a source of law. Which is plainly an absurd, insensate, weird conclusion.

If we consider the frame theory's theory of legislation (see Sect. 5.2, point 7, above), however, the conventional meaning variety's argument looks far from invincible.

First, the frame theory provides a clear criterion for distinguishing legal orders where legislation is a source of law from legal orders where legislation is not a source of law: the former are legal orders where there is a certain organ or body (the legislature) that produces *statutory provisions*; the latter are legal orders where no such organ or body exists, and, as a consequence, *no statutory provisions* exist.

Second, the conventional meaning variety assumes legislation to be a (true, genuine, effective) source of law, *if, and only if*, it not only produces statutory provisions, but it also produces statutory norms, corresponding, as we have seen, to the literal meaning of statutory provisions. In so doing, it makes an option that appears

[36] This is indeed the position of "older" supporters of the conventional meaning variety, as expressed in essays like Hart (1961), Carrió (1965), and Bulygin (1991).

[37] Diciotti (2014), pp. 60–61.

[38] Diciotti (2014), p. 61, italics added (ndr).

theoretically unjustified: one that denounces its adhesion to a "strong theory of legislation". Such a strong theory of legislation, however, is in fact a piece of normative ethics (see Sect. 5.4.1 above). Accordingly, it flies in the face of the ideal of ideological neutrality that should rule over genuine theoretical inquiries.

5.4.3 The Competitive Advantage of the Frame Theory

To conclude, there seem to be at least four more (good) reasons for adopting the frame theory and rejecting the conventional meaning variety. These reasons come from juristic commonsense, contemporary pragmatics, ideological neutrality and conceptual adequacy.

Juristic Commonsense The conventional meaning theory sets forth a highly counter-intuitive conceptual apparatus, far away from juristic commonsense. From its standpoint, the on-going ways of thinking about legal interpretation and legal integration, explicit and implicit norms, should be radically amended. This is not the case with the frame theory. Provided that it is clear that both interpretation and integration are practical argumentative games, on-going ways of thinking can be preserved. Why, if the reasonably arguable purpose of the legal provision "No dogs are allowed into restaurants" is keeping dangerous dogs out of restaurants, should we present the teleological norm "No dangerous dogs are allowed into restaurants" as an *implicit* norm?

Contemporary Pragmatics As we have seen in the previous chapter, from the standpoint of traditional literalism, the explicit meaning of a token sentence only consists in its semantic meaning, or semantically expressed proposition.[39] Contrariwise, from the standpoint both of semantic minimalism, which is an updated variety of literalism, and of contextualism, the explicit meaning of a token sentence consists both in its (full-fledged) semantic meaning (if any), and in some meaning corresponding to speaker's intention. From the standpoint of contemporary pragmatics, therefore: there are different, competing, views about the explicit meaning of a token sentence; the view defended by traditional literalism is minoritarian, and, what is more, is being criticized even by philosophers of language in the literalist camp.

If we consider the conventional meaning variety of the retrieval view from the standpoint of contemporary pragmatics, it looks like a form of traditional literalism applied to legal provisions. In so doing, however, it overlooks updated pragmatics and adopts a theoretically questionable theory of meaning. This is not the case with the frame theory, which, as regards to legal provisions, adopts instead a position of explicit meaning pluralism.

[39] See Chap. 4, Sects. 4.3 and 4.4, above.

Ideological Neutrality The conventional meaning variety can be charged, as we have seen (see Sects. 5.4.1 and 5.4.2.2 above), with (perhaps unaware) support to the Enlightenment case for the dignity and powers of legislatures: with endorsing a substantive, value-laden, conception of what the law is, and must be, in any legal experience whatsoever. On the contrary, no practical commitment whatsoever is to be found in the frame theory. The theory of interpretation (as an argumentative game) it sets forth is committed neither to any determinate set of interpretive rules, nor to any determinate "theory" of legislation. Purporting to be a genuinely descriptive theory, it is compatible instead with whatever set of rules, and whatever "theory" of legislation, may prevail in any given legal culture. It does not rule out that the lawyers (jurists, judges) working in a given legal order may hold that the legislature, by enacting legal provisions, produces the explicit norms corresponding to the conventional linguistic meanings of the provisions. Nor does it rule out that the lawyers (jurists, judges) working in a given legal order may adopt a different view about the proper way of conceiving legislation and interpretation: for instance, that they may hold that the legislature intends to produce constitutionally legitimate norms, comes what it may of linguistic meaning. All these contingent ideological postures are as many data for the frame theory to record, and account for, as possible features of on-going legal systems.

Conceptual Adequacy The conventional meaning variety suggests its own notions of legal interpretation and explicit norm to provide a better standpoint for establishing where lawyers simply "discover" the law (i.e., the objective meaning of legal provisions), on the one hand, and where, contrariwise, they "make" it, on the other.

From the standpoint of the frame theory, however, such a claim is objectionable on two counts.

First, the proposal is misleading. Lawyers playing at the interpretive or integration argumentation games never do simply "discover" the law. They always establish what the law is by their own decisions. Obviously, their decisions may fall upon the objective linguistic meaning of a legal provision. But, even in such a case, there is a decision for an interpretive sentence that is "correct" on the basis of an interpretive code that has been previously accepted as, in turn, "correct".

Second, the conceptual framework of the frame theory is perfectly equipped to capture and bring to the fore the difference between *literal* explicit norms (that are justifiable on the ground of the literal or conventional meaning argument), on the one hand, and, say, *teleological* explicit norms (that are justifiable on the ground of teleological argument from an assumed *ratio legis*), on the other.

One last remark seems in order. The frame theory's notion of interpretation may seem tautological. As you may recall, interpretation is (intra-linguistic) translation of legal provisions into explicit norms, according to arguments that the legal culture considers as being, *structurally*, *interpretive* arguments, namely, arguments about *what the legal provision* (if correctly interpreted) *says*. For the reasons I have tried to set forth, if there is any tautology here (which I doubt), this is a virtuous tautology: respectful of theoretical neutrality and serving explanatory comprehensiveness.

Chapter 6
Towards Pragmatic Realism

In sum, the child is (1) a wishful thinker who, (2) in the interest of his desire for harmony, chancelessness, security and certainty builds for himself an over-simplified, over-unified, novelty-less world, heedless of the lack of correspondence of this construction with the world of actual experience, and (3) who is aided in contriving this world by his implicit belief in the magic efficacy of words

—J. Frank (1930)

6.1 The Problem About Judicial Interpretation

Legal theorists still debate about the adequate description of judicial interpretation. The dispute turns on the following alternative: Is judicial interpretation necessarily (i.e., as a matter of empirical necessity) an evaluative, practical judgment-dependent, decisional activity, or is it, rather, at least sometimes, just a matter of knowledge, of a pure "grasping" of the content of the law? "Realism" (non-cognitivism, scepticism) sides with the first alternative, while "formalism" (cognitivism) sides with the latter.

My aim in this chapter is arguing for interpretive realism, and a construction conception of legal meaning, from the interpretive game, pragmatic point of view already put to work in the previous chapters.[1] The argument will have a five-steps development. In the first step, I will lay down a conceptual framework. In the second step, I will make clear what I consider interpretive realism and formalism to be. Here, I will contrast realism (non-cognitivism) with formalism in the two varieties of integral and limited cognitivism, and set forth a few criticisms of the latter. In the third step, I will offer an account of pragmatic formalism, the sophisticated version of limited cognitivism Andrei Marmor defends by resorting to the philosophy of language, and, particularly, to a semantics-geared, communication model, prag-

[1] See Chaps. 3, 4, and 5 above.

P. Chiassoni, *Interpretation without Truth*, Law and Philosophy Library 128,
https://doi.org/10.1007/978-3-030-15590-2_6

matic outlook. In the fourth step, the critical side of pragmatic realism will be set forth. It will be argued that philosophy of language, and pragmatics as a substantive part thereof, far from providing support for pragmatic formalism, suggests, rather, that it should be abandoned. In the fifth, and last, step, the proposal side of pragmatic realism will be outlined.

6.2 A Conceptual Framework

Realism (non-cognitivism) and formalism (cognitivism) purport to provide true descriptions of judicial interpretation.[2] Unfortunately, the descriptions they set forth are at odds. Telling which, if any, is the right one, represents still to these days a major jurisprudential concern. To the purpose of providing perhaps a clearer account of them, and also in order to prevent confusion, which is a plentiful commodity in the field, I will start by indulging in the clarification of a few key-terms. These are "interpretation", "integration", "interpretive discretion", "integration discretion", and "situation of interpretive discretion".

By *interpretation* I mean the activity, performed by a judge in order to decide a lawsuit, which consists in translating a previously identified legal provision into one or more explicit norms. These norms are explicit—i.e., correspond to "what the legal provision says"—since the judge presents, and, if necessary, defends them, by way of interpretive arguments, as the legally correct meaning of the legal provision at hand.[3]

---

[2] Barberis (2014), pp. 196–204, claims that realism and the so-called mixed theory—in my view, a variety of cognitivism that I will consider in a moment—would *both* provide correct answers, since they would aim at different questions. The mixed theory would provide a true answer to the question: "How is law being in fact applied by judges?" It would be concerned, accordingly, with so-called "concrete interpretation". Contrariwise, realism would provide a true answer to the different question: "How is law being in fact interpreted by jurists and judges?" It would be concerned, consequently, with the interpretation of legal texts apart from their application to individual cases, i.e., with so-called "abstract interpretation". I suspect, however, that the presumed way out suggested by Barberis depends on a confusion about the notion of "concrete interpretation", as I shall suggest in the following footnote.

[3] See Chap. 2, Sect. 2.2.1.1, Chap. 3, Sect. 3.6, Chap. 4, Sects. 4.2.2, 4.3, and Chap. 5, Sects. 5.2 and 5.4, above. Some authors—Guastini (2011b), pp. 138–140; Barberis (2014)—draw a distinction between *abstract interpretation* (interpretation *in abstracto*, "text-oriented interpretation") and *concrete interpretation* ("interpretation *in concreto*", "fact-oriented interpretation"). Abstract interpretation amounts (in my terminology) to translating a legal provision into an explicit general norm, without paying attention to the application of the norm to individual cases, while paying attention, instead, to overcoming ambiguity problems: that is to say, problems arising from the capability of legal provisions to be translated into a set of alternative (abstract) explicit norms. Concrete interpretation is concerned, contrariwise, with the qualification of individual cases according to previously identified abstract general norms; it focuses on the reference (denotation, extension, *Bedeutung*) of the descriptive expressions featuring in the general norms; it is meant to overcome problems of vagueness or open texture, if any, of the concepts to be used for qualifying cases. I think the notion of concrete interpretation, as it is usually defined, suffers from an ambigu-

By *integration* I mean the activity, performed by a judge in order to decide a lawsuit, which consists in identifying the implicit components of a positive legal order. In a very broad sense of the term, these implicit components are norms—principles, rules, criteria for conflict resolution, definitions, etc.—that, by hypothesis, are not explicit, since they cannot be presented and defended as the legally correct meanings, as the legally correct translations, of any definite legal provision whatsoever, their identification depending, contrariwise, on some integration process and technique (like, e.g., analogical or *a contrario* reasoning, reasoning from basic principles or the nature of things, etc.).[4]

By *interpretive discretion* I mean, for any judge whatsoever, and in relation to the interpretation of a previously identified legal provision, the power, (that is commonly assumed to have been) explicitly or tacitly conferred by the legal order, of choosing between two or more reasonable alternatives concerning the legally correct translation of the legal provision. It appears necessary defining interpretive discretion in terms of reasonable alternatives, in view of taking into account a basic aspect of judicial interpretation in our legal culture: namely, its being an argumentative game, belonging to the realm of rhetorics.[5] Reasonable alternatives are

---

ity that must be brought to the fore, in order to get a clearer, and finer, conceptual apparatus. Indeed it seems worthwhile distinguishing two notions of concrete interpretation. According to the first notion, concrete interpretation is a part of the activity of translating a legal provision into a general norm. This I shall call *concrete-interpretation-as-translation*. According to the second notion, contrariwise, concrete interpretation amounts to qualifying a certain individual fact in terms of a previously identified general norm. This I shall call *concrete-interpretation-as-qualification*. The output of concrete-interpretation-as-qualification is a qualification sentence: like, for instance, "John Smith's entering the park on roller-skates is—has the value of, amounts to, counts as—entering the park with a vehicle". On the contrary, the outcome of concrete-interpretation-as-translation is a norm, the logical form of which incorporates a parenthetic, denotative, definition of the relevant qualifying expression: like, for instance, "No vehicles (i.e., automobiles, motorcycles, bicycles, or roller-skates) are allowed into the park". In a well-designed judicial opinion, the outcome of concrete-interpretation-as-qualification logically depends on the outcome of a corresponding concrete-interpretation-as-translation. To be sure, the judicial process of interpretation-as-translation, broadly conceived, usually has its starting point in the description of an individual case ("John Smith entered the city park on roller-skates") and in a legal issue (a question of law) arising out of it ("Did John Smith's behaviour violate the Mayor's ordinance 'No vehicles into the city park'?"). The two notions of concrete-interpretation are precisely useful to emphasize this central aspect of adjudication.

[4] See Chap. 2, Sect. 2.2.1.2, Chap. 3, Sect. 3.6, and Chap. 5, Sects. 5.1–5.2, above.

[5] From the standpoint of judicial interpretation and integration, the law can in fact be considered as a rhetorical normative system. As a system, to wit, that consists, at any given time, of the totality of the rhetorical consequences of a given set of legal provisions. On this notion, see Chap. 2, Sect. 2.3.3.2, above. In current legal theory, the scholars of the Alicante School also emphasize the argumentative dimension of interpretation. See e.g. Atienza (2013) and Lifante Vidal (2018a). They claim, however, the "argumentative view" they defend to be a third way between interpretive formalism and interpretive realism. This is so because, according to the argumentative view, interpretation always involves both acts of knowledge and acts of will, and this would show any clear-cut distinction between knowing and deciding to be unsound. A few comments are in order, though in passing. First, acts of knowledge and acts of will are logically and psychologically distinct. Furthermore, as I have argued (see e.g. Chaps. 3 and 4 above), acts of knowledge occur within a

alternatives that, though they may be strongly disputable, even to the point of being considered as utterly "outrageous" by some sector of public opinion or the legal profession, are not, nonetheless, utterly "preposterous", "nonsensical", or "unserious". Ultimately, they are supported by some set of ethical principles—concerning justice, democracy, the constitution, the rule of law, the proper role of the judiciary within the institutional context, the proper interpretive method, etc.—the judges adopt as paramount on the basis of an (irrational) fundamental ethical option, one that is not itself liable to any conclusive justification.[6] Due to such argumentation requirement, interpretive discretion does not amount to an absolute, arbitrary, power to choose interpretive outputs. It is, rather, a power the exercise thereof is constrained by a burden of reasoning, however weak such a requirement may turn out to be in individual cases.

By *integration discretion* I mean, for any judge whatsoever, and in relation to the identification of the implicit components of a previously identified set of legal provisions, explicit norms and implicit norms, the power of choosing among two or more reasonable alternatives concerning the legally correct enrichment of that set

previously selected interpretive code. Therefore, the argumentative view is really no third way between formalism and realism, but, if anything, the Alicante Scholars notwithstanding, just a piece of refined realism.

[6] In a posthumous essay, Herbert Hart, after asserting that the exercise of "discretion occupies an intermediate place between choices dictated by purely personal and momentary whim and those which are made to give effect to clear methods of reaching clear aims or to conform to rules whose application in the particular case is obvious", emphasizes that every discretional decision always consists in the making of a "leap", for it can never be supported by conclusive reasons: "phrases often used to describe the exercise of discretion, such as "intuition" [and] "recognition of an implicit guiding purpose," may encourage the illusion that we never reach the point where we have to reconcile conflicting values or choose between them without some more ultimate principle to guide us. I think the suggestion that we never reach the "leap" is just as wrong as a description of discretion as a mere arbitrary choice would be. It seems to me clear that just because there is a point at which we can no longer be guided by principles and at the best can only ask for the confirmation of our judgment by persons who have submitted themselves to a similar discipline before deciding, that we have in discretion the sphere where arguments in favour of one decision or another may be rational without being conclusive": Hart (1956), pp. 658, 665; see also Hart (1961), "Postscript", 273–276. As it is well known, Ronald Dworkin singles out "weak" from "strong" discretion. The former obtains whenever an official's decision depends on a "use of judgment" that is "controlled by a standard furnished" by a particular authority: for instance, a sergeant is ordered by the lieutenant to "take his five *most experienced* men on patrol". The latter obtains whenever an official's decision is *not* "controlled by a standard furnished" by a particular authority, but must nonetheless keep within the limits set by the general standards of "rationality, fairness, and effectiveness": for instance, a sergeant is simply ordered to "take five men on patrol" (Dworkin 1977, pp. 31–33). Clearly, weak discretion and strong discretion differ not by quality, but, if at all, only by quantity: strong discretion obtains whenever the decision-makers (are assumed to) act under weaker constraints. Both notions can be captured by Hart's notion. On discretion in law, see also: Lifante Vidal (1989); Lifante Vidal (2018b), pp. 81–130; Ruiz Manero (1990), pp. 181–198; Iglesias Vila (1999), Laporta (2007), pp. 207–208 ("When the law is indeterminate, when its sentences are defeasible, when cases are hard cases, it shows up in front of us the riddle of judicial discretion").

(for instance, by adding one or the other of some implicit background principle or implicit norm of detail).

To the present purpose, I will leave integration discretion aside and focus, instead, on interpretive discretion. If we pay attention to the kinds of (reasonable) alternatives among which there may be room for choice, it seems worthwhile distinguishing two varieties of interpretive discretion. These are *selective discretion* and *applicative discretion*.

Selective discretion consists, for any judge whatsoever, and in relation to the interpretation of a previously identified legal provision, in the power—limited, of course, by the aforementioned burden of argumentation—of determining which, between two or more alternative interpretive codes, is (to be regarded as) "the legally correct one".[7]

Applicative discretion consists, contrariwise, for any judge whatsoever, and in relation to the interpretation of a previously identified legal provision, in the (limited) power of choosing between two or more alternative translations of the legal provision that are made possible by uncertainties showing up in the application of the rules of the previously selected interpretive code.[8]

To complete the present conceptual framework, one more notion is needed. This is the notion of "situation of interpretive discretion". By *situation of interpretive discretion* I mean, for any judge whatsoever, and in relation to the interpretation of a previously identified legal provision, the situation that consists in the possibility for the judge of exercising her powers of interpretive discretion: be it the power of selective discretion (discretion as to the choice of the interpretive code), or the power of applicative discretion (discretion in applying the rules of a previously selected interpretive code), or both.[9]

[7] On interpretive codes, see Chap. 2, Sect. 2.2.1.1, Chap. 3, Sects. 3.4 and 3.6, and Chap. 5, Sect. 5.1, above.

[8] Suppose, for instance, that the following situation occurs: (i) the interpretive code contains just one translation rule, prescribing to interpret statutory provisions "according to the original legislative intent as it can be gathered out of *travaux préparatoires*"; and (ii) competing reasonable interpretations are available of what the original legislative intent was, each one pointing to a different way of translating the legal provision at hand. In that case, following the interpretive code's default rule, the judge will exercise applicative discretion in view either of selecting what, all-things-considered, is to be taken as the governing legislative intent, or of deciding for a meaning dependent on some other interpretive resource.

[9] Are situations of interpretive discretion judge-dependent or judge-independent? For the reasons that will appear in the following, I am inclined to think that they depend on context, which, in turn, is neither always, nor wholly, waterproof to judicial beliefs, preferences, attitudes and expectations.

6.3 Three Theories

It is commonplace for legal philosophers distinguishing between three alternative views about the "nature" of judicial interpretation: formalism, realism, and the so-called intermediate or mixed theory.

Formalism ("the noble dream theory") claims judicial interpretation to be an activity of knowing the legally correct meaning of legal provisions ("grasping the true meaning of a law in view of its application to an individual case at hand").

Realism ("scepticism", "the nightmare theory"), contrariwise, claims judicial interpretation to be an activity that always, and necessarily, involves some practical evaluation and decision concerning the legally correct meaning of legal provisions.[10]

Finally, so-called *mixed* or *intermediate theory* ("eclecticism", "the vigil theory") claims judicial interpretation to be something enjoying of a hybrid nature: sometimes it is just knowledge ("law-finding"), sometimes it is practical evaluation and decision ("law-creation").[11]

The notions of interpretive discretion I have just defined suggest to draw a somewhat different, perhaps a little bit more precise, picture of such competing theories, where the featuring items are integral cognitivism, limited cognitivism and non-cognitivism.

6.3.1 *Cognitivism: Integral and Limited*

Integral cognitivism claims that, in relation to the interpretation of any legal provision whatsoever, judges can *never* find themselves in situations of interpretive discretion: neither in situations of selective discretion, nor in situations of applicative

[10] Sometimes two varieties of realism are singled out, according to the role they ascribe to interpretation in the determination of the meaning of legal provisions. Radical realism claims that there is really no meaning before interpretation: interpretation creates the meaning of legal provisions. Contrariwise, moderate realism claims that legal provisions are always open to a plurality of meanings. There are meanings before interpretation; interpretation, however, necessarily consists in deciding, for any case at hand, which is the (all-things-considered) correct one. See Guastini (2011b), pp. 150, 156–159; Troper (2001), pp. 69–84. The two varieties dissent, apparently, on the notion of "interpretation" they endorse. According to radical realism, whatever the interpreter decides to be the meaning of a legal provision *is* the meaning of that legal provision, even though it falls outside of the frame of methodologically possible interpretations of the provision. Contrariwise, according to moderate realism, whatever the interpreter decides to be the meaning of a legal provision *is* the meaning of that legal provision, if, but only if, it falls inside of the frame of methodologically possible interpretations of the provision. On frames of interpretations see above, at Chap. 5, Sect. 5.2.

[11] See, for instance, Carrió (1965), part II; Hart (1977); Diciotti (2003), p. 5 footnote 2; Guastini (2010), p. 121 ff.; Chiassoni (2011), ch. II. I have presented the basic ideas of the mixed theory, as an instance of semantic formalism or semantic quasi-cognitivism, in Chap. 4, Sect. 4.2.1, and, in the two varieties of the word-meaning and sentence-meaning theories, in Chap. 3, Sect. 3.2, above.

discretion. In other words, judges can never enjoy the possibility of exercising a (limited) power of interpretive choice: either in order to select the interpretive code, or in order to apply it.[12]

It is worthwhile pausing to consider the state of affair, if any, which must obtain for the claims of integral cognitivism to be true. Upon consideration, such a state of affair must amount to the existence of an *objective* interpretive code, *intrinsically endowed with strict normativity*, and characterized by the joint properties of *exclusivity* and *efficiency*. Such a code is *objective*, since it is an evident datum to every judge and jurist: something "out there", which exists independently of their beliefs and attitudes, and can just be known by any competent lawyer. It is *intrinsically endowed with strict normativity*, since, to any competent lawyer, it is in itself, by virtue of its very content, binding, and undefeasibly so, on interpretation.[13] It is *exclusive*, since no alternative objective code exists. If other codes are available, these are subjective in character, depending on interpreter's own beliefs and attitudes. It is, finally, *efficient*, since the translation rules of the objective code, combined with the relevant interpretive resources (the data that are necessary to apply them), *always* do point to (just) one definite interpretive output for any legal provision whatsoever. Such a code is, in other words, something any judge can simply know and follow.

Limited cognitivism claims that, in relation to the interpretation of any legal provision whatsoever, judges cannot find themselves in situations of selective discretion. This is so because interpreters face an interpretive code that is objective, intrinsically endowed with strict normativity, and exclusive. It may happen, however, that the code proves inefficient. It may occur that its translation rules, together with the interpretive resources available, do not point to (just) one definite translation for some legal provision at hand. In such cases, the interpreter finds herself in a situation of applicative discretion. There is a guidance failure in the rules of the objective code, and such failure must be fixed up in order to decide the case at hand. As a consequence, in those cases where the objective code runs out, interpretation cannot amount just to "finding" or "grasping" the legally correct meaning of legal provisions. It must amount, rather, to making ("creating") what is to count as their legally correct meaning.

[12] A staunch representative of integral cognitivism is apparently the German jurist Carl Friedrich von Savigny, the founder of the Historical School. For a recent account of his theory of legal interpretation see, e.g., Chiassoni (2016c), ch. IV, § 4.

[13] Legislatures can, and do in fact, dictate provisions concerning the interpretation of provisions. Such provisions, however, are not self-interpreting: no sentence in a natural language has such a portentous virtue. Accordingly, there must be a code that, by its very content, is (perceived and acted upon as) endowed with intrinsic and strict normativity. Such a code, of course, can be read by interpreters into certain legal provisions: can be presented as their legally correct meaning content.

6.3.2 A Few Perplexities

Both varieties of cognitivism—as general theories of judicial interpretation—depend, as we have seen, on the idea of there being, for every legal order and in every legal culture and experience, one interpretive code that is objective, intrinsically endowed with strict normativity, and exclusive, though they disagree upon one of its presumed virtues (efficiency). If my account of what makes cognitivism a workable view is correct, there must be a code like that, endowed with *all* those properties, if judicial interpretation is to be considered as a knowing-activity (as an "act of knowledge"): as a whole, or, at least, in a large part.

Let us leave the efficiency property aside, since it is put down even by the limited variety of cognitivism, and stop to consider the other ones. Even so, a few perplexities immediately arise. The very idea of there being, for *every* legal order, culture and experience, one interpretive code that is objective, intrinsically endowed with strict normativity, and exclusive is in itself, to say the least, open to reasonable doubt. Furthermore, even if we admit, for the sake of argument, that such an objective interpretive code does in fact exist for every legal order culture and experience, it seems nonetheless dubious that it would turn judicial interpretation into just a piece of knowledge. Let's cast a closer glance at these perplexing issues.

The first—"ontological"—perplexity can be phrased as follows: In which sense, if any, one may claim that "there is" an objective, intrinsically endowed with strict normativity, and exclusive interpretive code for every legal order culture and experience? To my mind, only two possibilities are conceivable: the existence of a code like that can be claimed either as a matter of *social fact*, or as a matter of *methodological naturalism.*[14]

Suppose, to begin with, that the existence, for every legal order culture and experience, of an interpretive code that is objective, intrinsically endowed with strict normativity, and exclusive, is claimed as a matter of social fact: as a cultural and institutional datum.

Two remarks seem in order by way of criticism. First, the existence of such a code would be a purely contingent social phenomenon: it would be a matter of how a legal and political culture, in a certain age, happens to be. Second, cognitivism would be a false account of judicial interpretation for most, if not all, of the legal cultures we know. Indeed, in our legal cultures there is, to be sure, an objective set of *interpretive rules* that is handed down by tradition, and, sometimes, is also sanctioned by positive laws. Unfortunately, however, that set of objective rules does not, by itself, make *one* interpretive code: it is interpreters that make codes out of them, according to their passing or stable interests. Besides, these objective rules about interpretation are usually very broad instructions, always calling for selective dis-

---

[14] A more complicated version of the argument would take into account the possibility of there being, in relation to any legal order, a (different) objective code like that for each sector of positive law (constitutional law, private law, administrative law, criminal law, etc.). This complication would not alter the gist of the argument.

cretion, in the form of precisifying otherwise broad, un-guiding, rules.[15] Finally, jurists are used to think both that new interpretive rules can be added, as time goes by, to the objective set handed down by tradition, and that any interpretation rule, be it old or new, far from being undefeasible, is typically (tacitly) accompanied by an "unless" clause.[16]

A second possibility must be considered, hoping for a better chance. This is the hypothesis according to which the claim that there is, for every legal order culture and experience, an interpretive code that is objective, intrinsically endowed with strict normativity, and exclusive, making of judicial interpretation just a matter of knowledge, is a piece of methodological naturalism. By "methodological naturalism" I mean the view according to which legal texts, in virtue of their essential properties, dictate the exclusive set of rules for their own correct interpretation. The problem of the correct interpretive method would become an issue of knowing the code dictated by the legal provisions selves, and faithfully following it, as we follow the rules of grammar and arithmetic.

If we pause for a moment, however, we cannot avoid feeling how queer, from the standpoint of institutional ontology, the idea of methodological naturalism is. Texts are nothing but inert strings of words. They cannot "dictate" anything at all. They do have properties, of course; but which out of these are their "essential properties" they cannot "tell" us. It is interpreters that, fatally, will pick up some of their properties as "essential" and draw interpretive instructions out of them.

Apparently, our reflexions upon the idea of there being, for every legal system culture and experience, one objective, intrinsically endowed with strict normativity, and exclusive interpretive code have led us to a disenchanting conclusion: cognitivism—in both varieties—seems to be doomed either to plain falsity, or to plain queerness.

Let's pass to the second—"epistemological"—perplexity I anticipated. Suppose, for the sake of argument, that one objective interpretive code, intrinsically endowed with strict normativity, and exclusive, *does* exist for a certain legal order culture and experience. Would that fact turn judicial interpretation (always or at least in many occasions) into an act of knowledge, as cognitivists claim?

The question commands a negative answer. There is apparently a quite simple reason for that. No code is a self-interpreting and self-applying entity. The application of any interpretive code whatsoever, even one having the properties cognitivists assume, presupposes the practical acceptance of the code: the decision to make use of it (for some moral or prudential reason) in view of interpreting some legal provision at hand. It may be, of course, a conformist decision. But a conformist decision still is a decision.

[15] Consider, for instance, the literal meaning rule as it is usually found in juristic textbooks and judicial opinions ("Interpret the legal provisions according to their literal meaning"). Does it instruct to take into account the literal meaning at the time the legal provision was enacted, or, rather, the literal meaning at the time of its application? This is something the rule, as usually understood in our legal cultures, leaves to the interpreters to decide.

[16] See e.g. Wróblewski (1985), p. 35 ff.; Wróblewski (1992), p. 87 ff.

6.3.3 Non-Cognitivism

Non-cognitivism claims that, in relation to the interpretation of any set whatsoever of legal provisions, judges necessarily find themselves in situations of selective discretion. Furthermore, depending on the interpretive code they have selected, they also can find themselves in situations of applicative discretion. The necessary presence of situation of selective discretion is a consequence of the trivial facts I have just mentioned: legal texts are not self-interpreting entities, nor they do "dictate" any interpretive directive at all for their own correct interpretation; the methodological traditions hands down to competent lawyers not one full-fledged interpretive code, but an evolving set of indeterminate, unordered and defeasible interpretive rules. Accordingly, any interpretive venture—the venture between a text and an interpreter—always depends on methodological and substantive options by the interpreter. These options, in turn, mirror the endorsement of some ideology of legal interpretation: the acceptance of some set of claims about how interpretation ought to be.

It may happen of course that, in a given legal culture, with regard to a certain kind of legal provisions, a certain interpretive code comes to be widely regarded by judges and jurists as the "correct" interpretive code, and acquires in that way the sort of contingent social objectivity I mentioned before. Also in those situations, however, interpreters will have occasions for exercising selective discretion. They will fatally be called to making reasoned choices about precisifying, putting into hierarchical order, and enriching the rules of the "objective" code.[17] To sum up, the point non-cognitivism makes is this: in any legal culture, selective discretion may have, in fact, different scopes for different judges and different kinds of legal provisions at different times. Because of structural features of legal interpretation, however, it is never a non-existent phenomenon, as integral and limited cognitivism (must and do) claim.

The case for non-cognitivism becomes even stronger, as we shall see now, by going into the details of a powerful version of limited cognitivism, pragmatic formalism, and bringing to the fore its many shortcomings.

---

[17] An example from history may perhaps help. The French jurists of the so-called Exegetical School apparently shared the same principles, which they regarded as evident, about the proper way of interpreting the *Civil Code*. These were the principle of "respect for the legislature" and the principle of "primacy of the text". These principles represented the core of the "objective" interpretive code considered as absolutely binding in French nineteenth century legal culture. Nonetheless, the two principles, due to their eminent indeterminacy, formed the basis for different, more specific, codes, adopted by individual interpreters. I provide a survey of the interpretive code(s) of the Exegetical School in Chiassoni (2016d), pp. 565–581. Similar considerations hold for those cultures where principles like "literal interpretation and legislative intent", "systemic interpretation", "constitution-oriented interpretation", "respect for the Constitution", etc., are paramount.

6.4 Pragmatic Formalism

In the foregoing attempt at providing a clear account of the properties that identify limited cognitivism, I took inspiration from a set of theories the archetype of which is usually thought to stay with Herbert Hart's well-known defence of a middle ground in between "the noble dream" of formalism and "the nightmare" of rule-scepticism.[18]

To be sure, somebody might feel shocked, or perhaps even horrified, by my claiming that Hart, while setting forth his view concerning legal interpretation, might have been committed—though tacitly, or by way of presupposition—to the idea of an objective interpretive code, intrinsically endowed with strict normativity, and exclusive. However, the sense of horror will perhaps wane, at least a bit, if we look at what can be considered as the more sophisticated version of the Hartian theory presently afoot. I mean the theory defended by Andrei Marmor.[19] One feature makes of Marmor's theory of judicial interpretation something particularly worth of attention from the standpoint of my present concern. This is Marmor's methodical resort to philosophy of language and pragmatics.

In the present section, I will briefly rehearse Marmor's own variety of limited cognitivism, i.e., *pragmatic formalism* as I shall call it, and suggest that the objective code hypothesis, so far as pragmatic formalism is concerned, seems to be endowed with sound explanatory power. The next section will be devoted to the critique of pragmatic formalism from the standpoint of pragmatic realism (Sect. 6.5). Finally, the last section of the chapter will outline the proposal side of pragmatic realism, as a pragmatic theory of judicial interpretation (Sect. 6.6).

Pragmatic formalism works out a theory of legal (and judicial) interpretation, setting it forth as a genuine piece of descriptive and explanatory theory, as a by-product of a theory of legislation. The core of pragmatic formalism consists in five main theses:

1. The production of laws by way of legislation is a communication enterprise that is properly represented, and accounted for, by means of a communication model (the communication model thesis);
2. Ordinarily, the full communicative content of any piece of legislation is, and can be, grasped by reasonable hearers through reasonable uptake (the reasonable hearer-reasonable uptake thesis);
3. Legislative communication can fail (the communication failures thesis);
4. Interpretation only steps in exceptionally, where reasonable uptake runs into situations of legal indeterminacy (the interpretation-as-exception thesis);

[18] See Hart (1958a, b), pp. 62–72, 84–87; Hart (1961), ch. VII; Hart (1977), pp. 124–143; a revised view is suggested in Hart (1967), pp. 105–106; Hart (1983a), pp. 6–8. On this variety of cognitivism, see also Chap. 3, Sect. 3.2, Chap. 4, Sect. 4.2.1, and Chap. 5, Sect. 5.3, above.

[19] See Marmor (2005), esp. chs. 2 and 6; Marmor (2011a, b), chs. 4 and 6; Marmor (2014).

5. Interpretivism, which claims interpretation to be a ubiquitous phenomenon in the ordinary working of any legal order, is false (the refutation of interpretivism thesis).

1. A Communication Model for Legislation Written law—and legislation as the foremost instance thereof—is evidently to be accounted for by resorting to a communication model, like the one that is usually employed in Gricean and neo-Gricean pragmatics to account for ordinary communication between ordinary people by means of ordinary language.[20]

Legislation is, in fact, a communication enterprise: each and every legislature intends to convey to judges, officials, and, above all, people at large, the full communicative content of its enactments. This content typically has both an explicit, and an implicit, component, amounting to what the legislature intends to say, and what the legislature intends to convey tacitly, without saying it, by way of implication, implicature or presupposition.[21]

On the one side, there is the legislature (the speaker) who sends a linguistic message having a certain communicative content; on the other side, there are judges, officials and people at large (the hearers), whose task is determining the full communicative content the legislature intended to convey by using certain strings of words.

2. Reasonable Hearers Performing Reasonable Uptakes In order to grasp the (full) communicative content of any piece of legislation whatsoever, judges (jurists, lawyers, people at large) must perform an act of understanding. This is to be conceived as "reasonable uptake": namely, as the understanding of the communicative content of a piece of legislation by a "reasonable hearer".[22]

Though Marmor does not put it in these terms, what he presents as "understanding" or "reasonable uptake", and, as we shall see in a moment, opposes to "interpretation" proper, encompasses apparently two distinct operations. These concern the two components of the explicit communicative content of any piece of legislation:

---

[20] The "communication model" resorted to by pragmatic formalism is a pragmatic model of linguistic communication, the original elaboration thereof is due Paul H. Grice, which purports to supplement and improve the semantic, "code model" of linguistic communication, used by John Locke and Ferdinand de Saussure, which reduces the communication content of speech acts to the conventional, explicit meaning of the uttered sentences. See, e.g., Korta and Perry (2015), § 3.

[21] Marmor (2014), p. 1 ff.

[22] Marmor explains the idea of "reasonable uptake", which corresponds roughly to what in previous essays qualified as "understanding", in the following terms: "the subjective intentions of the speaker are only partly constitutive of assertive content; speakers can sometimes fail to communicate all that they had intended to. Therefore, the content that is said or asserted by a speech act partly depends on its reasonable uptake. Assertive content, on this view (that I share), must be defined objectively as the kind of content that a reasonable hearer, with full knowledge of the contextual background of the speech, would understand the speaker to have intended to convey, given what the speaker expressed, the relevant contextual knowledge, and the relevant conversational norms that apply" (Marmor 2014, p. 19).

namely, the *semantic content* and the *pragmatic content*. I will refer to such operations as *semantic understanding* and *pragmatic understanding*, respectively.

Semantic understanding is a matter of grasping the "semantic content" of legal provisions, on the basis of the syntactic and semantic rules of the relevant natural language. It depends on linguistic skills. It is a necessary (unavoidable), un-reflexive, rule-determined, original, and independent cognition process.[23] In the plentiful situations of easy cases, Marmor argues, judges simply understand the semantic content of a legal provision. In those cases, the semantic content is, accordingly, tantamount to the "assertive content" (or "prescriptive content") of the legal provisions at hand ("what the law says"). By getting to know the semantic content of legislative utterances (legal provisions), judges get to know the law as it is (or, in other terms, what is the law for the question at hand), and give voice to it in their decisions.[24]

Coming to *pragmatic understanding*, it is not always, and indeed quite rarely, necessary in law.[25] It becomes necessary whenever the semantic content of legal provisions needs to be pragmatically saturated ("enriched") in order to get to the full "assertive" (or prescriptive) "content". This is the case whenever legal provisions contain context-sensitive expressions, like, e.g., personal pronouns ("it is not allowed for political crimes"), possessive ascriptions ("their behaviour shall be considered as …"), or domain quantifiers ("Everyone ought to abstain from piracy").[26] In these situations, the assertive (prescriptive) content of legal provisions, what the law says, is the output of a "defeasible inference" grounded on three factors: (a) the *semantic content* "of the expression used", (b) the *context* ("the contextual background that is common knowledge between speaker and hearer"), and (c) the relevant *conversational maxims* ("the relevant normative framework governing the conversation in question").[27]

---

[23] Marmor (2011a), p. 142: "Our ability to understand each other in a communicative context depends on a shared, at least tacit, understanding about the kind of conversation we are engaged in, and the norms governing it. Understandings of this kind are, of course, subject to occasional misunderstandings or deviations of various kinds, in which case, typically some aspect of the communication fails. None of this, however, is a matter of interpretation. From the fact that there is some normative framework governing the kind of conversation one is engaged in, it does not follow that a hearer's grasp of the communicative content hangs in the air, as it were, until she comes up with an interpretation of the relevant maxims. Maxims are typically common knowledge between speaker and hearer, in no need of interpretation"; 144–145: "Mostly, just like in an ordinary conversation, we hear (or read, actually) what the legal directive says and thereby understand what it requires. In some cases, it is unclear what the law says, and interpretation is called for".

[24] Marmor (2005), p. 10 ff. I have offered a synoptic table of the differences between understanding and interpretation in Chiassoni (2008), p. 257. See also Endicott (1994), pp. 451–479; Endicott (2016), § 2.2.

[25] Marmor (2014), p. 27, 28 ff., 33: "in the context of statutory law, the gap between semantic and assertive content is much more limited and infrequent compared with ordinary conversation". On context-sensitive expressions, see also Chap. 4, Sect. 4.3, above.

[26] Marmor (2014), pp. 22–27.

[27] Marmor (2014), p. 22 ff., 28 ff., 33–34, 108. In other parts of the book, pragmatic understanding, as part of the reasonable uptake of the full communicative content of a speech act, also concerns

Pragmatic understanding, on the basis of the relevant conversational maxims, is also afoot in determining the *implicit communicative content* of an enacted legal provision: in particular, its legislative implicatures. Here, however, as Marmor makes clear, and we shall see in a moment, its working can be impaired by the *strategic attitude* interpreters may choose to adopt.

3. Communication Failures Linguistic communication, ordinary and legislative alike, is sometimes unsuccessful. Concerning legislation, it happens any time reasonable uptake does not lead to one determinate outcome, because of some factors that undermine the law's determinacy. These factors are: (1) vagueness, (2) ambiguity, (3) gaps, (4) normative conflicts, (5) uncertainty about the correspondence between the semantic content and the assertive content of the legal provision at hand, and, finally, (6) uncertainty about the legal implicatures of the legal provision at hand.[28]

In all these cases, legislative communication fails, either because legislatures (speakers) "fail to communicate all that they had intended to", or because the communicative content, once the hearers (judges etc.) have come to determine it, proves troublesome.

Taking communicative failure into account, any theoretically sound description of the complex phenomenon jurists are used to identify by the generic phrase "legal interpretation" must draw a distinction between "understanding" ("reasonable uptake") of "what the law says", on the one hand, and "interpretation" proper ("interpreting it"), on the other hand.[29]

4. Interpretation-as-Exception Interpretation proper becomes necessary (unavoidable, a regular feature in the judicial application of statutory law), if, and only if, reasonable uptake (understanding) does not lead to one determinate outcome (see point 3 above). Unlike understanding, interpretation is a contingent, reflexive, not rule-determined, but, at most, paradigm-guided, parasitic, and evaluative activity.[30] In virtue of its contingent character, interpretation is—as Marmor emphasizes—"only the *exception* to understanding what the law says, not the standard way of grasping its content".[31] The exception amounts, as Marmor makes clear, to a dra-

the identification of the implicated content of the communication, beyond the assertive content. See, e.g., Marmor (2014), p. 49 ff. Marmor (2011a, p. 141) makes clear that: "every communicative interaction is guided by some norms that govern the kind of contribution to the conversation that speakers are supposed to make. Without such a normative framework, typically shared by the relevant conversational parties, communication would not be possible".

[28] Marmor (2011a), pp. 145–159; Marmor (2014), pp. 118–129 and ch. 3.

[29] See Marmor (2011a), p. 10, 97–108, 136–145; Marmor (2014), p. 19 ff., 107–109.

[30] Marmor (2005), ch. 2, 10ff.; Chiassoni (2008), p. 257.

[31] Marmor (2011a), p. 137; see also 9–10: against "Dworkin's argument that we can never grasp what the law says without interpretation", so that, given the partly evaluative nature of it, "understanding what the law requires is necessarily dependent on some evaluative considerations", Marmor wishes to argue that Dworkin's conception "of what it takes to understand a legal directive is based on a misunderstanding of language and linguistic communication […] when linguistic considerations are taken into account in the appropriate ways, we will realize that interpretation

matic change in the nature of the judicial application of law. Whenever a judge finds herself in need of (properly) *interpreting* a legal provision, she finds herself in need of performing a law-creation activity. Interpretation modifies—"completes"—the law: if only temporarily, by closing up the law's loose ends as to the individual case to be adjudicated.[32]

5. The Refutation of Interpretivism Some scholars—and notably, Ronald Dworkin—endorse an interpretivist account of law. They claim interpretation, as an evaluative and constructive (purpose-imposing, point-imposing, sense-imposing, meaning-determining) activity, to be ubiquitous in law.[33] But—Marmor argues—they are wrong.[34]

On the one hand, the ubiquity claim is at odds with ("flies in the face of") everyday experience, both outside of the law, and also inside of it. There are in fact plenty of cases where judges just understand the meaning of the legal provisions relevant to deciding the cases at hand.[35]

On the other hand, philosophy of language—which is obviously, evidently, relevant in dealing with theoretical legal problems, because of the linguistic, communicative, dimension of law[36]—shows that interpretation is a marginal phenomenon as regards to linguistic communication: both in general, and as regards to legal "conversations", i.e., to the linguistic transactions in law, like those among legislators, between legislatures and people at large, or between legislatures and judges or other officials. This is the case, Marmor maintains, in force of three factors: namely, (1) the circumscribed character of contextual dependence, (2) the irreducible normativity of conversational maxims concerning the uptake of legal provisions' assertive content, and, finally, (3) the limited scope of hearers' (judges etc.) strategic, non-cooperative, behaviours.

First, the contextual dependence of the meaning of utterances in general, and of legal provisions in particular, is an intermittent property, depending on the presence

becomes the exception, not the standard form of understanding what the law says"; Marmor (2014), pp. 107–109.

[32] See, e.g., Marmor (2014), p. 74.

[33] Dworkin (1985), pp. 145–166; Dworkin (1986), Stavropoulos (2014).

[34] Marmor (2005), Marmor (2011a), chs. 4 and 6; Marmor (2014), pp. 107–110.

[35] Marmor (2011a), pp. 107–108, 138: "When we conduct an ordinary conversation, it is not our experience that every utterance by a speaker is somehow followed by a pause, when the hearer thinks about ways to interpret what has been said. Under the normal circumstance of a conversation, we just hear the utterances and thereby understand what has been said". See also Marmor (2014), pp. 107–109.

[36] Marmor (2011a), p. 136: "Philosophy of language is central to an understanding of law for a different reason. Law, as we have seen in previous chapters, consists of authoritative directives. The content of the law is tantamount to the content that is communicated by various legal authorities. Authorities communicate, of course, in a natural language. Therefore, an understanding of how linguistic communication works and, in particular, how much is actually determined by various semantic and pragmatic aspects of language, is central to an understanding of what law is"; Marmor (2014), p. 1: "Language is to lawyers what a piano is to the pianist: the tool of trade".

of context-sensitive expressions. Besides, when it in fact shows up, it does not always require interpretation. In many cases, reasonable uptake (in the form, as we have seen, of pragmatic understanding) will do.[37]

Second, the conversational maxims ruling over the understanding of the assertive content of speech acts—ordinary and legal alike—make up a "normative framework" that cannot always be at the mercy of hearers and interpreters ("open for grabs"). Indeed, if that were really the case, communication would not be possible (the "parties to a conversation could not possibly engage in a communicative interaction").[38]

Third, and finally, the Judge-Legislature conversation (JLC) is, to be sure, characterized by the possibility that judges adopt a "noncooperative", "strategic", attitude towards legislation. However, noncooperative, strategic behaviours are to be regarded as phenomena at the margins of legal experience. They concern the area of implicit law: the content of positive law "that has only been implicated, but not actually asserted by the law".[39]

The five theses above should make clear why pragmatic formalism, in so far as it is also a theory of judicial interpretation, features as an instance of *limited cognitivism*.

To begin with—and this is the first point it is worthwhile emphasizing—it maintains that judicial interpretation—broadly conceived as the process leading to the identification of the meaning of a given legal provision in view of deciding a lawsuit—sometimes is just a matter of knowledge, sometimes is, instead, a matter of evaluation and law-creation. The former situation occurs whenever it simply amounts to the reasonable uptake (understanding) of the relevant legal texts. The latter situation occurs instead whenever, due either to the semantic indeterminacy of the legal provision (because of vagueness or ambiguity), or to other problems like the presence of gaps, normative conflicts or uncertainties about pragmatic implicatures, legal interpretation proper must be performed.

Furthermore—and this is the second point it is worthwhile emphasizing—in so maintaining, pragmatic formalism exhibits a tacit commitment to a view that might be dubbed "the objective code view". Indeed, it makes—sometimes, to be sure, tacitly—the following claims:

a. There is, in any legal order whatsoever, an objective interpretive code (a discrete set of interpretive rules), endowed with strict normativity (i.e., that hearers assume to be strictly binding), which prescribes using as the paramount transla-

[37] Pragmatic formalism adheres accordingly to one of the central tenets of literalism: see Chap. 4, Sect. 4.3.1, above.

[38] Marmor (2011a), p. 141.

[39] Marmor (2011b), pp. 83–104; Marmor (2014), pp. 35–36, 43–59; "The essential feature of strategic speech – as I will use the term here – is that the speaker strives to gain some advantage by implicating more (or less) than he would be willing to make explicit […] Hearers can be similarly situated in not being willing to fully acknowledge the uptake of content that goes beyond what is explicitly asserted" (Marmor 2014, pp. 45–59).

tion rule for legal provisions the literal meaning rule, pointing to the syntactic and semantic rules of the natural language to which the legal provisions belong.

b. When enrichment, and pragmatic understanding, become necessary, the literal meaning rule must be complemented by a likewise objective set of "conversational maxims", which, by the way, are the same maxims that, according to Grice, rule over ordinary conversations.[40]
c. The integrated set (literal meaning rule plus conversational maxims), however, may prove inefficient as a guide to the assertive or to the implicated content of the legal provisions.
d. When this happens, interpreters who put up with such inefficiencies really do not resort to some further set of interpretive rules; they do not follow anymore any rule; rather, they exercise an interpretive discretionary power in accordance with a default rule of the objective code.[41]

Now, limited cognitivism and the objective code view are disputable as genuinely descriptive, and true, claims about the phenomenon of legal (and judicial) interpretation. As we shall see in moment, pragmatic realism provides sound argument for such conclusion.

6.5 Pragmatic Realism: The Critical Side

Pragmatic realism is a non-cognitivist theory of legal (and judicial) interpretation, claiming that, whenever a judge, a jurist or a lawyer-at-large determines the meaning of some legal provision to the practical purpose of solving a legal problem "correctly" (or showing how it should be solved, to solve it "correctly"), the activity performed never amounts to an act of cognition (like Marmor's reasonable uptake); contrariwise, it always involves a fundamental practical choice about the "correct" interpretive code and the "correct" interpretive resources to be used, and such a

[40] Following Grice (1989), ordinary conversations are ruled by a "principle of cooperation" (roughly: "Make your contribution to the conversation adequate to the purpose and the stage of the linguistic interaction you are engaged in") and four related groups of more specific conversational maxims. The *maxims of quality* require each participant's contribution to the conversation to be qualitatively adequate: e.g., no statements that are known to be false or without adequate justificatory support are to be made. The maxims of quantity require each participant's contribution to the conversation to be quantitatively adequate: one must avoid saying more or less than is required by the stage of the conversation. The maxims of relation require each participant's contribution to the conversation to be relevant in content: one must avoid saying things that are not pertinent in relation to the topic of the on-going conversation. The maxims of manners require each participant's contribution to the conversation to consist in clear and ordered sentences.

[41] The default rule, for instance, may run as follows: "Whenever linguistic rules and the accepted maxims of legal conversation do not make it possible to identify a determinate assertive content for the legal provision at hand, make up the solution that best fits with the overall purpose of law application". On default interpretive rules, see Chap. 3, Sect. 3.4, above.

choice usually depends, in turn, on the interpreter's own normative vision (legal ideology, *Rechtsanschauung*) about her legal order and the law in general.[42]

From the vantage point of pragmatic realism, pragmatic formalism appears to be wrong and misleading as a descriptive, explanatory theory of legal (and judicial) interpretation. Five arguments support this conclusion. The first, second, and third argument point to the regular unavoidable ("necessary") presence of (constructive) interpretation well beyond the cases Marmor is disposed to concede (Sects. 6.5.2–6.5.4 below). The fourth and fifth arguments (Sects. 6.5.5 and 6.5.6 below) bring to the fore the self-defeating character of pragmatic formalism as a theory of law's indeterminacy. All arguments suggest that, if we take the pragmatic perspective seriously, the understanding-interpretation picture of legal (and judicial) interpretation should be abandoned.

6.5.1 Pragmatics and the Theory of Legal Interpretation

As a branch of semiotics and the philosophy of language, pragmatics is the theory of language from the standpoint of language users (speakers, hearers, writers, readers, authors, interpreters, senders, addressees, etc.). In its Gricean cast, pragmatics studies linguistic interactions ("conversations") in view of identifying the rules ("conversational principles and maxims") that characterize the several kinds of conversation afoot.[43]

Likewise, legal pragmatics is the theory of legal language from the standpoint of its users: legislators, legislatures, judges, officials, jurists, lawyers, people at large. In a Gricean-like cast, legal pragmatics studies legal "conversations" in view of identifying the conversational principles and maxims that single out several kinds of language games in law, marking each one's peculiarities.

What does legal pragmatics suggest about that key institutional "conversation" that is the "conversation" between judges and legislature (though, clearly, speaking of "conversation" here is talking metaphor)?

Pragmatic formalism, as we have seen, maintains the judges-legislature conversation (JLC) to be a special case of ordinary, cooperative, information conveying conversation (OC). It claims, as a consequence, that, like in any OC, context (shared contextual knowledge) and shared conversational maxims also intervene in JLC to help putting up with two problems. First, in order to saturate ("enrich") the semantic content of context-sensitive legal provisions, in the rare cases where this may be needed; second, in order to identify legal implicatures, that is to say, the implicated content of the legislative or constitutional communication. According to pragmatic formalism, in both situations the relevant conversational maxims are the maxims of

[42] I take the forerunner of pragmatic realism to be the Danish legal theorist Alf Ross (see Ross 1958, ch. IV). On pragmatic realism, see also Chap. 3, Sect. 3.2.2, above.

[43] On Gricean pragmatics and legal interpretation see Chap. 3 Sects. 3.5 and 3.6 above.

OC.[44] It concedes, nonetheless, that OC maxims (in particular, the principle of communicative cooperation) are liable to be defeated by the strategic, noncooperative, purposes and behaviours of the players, emphasizing that it is precisely this possibility that makes of the JLC a special case of OC.[45]

One point must be emphasized. Pragmatic formalism's view of the JLC as a special case of OC is instrumental to defending three inter-related theses about positive law in general:

First, the no-ubiquity of interpretation thesis, or the idea that interpretation is something exceptional also within the law (see Sect. 6.4 above).

Second, the idea that the content of the law—what the law is, what the law prescribes –, so far as written law is concerned, is tantamount to the (definite, determinate) linguistic meaning (semantic content or enriched assertive content) of legal provisions, plus the implicit content that can be inferred from the linguistic meaning.

Third, the idea the content of the law to be something that can simply be grasped by means of linguistic understanding (reasonable uptake), unless some crisis in communication occurs.[46]

The three theses, notice, do not only concern legal interpretation, being rather the cornerstones of a conventionalist positivism theory of law. For this reason, if pragmatic formalism succeeds in showing that they find support in philosophy of language and pragmatics, this would make the case for conventionalist positivism stronger.

From the standpoint of pragmatic realism, a few critical remarks are in order, though.

First, as pragmatic formalism concedes, there is not just one philosophy of language, not just one pragmatics, out there, telling good legal theories from bad ones. There are, instead, several and contrasting philosophies of language and pragmatics, which may bring support to a different view as to the JLC.[47]

Second, the business of the several philosophies of language and pragmatics is providing true, explanatory accounts of (ordinary) language and discourse. Can they really provide any support to questionable theories about "what the law is", like, e.g., pragmatic formalism's conventionalist legal positivism?[48]

Third, suppose we accept the philosophy of language and pragmatics pragmatic formalism has opted for. Does such a philosophical-linguistic outlook really support the three theses about the law I have listed above? Does it support, in particular, the

---

[44] On conversational maxims, see footnote 40 above.

[45] Marmor (2011b), pp. 83–102; Marmor (2014), pp. 35–59.

[46] The first and third ideas correspond to the interpretation-as-exception thesis and the refutation of interpretivism thesis: see Sect. 6.3 above.

[47] Marmor (2014), p. 19, 20. Think at the difference between traditional or Gricean pragmatics, on the one hand, and anti-literalist, contextualist pragmatics, on the other. See Chap. 4, Sects. 4.3 and 4.4, above.

[48] The self-delusion of thinking the philosophy of language to be capable of solving momentous problems in legal theory is analysed by Bix (2003).

no-ubiquity of interpretation thesis, which is the pillar of pragmatic formalism's theory of legal (and judicial) interpretation?

To the present purpose, only the last question matters, and will be considered. Now, that question commands a negative answer. It can be argued that, from the standpoint of the very pragmatic theory of language adopted by pragmatic formalism, the JLC is to be regarded as *a constructive interpretation game* (though not necessarily of the Dworkinian sort), *which judges* (together with lawyers and jurists) *play with the dummy* (that is to say, the legislature, who provides the legal provisions), *by means of a shared set of interpretive tools*, which tools they may select, combine, arrange, precisify, modify, revise, integrate, etc., according to the (spiritual or material) interests they happen to pursue. There is something of a paradox here: pragmatic formalism purports to refute interpretivism (see Sect. 6.4 above), but it cannot avoid running into it, though unwarily.

In the following, as anticipated, I will bring to the fore a few pieces of incoherence and some self-defeating points in pragmatic formalism. These, in turn, represent as many concessions to the ubiquity of (constructive) interpretation and non-cognitivism.

6.5.2 The Interpretive Relevance of Linguistic Meaning

A first flaw—a flaw of incoherence—that, from the standpoint of pragmatic realism, casts a dim light on pragmatic formalism shows up in the way it deals with the interpretive relevance of linguistic meaning (semantic content), on the one hand, and the interpretive relevance of lawgiver's intent, on the other.

Pragmatic formalism presents the interpretive relevance to law of the semantic content of legal provisions as a matter of course. That would be so, apparently, because legal provisions are sentences expressed in a natural language, and, as a consequence, they cannot but share in the fate of any natural language expression.[49]

Contrariwise, so far as legislative or framers' intent is concerned, pragmatic formalism agrees that Dworkin is right; the interpretive relevance of legislative or framers' intent, namely, its importance in view of a legally correct reading of legal provisions, depends on evaluative considerations:

> A very similar line of reasoning applies to the possible roles of intention of legislatures in the interpretation of statutes and the possible role of the framers' intentions in the context of constitutional interpretation. *Whether it makes sense to defer to such intentions must also*

[49] See, e.g., Marmor (2011a), pp. 138–139: "It is a very familiar aspect of natural language that the content communicated by a speaker is often partly determined by certain contextual and normative factors. These contextual and normative determinates of linguistic contents are called the *pragmatic* aspects of language. In other words, it is a well-recognized fact that semantics and syntax (meaning) are essential vehicles for conveying communicative content, but the content that is actually communicated is often partly determined by various pragmatic factors".

> *depend on a theoretical argument about where value lies in the relevant genre*, namely, the authority of legislation or the authority and legitimacy of a constitution.
>
> *Thus the conclusion so far is that the author's-intention model of interpretation only makes sense as an instance or application of the constructive [interpretation] model.*[50]

Now, such an asymmetric treatment seems unjustified from a theoretical standpoint. If deference to legislative or framers' intent depends on some evaluative, "theoretical argument" about authority and legitimacy, and is the outcome of a piece of constructive interpretation, why deference to semantic content (and literal meaning rule) should, instead, be something evaluation-free, something, so to speak, that stands *before* and *above* of any evaluation, and therefore outside of constructive interpretation?

Indeed, one may argue, the very claim according to which the interpretive value of the semantic content of legal provisions would be "above" and "outside" of the province of evaluative, theoretical argument, is not in itself an evaluative claim, one depending on some "theoretical argument" and some piece of constructive interpretation? How can we establish, as we must in fact do, the legal relevance of some interpretive resource (be it literal meaning, legislative intent, the purpose of the law, consistency with the constitution, etc.) *without* engaging in an evaluative "theoretical" argument? How can we do that, without taking side, and selecting (what we are ready to defend as) the "legally correct" translation rules (interpretive canons, methods, rules, directives) and the "legally correct" resources for reading the law "correctly"?[51]

6.5.3 *Art, Law and Ordinary Conversation*

The preceding argument, from the unwarranted asymmetric treatment of literal meaning and legislative intent, ended with a few rhetorical questions.

To these questions pragmatic formalism provides a reply: the law—so the argument goes—is, by its very nature, closer to ordinary conversation, than, say, to art, where constructive interpretation and evaluations are indeed ubiquitous. It is worthwhile quoting the passage where Marmor presents it:

> A work of art is not intended to convey a determinate communicative content that can simply be understood (or misunderstood); it is created with an intention to be somewhat indeterminate in content, or ambiguous in various ways, open to various interpretations. None

[50] Marmor (2011a), p. 105, italics added.

[51] There is indeed a simple test supporting the critique the present argument makes. If we ask why linguistic meaning should have an evident pride of place among interpretive resources, why the literal rule should have an evident pride of place among translation rule, we are likely to get the answer that it is so because the legislature evidently commands respect, and respect for the legislature requires reading legal provisions according to their literal, linguistic meaning. Such an answer, however, clearly depends on a piece of constructive interpretation as to the proper value, sense or point of legislation.

> of this, however, applies to law. In fact, art and law could not be less similar in this respect. Legal instructions are meant to generate concrete results, providing people with particular reasons for action, thus aiming to affect our conduct in some specified ways. The level of specification may vary, of course; some laws are very specific, instructing specific modes of conduct or avoidance of them, while others are much more general. And then, the more general the legal norm is, the more likely it is that circumstances will arise where interpretation is called for. *But, generally speaking, it is not in the nature of law, as it is in the nature of art, to become a cultural object that is detached from the specific communicative content it is meant to convey. Art is there to be interpreted; law is there to be acted upon.*
>
> Are there some other features unique to law that would make it the case that interpretation is always called for?.[52]

The argument looks convincing. It must nonetheless be rejected. Indeed, there is in fact something of a paradox in it. The above defence of the idea of law as being by its very nature unfit to interpretation has the unmistakable flavour of a piece of constructive interpretation.

First, in the passage just quoted, where Marmor establishes the essential character (the nature, the point, the purpose) of (the practice of) law, and contrasts it with the essential character of art, Marmor is clearly performing an act that, in Dworkin's and Marmor's own terms, qualifies as a piece of constructive interpretation. Indeed, Marmor is determining what is the point, the purpose, the essential character of law, and contrasts it with the (assumed) point, purpose, essential character of art.

Second, suppose Marmor retorts that such presumed "constructive interpretation" of the nature (point, purpose, essence) of law is really no interpretation at all, being rather the ascertainment of something that is altogether "evident" to everybody. Who would dare claiming that the laws are made to the purpose of being open to interpretations? Who would deny that the laws are done to the purpose of "generating concrete results", of "guiding behaviours", of "being acted upon"? Perhaps, Marmor is right; nobody could deny such platitudes. Unfortunately, however, they are perfectly empty; and that explains why they are so "evident" and "undeniable". As a consequence, once we have accepted this platitudinous view about the law (about its evident nature, essence, purpose, point), we still have to solve momentous problems: what does it mean that the law's purpose is "generating concrete results"? How the "guiding behaviours" purpose is to be understood and carried out? How the "acting upon" purpose is, again, to be understood, and, if I may say so, acted upon? If "the purpose" of the law is "generating concrete results", what about the very abstract, generic, and indeterminate constitutional clauses we commonly find in constitutional charters? Are they *not* law? All these questions, and many more that could be raised, are not open for evaluation-free, practical-commitment-free, answers. Marmor tries to throw constructive interpretation out of the window of the "Art *v* Law" divide. However, it always comes back. This happens, unavoidably, as soon as the empty platitudes, which would make of law a very different enterprise from art, must be set to work.

[52] Marmor (2011a), p. 143.

Third, the whole of Marmor's argument has an unmistakable scent of naturalistic fallacy. Indeed, Marmor pretends to derive, from the assumedly evident nature of law, practical consequences as to the (proper) way of dealing with law by people who have to determine the meaning of legal provisions and comply with them.

6.5.4 Which Easiness Easy Cases?

Another weak point in pragmatic formalism's defence of the understanding-interpretation divide, has to do with its theory of easy cases. Marmor cites easy cases, an evident phenomenon in everyday legal reality, as witnesses in favor:

> the truth is that both the laymen's picture of how determinate the law is, and the law students' impression of how indeterminate it is, are distorted. The law is much less clear than people tend to think, but it is much more clear than law students are led to believe, because they spend most of their studies focusing on the difficult or problematic cases that tend to reach the appellate courts.[53]

When the law is clear, so the argument goes, there is no need for interpretation. The phenomenon of clarity would show: first, that interpretation—and the evaluations going along with it—is not a ubiquitous, but, rather, a circumscribed, contingent, phenomenon in law; second, that there are cases where judges simply find the law, by means of understanding or reasonable uptake, and do not need to make it.

The argument seems invincible. And so has appeared to many scholars. Unfortunately, the impression is wrong. Indeed, the notion of easy case Marmor employs is questionable. Marmor characterizes an "easy case" as follows:

> An "easy case" [...] means that the relevant legal norm can simply be understood, and applied to the particular case without the mediation of the interpretation of the norm; we just understand what the law says, and know that it applies, or not, to the case at hand.[54]

Marmor's concept of an easy case is open to different readings. In fact, a legal provision (in Marmor's terms: a "legal norm") "can" make the case at hand "easy", i.e., can simply "be understood and applied", in no less than three different ways. It can have in fact the property of *linguistic easiness*, or, rather, of *methodological easiness*, or, else, of *ideological easiness*.

Linguistic Easiness A case is linguistically easy, if, and only if, by means of a simple linguistic understanding (reasonable uptake), the relevant legal provision is capable of providing the judge with a legal norm, corresponding to its semantic content or literal meaning, under which the individual case at hand clearly can, or cannot, be subsumed.

---

[53] Marmor (2011a), p. 138.

[54] Marmor (2005), p. 97.

Methodological Easiness A case is methodologically easy, if, and only if, when a judge provides a linguistic reading of the relevant legal provision, and applies the semantic content (literal meaning) so identified to the case at hand, her way of proceeding is fully justified according to an interpretive code the judge may invoke as the "proper" or "correct" code to be used.

Notice that from the perspective of this notion of an easy case, stopping at the linguistic understanding of a legal provision is not only a linguistically correct move; it is also a methodologically correct move, that is to say, one that is allowed for, and justified by, the rules of the interpretive code the judge deems proper ("correct", "right") to use.

Such a code, if we look at contemporary legal orders and cultures, would usually establish a defeasible presumption of legal correctness in favour of the linguistic meaning of legal provisions: one that can be defeated where the linguistic meaning is either indeterminate, or, in any case, legally "incorrect", "inappropriate", "inadequate", etc.

One point must be emphasized. The outcome of the judicial activity in a methodologically easy case is, by hypothesis, tantamount to the semantic content of the relevant legal provision. Such an outcome, however, does not depend on linguistic understanding *only*. On the contrary, it also depends on a reflexive activity, by means of which the judge considers whether staying with the semantic content of a legal provision is methodologically justified, or not. This reflexive activity, which goes beyond linguistic understanding, is part of what, in legal discourse, usually goes under the name of "interpretation".

Ideological Easiness A case is ideologically easy, if, and only if, when a judge provides a linguistic reading of the relevant legal provision, and applies the semantic content (literal meaning) so identified to the case at hand, her way of proceeding will be praised as endowed with substantial value ("reasonable", "good", "proper", fully "justified", "correct", etc.) by fellow judges, competent jurists, society-at-large, etc.

Notice that, from the perspective of this notion of an easy case, stopping at the linguistic understanding of a legal provision is not only a linguistically correct move. It is also a course of action that is in tune with (allowed, approved, justified by) the normative, ideological, axiological, attitudes of the generality of the relevant interpretive community, the public opinion, etc. Here again, the judge who applies a legal provision according to its semantic content does not only perform the supposedly un-reflexive activity of linguistic understanding. She also performs the reflexive activity of considering the ideological viability of that semantic content as the legally correct meaning of the legal provision at hand. This reflexive activity is, again, what in legal discourse is usually captured by the term "interpretation".

The different notions of easy case I have just brought to the light suggest a few considerations.

1. Marmor's notion of an easy case apparently mirrors the first view; it makes the easiness of a case to be a purely linguistic property, fully independent from interpretive methods and legal (and social) ideologies.
2. These latter ingredients, however, are a substantive part of the adjudication business, at least in our present legal cultures. As Frederick Schauer points out, according to juristic commonsense an easy case is not simply a linguistically clear case. It is, rather, a *linguistically clear* and *substantially sensible* case: that is to say, it is a case where the linguistically clear meaning of the relevant legal provision is, *at the same time*, not at odds with purpose, not at odds with superior legal principles, not at odds with morality, justice and convenience.[55]
3. As a consequence, Marmor's notion of an easy case flies in the face of juristic commonsense. What is more, contrary to Marmor's opinion, juristic commonsense suggests judicial interpretation to be at work *also* when an easy case is being decided. So far as judges are concerned, the identification of the general norm to be applied to a case at hand never is just the outcome of an un-reflexive process of linguistic understanding.[56] Marmor's conceptual framework however, due to its commitment to a sharp divide between understanding (reasonable uptake) and interpretation (proper), is not even equipped to capture this aspect of adjudication. In fact, it rules it out altogether from its account.

6.5.5 The Sting of Normative Conflicts

Pragmatic formalism uses the term "interpretation" broadly, to refer to the (contingent, marginal) activity that is needed for dealing with whatever sort of indeterminacy may upset the law.[57] Normative conflicts (antinomies), as we have seen, are listed among the situations calling for interpretation, together with gaps, vagueness, ambiguity, and pragmatic uncertainties (see Sect. 6.4, point 3, above).

From the standpoint of pragmatic realism, though, the pragmatic formalist's account of normative conflicts—as set forth by Marmor[58]—presents a few questionable points.

First, Marmor claims interpretation to be needed to cope with antinomies. In so claiming, however, he does not notice that, as he conceives of them, they are cases of *gap*. Indeed, he maintains that, whenever a determinate and pre-established conflict-solving criterion is available, there is really no conflict afoot: trousers have no holes, insofar as there are tailors capable of putting up with them!

---

[55] See Schauer (1984), p. 399, 414–423, 430–31; see also Dascal and Wróblewski (1988), pp. 203–224.

[56] Perhaps, that may be the case with ordinary people, but that's another story, to be carefully considered.

[57] Marmor (2011a), p. 145; Marmor (2014), pp. 107–109.

[58] Marmor (2011a), pp. 145–146; Marmor (2014), pp. 107–109, 118–120.

Second, Marmor seems to overlook that normative conflicts are interpretation-dependent, in the common juristic sense of "interpretation". In fact, no conflict can be *identified* unless on the basis of some previously selected interpretive code: be it even the "simple linguistic understanding", or "reasonable uptake", code that Marmor endorses.

Third, Marmor seems to overlook that the judges' preoccupation with normative conflicts, which Marmor correctly takes into account, suggests that there is always something more than simple linguistic understanding behind the judicial application of law. It suggests, more precisely, that judicial interpretation, in the common juristic sense of a reflexive and evaluative activity, is at work even when the relevant legal provision has a clear and determinate semantic content that can be identified by means of linguistic understanding. This is so because, once the semantic content of a legal provision has been identified, once the "literal" norm has been grasped, before applying it to the case at hand it must be evaluated in relation to other relevant norms of the system, in order to "see" whether any normative conflict is afoot. This consideration suggests that Marmor's dualistic, reasonable uptake-interpretation structural model of the judicial identification of the normative premises of judicial reasoning must be abandoned, and replaced by a model where interpretation is general. The point deserves a bit more of elaboration.

The judicial application of a legal norm to an individual case at hand presupposes that the norm to be applied has been previously identified. If the norm is a statutory norm, the starting point for its identification consists in identifying the text of the norm: the statutory clause, the legal provision of which the norm is, generally speaking, the meaning. This is something Marmor does not pay attention to, taking this preliminary activity for granted. His reasonable uptake-interpretation dualistic model encompasses three stages, as we have seen (see Sect. 6.4 above): the semantic understanding stage, the pragmatic understanding stage, and, finally and eventually, the interpretation stage. The first stage is devoted to the semantic understanding of the legal provision at hand, and represents, as we have seen, a necessary step. If the outcome is a clear semantic content, which is immediately applicable to the case at hand, the identification process is over. It may happen, however, that the semantic content needs to be pragmatically saturated (enriched). The judge moves then to the second stage. Here a process of pragmatic understanding is performed, which, by the way, may also cast light upon the implicit component of the full communicative content of the legal provision (as the output of a legislative speech act). It may happen, however, that reasonable (semantic and pragmatic) uptake does not lead to one determinate result: either in itself, or in relation to the individual case at hand. In that event, a third stage is needed. This is the stage of interpretation proper, where, fatally, judicial interpretation must be guided by some normative view about the proper allocation of power between judiciary and legislature.[59]

Now, it should be apparent why Marmor's theory of normative conflicts is incoherent with Marmor's reasonable uptake-interpretation dualistic structural model. Indeed, we may query, how do judges come to "know" that a certain semantic con-

[59] Marmor (2014), pp. 107–109.

tent is at odds with some other, superior, norms of the system? How do they proceed to identify normative conflicts, if any, calling for interpretation (in Marmor's sense)? Clearly, that would be altogether *impossible* if the judges just stayed with the simple linguistic understanding of isolated legal provisions. Normative conflicts cannot be identified outside of a systemic, holistic, consideration of law. This, in turn, makes the idea that the application of law depends, in many cases, just on a piece of linguistic understanding, a sheer illusion.

6.5.6 The Sting of Pragmatic Indeterminacies

Pragmatic indeterminacies are situations of context-dependent uncertainty about the full communicative content of a legislative or constitutional provision. Pragmatic formalism pays particular attention to two varieties of pragmatic indeterminacy: the mismatch problem (as I shall call it) and the legal implicatures problem. From the standpoint of pragmatic realism it can be argued that, while dealing with both problems, pragmatic formalism in fact endorses an interpretivist stance, which flies in the face of the rigorous reasonable uptake-interpretation model it avowedly stands for.

6.5.6.1 Mismatch Problems

A mismatch problem arises any time "what the words of the law say" apparently does not correspond to "what the law says (means, asserts)".[60] It is, in other words, a problem of mismatch between the semantic content (sentence meaning) and the assertive content (author's intended meaning) of a legal provision.

Marmor articulates his way out from such problems in a passage that is worthwhile quoting:

> Does it happen in the legal context that the law asserts something different from what it says? It could happen, but not very frequently. First, lawmakers would certainly try to avoid this since it would be too easy to misunderstand what they meant. Second, in the legal context, we would normally lack sufficiently rich contextual background to enable the conclusion that what the law asserts is obviously not what it says. Consider, once again, the "no vehicles are allowed in the park" rule. Suppose, for example, that the legislature of this rule had taken it for granted that only motor vehicles are meant here and that is the content it intended to assert. One can imagine some circumstances in which it would be obvious that this is the case, but those would have to be pretty special circumstances, knowledge of which is shared by all parties concerned. We can imagine, for example, that the "no vehicles in the park" is enacted as a response to specific complaints about pollution, that this is known to be the case, and maybe forms part of a larger legislative measure that curbs motor

[60] Marmor (2014), p. 28.

> vehicle pollution—then, yes, perhaps it is obvious that the ordinance is confined to motor vehicles. Otherwise, it is likely to remain an open question.[61]

The passage, notice, provides further evidence for concluding that a purely linguistic notion of an easy case and the reasonable uptake-interpretation dualistic structural model of the judicial identification of the normative premise are wrong, since they provide theoretically bad devices to cope with the reality of judicial application of law. A couple of remarks are in order.

1. Though we may find the cooperative conversation metaphor appealing, in fact a judge is *not* engaged in a conversation with the legislature: they are not together in the same place, chatting about the law to be applied, nor are they connecting by phone or any other long-distance communication device; they cannot talk to each other; they do not even know each other. As a consequence, how can a judge even come to think at a mismatch between the semantic content and the assertive content of a piece of legislation, unless she goes beyond both linguistic understanding, and the OC notion of a conversational context, to venture into the province of juristic theories, legal ideologies, legal policy, and legal interpretation (in the juristic commonsense acceptation)?
2. Once she has passed that border, she will find herself into another world. Here, the mismatch problem is evocated any time there are good axiological reasons for getting rid of the literal meaning of the legal provision at hand, and replace it with a wider or a narrower meaning, considered the "legally correct" one. Here, the technique of corrective interpretation is afoot, with the twin maxims "The law has said more than it wanted to say" (*lex magis dixit quam voluit*), and "The law has said less than it wanted to say" (*lex minus dixit quam voluit*). Here, to conclude, the very identification of a mismatch problem is not for reasonable uptake; it necessarily depends on some piece of holistic and purposive interpretation. It is not a matter of knowledge; it is, rather, a matter of interpretive politics.

6.5.6.2 Legal Implicatures Problems

A problem of legal implicature arises whenever there is uncertainty about the implicated content of a legislative or constitutional speech act. Suppose the legislature enacts a law saying "All X ought to f, unless F, G, or H". According to Marmor, from the standpoint of the maxims of OC (in particular, the maxims of quantity[62]), such a piece of legislation has a clear conversational implicature: it implies, conversationally, that *only if* F, G, or H the X have *not* the duty to f. It does often happen, however, that courts do not read legal implicatures that way; that, contrariwise, they do not (want to) see the implicature, and read instead a legal provision like that as providing an incomplete, open list of exceptions.

---

[61] Marmor (2011a), pp. 150–151.

[62] See footnote 40, above.

> The judicial decision in *Holy Trinity* is a case in point. To be sure, the fact that judges tend to ignore these kind of implicatures does not mean that the implicature is not there; judges tend to ignore them because they are skeptical, and perhaps rightly so, of a legislature's ability to determine in advance all the possible justified exceptions to the general norm enacted. But again, this testifies to the fact that the discourse between the legislature and the courts is not necessarily a cooperative business, and that the division of labour between legislatures and courts is a morally-politically contentious issue.[63]

This is a very telling passage. In his making reference to the noncooperative, strategic side of JLC, Marmor admits that the JLC is a very different sort of "conversation" from OC. He seems to think, however, as we have seen (Sect. 5.4 above), that the province of strategic behaviours and "morally-politically contentious issues" about the division of labour between courts and legislature, the province where the JLC is not cooperative, only, or mainly, concerns the identification of the legal implicatures of the asserted content of legal provisions. But why should that be the case? Why a noncooperative attitude on the part of the judges could not also affect the identification of legal provisions' asserted contents? Marmor does not see, apparently, that his admission about a noncooperative dimension in the JLC is tantamount to admitting that, after all, interpretivism is right. Interpretation—in the form of a reflexive and evaluative activity concerning the "legally correct" meaning and the "legally correct" implicatures of an enacted provision—is general (ubiquitous) all over the daily working of legal orders.[64]

6.6 Pragmatic Realism: The Proposal Side

The failure of pragmatic formalism is the failure of a theory of legal (and judicial) interpretation, centred on the distinction between the heterogeneous activities of understanding (reasonable uptake) and interpretation (proper),[65] which has been worked out as a derivative product of a communication model of legislation borrowed from philosophy of language and Gricean pragmatics.[66]

Pragmatic realism can be characterized, contrariwise and in very rough terms, as the combination of pragmatics (a pragmatic perspective on legal language and interpretation) with interpretivism (the idea of the ubiquity of interpretation, as a value-laden, reflexive, decisional activity, in the everyday working of legal orders).

I have already offered an account of pragmatic realism as an alternative view to semantic formalism.[67] In the following, I will provide a complementary outline of

---

[63] Marmor (2008), p. 30.

[64] This conclusion finds support in many passages by Marmor: see, e.g., Marmor (2011a), p. 151, 154, 157; Marmor (2014), chs. 5–6. In the present chapter, Marmor deals with constitutional interpretation in a thoroughly interpretivist way.

[65] What I have called "the dualistic structural model reasonable uptake-interpretation": Sects. 6.4 and 6.5 above.

[66] See Sects. 6.4 and 6.5 above; Marmor (2014), pp. 11–12.

[67] See Chap. 4, Sects. 4.2 and 4.4, above.

its major features and claims, by way of a comparison with pragmatic formalism, and focussing, in particular, on its view about judicial interpretation.

1. Two Views About the Judge-Interpreter In the background of pragmatic realism (which is a non-cognitivist theory) and pragmatic formalism (which is a limited cognitivism theory), there are two alternative views of the judge-interpreter.

According to pragmatic formalism, as we have seen, the judge-interpreter proceeds in the ordinary conversation way through linguistic "understanding" ("reasonable uptake") of legal provisions; and if, and only if, something goes wrong, if, and only if, some drawback shows up (in the form of vagueness, ambiguity, gaps, antinomies, etc.), she turns to the reflexive, speculative attitude inherent to "interpretation". The judge-interpreter, here, is an *intermittent speculator*.

According to pragmatic realism, on the contrary, every activity concerning the determination of the meaning of a legal text to be applied to a case at hand, be it understanding or interpretation proper, is performed in the shadow of a reflexive, speculative, background attitude. The judge-interpreter, here, is a *continuous speculator*. Linguistic understanding, so far as it goes, is never so-to-speak a purely spontaneous undertaking; it occurs instead, always by design. When a judge stays with the semantic meaning of a legal provision, she never simply "understands" it, but always also *decides* to stay with her understanding, if sufficient systemic, holistic, reasons make that course of action legally justified. This design dimension of understanding, which in hermeneutical theory is captured by the idea of the "postulate of reflexivity" ruling over the "pre-comprehension - text" hermeneutic circle, is totally overlooked by pragmatic formalism.

2. Two Views About the Pragmatic Model of the Interaction Between Judges and Legislatures (the "Judges-Legislature Conversation") Pragmatic formalism, as we have seen, is committed to a communication model of the JLC, one that presents such a "conversation" as basically of the same sort as any ordinary conversation, with strategic behaviours showing up at the edges where problems of legal implicatures arise (see Sects. 6.4 and 6.5.6 above).

Pragmatic realism maintains, contrariwise, that, if our business is working out a (genuine) general theory of legal (and judicial) interpretation, no definite pragmatic model about the JLC can be singled out as theoretically correct *a priori*, or by making an appeal to "the (very) nature of linguistic communication". That would be a Procrustean move, fatally saddled with (hidden) ideological commitments.

Pragmatic realism claims, furthermore, that, if we cast a cold glance on the legal experience of contemporary municipal legal orders, the pragmatic model of JLC that seems most in tune with it is something like a model informed by a different account of the "levels of meaning" of legal provisions, a different account of the basic "ingredients" of the JLC, and, from the standpoint of its "maxims", by the Principle of Prudent Interpretation and a few related maxims, as we shall see in a moment (see points 3, 4, and 5 below).

3. The Three Levels of Meaning of Legal Provisions Pragmatic formalism singles out, as we have seen, three levels, and sorts, of meaning in relation to any legal provision: the linguistic or semantic meaning, the speaker's explicit meaning (assertive content), and the speaker's implicit meaning (see Sects. 6.4 and 6.5.5 above).

From the standpoint of pragmatic realism as a theory of judicial interpretation, on the contrary, the proper way of accounting for the several levels of meaning of any given legal provision requires a different conceptual and terminological apparatus. This singles out (a) sentence meaning, (b) explicit systemic meaning, and (c) implicit systemic meaning.

Sentence meaning is the literal, conventional, a-contextual meaning, amounting to the purely semantic content of a legal provision.

Explicit systemic meaning is the meaning (assertive content, prescriptive content) of a legal provision, from the standpoint of the legal system and the proper way of interpreting its provisions. Explicit systemic meaning can be different from sentence meaning. According to the views that may be extant in a legal culture, explicit systemic meaning can be tantamount to the meaning corresponding to the legislature's ("the speaker's") intent. But that is a wholly contingent matter.

Implicit systemic meaning, finally, is the meaning or communicative content that is implicated by the explicit systemic meaning of a legal provision on the basis of "proper" integration rules. These rules, so far as the law is concerned, typically include, as we have seen, the *integration rules* of analogical reasoning, *a fortiori* reasoning, *a contrario* or *e silentio* reasoning, naturalistic reasoning, and reasoning from legal (constitutional, fundamental, general) principles.[68]

4. The Peculiarities of the Judges-Legislature Conversation Pragmatic formalism, as we have seen, adopts a Gricean legal pragmatics featuring the JLC as a sort of ordinary conversation ruled by Gricean maxims, with strategic behaviours at the margins (see Sects. 6.4 and 6.5.6 above).

Pragmatic realism considers the "Gricean project" a valuable contribution to the understanding of the JLC, insofar as it requires inquiring on, and reconstructing, the principle and maxims that rule upon it. It maintains, however, a fresh enquiry to be needed: one that, so far as the JLC is concerned, requires throwing the conversational metaphor overboard.

From the standpoint of pragmatic realism, three properties of the JLC must be emphasized, which make of it a very far cry from OC.

First, the JLC is a "conversation" with a dummy, the legislature, which cannot reply, at least not immediately. A new piece of legislation is needed, either to cancel any "wrong" judicial interpretation of a previous piece of legislation, or to "put the mutinous judiciary to its place". Furthermore, such a new law needs in turn to be interpreted, and its legal effects usually depend on a variety of factors, including, e.g., the principle against *ex post facto* laws. This suggests that the JLC really is an interpretive game that judges play with authoritative texts, by means of interpretive

[68] On integration rules, see Chap. 2, Sects. 2.2.2.2, Chap. 5, Sect. 5.2, above.

codes, within the contingent variable limits set by the public opinion and the ideologies and methodologies at work in the legal and political culture of the day.

Second, the JLC is an interpretive game where judges do not necessarily adopt the Gricean principle of cooperation as the purpose rule of their interpretive codes.[69]

Third, there is apparently a further level of prescriptions concerning the JLC, besides the interpretive rules making up interpretive codes. The JLC is an interpretive game played on legal provisions, by means of interpretive codes and the interpretive resources, out of the available multifarious set, that the codes selves make relevant to the task of getting to the "correct" legal meaning. Interpretive codes, as we have seen, are made of interpretive rules—basically: grammar, method and translation rules[70]—interpreters usually find in a toolbox handed down by the methodological tradition. They are selected and composed, mostly, out of rules the judges find in that (metaphorical) box. Now, if we cast a Gricean eye on the way judges, in "our" legal culture and experience, proceed to select and compose the codes they are going to use, such an activity appears to be ruled by a set of (higher-level) prescriptions. Any theory of judicial interpretation purporting to be descriptively adequate must bring that set of (higher-level) prescriptions to the fore. Tentatively, they can be articulated as follows.

5. The Principle and Maxims of Judicial Selection and Composition of Interpretive Codes When judges select and compose the interpretive code—with its grammar, method and translation rules—they are going to use for identifying or justifying the "correct" legal meaning of a legal provision in view of deciding a lawsuit, their activity is ruled, apparently, by five main prescriptions.

In the Gricean terminology of "principles" and "maxims", these prescriptions are: the Principle of Prudent Interpretation, the Combination Maxim, the Precisification Maxim, the Resource Selection Maxim, and, finally, the Integration Maxim.

The *Principle of Prudent Interpretation* can be regarded as a specification of a more general principle of methodological prudence. It states that judges are empow-

[69] See Chap. 3, Sects. 3.5 and 3.6, Chap. 4, Sects. 4.2.2 and 4.4, above. For instance, Italian judges in the late 1960s interpreted statutory law following a principle according to which cooperation was to be directed not to the actual, historical, flesh and blood, legislature, but, rather, to the "good legislature", that is to say, to a legislature that was presumed to make laws that were respectful of formal justice, logical consistency, instrumental rationality, non-redundancy, linguistic determinacy, systemic arrangement, and completeness (see Bobbio 1971, pp. 243–249). Likewise, in a constitutional state, judges often adopt a principle of interpretive cooperation with the Constitution (constitutional law and principles), which may result in adopting a principle of interpretive no-cooperation, or a principle of uncharitable interpretation, towards ordinary, sub-constitutional, legislation.

[70] See Chap. 2, Sect. 2.2.1.1, Chap. 3, Sects. 3.4 and 3.6, Chap. 5, Sect. 5.2, above. As you may recall, method rules encompass, in turn, purpose rules, selection rules, procedure rules, preference rules, and default rules. Translation rules, contrariwise, provide instruction for translating legal provisions into explicit norms. They are rules of linguistic, intentional, teleological, authoritative, systemic, and heteronomous interpretation.

ered with the maximum of (selective and applicative) interpretive discretion,[71] compatible with the need of presenting their interpretive outputs as imposed by, or, at any rate, derived from, legal materials, in observance to the adjudication legality principle ("Judges ought to adjudicate according to the law", "*Iudex iudicare debet secundum ius*"). Clearly, the principle of prudent interpretation is compatible with, and allows for, a wide array of purpose rules, according to each judge's attitudes and goals.

Like in the Gricean model, the four maxims for the selection and composition of judicial interpretive codes I have just mentioned work as many maxims of detail: they entitle judges to specific courses of action, within the (loose) limits set by the principle of prudent interpretation.[72]

The *Combination Maxim* allows each judge to combine the translation rules available to form the interpretive code that she considers to be the best in order to present her interpretive output as the legally correct one, in the light of the case at hand, the principle of prudent interpretation, and the purpose she thinks proper and paramount to pursue.

The *Precisification Maxim* allows each judge to precisify available translation rules, in order to adapt them to the decisional and justificatory needs of the case at hand, always within the limits of the principle of prudent interpretation.

The *Resource Selection Maxim* allows the judge to choose the interpretive resources needed to apply the previously selected translation rules in such a way as to favour the identification of what she considers the legally correct interpretive output, again within the limits of the principle of prudent interpretation.

The *Integration Maxim*, finally, allows the judge to add new translation rules to the toolbox of the already available ones, provided the principle of prudent interpretation is, again, respected.

6. The Context of Legal Provisions According to pragmatic formalism, as we have seen, the "context" of the JLC concerning the judicial interpretation of any piece of written law whatsoever, is an objective background of shared information or shared data, as the standard pragmatics of OC maintains (see Sect. 6.4 above).

Pragmatic realism maintains such a view to be wrong, so far as we are looking for a genuine theoretical and true account of judicial interpretation of legal provisions in contemporary legal experience. Pragmatic realism claims in particular that, due to the specificity of the JLC, the interpretive "context" of legal provisions, far from being an objective set of data shared by judges and the legislature, corresponds, rather, to the set of data that each judge-interpreter herself selects as relevant to the interpretation of the legal provisions at hand. These data are nothing else but *interpretive resources*. They are identified on the basis of the translation rules of the code that the judge has selected to perform her task. Among the prominent factors bearing on the determination of the context of any legal provision, do feature

[71] On selective and applicative interpretive discretion, see Sect. 6.2 above.

[72] For a thought experiment concerning the maxims of a code of judicial interpretation, see Chiassoni (2000b), pp. 79–99, at 95–97 and Chap. 3, Sect. 3.6, above.

the interests which the interpreter pays allegiance to: material or ideal interests, including principles of justice, religious beliefs, ideologies about the proper role of the judiciary according to the constitution, etc.

7. The Pragmatic Enrichment of Legal Provisions From the standpoint of the communication model of legislation adopted by pragmatic formalism, as we have seen, there is really very small room for pragmatic enrichment in JLC (see Sect. 6.4 above).

According to pragmatic realism, however, such a conclusion follows from a Procrustean projection of OC, with its rules of pragmatic enrichment, upon judicial interpretation.[73] If we look at the way judicial interpretation actually works, it appears that pragmatic enrichment has a wider scope (concerning, for instance, making explicit the "unarticulated components" of legal provisions), and depends, ultimately, on the translation rules the judges decide to select and use.[74]

8. Legal Implicatures Pragmatic formalism, as we have seen, presents the legal implicatures of legal provisions' assertive content as *data out there* that, nonetheless, judges often overlook for strategic reasons (see Sect. 6.4 above).

Pragmatic realism, which rejects the Gricean communication model of the JLC endorsed by pragmatic formalism, propounds a different view. Roughly speaking, the view centres on the idea of *methodological* and *ideological dependence* of legal implicatures. Which implicatures a legal provision has is something that depends on the integration rules, concerning the identification of "implicit" or "implicated" law, which are selected and applied by judges, and by the integration resources they resort to.[75] Implicit, unwritten laws are not an objective reality out there, waiting to be grasped by faithful interpreters, as pragmatic formalism suggests. They are, rather, through and through, the dependent variables of judicial (and juristic) ideological and methodological options.

[73] On theoretical Procrusteanism, see Chiassoni (2000a) and Chap. 3, Sect. 3.1, above.

[74] On "unarticulated constituents" see Chap. 4, Sects. 4.3.2 and 4.4 above.

[75] On integration rules see Chap. 5, Sect. 5.2 above.

Chapter 7
Legal Gaps

Sed quia divinae quidem res perfectissimae sunt, humani vero iuris condicio semper in infinitum decurrit et nihil est in ea, quod stare perpetuo possit (multa etenim formas edere natura novas deproperat), non desperamus quaedam postea emergi negotia, quae adhuc legum laqueis non sunt innodata

Codex Iustinianus

Mon exposé va porter sur un vieux sujet assez poussiéreux: les "lacunes du droit"

—R. Dworkin (1989)

7.1 Two Traditions

At its outset, in the writings of early analytical jurists like Jeremy Bentham and John Austin, jurisprudence was a comparative enterprise, dealing with the basic concepts of Western legal thought. In the well-known inventories of Bentham and Austin, however, neither "legal interpretation", nor "legal gaps" show up: though the two authors deal with both subjects. They are, however, basic concepts, like "law", "right", "duty", "sanction", etc., though they play a somehow less evident role in legal discourse. Furthermore, like "law", "right", "duty", etc., the concepts of "legal interpretation" and "legal gaps" are theory-dependent: any definition thereof, unless freely floating on the wings of imagination, is expected to be a part of a larger, well-formed and well-argued, discourse ("a theory"), and is to be read against such a larger, background, discourse.

The purpose of the present chapter is providing an account of a few theories of gaps in contemporary jurisprudence. I will focus on the different ways of dealing with "gaps" on both sides of the Atlantic. In doing so, I will also consider interpretation, the core subject of the present book.

On both sides of the Atlantic, gaps feature as sources of concern, for legal practitioners (judges, jurists, barristers, attorneys at law, etc.) and legal theorists alike. On the one hand, gaps challenge the practitioner's skills in coping with cases that—as lawyers like to say—are (somehow) "unprovided for" by the law. On the other

P. Chiassoni, *Interpretation without Truth*, Law and Philosophy Library 128,
https://doi.org/10.1007/978-3-030-15590-2_7

hand, gaps are a powerful test for legal theorists' ability to provide careful, practice-sensible and practice-oriented accounts of a tangled phenomenon. Indeed, as soon as one leaves the (apparently) sound lands of practitioners' common sense, as soon as one departs from lawyers' (apparently) smooth "intuitions" (that is to say, fuzzy and unreflective everyday notions), a host of overwhelming questions suddenly pops up. And it is conceptual quick-sands everywhere. *What* a gap in the law *really is*? *Really* are there *gaps* in the law? What is it, for a judge, to *find* a gap in the law, if any? Assuming there is a gap in the law, how is it to *be filled up* properly by the law-applying agencies? And so forth.[1]

The present enquiry will dwell, as I said, on a meta-theoretical level. It will be an enquiry about *theories* of gaps, including two main parts plus a few final remarks. In the first part, I will provide an outline of what, in my opinion, can be regarded as the Standard Civil Law View. In the second part, I will provide a very sketchy account of a few among the most sophisticated theories of gaps that have been worked out, within Common Law jurisprudence, from the 1970s onwards. In the concluding section, I will make a few comments on the two sets of theories, from the point of view of a comparative analytical (meta) jurisprudence. It goes without saying that the whole chapter is meant to extoll the virtue of a realistic approach to the matter.

7.2 The Civil Law Side

The Civil Law tradition—from the ages of the great Roman jurists and emperor Justinian, up to the nineteenth century codification processes—was well aware of gaps. Gaps represented, however, what, at present, would be regarded as a political and a methodological issue. Indeed, both the Roman jurists and their *ius commune* followers (Glossators, Commentators, etc.) took for granted that gaps were, so to speak, a fatal side-effect of any piece of written law: something naturally going along with it, like a shadow. Accordingly, they were concerned with—either, or both, of—the two following problems. First, there was the problem of *authority*: *who* should be regarded as entitled to fill them up? Here, the alternative was whether such a power competed to the sole emperor or the sole legislative authority, or was also vested in judges and jurists, according to their respective roles. Secondly, there was the problem of *method*: *how* were gaps to be filled up? Which techniques were appropriate in proceeding to the so-called *extensio legis*?[2] By mid-nineteenth

[1] Practitioners and theorists—it is worthwhile noting, though in passing—do not live into separate, far away, worlds, as the previous remarks of mine may have suggested. On the contrary, they dwell on the same "premise", and do co-operate—though at different levels and in different ways—in shaping and making it what it is. Accordingly, theorists' ideas about the nature of legal gaps and other related issues are not just a bundle of self-serving speculations on practitioners' (supposedly) crude views. They do strike back on practitioners' conceptual frameworks, affecting their ways of looking at, and dealing with, such puzzling events. This plain fact makes, in turn, the whole gaps-business even more worthwhile of a careful, and detached, scrutiny.

[2] For a very sketchy account of these points, see, e.g., Chiassoni (1998), pp. 208–209, 221–222;

century, however, as an outcome of the working of several factors (codification; Enlightenment ideologies about legislatures' omnipotence, separation of powers, rule of law, and judges' passivity; the organicist and holistic conception of positive law advocated by the Historical School and Legal Dogmatics; etc.) the Civil Law world was apparently stung by the "positivistic" dogma asserting that legal systems are, by their very nature, *gapless* sets of norms, providing for any possible case whatsoever. As a matter of fact, a random survey of the methodological writings of nineteenth century positivists (like François Laurent, Charles Demolombe and Friedrich Carl von Savigny) shows that their adherence to the dogma was neither so *new* (recall the old *ius commune* saying "*omnia in corpore iuris inveniuntur*"), nor so methodologically *naïf*, as it is commonly depicted in the galleries of legal curiosities.[3] Be it as it may, however, by the end of the nineteenth century onwards, the so-called anti-formalists movements (like, for instance, the *Freirechtsbewegung* in Germany) opposed the official, positivistic ("scholastic", "formalistic"), outlook, centred on the doctrine of the completeness of legal orders, claiming, by contrast, legal systems to be *necessarily* replete with gaps positive laws cannot prevent.[4] Among the different reactions to the anti-formalist criticism of the doctrine of the completeness of legal orders, one may record, along with value-laden efforts purporting to establish the "logical" completeness of legal orders (for instance, by Ernst Zitelmann and Donato Donati), the development of a line of genuine, value-free, theoretical inquiries about legal gaps. Hans Kelsen's theory of gaps, dating from the early 1930s, provides, though in part, a clear sample of this new attitude of legal scholars.[5] After World War II, theoretical investigations on gaps improved greatly in the Civil Law world, as a consequence of the use and refinement, by a few legal theorists, of some conceptual tools worked out by analytical philosophers (like Ludwig Wittgenstein, Rudolf Carnap, Gilbert Ryle, John Langshaw Austin, and Georg Henrik von Wright, to mention the most prominent representatives). Norberto Bobbio's 1963 entry *Lacune del diritto* (Legal Gaps), on the one hand, and Carlos E. Alchourrón's and Eugenio Bulygin's 1971 book *Normative Systems*, on the other hand, represent two of the most thoughtful contributions within the (new) analytical perspective.[6]

The several analytical theories of gaps so far set forth share a few, basic, tenets. On the whole, these tenets make up the backbone of what I am going to consider the "Standard Civil Law View" on gaps. They run, roughly, as follows.

Chiassoni (2005), p. IV.

[3] I have offered a survey of Exegetical School, Historical Schools and German Dogmatics on gaps and interpretation in Chiassoni (2016d), pp. 565–600.

[4] For survey of *Freirechtsbewegung* on gaps and interpretation, see e.g. Chiassoni (2016e), pp. 608–618.

[5] See, e.g., Kelsen (1934), pp. 127–135.

[6] Bobbio (1963), pp. 89–102; Alchourrón and Bulygin (1971), ch. 1; Conte (1962), Conte (1968), pp. 15–37; Rodríguez (2002), ch. I; Guastini (2004), ch. XII; Chiassoni (2011), ch. 3; Guastini (2011b), pp. 128–154.

1. The *existence* of gaps is neither a necessary, nor an impossible, feature of positive legal orders. It is, on the contrary, a mere *possibility* for every given legal order, or any section thereof (Contingent existence thesis).[7]
2. The identification of a gap in the law, by a judge or a jurist, is not the outcome of a purely mechanical or logical job. On the contrary, it depends—directly or at least indirectly—on interpretive activities. These activities, in turn, are—or may be in at least some cases—value-laden and decision-dependent (Optional identification thesis).
3. There is no necessary, universal, way of filling gaps up in the Western legal tradition. On the contrary, whenever a judge thinks there is a gap in the law, she may usually choose among a set of alternative gap-filling techniques, that are likely to lead to different outcomes (Optional integration thesis).
4. From the perspective of a practice-sensible and practice-oriented theory, it is worthwhile distinguishing several different concepts of a gap, so as to casting light on, and put an order to, the fuzzy, everyday, intuitions legal practitioners entertain on the matter (Conceptual pluralism thesis).

The major differences among the several analytical theories of gaps within the Civil Law tradition concern the optional identification thesis and the conceptual pluralism thesis.

As regards the *optional identification thesis*, a basic distinction may be drawn between three kinds of theories.

First of all, there are theories (like, for instance, Bobbio's theory) that simply *presuppose* the optional identification thesis, without giving it any due, express, consideration.

Second, there are theories (like, for instance, Alchourrón's and Bulygin's theory) that regard the identification of gaps as being, *directly*, the outcome of a *logical process* consisting in the determination of the solutions provided by a previously identified, limited, set of norms for a previously identified, limited, set of cases. These theories consider interpretation as an "empirical" (not-logical) activity, which affects the identification of gaps only in an indirect way, and, furthermore, involves decision-making in hard cases only.[8]

Third, and finally, there are theories (like, for instance, the theories developed by representatives of the Genoese Realistic School) that, on the contrary, claim the identification of gaps to depend on activities of textual and meta-textual interpretation, which are necessarily value-laden and decisional in character.[9]

Coming to the *conceptual pluralism thesis*, provided legal theory should supply legal practice with a set of carefully defined concepts of gap, it must be noticed that

[7] For instance, in the case of *normative gaps proper*, their existence as to a given set of norms depends: (a) on the content of the norms of the set and (b) on the (explicit or implicit) criteria concerning the legal relevance of cases, both of which do usually vary from time and place. On relevance criteria, see Chiassoni (2011), ch. 3.

[8] As we have seen, this claim represents the core of semantic formalism: see Chap. 3, Sect. 3.2, and Chap. 4, Sect. 4.2.1 above.

[9] See Chap. 2, Sect. 2.2.1, Chap. 5, Sect. 5.2, above.

several sets compete in the extant literature. Taking into account the most influential set so far worked out—namely, the one proposed by Alchourrón and Bulygin in *Normative Systems*[10]—while, at the same time, revisiting it in the light of a realistic conception of law and interpretation, it seems worthwhile distinguishing three basic concepts of a *normative gap—i.e.*, of a gap as a situation where, generally speaking, some norm is assumed to be "missing" for a given case—, namely: *normative gaps proper*, *switchover gaps*, and *adding-up gaps.*[11]

7.2.1 Normative Gaps Proper

A normative gap proper, or properly so-called, may be characterized as:

> the absence, in relation to a given set of legal materials LM_i, of a legal norm providing a solution to a legally relevant question QL_j.

This characterization makes clear that the absence of a norm is a gap relative to:

1. A *given* set of *legal materials* (legal provisions, explicit norms, implicit norms), and
2. A *legally relevant question* (*quaestio iuris*), that is to say, a problem concerning the legally correct normative consequence for a given "fact" (behaviour, situation), which judges have the duty to solve.

The characterization above is to be regarded as a mere starting point. It provides a broad notion, in need of precisification. Indeed, much confusion about gaps—and the related claims concerning their necessary, impossible or merely possible existence—is likely to be cured, though only in part, if we are careful enough to distinguish between two basic types of normative gaps proper: namely, *explicit* gaps and *implicit* gaps, respectively.

An *explicit gap* may be characterized as:

> the absence, in relation to a given set of legal provisions LP_i, and to an interpretive code IC_k, of an explicit norm providing a solution to a legally relevant question QL_j.

On the contrary, an *implicit gap* may be characterized as:

> the absence, in relation to a given set of legal norms SN_y, and to an integration code IGC_k, of an implicit norm providing a solution to a legally relevant question QL_j.

By definition, an explicit norm is a *meaning*: and, more precisely, it is the (assumedly) legally correct meaning of a legal provision (what the legal provision

[10] See Alchourrón and Bulygin (1971), ch. I.

[11] The distinction between "normative gaps proper" and "switch-over gaps" mirrors, though with some changes, a distinction to be found both in Bobbio ("normative gaps proper" v. "ideological gaps") and in Alchourrón and Bulygin ("normative gaps" v. "axiological gaps"). The idea of an "adding-up gap" is somehow a new entry, purporting to complement the main distinction above. For a more detailed account of normative gaps, see Chiassoni (2011), ch. 3.

says).[12] Accordingly, the identification of an explicit norm depends on three basic factors: (a) a legal provision; (b) an interpretive code, that is to say, a discrete set of interpretive rules the interpreter has selected in order to translate the norm-formulation into one or more explicit norms; (c) a set of interpretive resources.[13] Thus, an explicit gap occurs when, for a legally relevant question, no suitable meaning can be ascribed to any of the provisions available on the basis of a given set of interpretive rules.

By definition, implicit norms are derived from previously identified (explicit or implicit) norms, by means of some norm-creating, integration technique: like, for instance, analogical, *a contrario* or *a fortiori* reasoning (in their productive versions), so-called legal induction, and appeal to general or fundamental principles of law. Accordingly, an implicit gap occurs whenever, for a given legally relevant question, no suitable implicit norm can be identified from a given set of norms on the basis of a given set of integration rules.[14]

While explicit gaps are usually considered as a matter of course, implicit gaps are considered, contrariwise, to be a very rare, if not at all impossible, event.

A further distinction is useful making, besides the one I have just mentioned between explicit and implicit gaps. It runs between *ordinary gaps* and *methodological gaps*. Very roughly speaking, *ordinary gaps* occur whenever what is (apparently) missing, and needed for, is an *ordinary legal norm*, concerning somebody's rights, duties, powers, liberties, etc. *Methodological gaps* occur, by contrast, whenever what is (apparently) missing, and needed for, is a *methodological norm*: namely, some higher-order definitional, interpretive, gap-filling, or conflict-resolution rule, establishing which definition of a legal term, which interpretation of a legal provision, which way of filling-up an explicit gap, or which way out to a normative conflict ought to be followed (preferred) in a given case.[15]

7.2.2 Switchover Gaps

A switchover gap may be characterized as:

> the absence, in relation to a set of legal norms SN_y, of the first-best norm FBN_w which, for reasons of justice or public policy, should regulate a legally relevant question QL_w, instead of the second-best norm SBN_w which, at least prima facie, actually regulates it.

Normative gaps proper occur whenever, for a legally relevant question, the law provides no—explicit or implicit—norm whatsoever. By contrast, switchover gaps occur when, for a legally relevant question, the law *does* provide a norm that it *should not* provide (the second-best norm), and, *at the same time*, *does not* provide the norm it *should* provide (the first-best norm). Thus, the problem interpreters

---

[12] See Chap. 2, Sect. 2.2.1.1 and Chap. 5, Sect. 5.2 above.

[13] See Chap. 3, Sects. 3.4 and 3.6, Chap. 5, Sect. 5.2, Chap. 6, Sects. 6.2, 6.3 and 6.6 above.

[14] On integration rules, see Chap. 2, Sect. 2.2.1.2, and Chap. 5, Sect. 5.2 above.

[15] On this distinction, see Chiassoni (2011), ch. 3.

apparently face, when a switchover gap is afoot, consists in *replacing* the second-best norm (getting somehow rid of it) with the first-best one.

Alchourrón and Bulygin—and many other theorists, on their footsteps—call these gaps "axiological gaps", so as to emphasize that their existence depends on some pretended value-unfitness of some piece of a legal order. Kelsen and Bobbio were used to name by "ideological gaps" roughly the same situations. Axiological inadequacy of legal norms can be either *internal* or *external*. It is *internal* whenever, by hypothesis, the axiological inadequacy of a certain legal norm is being measured against (higher) principles (or values) that belong to the *same* legal order (*e.g.*, constitutional principles and fundamental rights). By contrast, the axiological inadequacy of a norm is *external*, whenever, by hypothesis, it is being measured against (higher) principles (or values) that belong to a *different* normative order the interpreter is committed to: like, for instance, some natural law system or any other given system of morals.

There are good reasons, I think, to maintain that switchover gaps ("axiological gaps") are nothing else, but a particular kind of *normative conflict*, though in a disguised form. This latter point, however, would carry us too far away.[16]

7.2.3 Adding-Up Gaps

Finally, an adding-up gap may be characterized as:

> the absence, in relation to a given set of legal norms SN_y, of a norm providing a solution to a legally irrelevant practical question $PQ_{j.}$, whereas such question should be legally relevant from the standpoint of moral principle MP_i.

A practical question is legally irrelevant from the standpoint of adjudication when, by hypothesis, either judges ought not to decide it (imperative irrelevance), or they can decide, at their own discretion, whether to decide it or not (discretionary irrelevance). Think, for instance, at those situations falling within the *De minimis non curat Praetor* rule. Thus, in order to fill an adding-up gap, some change in the criteria of legal relevance of the problem at stake needs to be made first. Adding-up gaps are axiological gaps, where the presence of the missing norm within a given legal order is usually required by some *external* moral principle the interpreter is committed to.[17]

---

[16] For further details, see Chiassoni (2011), ch. 3, § 8, where a more precise definition is provided.

[17] It may also occur that a legal order, while making a practical question not decidable by judges, puts the duty to decide it upon the legislature. In such an event, the practical question is legally irrelevant from the standpoint of adjudication, while it is legally relevant from the standpoint of legislation. See Chiassoni (2011), ch. 3, § 9.

7.3 The Common Law Side

The Civilian who, stepping outside of her tradition, casts an inquiring glance at the theories of gaps worked out by Anglo-American jurisprudents in the last forty years or so, will probably be amazed by the following facts. No full-fledged book (nor any chapter thereof) has ever been expressly devoted to legal gaps by any Common Law jurisprude whatsoever. On the contrary, with a few notable exceptions, in their writings dedicated to "legal reasoning" or "interpretation", Common Law legal theorists usually spend on "gaps" (provided they even use such a word) just a few pages, if not a few lines.[18] These facts suggest that Common Law theorists, though acknowledging gaps to be a source of concern, appear to be not so obsessed with them, as their Civil Law colleagues seem instead to be. I will leave any (tentative) explanation of this latter fact for the conclusion.[19] By now, I will consider, in turn, the theories of gaps set forth by Frederick Schauer, Brian Bix, Jules Coleman and Brian Leiter, together with the older views entertained by Ronald Dworkin and Joseph Raz. In so doing, I will focus on the solutions each of the several theories examined does apparently provide to the existence, identification, and conceptual problems I mentioned while dealing with the Civil Law side. This will provide the basis for a few comparative remarks.

[18] Two examples should do, to corroborate my claim. On the one hand, the way Herbert Hart, the most distinguished English legal philosopher of the twentieth century, deals with "gaps" or "unregulated cases": see Hart (1983a), pp. 7–8; Hart (1967), pp. 105–108; Hart (1977), pp. 134–140; Hart (1961), "Postscript", 272–276. On the other hand, the fact readers will not find any reference to "gaps" or "unregulated cases" in the analytical index of what represents the compendium of the theoretical achievements of Common Law jurisprudence at the turn of the century: I mean *The Oxford Handbook of Jurisprudence and Philosophy of Law* (Coleman and Shapiro 2002). See also, Lucy (2002), pp. 206–267, where the author basically follows MacCormick's theory of "hard cases", where gaps are treated under the heading of "problems of relevancy", and appears to be concerned with *justifying* adjudication, rather than providing an analytical account of its structure and typical operations. The same remarks apply to the essays in *The Blackwell Guide to the Philosophy of Law and Legal Theory* (Golding and Edmunson 2005). See also MacCormick (2005), pp. 47–51. In the more recent literature "gaps" are dealt with by Marmor (2011a, 2014), Gardner (2012), pp. 34–35 (while considering "Positivistic adjudication", and endorsing the standard common law view that "gaps" do not amount to cases where "the law is silent", but, rather, to cases where the law is either linguistically "indeterminate", or does not contain a norm for resolving a "normative conflict"). I have analysed Marmor's theory of gaps above, at Chap. 6, Sects. 6.4 and 6.5.

[19] See Sect. 7.4, below.

7.3.1 Schauer

Frederick Schauer deals with legal gaps in a few, dense, pages of his well-known 1991 book *Playing by the Rules*, where he revisits thoroughly the more conventional view on the subject he endorsed in the 1985 essay *Easy Cases*.[20]

In *Easy Cases*, Schauer upholds the following view:

1. Gaps are cases that, though they are "not regulated" by any "law" whatsoever, are nonetheless submitted to judicial decision ("the cases are still for some reason before a court for decision")[21];
2. Gaps are a variety—along with the cases of vagueness, ambiguity, and obscurity of rule-formulations—of those "hard cases" where it is not possible to find an answer to a question of law, simply by appealing to the most immediate literal meaning of rule-formulations ("a straightforward reading of the rules")[22];
3. Gaps are, at any rate, *quite rare* occurrences in contemporary, mature, legal systems, "given the pervasiveness of contemporary legal norms".[23]

In *Playing by the Rules*, Schauer settles for a more complex view about gaps, which, as we shall see in a moment, is built on a peculiar theory of legal rules and has a clearly ideal import, for it connects to a proposal showing how the values of legal certainty and the rational (purpose-inspired) legal regulation of facts might be served, at once, by a working legal system. The basic points of Schauer's "second" theory of gaps run as follows.[24]

1. A "gap" is the absence, within a system of *regulative rules* that *aims at being comprehensive* (i.e., one that includes, or "makes", a claim to completeness), of a rule connecting some specific legal consequence ("result") to a given case.

   We have here, apparently, the only theoretically proper concept of a "legal gap" Schauer thinks suitable. By contrast, indeed, no gap can be envisaged when *jurisdictional rules* are at stake. This is so, because jurisdictional rules are voluntarily inchoate pieces of legislation. Their scope of application is left open and indeterminate by design, for their formulations include general clauses like "equal protection of the laws", "restraint of trade", "during good behaviour", "cruel and unusual punishment", etc.[25]

---

[20] See Schauer (1991a), Schauer (1984), p. 415 ff.; Schauer (2009), pp. 158–163, under the heading "When the Text Provides No Answer" deals with the phenomenon of statutory vagueness.

[21] Schauer (1984), p. 415, footnote 42.

[22] Schauer (1984), p. 415.

[23] Schauer (1984), p. 415, footnote 42.

[24] Schauer (1991a), p. 224 ff.

[25] Schauer (1991a), p. 227: "It is exactly the purpose of such rules [jurisdictional rules, ndr] to empower the interpreters to work out the results on the basis of factors not themselves contained in the rule, and thus an interpreter engaging in that task is doing something different than [when, ndr] is forced into an interpretive act by the limitations of language, by the limitations of the foresight of the rule-maker, or by the in eliminable factor of open-texture".

2. Gaps are possible features of *systems* of regulative rules *only*: no gap may properly be identified on the basis of a single, isolated, regulative rule.[26]
3. The existence of gaps in any system of regulative rules whatsoever is a contingent fact, that depends—according to Schauer: "exclusively"—on the satisfaction of two conditions. First, as it appears from Schauer's definition of a gap, the system of regulative rules must include a claim to completeness, i.e., a claim to regulate whichever case may arise by means of acts of interstitial judicial law-making. Second, the system must not contain any "closure", or "default", rule for "unprovided cases", for this would carry out its completeness automatically, ruling out gaps beforehand.[27]

   It must be noticed, in passing, that both conditions hardly refer to hard-and-fast facts. On the one hand, legal systems do not "claim" anything: this being clearly a metaphorical way of speaking, by means of which jurists impose "claims", "purposes", "intentions", etc., to unanimated sets of rules. On the other hand, closure rules may be, of course, explicitly stated pieces of written law—and surely Schauer had such a situation in mind, when he talked about the second condition for a system to have gaps. Closure rules, however, may also be regarded, and argued for, as being an implicit (and controversial) part of a legal system.
4. As to the *identification* of gaps within a system of regulative rules where there can be gaps, Schauer does not apparently consider such issue in a clear and direct way. However, a reading of *Playing by the Rules* according to the so-called principle of charitable interpretation provides the following suggestions. Regulative rules are rules laid down by normative authorities by means of the enactment of rule-formulations. Thus, the identification of a gap, if any, within a given system of regulative rules, depends on the interpretation of the relevant rule-formulations. Following Schauer, one may distinguish between (at least) two different interpretive approaches: the "modest interpretation" approach, on the one hand, and the fully "purpose-oriented" interpretation approach, on the other. The modest interpretation approach requires that rule-formulations be translated into rules that may be regarded either as their *literal meanings*, or as meanings suggested for them by a *first-* or, in any case, a *lower-order*, teleological interpretation. In these ways—according to Schauer—the interpretive reasonings by law-applying agencies would be "from and through the rule itself" ("on the basis of factors

[26] Schauer (1991a), p. 224: "If we are thinking about just one regulative rule, [...] it seems hard to generate the idea of a gap. The failure of the "No Dogs Allowed" rule to exclude men without neckties is hardly a "gap" in the rule [...] one rule cannot generate the idea of a gap". See, however, contrariwise, Alchourrón and Bulygin (1971), ch. I. For them, the normative set containing, say, just the norm "Dogs are not allowed into restaurants" would be gappy as to the complementary class of relevant cases identified by the "no-dog" property. For lions, rattlesnakes and bonobos—all instances of no-dog entities—the norm does not provide any solution.

[27] Schauer (1991a), p. 225: "Gaps are *exclusively* a product of the conjunction of two distinct conditions, existing only within systems purporting to be comprehensive, *and* which provide no default (or closure) rule for unprovided cases" (italics added, ndr). On Schauer's exclusivity thesis I will come back in a moment, while dealing with the identification of gaps.

[…] themselves contained in a rule"), and may actually result in the identification of cases unprovided for by the law. By contrast, if judges were to appeal to a fully purpose-oriented interpretive approach, they would—"trump the rule" and—hardly identify any gap at all in any system of regulative rules. Indeed, such an approach "would leave no room for gaps", since it would always provide rectifying, extensive re-interpretations of the relevant rule-formulations, so as to rule out beforehand whatever gaps there might be if a modest interpretation perspective were adopted instead.[28]

In this way—we can notice, in passing—the existence of gaps within a system of regulative rules is made to bear on a further, *third* condition, besides the two basic ones I have just recalled at point 3. This is the paramount condition that consists in endorsing, and following, a modest interpretation approach. It must be emphasized that the satisfaction of such a condition involves a fundamental methodological option; one that depends ultimately on the interpreters' ideologies about their own institutional role, powers, and duties. As a consequence, Schauer's theory of gaps either does work only for those legal realities where law-applying agencies actually endorse the modest interpretation approach (which, to my knowledge, are quite rare, if not imaginary at all), or is no general, descriptive, theory at all; being, rather, an idealized picture about how gaps—and their existence and identification—should properly be conceived of by lawyers, if certain goals (like legal certainty or the claim of some reasonable positivistic outlook) are to be fostered.

7.3.2 Bix

In a few passages of his 1993 book *Law, Language, and Legal Determinacy*, while dealing with Hart's theory of law, Brian Bix addresses one of the basic problems concerning gaps: namely, the conceptual problem, the problem about the *proper* or

[28] See Schauer (1991a), pp. 222–223, 224, 227. The difference between first- or lower-order teleological interpretation of a rule(-formulation) and full purpose-oriented (or, as we may say, "higher-order teleological interpretation) may be drawn, following Schauer, in this way. Take the rule(-formulation): "No dogs allowed". Its literal meaning states that no dogs are allowed (in a certain restaurant: be they large or small, dead or alive, quiet or rabid, etc.). A possible lower-order teleological interpretation would focus, for instance, on the goal of "excluding from the restaurant those agents likely, by their annoying behaviour, to interfere with the dining pleasure of others in restaurant" (pp. 222–223). In this case, the teleological meaning of the same rule(-formulation) would state, e.g., that no large, alive and rabid animals are allowed into the restaurant. However, we may settle on an even broader goal for the rule(-formulation): claiming, e.g., that it purports to maximize "the dining pleasure of […] patrons" (p. 223). In this latter event, whatever—animated or soul-less—thing the receptionist would regard as obnoxious to the dining pleasure of patrons will not be allowed into the restaurant. Such an interpretation will make the original rule to disappear entirely (it would "trump it", in Schauer's words). I leave aside, here, the puzzling issue about where, and how, to draw the line between what is within and without any "rule".

adequate notion(s) of a gap to theoretical or practical purposes. In so doing, Bix distinguishes three concepts of a gap.

To begin with, there are (what I shall call) *semantic-exhaustion gaps*. They occur whenever the law does not provide *one single right answer* to a problem at hand, because:

> [T]he meanings of the relevant materials have simply "faded" so much at the periphery that they no longer determine a particular answer or interpretation, even though they do establish a range of permissible (and, by inference, a range of impermissible) answers and interpretations.[29]

Secondly, there are (what I shall call) *material-exhaustion gaps*. They occur whenever the law does not provide *one single right answer* to a problem at hand, because:

> language, rules, or the law have "run out" entirely.[30]

According to Bix, however, the two notions of gap above are quite useless as efficient conceptual devices, being framed on metaphorical, elusive, expressions. Therefore, on the footprints of a short 1988 essay by John Gardner (*Concerning Permissive Sources and Gaps*),[31] Bix proposes to adopt the following concept of gap—a concept that, *inter alia*, would capture the gist of Hart's position. A *gap*—says Bix—is *any situation where judges cannot decide on an issue, without resorting to extra-legal criteria.*

Apparently, if we require concepts to be efficient intellectual devices, Bix's own concept of gap seems to fall short—at least in part—of such a standard, on two basic counts.

On a first count, Bix's concept of gap appears to be overly general. In order to make (more) sense of it, it needs to be supplemented, for instance, with a list of the extra-legal criteria judges may have to resort to, in deciding a case—a list, I would add, to be drawn from the perspective of these criteria's likely *content*. Accordingly, one might make clear that the missing legal criterion may be, for instance, of the following kinds: rules of conduct; criteria and meta-criteria for settling a normative conflict; statutory definitions of words and phrases appearing in rules-formulations, together with default rules for coping with indeterminacy situations; interpretive rules concerning which, out of competing interpretations of the same rule-formulation, ought to be preferred; rules concerning which, out of competing filling-up techniques, ought to be preferred; etc.

On a second count, and contrariwise, Bix's concept of gap appears to be overly specific. In fact, by identifying gaps with any situation where judicial decisions depend on extra-legal standards, Bix seems to overlook the distinction (I have drawn while dealing with Civil Law theories) between *explicit* gaps (which may be filled-up by means of legal criteria, like, e.g., analogy or an appeal to general principles of

[29] Bix (1993), p. 25.

[30] Bix (1993), p. 25.

[31] Gardner (1988).

the law), on the one hand, and *implicit* gaps, which are likely to need extra-legal criteria for being filled-up, on the other hand—tacitly suggesting the only, *real*, gaps to be *implicit* gaps.

The ultimate outcome of Bix's view, thus, amounts to providing legal practitioners with an impoverished set of concepts of a legal gap: a set that, by the way, seems even poorer than legal practitioners' own current set.[32]

7.3.3 Coleman and Leiter

In the 1995 essay *Determinacy, Objectivity, and Authority*, Coleman and Leiter outline a theory of gaps basically concerned with the conceptual and the existence issues.[33]

As to the concept of gap, they ground their view on the distinction between those situations that are "genuine gaps", on the one hand, and those situations that, on the other hand, are *not* gaps. These, as they make clear, are situations (*i*) where the arguments in favour of a given solution are *substantially weak* ("the relationship between the norms and any outcome a judge might reach is too weak to warrant or justify the decision"), or (*ii*) where there is a plurality of competing solutions.[34] Accordingly, Coleman and Leiter define a *genuine gap* as any situation where:

> [N]o binding source – principle or rule – is available as a legitimate resource to enable a judge to think fruitfully about a dispute before her.[35]

It is worthwhile noticing that, due to its formulation, Coleman's and Leiter's concept of gap sets a quite demanding test for the existence of any gap in any legal system. In fact, for there *not* being a "gap", it is enough that a judge may find in the law some binding sources that enable her simply to *think fruitfully* about a dispute. Indeed, Coleman and Leiter endorse a view about the *existence* of gaps in "mature" legal systems that smells of "eliminationism". As they make clear:

---

[32] On Common Law practitioners' views, see, e.g.: MacCormick and Bankowski (1991), pp. 362–364, 373–374, where they distinguish between "interpretative gap-filling" (which is deemed "acceptable", or "legitimate", by English judges) and "substantive gap-filling" (which, contrariwise, is not "legitimate"); Summers (1991), pp. 411–412, 419 ff. According to Summers, "A gap in a statutory scheme may be said to exist when a statute includes a general clause or other terms which grant discretion to courts or administrators, when the implementing language of a statute is undergeneral in relation to its purpose, when an integral part of a statute is omitted, when a statutory scheme is left in fragmentary form, left unspecified, or left implicit in some respect [e.g., "a statute will purport to treat a topic exhaustively but an 'unprovided case' will arise", ndr], and when the relation between subsections or sections is left unspecified. There is little systematic scholarly analysis of the nature and varieties of gaps and gap-filling. Nor have the courts adopted a uniform typology". Both essays are clearly infused with a Civil Law-like concern about gaps.

[33] Coleman and Leiter (1995), pp. 203–278.

[34] Coleman and Leiter (1995), p. 226 ff.

[35] Coleman and Leiter (1995), pp. 225–226.

> the claim that there are genuine gaps in mature legal systems [...] is misleading at best. Given the set of standards and accepted tools for thinking about the relationship between binding standards and various fact patterns available in a reasonably mature legal system, it is unlikely that genuine gaps exist. For almost any dispute that we could imagine arising, there exist some legal norm or rule that bears on its resolution.[36]

Like in the case of Bix's theory, we may note in passing, such a conclusion by Coleman and Leiter is liable to be questioned on two different, though related, grounds. First, it is plainly at odds with practitioners' common sense view, and experience, of the matter. Secondly, it is bought at the price of a simplified—one may suggest: an overly simplified—conceptual framework, where there is no trace of the distinction between explicit and implicit gaps, which is usually presupposed in ordinary legal discourse.

7.3.4 Dworkin

So far, I have provided a bird-eye survey of a few of the most sophisticated *fin de siècle* theories of gaps in the Common Law tradition. It is time to consider two samples from an earlier generation of legal theorists. I mean Dworkin's and Raz's theories.

Like in the case of Schauer, we can distinguish *two* theories of gaps in Dworkin's jurisprudence. The first theory of gaps belongs to the *pre-interpretive stage* of Dworkin's legal thought; it is at work, for instance, in the famous 1975 essay *Hard Cases* and in the 1977 essay *No Right Answer?*.[37] Here, like in most Common Law jurisprudence, the idea of a gap is buried into the notion of a "hard case". Hard cases—Dworkin makes clear—are those puzzling situations where the following conditions occur: (*i*) "no settled rule dictates a decision either way"; (*ii*) "reasonable lawyers and judges" may, and do, "disagree about" the "legal rights" of the parties; (*iii*) "no procedure exists, even in principle, for demonstrating what rights the parties have"; but nonetheless, (*iv*) the idea that parties do have rights that can, and ought to, be enforced by judges is to be accepted as the only viable one, for philosophical and practical reasons alike.[38]

---

[36] Coleman and Leiter (1995), p. 225.

[37] Dworkin (1975), pp. 81–130; Dworkin (1977), pp. 58–84.

[38] See Dworkin (1975), p. 81, 83. Sometimes, the line between gaps and hard cases seems to disappear altogether, for hard cases are regarded as tantamount to gap situations. Dworkin seems to think such a blurring to be a central trait of positivist theories of law: "How should judges reason in hard cases? Under the simple package of positivism and utilitarianism that I described, judges must make fresh judgments to fill gaps in the law" (see Dworkin 2006, p. 251, and also pp. 247–248, 242). Dworkin's opinion is common to anti-positivist positions: see, e.g., Dyzenhaus (2004), p. 52: "in most hard cases, cases in which there is reasonable disagreement about what the law requires, there will be no answer picked out by the Sources Thesis. Here variously described, there is a "gap" in the law, or the judge is in a "penumbra" of "unsettled" law in contrast to the "settled" law". A further example of such a blurring—at the level of ordinary juristic thinking—is provided by the passage from Summers (1991), I quoted above (footnote 24).

Dworkin's characterization of hard cases is, by design, overly general. Indeed, when is it the case that no "settled rule dictates a decision either way"? Dworkin's examples make clear that hard cases, in his view, include situations where no explicit rule at all is available for a case at hand (like, e.g., the *Spartan Steel* case), along with situations that a Civilian would rather classify as mere interpretive problems (like, e.g., the *Everson* case, where the issue was about whether a statute, granting free busing to children in parochial schools, was an act "establishing a religion"). Thus, Dworkin's early notion of a legal gap is apparently the common sense one seeing "gaps" whenever a case is not, or not clearly, regulated: without any further theoretical refinement. This—as I said—is done by Dworkin on purpose. In fact, one may safely suggest that Dworkin was not interested at all in carrying out any detailed conceptual analysis of the notion of a "hard case"—even less so, as to the notion of a "gap": a term he uses mostly while reporting on *positivists'* theories of law (for, in his view, "gaps" are *positivists'* typical business and misguided obsession). All of Dworkin's efforts are devoted, on the contrary, to defend a picture of adjudication, descriptive and normative at once, that is centred on the one-right-answer thesis, *i.e.*, on the claim that, even in hard cases of whichever variety,

> For all practical purposes, there will always be a right answer in the seamless web of our law,[39]

provided, of course, we assume the perspective of Hercules, Dworkin's mythical judge, and proceed in the way he is able to.

The second Dworkinian theory of gaps belongs to the *interpretive stage* of his thought: from around the mid-1980s, when Dworkin performed—and advocated the general need for—an *interpretive turn* in legal theory. This theory of gaps is at work, for instance, in the 1986 book *Law's Empire* and, in an unusually explicit way, in the 1989 essay *La complétude du droit*,[40] which will provide the basic source for the present account. Dworkin's second theory of gaps—unlike the ones by Bix, Coleman, and Leiter, on the one hand, and like Schauer's theory, on the other—deals with all the basic problems concerning gaps: namely, the conceptual, the existence, the identification, and the integration (or filling-up) problems. Let's have a swift look at its basic points.

1. As regards the concept of gap, Dworkin suggests that, from the perspective of an interpretive theory of law (according to which, the law is an ongoing, complex, historically-grounded, practice of constructive and purposive interpretation of materials provided by political authorities), gaps are those situations where:

[39] See Dworkin (1977), p. 84.

[40] See Dworkin (1986), Dworkin (1989), pp. 127–135.

[*a*] there are two interpretations – for instance, two different ways of reading a statute – the one for the plaintiff, the other for the defendant […] and [*b*] there is no way to choose among the two; that is to say […] there is no *reason* to say that one of the two readings of the statute and its history makes of it a better sample of political wisdom than the other.[41]

As Dworkin makes clear, for there being a *real* (interpretive) *gap* in the law—*from the point of view of a well-trained interpreter*—it is necessary that the competing interpretations of the same legal materials (texts and past interpretive practices) appear to be *argumentatively incomparable*: to wit, the interpreter *believes* she cannot rank them, that is, she cannot establish a reasoned, all-things-considered, order of preference between the two interpretive alternatives; and, furthermore, the incomparability of the competing interpretations is *argumentative*: it cannot be established as an objective matter of fact, but is itself part of what is to be argued for, and depends, ultimately, not on the interpreter's "ontological commitment" as to the real nature of law, but on her "political [and moral] convictions".[42]

This interpretive—and argumentative—concept of gap Dworkin opposes to the positivist concept, according to which a gap is an institutional failure: namely, the failure, by normative authorities, to enact the rule exactly suiting to a certain case—so that gaps are, on this view, like empty pigeonholes on the hard-and-fast, historical, shelf of legislatures, judges, and customs-producing communities.

2. As regards to the problems concerning the existence and identification of a gap, Dworkin holds the following views. First, gaps may contingently exist in a legal system, though they are likely to be quite rare in complex, mature, legal systems like ours.[43] Second, their *identification* (*i.e.*, the conclusion according to which *there is* a gap on a certain issue), far from being a pure statement of fact, depends, as we have seen above, on each interpreter's *political convictions*, for it depends on a judgment of argumentative incomparability concerning the reasons that may be brought in support of each of the competing interpretations for the same piece of written law.[44]
3. Finally, as regards to the integration or filling-up problem, Dworkin argues apparently as follows. In the very rare cases where a genuine gap has been identi-

[41] Dworkin (1989), p. 133: "existent deux interprétations, deux façons de lire une loi (par exemple), l'une donnant raison au demandeur, l'autre au défendeur et […] il n'y a aucun moyen de choisir entre les deux; c'est-à-dire lorsqu'il n'y a aucune raison de dire que l'une des lectures de la loi et de son histoire est un meilleur exemple d'habileté politique que l'autre".

[42] Dworkin (1989), p. 135; see also Dworkin (2006), p. 254.

[43] Dworkin (1989), p. 127: "j'ai à ce propos des idées bien arrêtées. Elles peuvent ainsi se résumer: "Les lacunes du droit sont très rares; il existe presque toujours une réponse exacte à une question juridique"".

[44] Dworkin (1989), pp. 134–135, where, in support of the claim that gaps are very rare events indeed, he emphasizes that: "dans le domaine très restreint où on peut comparer différentes interprétations d'une loi précise dans le contexte général de la culture politique dans laquelle cette loi a été édictée, dans le domaine très limité de cette comparaison, *l'expérience montre que l'on peut presque toujours avoir une opinion*" [italic added, ndr].

fied, provided the competing interpretive solutions are by definition argumentatively incomparable, the elimination of the (presumed) gap must depend on each judge's best political, and moral, considerations.[45]

On the existence and identification problems, Dworkin's position—any claim to difference notwithstanding—is, paradoxically, pretty close to the one defended, from a different theoretical perspective, by his long-time target, and former mentor, Herbert Hart. Indeed, according to Hart:

> Very often in deciding such cases [hard cases, ndr] courts cite some general principle or general aim or purpose which a considerable area of the existing law can be understood as exemplifying or advancing, and which points towards a determinate answer for the instant case. But to admit this is not to admit the correctness of a general holistic theory of law as a gapless system of entitlements, such as Dworkin has advanced [...] For though the search for and use of principles underlying the law defers the moment, it cannot eliminate the need for judicial-lawmaking, since in any hard case different principles supporting competing analogies may present themselves and the judge will have to choose between them, relying like a conscientious legislator on his sense of what is best and not on any already established order of priorities among principles already prescribed for him by the law. Only if for all such cases there was always to be found, as Dworkin's theory implies, implicit in the existing law some unique set of higher order principles assigning relative weights or priorities to competing lower order principles would the moment for judicial law-making be not merely deferred but eliminated.[46]

One difference must be emphasized, though perhaps is more apparent than substantial. Hart's theory presents gaps as a widespread phenomenon in mature legal systems. Dworkin's theory, on the contrary, presents the cases of genuine argumentative incomparability as quite rare, marginal ones. However, it must be kept in mind that, according to Dworkin, when arguments pushing to opposite solutions appear nonetheless *comparable*, such a comparability is not a matter of demonstration, but, rather, a matter of constructive interpretation and (rhetorical) argument.

7.3.5 *Raz*

Being a legal positivist, Joseph Raz regards gaps, unlike Dworkin, as something that has to be accounted for carefully inside of a well-built theory of law. In the 1979 essay *Legal Reasons, Sources and Gaps*, while setting forth what represents, perhaps, the most articulated theory of gaps in Anglo-American jurisprudence, Raz

[45]This conclusion, implicit in the 1989 essay, is made more explicit in Dworkin (2006), p. 242 ff., 254. Hard cases usually require judges to make "a fresh judgment", the content of which is "controversial" and engage "judicial responsibility". Now, says Dworkin, "On no conception of law – positivist or interpretivist – can judges in complex pluralistic communities acquit their institutional responsibilities without relying on controversial moral convictions", i.e., without referring to "moral opinions that he but not others think right".

[46]Hart (1983a), p. 7; see also Hart (1961), "Postscript", 274–275.

deals with two of the four basic problems concerning gaps: namely, the conceptual problem and the existence problem.[47]

1. As regards the concept of gap, Raz distinguishes, to begin with, between *jurisdictional gaps* and *legal gaps* proper.

Jurisdictional Gaps A legal system is jurisdictionally complete if its courts have jurisdiction over all legal questions. It has a jurisdictional gap if its courts lack jurisdiction over certain legal questions;

Legal Gaps A legal system is legally complete if there is a complete answer to all the legal questions over which the courts have jurisdiction. It contains a legal gap if some legal questions subject to jurisdiction have no complete answer.[48]

The notion of *jurisdictional gap* brings to the fore the issue of the scope of jurisdiction in relation to "legal questions". There may be practical questions, Raz suggests, that are "legal", but that, nonetheless, cannot be brought in front of a court.[49] Thus, the notion of jurisdictional gap captures a species of situations similar to the adding-up gaps I considered while dealing with the Civil Law side. Indeed, they are situation were some legally relevant question is not jurisdictionally relevant—and, maybe, should be jurisdictionally relevant from the standpoint of the principles of some critical morality.[50]

The notion of legal gap is quite in tune with lawyers' common sense. It is meant to be a more precise and rigorous notion, though. As Raz makes clear, there are two kinds of situations where the law has a gap for not providing "a complete answer" to a question "subject to jurisdiction". On the one hand, there are *simple indeterminacy gaps*. These occur either (a) when a rule-formulation contains vague or ambiguous terms (*linguistic indeterminacy*), or (b) when legislative intent, being assumed as a relevant interpretive resource, proves indeterminate (*indeterminacy of intent*). On the other hand, there are *unresolved conflict gaps*. These occur whenever the law provides no criteria for settling a conflict between two norms ("reasons"). In Raz's terms, clearly echoed by Dworkin's later definition of a gap:

> a situation of unresolved conflict […] arises when conflicting reasons fail to override each other, not because they are equally matched, but because they are not matched at all: for whatever reason, the conflicting reasons are incommensurate in strength.[51]

---

[47] Raz (1979), pp. 33–77. Raz's theory, above all as to its theses on the existence issue, has been widely criticized: see, e.g., Moreso (1997a), pp. 99–107; Moreso et al. (2000), Endicott (2001), pp. 367–393, Bulygin (2004), pp. 21–28.

[48] Raz (1979), p. 70.

[49] According to Raz (1979), p. 71: "Gaps present legal and philosophical problems only if they arise from questions over which there is jurisdiction […] Since the law is identified through the eyes of the courts, legal gaps should be so identified too".

[50] See Sect. 7.2.3 above.

[51] Raz (1979), p. 72 ff.

2. As regards to the problem concerning the existence of gaps, in a much quoted (and much criticized) passage of his essay, Raz makes clear his position in the following terms:

> legal gaps [...] arise [...] where the law *speaks with an uncertain voice* (simple indeterminacy) or where it *speaks with many voices* (unresolved conflicts). Contrary to much popular imagining, there are no gaps where the law is silent. In such cases closure rules, which are *analytic truths* rather than positive legal rules, come into operation and prevent the occurrence of gaps.[52]

Raz's position about the existence of gaps—it must be noticed—is at odds, at the same time: with lawyers' ordinary intuitions about gaps, according to which there are gaps precisely when the law *is* silent; with Schauer's and the Civil Law theory, both of which focus on different concepts of gap and deny that closure rules might be simple "analytic truths", being rather contingent positive legal rules.[53]

7.4 Comparative Jurisprudence

It is time to take stock of the preceding survey. In the following, concluding, remarks, I will outline a very tentative comparison between the Standard Civil Law view, on the one side, and the several, Common Law, theories of gaps mentioned above, on the other side. To do so, I will pay attention: first, to their content; second, to their institutional context; third, and last, to the overall theoretical attitudes that respectively inspire and pervade them.

7.4.1 Puzzle-Theories v. Servants-Theories

From the standpoint of their respective contents, the differences between the Civil Law and the Common Law theories of gaps may be captured by the distinction between *puzzle-theories* and *servants-theories*.

Common Law theories of gaps are *puzzle-theories*. In defining gaps, Anglo-American jurisprudents usually emphasize that they are *critical* situations, and sometimes *extremely* so, for judges and legal practitioners. Indeed, with the notable exception of Schauer's theory, the other theorists, in their definitions of gaps, emphasize that the law appears to be working ill there: *legal* criteria have *run out entirely*; they do not allow judges to *think fruitfully* about a case; the law *speaks with an uncertain voice*; the law *speaks with many, confusing, voices*, giving way to competing and incomparable alternative interpretations.

---

[52] Raz (1979), p. 77, italics added.

[53] For a radical critique, see Bulygin (2004), pp. 21–28.

By contrast, Civil Law theories of gaps are, so to speak, *servants-theories*. Any sense of (ultimate) uncertainty and overwhelming, titanic, challenge is altogether absent from the Civil Law view. Here, the concepts of gaps bear no trace of interpreters' strains. On the contrary, they are like torch-bearing servants in the darkness of ordinary legal practice. They help lawyers, by showing them, in a clear light, *which* sort of "gap" problems they may run into, and *where*, and *how*. And this is the starting point for any fruitful groping for way-outs.

7.4.2 Jealous Statutes v. Generous Codes

The Civil Law view bears no trace of concern about emphasizing that gaps—*real* gaps—are to regarded as quite rare events in legal orders. In fact, the distinction between genuine, or real, gaps and the situations that are not "really" gaps at all, seems to have no central place in it. Though we find in the Civil Law view a distinction—between *explicit* and *implicit* gaps—that may be regarded as pointing to a similar distinction within lawyers' common sense: I mean the distinction between *apparent*, or *prima facie*, gaps, on the one hand, and *real*, *all-things-considered* gaps, on the other.

By contrast, many Common Law theorists—like, e.g., Coleman, Leiter, and Dworkin—claim, for different reasons, that real gaps are very rare events in the law. Why is that so? On this point, I venture—for the sake of the argument—a possible, partial, and remote explanation, having to do with the institutional contexts of the two sets of theories, and, more precisely, with background doctrines of legislation. To do so, the basic tool I propose to use as an explanatory device consists in the distinction between two quite different *legal deities*: these are *jealous statutes* and *generous codes*, respectively.

The deities ruling over Common Law theories of gaps are (still) *jealous statutes*. Here you are the English depiction of these deities. Statutes float on the high seas of the common law. They are presumed to be complete in themselves: they do not have any *real* gap, and, in such an unfortunate case, the gap would not be for judges to cope with, this being a job for the sole legislature. Of course, problems about some *casus omissus* may arise. *Casus omissus*, however, are not *real* gaps: they are just interpretive problems judges may—and ought to—fix, by means of ordinary interpretative rules.

By contrast, the deities ruling over Civil Law theories of gaps are, so to speak, *generous codes*. After the extreme, unrealistic, claims to completeness (if ever seriously made) faded away, and *référé législatif* proved unviable, codes came to be regarded by lawyers as generous deities, providing them with most of their legal certainties, but waiting, at the same time, for lawyers' (and judges') help as to the correct interpretation of their provisions and the filling-up of their (explicit) gaps. This is apparent, for instance, from François Laurent's view about the proper reading, and function, of article 4 of the "Preliminary Title" to the Code Napoléon, which he interprets as a clear instance of delegation of interstitial law-making power to the judges.[54]

7.4.3 *Philosophers v. Watch-Repairers*

Finally, I will suggest that the Civil Law and the Common Law views about gaps are different—contents and institutional settings apart—also from a third point of view: namely, as to the basic attitudes of the legal theorists. Here, the distinction between *philosophers* and *watch-repairers* seems to provide an appropriate comparing device.

On the one hand, Civil Law theorists look at gaps as watch-repairers would. They think they have to deal with a clumsy conceptual machinery laid down by tradition and embodied in lawyers' common sense. They think their job to be taking it to pieces, polishing it, and giving it back to practitioners, in a glittering improved shape for everyday use.

On the other hand, Common Law theorists cast on gaps the highbrow look of legal philosophy. From their perspective, gaps are just one issue of detail, among others, pertaining to what they perceive as the real, big, theoretical (and practical) issues at stake: namely, the inter-related issues concerning judicial discretion, the existence of right answers to legal problems, and law's determinacy (or indeterminacy). They think, furthermore, that all these big issues point out, in turn, to an even bigger issue. This is the issue concerning—nothing less than—the very nature and guiding-powers of legal rules: and, ultimately, whether the Law is reality or delusion. All this, of course, along with the lines drawn by Herbert Hart in chapter VII of his 1961 *The Concept of Law*: the Bible, for better or worse, of late twentieth century Common Law jurisprudence.[55]

---

[54] On this point, see e.g. Chiassoni (2016), pp. 579–580.

[55] See Hart (1961), pp. 124–154. On the genesis, and cultural context, of Hart's masterpiece, see Lacey (2004), ch. 9.

Chapter 8
Judicial Fictions

> *Quand doit-on recourir à la fiction en droit? Quand [...] les catégories et les techniques juridiques reconnues, celles qui font partie de la réalité juridique admise, ne fournissent pas de solution acceptable au problème de droit que l'on doit résoudre*
> —C. Perelman (1974)

8.1 The Need for Clarification

My aim in this chapter is carrying out a conceptual investigation about judicial fictions.[1] The enquiry will proceed in two steps. In the first step, which is dedicated to conceptual survey, I will consider a few characterizations of judicial fictions, some of which coming from very influential authors. In the second step, which is dedicated to conceptual reconstruction, I will argue that those characterizations, which surely contain many valuable ideas, are nonetheless unsatisfactory. I will set forth, accordingly, a different characterization of judicial fictions. I wish to emphasise, however, that the characterization I will propose purports to capture the valuable ideas conveyed by the extant characterizations analysed. Hence, my conceptual proposal should be regarded as an explanatory stipulation, or rational reconstruction, about the concept of judicial fiction.[2]

In the second step of my enquiry, while analysing extant characterizations of judicial fictions and setting forth a different one, I will also deal, though in passing, with two persistent problems in the theory of judicial fictions. These are: (1) the problem concerning the proper way of understanding, and accounting for, the

---

[1] A previous version of this chapter was presented at the International Conference "Legal Fiction", Maison Française d'Oxford & St. Hilda College, Oxford, March 11, 2015. I wish to thank all the participants for their questions and comments. I am particularly indebted to prof. William Twining and prof. Maksymilian Del Mar for a very fruitful, post-conference, discussion which allowed me to "think like a common lawyer".

[2] On conceptual analysis and rational reconstruction, see e.g. Hospers (1967), pp. 18–67; see also Chap. 1, "Introduction: The Path of Analytical Realism", Sect. 1.3, above.

P. Chiassoni, *Interpretation without Truth*, Law and Philosophy Library 128,
https://doi.org/10.1007/978-3-030-15590-2_8

relationship between judicial fiction, judicial law-making, and analogical reasoning and interpretation; (2) the problem concerning the proper way of understanding, and accounting for, the relationship between judicial fictions and truth.

8.2 A Few Extant Characterizations

In jurisprudential literature, judicial fictions are usually treated inside of broader theories on "legal fictions".[3] In the following, I will consider in turn the characterizations of judicial fictions as they may be gathered from the theories of legal fictions provided, respectively, by Hans Kelsen, Alf Ross, Gidon Gottlieb, Frederick Schauer, and Maksymilian Del Mar. To be sure, the list is far from exhaustive. Nonetheless, I think it offers a fair showcase of the current status of the art, and represents an authoritative and useful starting point for further enquiry.[4]

8.2.1 Kelsen

In a 1919 essay, commenting upon Hans Vaihinger's theory of *epistemic fictions* (fictions supposedly working as tools for improving our knowledge of the world), Hans Kelsen draws the distinction between two kinds of legal fictions: "theoretical legal fictions" and the "fictions of legal practice".[5]

Theoretical fictions are fictions properly (*à la* Vaihinger): they are statements that stand in opposition to *factual* reality; and, furthermore, legal theorists make use of them in order to describe, and account for, (aspects of) positive law.[6]

Fictions of legal practice, on the contrary, are not fictions properly (*à la* Vaihinger). This is so because—as Kelsen claims—they are in fact *norms*. Being norms, they neither can be at odds with ("stand in opposition to") factual reality, nor are they resorted to for the purpose of cognition (i.e., advancing either our knowledge of law in general, or of some part of some legal order).

According to common opinion, there are two varieties of fictions of legal practice: these are "legislative fictions" and "fictions in the application of law". Kelsen, however, claims the received wisdom to be wrong.

---

[3] See, e.g., Fuller (1967).

[4] See Del Mar and Twining (2015).

[5] Kelsen (1919), § II.

[6] According to Vaihinger, a fiction is any claim that (a) is made to a cognitive purpose, (b) stands in contradiction (opposition) to reality in such a way that it can never become true, (c) is always provisional (i.e., likely to be abandoned as soon as a better tool of cognition is found), (d) is openly made (i.e., without any intention to deceive), and (e) is actually useful to the purpose (pragmatic justification). See Kelsen (1919), pp. 4–9; Frank (1949b), pp. 313–314; Del Mar (2015a), p. xii, xx.

To begin with, he maintains that so-called "legislative fictions" are nothing but cases where the legislature (or, in general, any person or body of persons vested with law-making power) extends the legal consequences of some norm, by establishing ("positing") that certain further situations or behaviours ought to be treated in the same way as the situations or behaviours to which that norm immediately applies. For instance, the legislature "decrees" that adoptive sons ought to be treated *just as* actual sons ought to be treated. As a consequence, legislative fictions are no "fictions" at all: not only from the standpoint of factual reality, but also from the standpoint of *legal* reality ("the legal order"). They—Kelsen maintains—stand "in opposition to *nothing*". In particular, they *cannot* stand in opposition to legal reality; and this is so because, whatever the legislature posits, that *is* (coincides with, makes, amounts to) legal reality: "Within his realm, the legislator is *almighty* [...] A *fiction of the legislator* would thus be *as impossible as a fiction of nature itself*".[7]

Coming to "fictions in the application of law", Kelsen underscores three properties.

First, from a technical point of view, fictions in the application of law are *norms created by means of analogical reasoning*. In Kelsen's words: they are "identical with the cases of interpretation by means of analogy". They do not consist, as common opinion mistakenly believes, in judicial assertions like, for instance, that "Public telephones are (as if) public telegraphs". They consist, rather, in judicial prescriptions like, for instance, that "Public telephones ought to be protected in the same way as public telegraphs".[8]

Second, fictions in the application of law are the *outputs of a dissimulated usurpation of law-creating power*: they are "invalid" norms that judges (and other law-applying officials) present, and treat as, "valid" according to pre-existing law.[9] As a consequence, "a fiction of someone applying the law is completely inadmissible, since it is *in violation of the purpose of the law*".[10]

Third, the *existence* of fictions in the application of law *depends on the condition that judges be, as to the cases at hand, purely law-applying organs*, that is to say,

---

[7] Kelsen (1919), pp. 12–13, italics added.

[8] Kelsen (1919), p. 15. Kelsen provides the following example: "If one wishes to subsume a certain case under a norm, which does not capture this case, then a fiction may seem expedient: to treat the case *as if* it fell under the legal norm. The law threatens a sanction for the damaging of a public telegraph, but leaves a similar damaging of a public telephone without threat of sanction [...] then it is a fiction if the judge applies to someone who damages a public telephone a sanction, which the law had intended only for someone damaging a public telegraph, in that he uses the norm intended to protect the telegraph to protect the telephone; the judge here does not proceed *as if* the telegraph were a telephone, this is not what the judge claims and wants to claim, but he proceeds as if the law threatened the same sanction to a damaging of a telephone as it does to the damaging of a telegraph. The juridical fiction can only involve a fictitious *legal* claim, and not a fictitious *actual* [*factual*] claim".

[9] Kelsen (1919), p. 15: "His [the judge's] claim, which stands in opposition to the *legal* order and not to actual reality, is: the public telephone, too, *must* not be damaged. Claiming the validity of an—invalid—general norm is the means by which he reaches the correct judgement, at least the one intended by him. It is not the claim that a telephone is a telegraph".

[10] Kelsen (1919), p. 16.

officials not endowed with law-making power. Indeed, whenever judges are—according to the "constitutional law" of the land—law-making organs, whenever "the fiction" that treats judges as "merely applying the law", and denies they are "delegated legislators", "falls away", fictions "in the application of law" really are tantamount to legislative fictions, and so become "impossible".[11] They become, in fact, just cases where *authorized* law-making officials, while making new valid law, simply pretend to apply pre-existing law.

8.2.2 Ross

In a 1969 essay, Ross distinguishes three kinds of "legal fictions": namely, "creative" fictions, "dogmatic" fictions, and "theoretical" fictions.[12]

Dogmatic fictions are tools helping in the presentation of complex sets of legal norms—like, e.g., the fiction of the corporation as a "legal person".[13] They correspond, roughly, to Kelsen's theoretical fictions.

Theoretical fictions are false and misleading theoretical representations of legal reality. Ross quotes as an example the ("mythical") fiction according to which judges do not make law, but only apply it, claiming it gets support from creative fictions.[14]

Creative fictions, finally, from the standpoint of the subjects who put them afoot, are mostly judicial fictions. They characterize as follows.

First, they are *a technique of undercover judicial lawmaking*: they are a "practical means" judges employ "for expressing new legal rules" under the pretence of performing a purely law-applying activity.[15]

Second, they are a judicial law-making technique consisting in *a peculiar, dissimulated, form of analogical extension of legal rules*, which is carried out by means of (we may say) *fictional sentences* (sentences the standard grammatical form thereof is: "A is B"). In Ross's own words:

> It has long been recognized that such fictions [creative fictions] are *no more than a peculiar technique for the analogical extension of legal rules*. To say that a barbarian is a Roman citizen *amounts to extending to* foreigners the application of the procedural rules that have hitherto been confined to Roman citizens. To say that Bordeaux is in Middlesex *amounts to saying that* the rules, according to which the competence of English courts has hitherto been confined to claims originating in England, are now to be extended so that this

[11] Kelsen (1919), p. 14.

[12] Ross (1969), pp. 217–234.

[13] Ross (1969), p. 220.

[14] Ross (1969), p. 220: "The *theoretical* legal fiction is often conflated with the creative legal fiction, but differs from the latter despite a functional relationship between the two. We have already cited some cases of creative fictions: the "barbarian" being considered a Roman citizen and Bordeaux being supposedly located in Middlesex. Now, the use of such fictions can serve to sustain a further fiction, namely, that the courts do not create law".

[15] Ross (1969), p. 220.

> competence also embraces claims originating in other countries [...] *Subjected to logical analysis, the creative fiction reveals no special oddity.* To "pretend" that A is B is *merely an odd way of expressing the thought that, for purposes of law, A is to be treated as subject to the same rules as apply to B.*[16]

8.2.3 Gottlieb

In a 1968 book, Gottlieb devotes a few pages to "legal fictions",[17] by which phrase he seems to refer in fact to the subset of *judicial* fictions. Gottlieb characterizes judicial fictions as consisting in

(a) establishing a finding of facts knowingly "at variance with truth" (*untrue fact-finding*), on the basis of which
(b) a revised rule is in fact applied in lieu of the rule which appears to be applied (*undercover application of a revised rule*), so that
(c) the law on the books is substituted by another "more lenient law" (*substitution effect*).[18] In Gottlieb's own words:

> When fictions are used, the facts that are *formally taken* as the basis of the decision have little or no reference to the actual events in the case [...] *the judge or the jury find facts which they know are at variance from the truth* [...] In such cases, *a revised rule is in practice applied in lieu of the rule which appears to be applied*, and there is then a *de facto* nexus between the facts and the rule, [...] between the "is" and the "ought".[19]

[16]Ross (1969), p. 222, 223, italics added. Several authors share a similar position, which, by the way, is roughly the same Kelsen upholds while dealing with "fictions in the application of law" (see Sect. 7.2.A above). According to P. Foriers, provided legal fictions are relevant for "the theory of the extension of the legal norm", "judicial fiction"—"la fiction jurisprudentielle"—consists in a "operative process that makes the law to progress and is used by the judge when he desires to create an evidently inexact assimilation, but necessary to obtain a desired result" (Foriers 1974, p. 8, 23). According to R. Guastini, fiction is "a judicial technique that aims at innovating – without making it apparent – an existing norm, at present perceived as unjust or inadequate, so as to adapt it to the changed social conditions"; the technique employs consciously false statements in order to make possible subsuming "a fact under a norm that – according to common sense [...] or [...] the on-going interpretation – would not be applicable to that fact"; "The effect of the fiction would be to extend to" a certain category of subjects the same form of legal protection "*so far reserved*" to a different category of subjects; "Clearly, the technique of legal innovation, that goes under the name of "legal fiction", does not differ, but perhaps for a nuance, from ordinary analogical application" (Guastini 1992, pp. 158–159). Finally, according to R. Gama, judicial fictions are "operations" by which "a judge extends the application of an existing rule to a situation of fact that cannot be subsumed under that rule, and in so doing he creates a new rule" (Del Mar 2015a, p. xxiii).

[17]Gottlieb (1968), pp. 43–44.

[18]Gottlieb (1968), p. 44.

[19]Gottlieb (1968), p. 44.

For instance, referring to the Macallister case, Gottlieb observes that there "a jury found a £ 10 Bank of England note [...] to be worth only 39 shillings"; and concludes that, by means of that manoeuvre:

> The jury, without apparent disrespect for the law on the books, *applied another law* [i.e., the law "governing thefts of less than forty shillings"] by means of the fiction about the true value of the banknote [...].[20]

8.2.4 Schauer

In a 2015 essay, Schauer distinguishes three kinds of "fictions"; these are "presupposition fictions", "presumption fictions", and "prevarication fictions".[21]

All these fictions—be they either within, or without, the law—share the property of being, "by definition, untrue".[22]

Legal fictions, however, look, at least *prima facie*, as being *questionably* untrue: "A legal fiction, *an intentional untruth in the law*, [...] seems an especially odd thing for an institution allegedly committed to truth-finding to tolerate".[23] Schauer claims, nonetheless, that, on closer scrutiny, questionability does not necessarily affect every sort or instance of legal fiction.

To begin with, there seems to be nothing wrong with *presupposition* legal fictions. Indeed, these are fictions that legal theorists employ in order to account for some aspect of the legal order. This is the case, for instance, with Kelsen's fiction of the "basic norm": the epistemological device by means of which he grounds the objective validity of positive legal orders.

Furthermore, and again, there seems to be nothing wrong with *presumption* legal fictions. Indeed, these fictions consist in (typically defeasible) generalizations that treat *what is ordinarily* the case *as being always* the case—like, for instance, the presumption according to which "the husband is the father of the children his wife gave birth to during marriage".

Contrariwise, something wrong may be seen in *prevarication* legal fictions. Schauer characterizes prevarication fictions—which are typically to be found in judicial decisions—by means of three properties.

First, they are *derogation devices*: they serve to defeat existing rules (they are "devices for effectuating the defeasibility of legal rules").

Second, they consist in *untrue re-descriptions of the relevant facts of the case* (for instance, "the *re-description* of an X (or the class of X's) as a Y"), which are *made in order to realize justice in the individual case*, by opening the way for the right decision ("right result") and avoiding "embarrassing" outcomes.[24]

---

[20] Gottlieb (1968), p. 44.

[21] Schauer (2015), pp. 113–129.

[22] Schauer (2015), p. 114.

[23] Schauer (2015), p. 114, italics added.

[24] Schauer (2015), p. 115: "the *re-description* of the facts of some event in order to make those facts

Third, they are devices to which judges resort in legal cultures characterized by a *preference for "judicial prevarication" over "judicial activism"*:

> it has long been considered more acceptable *in the pursuit of justice in the individual case* to *re-describe* the facts in order to achieve the right result than to *rewrite a law* in order to do the same thing, even though, in reality, *re-describing (and thus mis-describing)* the facts to make them fit the law is little different from *re-describing* the law in order to make it fit the actual facts [...] Despite this similarity between the two approaches, for a long time, and perhaps precisely *because of the psychological and political reasons just noted*, the *re-description of facts* in order to produce a just result has seemed preferable to the more overt *re-writing of a legal rule*, and from this preference – a *preference for judicial prevarication over judicial activism* – there emerges an important version of the legal fiction. Thus we see the classic example of *Mostyn v. Fabrigas* [i.e., the famous "Minorca fiction"] decided by the King's Bench court in 1774.

8.2.5 Del Mar

Finally, in a recent essay, Del Mar characterizes a "legal fiction"—that is, more precisely, a *judicial* fiction—by means of two properties. It consists in (a) the *momentary "suspension" of an operative fact,* that is typically performed (b) in order *to secure a right result for the individual case at hand.*[25] Such "suspension", as Del Mar makes clear, amounts to *making the operative fact to which a norm connects some normative consequence, either momentarily irrelevant, or momentarily unnecessary, in order to retain the imposition of that normative consequence.*[26]

Del Mar stresses that occasional suspensions may work as an invitation to future courts to develop them into a rule, and may in fact be developed by courts into "a new rule or principle", i.e., into a standard *generally binding.*[27] This possibility suggests, according to Del Mar, that judicial fiction's "bad reputation" is unwarranted. Indeed, they can be seen:

> as forms of tentative cognition that enable courts to communicate with each other, exploring whether *a certain change in the law* (i.e. precisely a suspension of a required operative fact in the imposition of a certain normative consequence) ought to be introduced *at a more explicit level*. Under the guise of this relational reading of legal reasoning, legal fictions become *an instrument of careful experimentation* — a way of testing the extent to which the potential introduction of a rule will be beneficial. Seen in this light, legal fictions are by no means signs of the immaturity of the system; they are, instead, dynamic resources that

---

compatible with the rule while at the same time permitting what appears to be the right result [...] the *re-description* of an X (or the class of X's) as a Y *in order to avoid an embarrassing outcome*", italics added.

[25] Del Mar (2015a), p. xxii; Del Mar (2015b), p. 225 ff., 250.

[26] The judge will decide to consider the *presence* of an operative fact *irrelevant*, when she wants to retain the normative consequence that its presence would rule out. She will decide to consider an *absent* operative fact *unnecessary*, when she wants to retain the normative consequence that its absence would rule out.

[27] Del Mar (2015a), pp. xxii–xxiii.

allow courts, over time, to balance flexibility and responsiveness with stability and predictability.[28]

8.3 Characterizations Analysed

Let's analyse the several characterizations of judicial fictions so far considered.

1. All the different characterizations converge, apparently, on two points. First, judicial fictions, whatever they are, are *related to* (*have to do with*) *judicial lawmaking*. Second, judicial fictions, whatever they are, are typically related to *unavowed* (dissimulated, oblique, undercover) judicial lawmaking. They are typically afoot when judges somehow *make new law under the pretence of merely applying pre-existing law*. This, notice, may happen both when judges are, by hypothesis, authorized to make new law, acting as delegated legislators, and when they are, by hypothesis, denied such authorization, and so recourse to fiction amounts to an usurpation of the lawmaking function.

   Beyond these two, very broad, points, however, there is apparently no identity of theoretical views.
2. Some theorists—notably, Kelsen and Ross—adopt a *normative conception* of judicial fictions. Fictions—they claim—are (nothing but) *norms*; they are new norms—usually, new norms of conduct, new regulative rules—that are being created under the pretence of merely applying pre-existing law. Other theorists—Gottlieb and Schauer among others[29]—adopt instead a *propositional conception* of judicial fictions. Fictions—they claim—are *false*, *untrue*, *sentences about the facts of the case* ("finding of facts at odd with truth", "untrue re-descriptions of facts") that judges use in view of presenting some law-making activity as one of merely applying pre-existing law. As I shall argue in a moment, however, there seems to be room for a third view about judicial fictions: one that is neither normative, nor propositional, being centred instead on the role played by fictional sentences as a kind of constitutive or stipulative sentence.
3. Different authors characterize differently the lawmaking operation to which judicial fictions are related. Indeed, as we have seen, fiction-related lawmaking is claimed to consist:

[28] Del Mar (2015b), p. 224, italics added.

[29] A propositional account of fictions is detected, e.g., by Fuller (1967, italics added), 9: "To sum up the results of our discussions, and to attempt a definition of the fiction that will at least approximate current usage, we may say: A fiction is either (1) a *statement* propounded with a complete or partial *consciousness of its falsity*, or (2) a *false statement* recognized as having utility"; it is maintained, e.g., by Tuzet (2011), pp. 541–542, and Tuzet (2015), p. 272, 274–275, where he characterizes a "justificatory fiction" as "a *consciously false assumption* but accepted in order to determine a good legal consequence" (italics added); Lind (2015), p. 100: "legal fictions" are "*true legal propositions* asserted with conscious recognition that they are *inconsistent in meaning or otherwise in semantic conflict with true propositions asserted within some other linguistic system* (or elsewhere within the law)" (italics added).

(a) in the *analogical extension* of existing norms (Kelsen, Ross);
(b) in the *substitution* or *replacement* of existing norms, based on a formal fact finding consciously departing from truth (Gottlieb);
(c) in *derogating (defeating)* existing norms by means of an untrue re-description of the relevant facts (Schauer);
(d) in the *suspension of operative facts* to get to the just result for the individual case (Del Mar).

Let's cast a closer glance upon each of these different characterizations.

4. Kelsen and Ross (and others[30]) see judicial fictions as dissimulated forms of analogical reasoning. The core of judicial fictions—they claim—is made by an instance of analogical reasoning (analogical "interpretation", analogical "extension"). Are they right? Two remarks seem to undermine their analogical account of judicial fictions.

First Remark Analogical reasoning turns upon an *analogy judgment* according to which the (already) regulated fact X and the (so far) unregulated fact Y do share a certain relevant property ("Y is similar to X as to the relevant property P in relation to the norm N"), and such sharing makes the (so far) unregulated fact Y eligible for the same legal consequence provided for the already regulated fact X, according to the analogy principle "Treat like cases alike". When judicial fictions are at hand, however, two different facts (say, being a Roman citizen and being a foreigner) are treated *as if* they were the same thing ("A*s* are B*s*", "A*s* are as if B*s*"), although they are neither the same thing, nor they are alike. The equivalence that a fictional sentence establishes is a matter of pretence and *fiat*; it is the outcome of a stipulative or constitutive speech act, on the background of which there is the full consciousness, on the part of the judge, that *the two facts do not share* the relevant property in virtue of which the regulated fact has been regulated in a certain way. For instance, in order to entitle foreigners to certain actions (like, e.g., the *actio furti*), they are considered *as if* they were Roman citizens, on the background assumption that, from the standpoint of *previous legal reality*, they neither are Roman citizens, nor they are alike to Roman citizens. In other words: reasoning by analogy and the technique of fiction are *structurally different*. A fictional sentence ("A is (as if) B") is *not* an analogical judgment ("A is similar to B (as to the relevant property P in relation to the norm N)"); it does *not* claim to point to an *actual* legally relevant *similarity* between two (classes of) cases. Rather, it establishes a pretended, fictional (and unprecedented) *legal equivalence* between them. Consequently, a fictional sentence cannot be reduced to an oddly formulated analogical judgment, without throwing away a peculiar aspect of judicial fictions.

Second Remark Analogical reasoning—interpretation by means of analogy, analogical extension—is a tool that is ordinarily employed to overcome situations of *normative gap proper*.[31] These are situations where a class of cases is, by hypothesis,

---

[30] See, e.g., Guastini (1992), quoted above at footnote 13.

[31] On normative gaps proper, see Chap. 7, Sect. 7.2.1, above.

not (yet) regulated by law: situations where the law, by hypothesis, provides *no answer* whatsoever. However, some characterizations (e.g., those by Gottlieb and Schauer[32]) suggest—in my view, correctly—that the problem, when judicial fictions show up, is not an ordinary problem of normative gap proper. Gottlieb, as we have seen, characterizes legal fictions as establishing a formal fact finding at odds with truth, not in order to fill up a gap by providing a new rule for a so far unregulated case, but in order to *replace* or *substitute* a legal rule "on the books", the application of which would produce a *bad answer*, with "a revised rule" or "another law", leading to a *good answer* ("more lenient"). Likewise, Schauer characterizes creative fictions as meant *to defeat* the application of an otherwise applicable rule. This suggests that, without resorting to fiction, the case at hand would in fact be regulated by an already existing rule; such a rule, however, appears to the judge as deserving to be set aside in view of realizing justice in the individual case.

To sum up: if we consider the structure of genuine analogical reasoning, and, besides, we look at judicial fictions from the standpoint of certain accounts (like those by Gottlieb and Schauer, among others), the theory of judicial fictions offered by Kelsen and Ross appears to be misleading and impoverished. The theory is misleading: judicial fictions do not work, technically speaking, just as a form of analogical reasoning. True, the discipline provided by an existing norm N for fact X is also applied to fact Y; such an "extension", however, is not analogical in kind: it does not depend, as we have seen, on a genuine *analogy judgment*, depending, rather, on a *fictional sentence*. The theory is misleading and impoverished, furthermore, because the situations where judicial fictions show up look different from, and somehow more complex than, the situations of normative gap proper where analogical reasoning is commonly employed.

The last point suggests a further point that, in my opinion, is particularly relevant in view of a proper (clearer, explanatorily stronger) characterization of judicial fictions. The point is the following: the situations, different from normative gaps proper, where the law provides a bad answer and where judicial fictions show up, *identify a definite sub-set* of a class of troublesome situations in law. The class of troublesome situations is what, in Continental Jurisprudence, goes under the name of *ideological*, *axiological* or *switchover* gaps[33]: the law provides an answer to a case at hand, but, unfortunately, the answer is (considered to be) a "bad" answer, usually from the standpoint of justice and higher, fundamental, legal principles. As a consequence, the problem, when axiological gaps are afoot, does not consist in making an appropriate new rule for a so far unregulated case. It consists, rather, in getting rid of the bad answer—and the "bad rule" that provides it—and replacing it with a good one.

5. Gottlieb points in the right direction when he pictures the technique of fiction as involving the replacement or substitution of an extant rule. Sound theory requires,

[32] See e.g. Guastini (1992), pp. 158–159; Chiassoni (2002), pp. 73–80.

[33] See for instance Bobbio (1963), pp. 72–73; Alchourrón and Bulygin (1971), ch. VI, §§ 5–6. On axiological or switchover gaps, see above, Chap. 7, Sect. 7.2.2.

however, that we are absolutely clear, I would say, clear beyond any reasonable doubt, about the sort of replacement or substitution that is at stake. Gottlieb's account is, unfortunately, too scanty and broad to provide an exact characterization as required by the clarification principle.[34] Let's nonetheless have a closer look at it, in view of advancing towards a more precise account. As we have seen, Gottlieb claims that, on the basis of an untrue formal finding of facts, "a revised rule is in practice applied in lieu of the rule which appears to be applied"; he also claims that, in cases of fiction, "another law is applied".[35] Gottlieb's language is a bit mysterious. Rehearsing the Macallister case will perhaps help us in getting a clearer view of the matter. In front of a theft of a £ 10 note (which is worth 200 shillings), the court declares ("finds") that it is a theft worth 39 shillings. On the basis of that *individual fictional premise*, the court applies "another law": namely, it applies the rule concerning the stealing of objects worth up to 39 shillings (let's call it R1: "If somebody steals something worth up to 39 shillings, he ought to be sentenced to jail"), *instead of* the rule concerning the stealing of objects that are worth 40 shillings or more (let's call it R2: "If somebody steals something worth 40 shillings or more, he ought to be sentenced to death"). Gottlieb also claims, however, that in such a case the judges are applying *a revised rule in lieu of the rule that appears to be applied*. Which is such a revised rule? We can only make a guess. A reasonable guess seems the following. The rule that *appears* to be applied is the rule R1, according to which, "If somebody steals something worth up to 39 shillings, he ought to be sentenced to jail". From a realistic point of view, however, one may suggest that the court has in fact applied a different rule, and, furthermore, that this is, say, the rule R3, which runs roughly as follows: "If somebody steals something worth 40 shillings or more, *and* the seriousness of the offence is modest, he ought to be sentenced to jail". So, in the Macallister case, if we follow Gottlieb, recourse to fiction would involve apparently three ingredients: (1) a formal "finding of facts" at odds with truth (the individual fictional premise); (2) the *apparent* application of the rule R1, *instead of* the rule R2, which, without that formal finding of facts, would have to be applied (apparent substitution of the rule R2 by the rule R1); (3) the *actual* application of the rule R3, that is a different rule from the apparently applied rule R1, *instead of* the rule R2 (actual substitution of the rule R2 by the rule R3).

I hope I have offered a fair, charitable, reconstruction of Gottlieb's theory of judicial fictions. If my reconstruction is correct, however, Gottlieb's theory of fictions appears to be troublesome on two counts.

First, from a logical point of view, the rule R3 derives from the combination of the rule R1 plus a *general fictional premise* FP:

R1: "If somebody steals something worth up to 39 shillings, he ought to be sentenced to jail"

[34] On the clarification and other principles of analytical investigations, see Chap. 1, Sect. 1.2, above.

[35] Gottlieb (1968), p. 44.

GFP: "If somebody steals something worth 40 shillings or more, *and* the seriousness of the offence is modest, he steals something worth up to 39 shillings"

R3: "If somebody steals something worth 40 shillings or more, *and* the seriousness of the offence is modest, he ought to be sentenced to jail".

As a consequence, we must reject Gottlieb's claim that the judges *only apparently* applied the rule R1, while *in fact* they applied the rule R3. Indeed, as the above fragment of the logical structure of the Macallister case suggests, since the rule R3 is logically derived from the rule R1, the application of R3 to the case at hand is also, at the same time, an indirect application of R1: R1 represents, in fact, the second-order *ratio decidendi* of the case.[36] Furthermore, it must be observed that the judge could have applied the rule R1, on the basis of GFP and the relevant premises of individual subsumption (ISP1: "Macallister stole something worth 40 shillings or more, *and* the seriousness of the offence is modest"; ISP2: "Macallister stole something worth up to 39 shillings"), *without* applying R3. Indeed, a chain of reasoning including R1, GFP, ISP1 and ISP2 (but not also R3) would be logically valid, and lead to the conclusion D: "Macallister ought to be sentenced to jail".

Second, if, contrary to my reconstruction, we consider R1 and R3 as two independent standards, and assume that the *only* rule that was "really" applied in the Macallister case is the rule R3, then the case becomes an ordinary case of defeasibility, where recourse to fiction is utterly *superfluous*. Let's see why. If we consider the rules R1 and R3 as independent standards, then the rule R3 would not derive from R1, plus the fictional premise GFP; rather, R3 would be the outcome of a reasoning involving the direct defeating of the rule R2:

R2: "If somebody steals something worth 40 shillings or more, he ought to be sentenced to death".

R2*: "If somebody steals something worth 40 shillings or more, *and* the seriousness of the offence *is not* modest, he ought to be sentenced to death".

R3: "If somebody steals something worth 40 shillings or more, *and* the seriousness of the offence *is* modest, he ought to be sentenced to jail".

R2* replaces R2. As an effect of that substitution, a case like Macallister becomes a case of normative gap. Then R3 is created to fill up the gap.

Now, however, we face an overwhelming question: if *that* way of directly defeating R2, by replacing it with R2*, was available to the judges, why did they bother to introducing the fictional premise GFP? Why did not they focus exclusively on the rule R2, and defeat it by R2* in the name of some principle of retributive justice? The answer seems evident. They did not do so, because the direct, fiction-less, defeating of the rule R2 by R2* was not a viable course of action, from the standpoint of its acceptability in the legal culture of the time.

Let's take stock of the previous analysis. If my criticism of Gottlieb's theory of judicial fiction is correct, it seems possible to add a further link in view of a better

[36] On this variety of *ratio decidendi* see Chap. 9, Sects. 9.3 and 9.4, below.

characterization of judicial fictions. As I said, the situations where judicial fictions occur identify *one sub-set of the class of axiological gaps*. Axiological gaps involve the presence of a second-best, bad rule, which provides a bad answer. Axiological gaps pose the problem of getting rid of the bad (wrong) rule, and replace it with a good (right) rule. Now, as the Macallister case suggests, the situations of recourse to judicial fictions are situations of axiological gap, where the bad rule cannot be eliminated by *directly defeating* it with the aid of ordinary interpretive techniques. The legal culture, by hypothesis, would not tolerate that kind of move. Only *indirect defeasibility* is viable. Accordingly, the only way of getting rid of the bad rule is by making its complementary rule applicable instead. To get rid of the rule R2, it is necessary to make applicable, instead, its complementary rule R1. To this purpose, fiction steps in, in order to make possible extending the application of the rule R1 to cases that, without fiction, would fall within the scope of application of the rule R2. Indirect defeasibility of a rule passes through the fictional extension (i.e., extension by means of a fictional premise, be it individual or general) of the scope of application of the complementary rule; to such fictional extension corresponds, obviously, an equivalent restriction of the scope of application of the indirectly defeated rule. Two rules are at stake. By playing with the semantics of both of them by means of a fictional sentence, the judge finally gets to the right result.

7. Schauer, as we have seen, characterises judicial fiction as a technique that involves defeasibility: fictions—he claims—*serve to defeat existing rules.* According to him, furthermore, the specific property making of judicial fictions something different from other "devices for effectuating the defeasibility of legal rules" consists in the recourse to an *untrue re-description* of the relevant facts of the case.

I agree that we can look at judicial fiction from the standpoint of defeasibility.[37] Provided we make clear, as we have just seen, that judicial fiction is a technique for *indirectly* defeating the bad rule at stake. I think, however, that Schauer's claim about what makes of judicial fictions a specific device for effectuating the (indirect) defeasibility of legal rules—the recourse to an *untrue re-description* of the relevant facts of the case—is misleading and suffers, so to speak, from an information gap. First, speaking of an "untrue re-*description* of the relevant facts" is misleading, insofar as it suggests—perhaps unwillingly, perhaps to simple-minded readers—that fictional sentences belong to the descriptive use of language, and are, accordingly, subject to truth-values. To this thorny issue I will devote some comments in the following section. Second, in selecting the untrue re-description of the relevant facts as the property accounting for the specificity of judicial fictions as a defeasibility technique, Schauer's account faces an information gap: it does not make clear, as required by the complexity of the matter, that the typical situation where judicial fictions show up is the situation where an axiological gap is afoot.

[37] On defeasibility, see Chap. 10 below.

8. Coming, finally, to Del Mar, he characterizes judicial fictions, as we have seen, in terms of making some operative fact irrelevant or unnecessary in view of retaining some associated normative consequence. To be sure, the characterization is appealing. Nonetheless, it suffers from the same information gap as Schauer's. Indeed, by focussing on the "suspension" of operative facts to secure in any case a certain normative consequence, Del Mar does not make clear that the purpose of these acts of suspension consists in overcoming an axiological gap: namely, a situation where the court assumes it has to get rid of a bad rule, in order to getting to the right result.

8.4 A Further Characterization

The previous analysis makes possible articulating what is perhaps a clearer and more informative characterization of a judicial fiction, while retrieving and retaining the valuable suggestions coming from the several notions considered. The characterization I propose can be presented in the following terms:

A Judicial Fiction is (a) a technique for overcoming axiological gaps, (b) to which the judges resort when the bad rule at hand cannot be directly defeated by means of ordinary interpretation techniques, (c) that consists in laying down an individual or a general fictional sentence, (d) on the basis of which the individual case at hand can be regulated by the good rule at hand, (e) which technique the judges assume to be authorized to employ, in virtue of a tacitly vested lawmaking power that is not preposterous from the standpoint of legal tradition, and is in tune with society's aversion to judicial activism.

A few explanations are in order.

1. A judicial fiction is an extra-ordinary tool, the core of which consists in playing with the semantics of two pre-existing rules, the bad rule and the good rule, in such a way as to change their respective, previous, ordinary scopes of application, by moving one individual case or one class of cases from the scope of application of the bad rule into the scope of application of the good rule.
2. The fictional sentence, which stays at the core of judicial fictions, does not belong to the descriptive use of language. It belongs, rather, to the constitutive or stipulative use of language that is typical of law and judicial decisions. By saying that "Stealing a £ 10 note does amount to stealing 39 shillings" (general fictional premise) or that "The stealing of a £ 10 note by John Macallister does amount to stealing 39 shillings" (individual fictional premise), the court is not misdescribing the fact of the case. It establishes—stipulates, constitutes—that stealing a £ 10 note does amount to stealing 39 shillings, that the stealing of a £ 10 note by John Macallister does amount to stealing 39 shillings. The fictional sentence is, thus, neither true nor false. It would be false, if it were set forth as a genuine descriptive sentence, with all the speech act commitments that go along

with making statements of facts.[38] But that is not the case. The idea that such a sentence would belong to the descriptive use of language originates, perhaps, from the traditional conception of the so-called "minor premise" of the judicial syllogism. This view claims that the minor premise represents the "factual premise", the "premise as to the fact". All thieves shall be sent to jail. John Smith is a thief. John Smith shall be sent to jail. Unfortunately, the traditional conception is wrong. The minor premise is not a factual premise. It is, contrariwise, an interpretive, qualifying, premise, by means of which the judge qualifies something according to a normative predicate (in our example: "thief") in view of subsuming that something under the relevant rule.

3. Until now, I have avoided any direct analysis of the phrase "judicial fiction". It may be worthwhile considering, however, that such a phrase is eminently ambiguous. Indeed, whatever view we adopt about it, "judicial fiction" can be used to refer, alternatively, to not less than four different things, namely:

   (a) A *fictional*—individual or general—*sentence*: "A is (as if) B", which, if it expresses a general sentence, may be also formulated by means of the conditional: "If something is A, then is (as if) B" (fiction-sentence);
   (b) The *technique that employs a fictional sentence in order to overcome a situation of axiological gap, where direct defeasibility of the bad rule by means of ordinary interpretive tools is not viable* (fiction-technique);
   (c) A *fictional rule*, that is to say, a rule that is applied on the basis of a fictional premise laid down while putting the fiction technique to work (fiction-rule);
   (d) A *fictional reasoning*, that is to say, a reasoning involving a fictional sentence and leading to the application of a fictional rule (fiction-reasoning).

So far I have provided only fragmentary evidence of my central explanatory claim: namely, of the claim according to which the technique of judicial fiction is, at least typically, a tool for overcoming axiological gaps where the direct defeasibility of the bad rule, by means of ordinary interpretive techniques, is not viable. To remedy to this defect, I will provide, in turn, two examples of axiological gaps not requiring recourse to fiction, and two examples of axiological gaps where recourse to fiction is, on the contrary, performed.

8.4.1 *Solving an Axiological Gap Without Fiction: The Sweeping Abortion Prohibition*

Suppose a legal order, LO_j, contains in its criminal code a provision according to which:

D: "Whoever performs an abortion shall be sentenced to jail".

[38] On this point, see e.g. Searle (1974–1975), p. 65 ff.

Suppose, furthermore, that the on-going interpretation of D, up to the time t_1, reads it as follows:

N: Whoever performs an abortion shall be sentenced to jail.

The norm N concerns, and punishes, *any sort* of abortion. To be sure, it concerns, and punishes, *both* any abortion performed for not-therapeutic reasons, *and* any abortion performed for therapeutic reasons. From this standpoint, D—by way of N—may be regarded as jointly expressing *two* norms:

N1: Whoever performs a not-therapeutic abortion shall be sentenced to jail.
N2: Whoever performs a therapeutic abortion shall be sentenced to jail.

Suppose, now, that in time t_2, a case is brought in front of a court, where an abortion has been performed to save the life of the mother, and such a legal good (the life of the mother) is considered paramount in the legal culture of the time. The court faces an axiological gap. The individual case *is* indeed regulated by the law—and, more precisely, by the norm N2; unfortunately, N2 is a *bad rule*: it provides a bad answer to the case at hand. How can the court overcome the gap? There is, apparently, a way out in three steps.

First step: The court rejects the on-going interpretation of D, and replaces it with a restrictive interpretation supported by, say, a mix of evolutionary, intentional, purposive and principle arguments. This means that

D: "Whoever performs an abortion shall be sentenced to jail"

is restrictively re-interpreted to express *only* the norm:

N1: Whoever performs a not-therapeutic abortion shall be sentenced to jail.

The norm N2 has been eliminated by way of interpretation: more precisely, by resorting to the ordinary restrictive technique of dissociation.

Second step: the courts declares that, from the standpoint of D, as properly interpreted to mean N1, the criminal law does not provide any norm punishing the performance of a therapeutic abortion. There is in other terms, at least *prima facie*, a *normative gap proper* in the criminal system of the legal order LO_j.

Third step: the court concludes that the normative gap proper ought to be filled up by applying the "general exclusive norm", according to which whatever is not (expressly) prohibited is permitted. On the basis of that (closure) norm, the court assumes the existence of the norm

N3: Whoever performs a therapeutic abortion shall not be sentenced to jail.

In technical terms, the norm N has been defeated, by replacing it with the norm N1. The norm N2 has been eliminated, and replaced with the (opposite) norm N3. The whole operation turns on an interpretive move according to ordinary interpretive techniques. No fictional sentence has been laid down.

8.4.2 *Solving an Axiological Gap Without Fiction: Mothers' Parental Leave*

Suppose a legal order, LO_j, contains in its labour code a provision according to which:

D: "Mothers have the right to parental leave in case of adoption".

Suppose, furthermore, that the on-going interpretation of D, up to the time t_1, reads it as follows:

N: Mothers have an exclusive right to parental leave in case of adoption.

The norm N is considered, in turn, to be tantamount to the conjunction of two norms:

N1: Mothers have the right to parental leave in case of adoption
N2: Not-mothers do not have the right to parental leave in case of adoption.

Since, however, "parental leave" is strictly construed, in LO_j, to concern *parents* only, the class of "not-mothers" is understood to be exhausted by the fathers of adopted children. Accordingly, the norm N is considered to be tantamount to the following conjunction of norms:

N1: Mothers have the right to parental leave in case of adoption
N2*: Fathers do not have the right to parental leave in case of adoption.

Suppose, now, that in time t_2, a case is brought in front of a court, where a father asks for a parental leave in case of adoption. The action is evidence of a new, widespread, cultural attitude towards the parental role of fathers, one that favours fathers' active involvement in the upbringing of children. The court faces an axiological gap. The individual case *is* indeed regulated by the law—and, more precisely, by the norm N2*; unfortunately, N2* is a *bad rule*: it provides a bad answer to the case at hand. How can the court overcome the gap? There is, apparently, again a way out in three steps.

First step: The court rejects the on-going interpretation of D, and replaces it with a not-exclusionary interpretation supported by a mix of evolutionary, purposive and principle arguments. This means, technically speaking, that

D: "Mothers have the right to parental leave in case of adoption".

is re-interpreted, in a not exclusionary way, to express *just one* norm, namely the (literal) norm:

N1: Mothers have the right to parental leave in case of adoption.

The norm N2* has been eliminated by way of interpretation: more precisely, by resorting to the ordinary technique of dis-exclusionary interpretation.

Second step: the courts declares that, from the standpoint of D, as properly interpreted to mean N1, the labour law does not provide any norm concerning fathers' parental leave in case of adoption. The law only regulates mothers' parental leave, being silent as to fathers. There is, accordingly, a *normative gap proper* in the labour law system of the legal order LO_j.

Third step: the court concludes that the normative gap proper ought to be filled up by analogical reasoning: namely, on the basis of the relevant similarity between mothers and fathers as to the right to parental leave. As a consequence, the courts concludes for the existence, in the labour law of LO_j, of the following, by hypothesis implicit, norm:

N3: Fathers have the right to parental leave in case of adoption.

In technical terms, the norm N has been replaced with the norm N1 by means of a dis-exclusionary re-interpretation of D. The norm N2* has been eliminated, and replaced with the (opposite) norm N3. The whole operation turns on an interpretive move according to ordinary interpretive techniques. Neither defeasibility, nor recourse to fiction, has been performed.

Keeping these two examples in mind, let's analyse, in turn, two of the most famous examples of judicial fiction in the history of Western legal culture, namely: the common law fiction in the *R. v. Macallister* case and the common law fiction in the *Mostyn v. Fabrigas* case.

8.4.3 Solving an Axiological Gap by Fiction: The Macallister Case

We have already approached the Macallister case through the lens of Gottlieb's theory of judicial fiction.[39] Let's look at it from the standpoint of the characterization of judicial fiction I propose.

Macallister steals a £ 10 note, amounting to 200 shillings. There is no doubt about that. The law of England as to theft contained two rules:

R1: If somebody steals something worth up to 39 shillings, he ought to be sentenced to jail.

R2: If somebody steals something worth 40 shillings or more, he ought to be sentenced to death.

In combination, the two rules provide an exhaustive regulation of theft. Accordingly, the problem the court faces is not due to a situation of *normative gap proper*. It is, rather, a problem arising out of a situation of *axiological gap*. The individual case—what Macallister did—is clearly regulated by the law. Unfortunately, from the standpoint of current legal culture, the law provides a bad rule for the case: a rule leading to a bad result, represented by the outrageously high penalty of death for a £ 10 worth theft.

[39] See Sects. 8.2 and 8.3, point 6., above.

Two ways were available to the court to set aside the bad rule and apply—directly or indirectly—the good rule instead (i.e., R1): on the one hand, the direct defeasibility of the rule R2; on the other hand, its indirect defeasibility, by means of a fictional sentence.

Direct defeasibility could be achieved, technically, by the ordinary technique of dissociation. By claiming that, in rule R2, stealing something worth 40 shillings or more is not, really, the sufficient condition for the legal consequence of the death penalty; by claiming, thus, such a condition to be *necessary*, but *not sufficient*, since a further condition must be met for the death penalty to apply. As we have seen, this way of proceeding amounts to changing the rule R2 into a different rule. For instance, into a rule like R2*:

R2*: If somebody steals something worth 40 shillings or more, and the seriousness of the offence is not modest, he ought to be sentenced to death.

Notice that, from the standpoint of R1 and R2*, the criminal law of England would present a *normative gap proper* as to the Macallister case. This is perhaps one of the reasons why the court opted for indirectly defeating R2 by means of fiction. Indeed, by introducing the individual fictional sentence IFS:

IFS: "The stealing by Macallister of a £ 10 note amounts to stealing something worth up to 39 shillings"

the court opened the way to make R2, the bad rule, not applicable to the case, and apply instead R1, the good rule. It moved the Macallister case from the scope of application of R2, to the scope of application of R1.[40]

8.4.4 *Solving an Axiological Gap by Fiction: The Minorca Case*

In *Mostyn v. Fabrigas*, the London court of King's Bench affirmed its jurisdiction on a case occurred in the Spanish island of Minorca, during British occupation, on the fictional premise according to which Minorca is situated within the borders of the city of London. Here again, the law of England contained indisputably two, jointly exhaustive, rules:

R1: If a case arises out of facts that occurred in the city of London, the court of King's Bench shall hear the case

R2: If a case arises out of facts that did not occur in the city of London, the court of King's Bench shall not hear the case.

[40] I have reconstructed the opinion as resorting to an individual fictional premise. Judicial fictions, however, may also resort to general fictional premises. In such cases, judicial reasoning would contain a premise like, e.g., "If somebody steals something worth £ 10, he steals something worth up to 39 shillings".

Here, again, in front of Fabrigas's complaint, the court considers to be in front of an axiological gap. The law provides in fact a clear answer about the court's jurisdiction, but that is (deemed) a bad answer. The problem is, again, how to set aside the bad rule (R2) and apply the good one, instead. Again, the problem could have been solved by means of directly defeating the rule R2, by adding to it, by means of interpretation, a further, negative condition of application.[41] This, in turn, would have created a normative gap proper, to be filled up, say, by means of an analogical application of the rule R1.

The court, however, preferred the way of indirect defeasibility. It introduced, accordingly, the well-known fictional premise I have recalled above ("The case Y, involving a British subject, that occurred in the island of Minorca, is a case that occurred in the city of London"). Again, the reason why the court preferred the way of indirect defeasibility to the way of direct defeasibility has to do, probably, with the cultural acceptability of its move. With what Schauer calls a cultural preference for judicial prevarication over judicial activism.

[41] The output of this way of proceeding could have been, for instance, a new rule R2* according to which "If a case arises out of facts that did not occur in the city of London *and the facts do not concern people's liberty rights*, the court of King's Bench shall not hear the case".

Chapter 9
Precedent

> *It is a basic principle of the administration of justice that like cases should be decided alike*
>
> —R. Cross (1977)

9.1 The Philosophy of Precedent: Two Varieties

The philosophy of precedent can be conceived as a critical enquiry on topics like "the structure of legal precedents", their "philosophical foundations", their "relevance for legal theory", their "relevance for legal practice", the "methodological problems" jurists and judges must cope with in order to "recognize", "interpret", and "follow" precedents.[1]

Two varieties are to be singled out. A philosophy of precedent can be a *normative theory* of precedent. In such a case, it is a discourse that, in relation to some legal order or set of legal orders, purports to provide answers to constitutional policy questions concerning the axiologically correct way of defining the very notion of "precedent", determining the place, if any, of judicial precedents among the sources of positive law, and determining the principles that should regulate the interpretation and the use of precedents. It goes without saying that the axiological adequacy of any such theory ultimately depends, and must be measured, on some background ethical view: usually, on some principles of public morality the philosopher is committed to. However, a philosophy of precedent can also be an *analytical theory* of precedent. In such a case, it is a discourse devoted to conceptual analysis and reconstruction, the core business of which consists in dealing with the terminology, the concepts, and, at a meta-theoretical level, the "theories" concerning judicial precedent as regards to a certain legal culture, in order to get to a better terminology, better concepts, and better ways of thinking, from the standpoint of the rationality values of clarity, precision, discrimination and justification.

[1] See e.g. Bustamante and Bernal Pulido (2012a), pp. 7–10, and the essays collected in Bustamante, Bernal Pulido (2012b).

P. Chiassoni, *Interpretation without Truth*, Law and Philosophy Library 128,
https://doi.org/10.1007/978-3-030-15590-2_9

There are obvious connections between the philosophies of precedent of the two varieties above. On the one hand, a normative philosophy of precedent is doomed to failure—to dwelling in the rhetorical world of hazy discourses—unless it is enlightened, supported, and, if necessary, cured, by an equipment of clear and distinct concepts, views, and modes of thought. On the other hand, an analytical philosophy of precedent, to do its job properly, needs full consciousness about the fact that judicial precedent is a matter for practical disputes and ideological allegiances.

My aim in this chapter is providing an outline of a few tiny pieces of a philosophy of precedent in the analytical mood. By way of a piecemeal, explanatory, axiologically uncommitted, analysis, I will deal, in turn, with three issues: first, the issue concerning an analytically proper definition of the key-notions of *judicial precedent*, *ratio decidendi* and *obiter dictum* (Sects. 9.2 and 9.3 below); second, the issue concerning an analytically proper theory of the interpretation of judicial precedents (really, an explanatory meta-theory, as we shall see) (Sect. 9.4 below); third, and finally, the issue concerning an analytically proper theory about the practical relevance of judicial precedents (Sect. 9.5 below).

9.2 "Judicial Precedent"

What is a "judicial precedent"? The phrase occurs in loose talk. By way of clarification, it seems useful distinguishing three (mutually related) notions, namely: *precedent-judgment*, *precedent-ratio*, and *precedent-order*.

To begin with, a *judicial precedent* may be taken to consist in (i) a *judicial decision*, i.e., the combination of the *opinion* and the *individual determinations* issued for an individual case at hand; (ii) *pronounced in a previous time* t^{-1}; (iii) *usefully reported*, i.e., reported in such a way as to be liable of being known and used in the future by the judges and lawyers working in the concerned jurisdiction; and (iv) *bearing on the same or like* (kind of) *facts and questions* as the facts and questions to be adjudicated at present time *t*. This I will call *precedent-judgment*.

Furthermore, and alternatively, a *judicial precedent* may be taken to consist, more narrowly, in the sole *ratio decidendi* of a precedent-judgement, whatever one may mean by *ratio decidendi*. This I will call, for brevity's sake, *precedent-ratio*.

Finally, a *judicial precedent* may be taken to consist, again in a narrow way, solely in the *individual determinations* of a precedent-judgment: i.e., in the set of individual norms or orders the judge has issued concerning the rights, duties, responsibilities, etc. of the parties to the decided lawsuit. This I will call *precedent-order*.

9.3 "Ratio Decidendi", "Obiter Dictum"

Sometimes, as we have seen, it may happen that "judicial precedent" just refers to the *ratio decidendi* contained in a precedent-judgment, i.e., in a judicial decision previously pronounced, usefully reported, and bearing on the same or like (kind of) facts and questions as the facts and questions to be presently adjudicated (Sect. 9.2 above). What is, however, a *ratio decidendi*? What do lawyers mean by that key-term of legal language? What can they mean?

A survey, even one dwelling on the surface, of the immense civil and common law literature results in a multiple-headed inventory. In fact, the *ratio decidendi* of a case (i.e., occurring in the decision of a particular cause, controversy or lawsuit) has been characterized in not least than (I am afraid to say) eleven different though, of course, related ways. Let's have a look:

(RD1) *Ratio decidendi* is the *element* in the opinion that represents the *necessary premise*, or the *logically necessary step*, for the decision of a case;

(RD2) *Ratio decidendi* is the *legal principle* that, in a judicial decision, is *sufficient* to decide the case at hand;

(RD3) *Ratio decidendi* is the *argumentation necessary or sufficient* to decide a case at hand;

(RD4) *Ratio decidendi* is the *norm* (*rule*, *principle*) that represents, alternatively: (*a*) the *necessary and sufficient* condition, (*b*) the *sufficient but not necessary* condition, or even (*c*) any *necessary but not sufficient* condition of the decision of a case at hand;

(RD5) *Ratio decidendi* is the *norm* for the facts of a case that, as a textual analysis of the precedent-judgment discloses, the judge who decided the case has *actually established or followed*, *whatever* she may have *stated* or *thought to have stated*;

(RD6) *Ratio decidendi* is the *norm* for the facts of a case that the judge who pronounced the judgment either has *expressly declared to have established or followed*, or *tacitly believed* to *have established or followed*;

(RD7) *Ratio decidendi* is the *norm* for the facts of a case that the judge has *expressly or tacitly treated* as being *necessary* to decide the case;

(RD8) *Ratio decidendi* is the *norm* for the relevant facts of a case that—according to existing law, facts, and precedents—the judge who decided the case *should have established or followed*, in order to decide the case *properly*;

(RD9) *Ratio decidendi* is the *norm* for the relevant facts of a case that, according to the subsequent judge J_s, the previous judge J_p, who decided the case, *believed to have established or followed*;

(RD10) *Ratio decidendi* is the *norm* for the relevant facts of a case that, according to the subsequent judge J_s, the previous judge J_p, who decided the case, *has in fact established or followed*, whatever she *may have meant* to do;

(RD11) *Ratio decidendi* is the *norm* for the relevant facts of a case that subsequent judges J_{ss} *should have regarded* as having being established or followed by the previous judge J_p, in the relevant precedent-judgment.[2]

All the notions of *ratio decidendi* above are indeterminate, though in different ways and degrees. Some bit of rational reconstruction is, therefore, necessary. Before doing so, however, a few comments must be premised.

1. The several notions above mirror different conceptions about the nature of a *ratio decidendi*, and suggest distinguishing different sorts of *rationes decidendi*, in relation to their *mode of communication*, the *relevance* of the *intention of the judge* who established and applied ("followed") them in order to decide a case, their *objective relevance* for the decision of a case, their *systemic standing*.
2. As regards to the *nature* of the *ratio decidendi*, there are apparently two conceptions at stake.

   On the one hand, *rationes decidendi* are sometimes characterized as *reasons*, *premises*, *logically necessary steps*, *necessary or sufficient argumentations* of a precedent-judgment (as it is the case, for instance, with the notions RD1 and RD3). These characterizations mirror an *argumentative conception* of the *ratio decidendi*.

   On the other hand, *rationes decidendi* are also characterized as general *norms*, *rules*, or *principles* (see, e.g., RD2, RD4, etc.). These characterizations mirror a *normative conception* of the *ratio decidendi*.

   Both conceptions are ultimately grounded on the semantics of the Latin word "ratio", which includes both the idea of a *reason* and the idea of a *rule* (a measure, a criterion of judgment). The *general norm* applied by a judge to decide a case is a *reason* (the *normative reason*) that justifies that decision. It works as a *premise* (the *normative premise*) of a reasoning the conclusion of which is a judicial order. If we look at any judgment as to a piece of reasoning provided with a logical structure, the general norm applied by the judge may also be regarded as a *logically necessary step* (the logically *necessary condition*) in that reasoning. The normative conception of the *ratio decidendi* is, thus, perfectly in tune with the argumentative conception. It leads, however, to more determinate notions. From an analytical point of view, therefore, it seems preferable regarding the *ratio decidendi* of a case as the general *norm*, *rule*, or *principle* that plays a fundamental role (let's by now be content with this) in the justification of the individual determinations (orders, norms) issued by the judge.
3. As regards to the *mode of communication* of the *ratio decidendi*, the several notions above suggest distinguishing between *explicit* and *implicit rationes* (consider, e.g., the notions RD7 and RD10).

   A *ratio decidendi* is *explicit*, when it has been provided with a discrete formulation: when it has been expressed, stated, or (as it is sometimes said) "announced"

---

[2] The analysis in the present section is based on Chiassoni (2005b), pp. 75–101, to which I refer also for bibliographical references.

by the judge in the opinion of a precedent-judgment by means of one or more sentences.

By contrast, a *ratio decidendi* is *implicit*, when it is the *tacit* normative premise of a judicial reasoning: when it has not been formulated, stated, announced, though—somebody claims—it has been established and applied to decide a case.

In due contexts, the (presumed) *implicit ratio decidendi* of a precedent-judgment may be played against its (presumed) *explicit ratio*. Indeed, by combining this distinction with the further distinction, concerning instead the *objective relevance* of a *ratio*, between *real ratio* and *apparent ratio*, one may argue, for instance, that the explicit *ratio* of a precedent-judgment, though carefully formulated by the judge, is just a sham; it is only the *apparent ratio*, which should be turned down in order to pay to the *real ratio*, i.e., the *tacit*, *implicit*, *unformulated*, *not-announced* one, the respect it deserves (it ought to have) in subsequent judicial decisions.

From an analytical point of view, the two distinctions—between explicit and implicit *ratio decidendi*, and between real and apparent *ratio decidendi*—are worthwhile keeping in mind, above all for their use as tools in the practical art of reasoning with precedents. One *caveat* is in order, however. To make sense from an analytical perspective, the distinction between explicit and implicit *ratio decidendi* should be recast in such a way, that a reasonably objective procedure may be followed to identify them by means of a textual analysis of a precedent-judgment. This suggests appealing to the logical structure of judicial decisions, as we shall see in a moment.

4. Sometimes, the notion of *ratio decidendi* is defined in such a way as to take into account the (presumed) *intention* of the judge who pronounced the precedent-judgment (see, e.g., RD6, RD7, RD9). Sometimes, on the contrary, this is not the case (see, e.g., RD1, RD2, RD3, RD4).

The notions of the former kind we may call *intentionalist* or *subjective* notions of *ratio decidendi*: according to them, the *ratio decidendi* is the *intended ratio*, the one the judge *meant* to establish and apply.

The notions of the second kind, by contrast, we may call *de-psychologized* or *objective* notions of *ratio decidendi*: according to them, the *ratio decidendi* is to be identified, and dealt with, as a purely unintentional object, as a piece of discourse the meaning, sense or value of which are to be determined and appreciated without making any reference, or paying any attention, to the intention (purpose, beliefs, attitudes) of its author.

The notions of *ratio decidendi* defined by civil law jurists are usually objective. By contrast, the notions defined by their common law colleagues are frequently subjective.

The distinction between subjective and objective *rationes decidendi* is relevant from two related perspectives. On the one hand, it is, at least apparently, at the core of two different models concerning the "interpretation of precedents": the subjective (or mixed) and the objective models (as we shall see at Sect. 9.4 below). On the other hand, the distinction has an argumentative use, like the ones I considered in the previous point. Indeed, in due contexts, one may play the (presumed) *subjective ratio* of a precedent-judgment against its (presumed) *objective ratio* (this way of proceeding is suggested, by the way, by the notions RD5 and RD10), claiming, for instance, that the subjective *ratio* is just the *apparent ratio*, while the *real ratio* corresponds to the objective one.

5. Sometimes, the notion of a *ratio decidendi* is defined in such a way, to include a reference to its *systemic standing* (see, e.g., RD8, RD11). Here, what is being defined is, more precisely, a—rather vague—notion of the correct, proper or right *ratio decidendi* for a case. The use of this notion clearly belongs to the critique, either by appeal judges or by jurists, of some (assumedly) erroneous precedent-judgment.

We are now in the position to proceed to the next, and final, step of the present enquiry. This requires providing an analytically adequate re-definition (rational reconstruction) of the several notions of *ratio decidendi* previously brought to the fore.

Apparently, if we take into account the presence of subjective and objective notions of *ratio decidendi* in juristic thinking, and keep in mind the need to downsize indeterminacy in the identification of *rationes decidendi* inside of precedent-judgments (curing, for instance, any loose talk in terms of "necessary" and/or "sufficient" "condition"), an analytical reconstruction, to be of some use, should meet the following requirements.

First, three concepts of *ratio decidendi* are to be defined, namely: an *objective*, a *subjective*, and a *mixed* concept. It will be up to jurists and judges *choosing* which *one* to adopt, if any, in their practice, which will fatally depend both on their purposes and on the checks and nudges provided by their legal culture.

Second, in defining the objective concept of *ratio decidendi*, reference is to be made to the *logical structure* of judicial decision. Such a structure should be conceived in turn, in its minimal form, as a normative *modus ponens*, where a normative individual categorical conclusion (the judicial order) follows from a normative general conditional premise (the applied general norm) and a qualificatory or subsumptive individual categorical premise.

Third, the use of the logical structure of judicial decisions, which brings back the centuries-old idea of judicial syllogism, should be immune from whatever sort of "formalism" or "logicism". The idea that precedent-judgments have a logical structure, indeed, does not by itself imply any commitment to the mistaken view of judicial reasoning as a logical reasoning from evident premises. On the contrary, the idea of the logical structure of judicial decision (in Wróblewski's original term: the idea of the "internal justification" of judicial decisions) is to be conceived just as a useful *tool* of analysis and criticism of judicial decisions, that is perfectly compatible with the view that the premises of the internal justification are necessarily *chosen* by the judge, and should be provided in turn with an (adequate) "external" justification".[3]

[3] See e.g. Wróblewski (1969, 1971) and Alexy (1978).

Keeping these requirements in mind, the three concepts of *ratio decidendi* may now be defined, tentatively, as follows.

Ratio decidendi (*objective concept*) = Df. A general norm (rule, principle, ruling), that is either *expressed* by a sentence in the text of a precedent-judgment, or *implicit* in it, is the *ratio decidendi* of a case in relation to a certain question of law to be decided, if, but only if, it is the normative general premise of the *modus ponens* inference from which, together with at least another premise (the individual subsumption premise), the issued judicial order may be derived.

Notice that this concept does not rule out, and indeed allows for, two situations that may occur in practice, and should be briefly considered. To begin with, it may happen that the *same* judicial order may be derived, in the text of the judicial decision, from different, but convergent, *modus ponens* inferences. In this case, there are as many *rationes decidendi* as are the different, but convergent, *modus ponens* inferences at stake. In such a situation, there is a *plurality* of different, but convergent, *first-degree modus ponens inferences*, and, consequently, a *plurality* of different, but convergent, *first-degree rationes decidendi*. Furthermore, it may also happen that the logical structure of the judicial decision is a *chain* of inter-connected *modus ponens* inferences, where the normative general premise of the lower-degree inference is, at the same time, the normative general conclusion of the higher-degree inference. In such event, we may distinguish for instance, within the logical structure of a precedent-judgment, a first-degree *modus ponens* inference, a second-degree *modus ponens* inference, a third degree … and so on, up to the nth-degree, highest or ultimate, *modus ponens* inference. In a situation like this, there are, *from a logical point of view*, several *rationes decidendi*: from the lowest, and less abstract one, working as the normative premise of the first-degree *modus ponens* inference, up to the highest, and more abstract, one, working as the normative premise of the nth-degree, ultimate, inference. In both cases, which *ratio decidendi*, among the several identified on the basis of the logical structure of a decision, should be treated as provided with *precedential value* is not something that the logical structure as such—and this concept of *ratio decidendi*—can tell. Only a doctrine of precedent—providing some legal-policy-committed criterion—can do that job. In common law countries, by the way, one such criterion seems precisely to be the *intention* of the judge: this brings into the fore the subjective and mixed concepts of *ratio decidendi*.

Ratio decidendi (subjective concept) = Df. A general norm (rule, principle, ruling), that is either *expressed* by a sentence in the text of a precedent-judgment, or *implicit* in it, is the *ratio decidendi* of a case in relation to a certain question of law to be decided, if, but only if, the judge who decided the case has *intended* it to be (*a*) the *paramount legal prescription* for the correct decision of the case at hand, and (*b*) provided with *precedential value* for subsequent decisions.

Ratio decidendi (*mixed concept*) = Df. A general norm (rule, principle, ruling), that is either *expressed* by a sentence in the text of a precedent-judgment, or *implicit* in it, is the *ratio decidendi* of a case in relation to a certain question of law to be decided, if, but only if: (*a*) it is the normative general premise of a *modus ponens* inference from which, together with other premises, the issued judicial order may be derived; (*b*) the judge who decided the case *intended* it to be (*b1*) the *paramount* legal prescription for the correct decision of that case, and (*b2*) provided with *precedential value* for subsequent decisions.

Clearly, from the viewpoint of certainty in the identification of the *ratio decidendi* of a case, the subjective and the mixed concepts fare worse than the objective concept. This is so, however, since the objective concept is defined in such a way, to leave the problem of precedential value aside. The other two concepts, contrariwise, take into account also this important problem. Together, the three concepts bring to the light where the borders between logical analysis, on the one side, and legal standards and policy, on the other side, run: they show up to which point logical analysis may help clearing the way, and where some doctrine (normative theory) of precedent has to step in. From the standpoint of an analytical philosophy of precedent, of course, the limited reach of logical analysis is by no means a drawback. On the contrary: everything is given its due (*unicuique suum*); and doctrines (normative theories) of precedent come to the fore as a further, relevant, subject for analytical enquiry and rational reconstruction.

Ratio decidendi is usually opposed to *obiter dictum*. The same sentence in the text of a judgment cannot be, at the *same* time, and from the *same* conceptual perspective, both *ratio* and *dictum*. Having provided a few concepts of the former, the latter may be defined negatively: as anything, in a precedent-judgment, that is not a *ratio decidendi* according to the objective, subjective or mixed concept of *ratio decidendi*.

9.4 "Interpreting Precedents"

What exactly do we interpret, when we "interpret precedents"? As the preceding analysis suggests, the question commands an articulated answer.

1. Provided a "precedent" can be a precedent-judgement, or a precedent-*ratio*, or else a precedent-order, interpreting a precedent may consist in interpreting a precedent-judgement, or in interpreting a precedent-*ratio*, or else in interpreting a precedent-order.
2. Judges, jurists and lawyers interpret a precedent-judgment—usually, one coming from a superior or supreme judicial body—in order to identify its *ratio decidendi* (of course, they can be more then one). Judges (of appeal) and lawyers also interpret a precedent-judgement in order to identify which *individual determination*(*s*) have been issued. In these situations, the precedent-judgment (the full text of a judicial decision: Sect. 9.2 above) is the *object* of interpretation (what is being interpreted); contrariwise, the *ratio decidendi* and the individual determinations are the *outputs* of interpretation (what interpretation aims, and gets, to). We may call such an activity *textual interpretation* of precedent-judgments.
3. Let's leave precedent-orders aside, and focus instead on precedent-*rationes*. These too can be the *object* of interpretation. This presupposes, of course, that

they have already been identified and formulated by means of a set of sentences. A (previously identified and formulated) *ratio decidendi* can be the object of two different sorts of interpretation: namely, both of *textual* and of *meta-textual* interpretation.[4]

4. Most of the traditional common-law techniques for dealing with precedents are, in fact, techniques concerning either the textual, or the meta-textual, interpretation of a previously identified *ratio decidendi* of a case (as we shall see in a moment: Sects. 9.4.1 and 9.4.2 below).
5. It is commonplace talking about "determining the *ratio decidendi* of a case". From an analytical point of view, such a phrase is highly indeterminate. Indeed, according to the context, it may refer to the three sets of operations above at once (i.e., textual interpretation of a precedent-judgment, textual interpretation of a *ratio decidendi*, meta-textual interpretation of a *ratio decidendi*), or just to some of them.

9.4.1 Interpreting the Ratio Decidendi*: Textual Techniques*

The techniques of textual interpretation of the *ratio decidendi* are suitable for re-interpreting (what is assumed to be) the original meaning (and normative scope) of a previously identified *ratio decidendi*.[5] To make the point clearer, it is useful introducing the distinction between *declarative* and *corrective* interpretation of a *ratio decidendi*.

Declarative interpretation aims at establishing the correct meaning and normative scope of a *ratio decidendi*, basically in two different situations: when the original meaning proves to be indeterminate as to a case at hand; when (it is alleged that) the original meaning has been misconstrued by some other judge in some previous decision. Here, common-law jurists use to speak of "construing", "measuring", or "explaining" a "precedent".

Corrective interpretation, by contrast, aims at coping with a (presumed) discrepancy between the *real* and the *apparent ratio decidendi* of a case. The previously identified, apparent, *ratio*—i.e. the *prima facie ratio* established by a superficial reading of a precedent-judgment (and often approved by public opinion)—is being re-interpreted, to make it matching with the (presumed) *real*, and *correct*, *ratio*. This means, in turn, that the apparent *ratio* has to be either *narrowed*, by way of a restrictive interpretation (*interpretatio restrictiva*), or else *extended*, by way of an extensive interpretation (*interpretatio extensiva*). In the former case, common lawyers talk of "refining", "reducing", "confining", "pruning", "nu-ancing", and per-

[4] On textual and meta-textual interpretation of legal provisions see Chap. 2, Sect. 2.2 above. The notions, as we shall see in a moment, can also be used, with due adaptations, in relation to precedent-*rationes*.

[5] For this and the following section, I have found a very useful, though totally unstructured, catalogue of common-law techniques in Marshall (1996), p. 29 ss.

haps, again, "measuring" the *ratio decidendi* of a case; in the latter, they talk of "extending" or "loosening" it.

9.4.2 *Interpreting the* **Ratio Decidendi***: Meta-Textual Techniques*

The techniques of meta-textual interpretation of the *ratio-decidendi*, by contrast, fall into two groups.

On the one hand, there are the techniques that concern the use of an established, precedent-*ratio* to cope with a case of first impression. This involves, usually, proceeding by analogy from the established *ratio* to a new *ratio* for the new case at hand.[6]

On the other hand, there are the techniques that concern the *precedential value* of a previously identified *ratio decidendi*. They deal with its having, or not having, the *force* or *authority* of "precedent" (with its being, or not being, the right normative premise) as to an individual case to be decided here and now. Some of these techniques are meant to *erase* or *weaken* the authority of a precedent-*ratio*; others are meant, alternatively, to *strengthen* it. To these purposes, common lawyers perform operations like, for instance, (a) *dictum-ising* (saying that a *ratio* is not really *ratio*, but mere *dictum*), (b) *undermining* (claiming there are reasons for not taking a *ratio* as authoritative), (c) *per-incuriam-ing* (saying that a *ratio* was pronounced out of mistake), (d) *outflanking* (saying that a *ratio* was pronounced by way of a mere experiment, without the serious intention that it should have precedential value), (e) *quondam-ing* (saying that a *ratio* was pronounced very long time ago, and, of course, a lot of things have changed since …), (f) *garnishing* (presenting a *ratio* in a better light than usual), and (g) *napping* (presenting a *ratio* as part of a rooted line of decisions).

Other techniques of meta-textual interpretation, finally, aim at getting rid of a precedent-*ratio* by maintaining that, though surely provided with precedential value in itself, it cannot nonetheless be applied to a specific case at hand. Among these techniques of precedent-*ratio* neutralization, *distinguishing* plays a central role. There are, apparently, two different kinds of *distinguishing*: to wit, *internal*, or *rule*-, distinguishing, and *external*, or *fact*-, distinguishing.

External distinguishing is the technique showing that a precedent-*ratio* ought not to be applied to a case at hand, because, in the present case, the material facts are different from the ones encompassed by the *ratio*—though, at a first glance, they

---

[6] Sometimes, it is alleged that the gist of reasoning with precedent is analogical reasoning. This suggestion has, however, to be resisted. Analogy plays in fact a role in seeing whether the facts of the case at hand are of the same, or like, kind as the facts ruled by a precedent-*ratio*. But this, important as it may be, does not exhaust neither the techniques of common law reasoning, nor captures the axiological foundation of the authority of precedents. On this issue, see Schauer (2008), pp. 454–460; Schauer (2009), pp. 85–92.

may have appeared to be like the facts decided by the precedent-*ratio*. Here, the jurist changes the previous description of the facts of the case, in order to claim that, all-things-considered, they are materially *different* from the facts governed by the precedent.

Internal distinguishing, on the contrary, is the technique showing that a precedent-*ratio* ought not to be applied to a case at hand, because, at a careful reading, the material facts actually encompassed by the *ratio* are different from what they appeared to be at first sight, and, consequently, they are different from the material facts of the present case. Here, accordingly, the material facts of the actual case stand, while the jurist changes the description of the relevant (material, substantive) facts ruled by the precedent.

External distinguishing leaves the precedent-*ratio* unscathed, though it leads to its non-application to a case at hand. *Internal distinguishing* is, instead, a form of re-interpreting the precedent-*ratio*. It belongs, consequently, to the techniques of textual interpretation of the *ratio decidendi*; apparently, it is sometimes conveyed under the label of "confining a precedent".

9.4.3 *Models for Determining the* Ratio Decidendi *of a Case*

A *ratio decidendi* is also, and first of all, the *output* of textual interpretation of a precedent-judgment. Two families of normative models about the "proper" way of identifying the *ratio decidendi* of a case are extant in the current literature.

On the one hand, there are Common-law models: like, e.g., the well known models by Eugene Wambaugh, Arthur Goodhart, and Rupert Cross.[7] They are intentional, mixed-models, where the interpretive contribution of the logical structure of the judicial decision either is not openly recognized, or steps in, apparently, as a default-device.

On the other hand, there are Civil Law or Continental models, like, e.g., the one that may be derived from the writings of Jerzy Wróblewski and Robert Alexy concerning the justification of judicial decisions.[8] They are objective, utterly de-psychologized, models, where the logical structure of the judicial decision is paramount.

9.5 The Practical Relevance of Judicial Precedents

While accounting for the practical relevance of judicial precedents, and, more precisely, of the *rationes decidendi* of precedent-judgments, phrases like "persuasive force", "binding force", "vertical binding force", "horizontal binding force", "*de*

[7] See e.g. Cross (1977), ch. II; Schauer (2009), ch. 3.

[8] See e.g. the references in footnote 3 above.

facto persuasive force", "formal bindingness", etc., are employed. They are, nonetheless, far from having a settled and clear meaning, passing the muster of analytical adequacy. I will proceed as follows. First, I will introduce a few distinctions necessary to cast light on the "relevance of precedent" issue (Sect. 9.5.1 below). Second, I will briefly report on what seems to be, even to-date, the most sophisticated theoretical attempt at dealing with the practical relevance of judicial precedents: namely, the one performed by the scholars of the so-called *Bielefelder Kreis* (Sect. 9.5.2 below). Third, and finally, I will provide a sketch of eight ideal-typical systems of judicial precedent, from the vantage point of the formal (*de iure*) relevance they allow for (Sect. 9.5.3 below).

9.5.1 A Few Distinctions

Concerning the *practical relevance* of judicial precedents—if by that phrase we mean, in a very broad and uncompromised way, the relevance of judicial precedents, or, more precisely, of precedents-*ratio*, for the practice of adjudication—it is useful distinguishing between *formal* (*normative, de iure*) relevance and *factual (empirical, de facto*) relevance.

Formal (normative, *de iure*) relevance is a matter of positive legal norms. It is constituted and regulated by the norms (rules, standards, principles) of a positive legal order. It consists in the relevance (authority, force, influence, importance, consideration) that judicial precedents (as defined by legal norms) *may* or *ought to* have as to the decision of subsequent cases.

Contrariwise, *factual* (empirical, *de facto*) relevance is a matter of fact. It is the relevance (authority, force, influence, importance, consideration) that judicial precedents do have in fact, in a certain legal experience, as to the decision of subsequent cases.

Formal relevance and *factual* relevance are not necessarily at odds. In fact, they point to logically independent, though not necessarily unrelated, aspects of the legal world.

From the standpoint of the norms about the formal relevance of precedents in a legal order, we may distinguish three kinds of *factual* relevance: according to the law (*secundum legem*); against the law (*contra legem*); beyond the law (*praeter legem*).

Factual relevance according to the law (secundum legem): the factual relevance of precedents, whatever it is, is the effect of judges' observance of the positive legal norms concerning precedents, of their faithful allegiance to the positive law doctrine of precedent. It is, in other words, how it ought to be.

Factual relevance against the law (contra legem): the factual relevance of precedents, whatever it is, is the effect of judges' violation of the positive legal norms concerning precedents, of their behaviours flying in the face of the positive law doctrine of precedent. It is, in other words, how it ought not to be.

Factual relevance beyond the law (praeter legem): by hypothesis, the law is assumed not to say anything about the relevance of judicial precedents, and to be, indeed, *indifferent* regarding it. In such a situation, the factual relevance of precedents, whatever it is, is the effect of a judicial practice beyond the law (*extra* or *praeter legem*). It has been established outside of positive law, possibly, but not necessarily, following some normative model of good judicial practice supported by the public opinion of the legal culture.

Scholars frequently refer to precedents having *persuasive force*, as opposed to precedents having *binding force*. Sometimes, the distinction is meant to be tantamount to the distinction between the *factual* and the *formal* relevance of precedents: precedents having *persuasive force* have a merely *factual* relevance—usually, we would say, a *factual* relevance *praeter legem*; while, on the contrary, precedents having *binding force* have a *formal* relevance. Sometimes, however, the distinction between the *persuasive* and the *binding* force of precedents seems to refer to two different forms of *formal* relevance of judicial precedents.

A further distinction, which like the one just recalled belongs to the current theory of judicial precedent, must be mentioned in passing. This is the distinction between the *horizontal* and the *vertical* relevance of precedents. For clarity's sake, it might be useful to combine it with the distinction between *factual* and *formal* relevance. Most of the time, however, it refers to two forms of *formal* relevance.

9.5.2 The **Bielefelder Kreis**

The scholars belonging to the *Bielefelder Kreis* (Aulis Aarnio, Robert Alexy, Zenon Bánkowski, Gunnar Bergholtz, Svein Eng, Francisco Laporta, Neil MacCormick, Geoffrey Marshall, Lech Morawski, Enrico Pattaro, Aleksander Peczenik, Alfonso Ruiz Miguel, Robert S. Summers, Michele Taruffo, Michel Troper, Marek Zirk-Sadowski, etc.[9]) have worked out, as I said, what is perhaps the most sophisticated theoretical account to-date of the practical relevance of precedents-*ratio*. Their account turns on four basic forms of relevance:

1. Formal bindingness;
2. *De facto* persuasive force;
3. Complementary justificatory force;
4. Mere illustrative force or other like value.[10]

1. *Formal bindingness* = Df. "a judgment not respecting a precedent's bindingness is *not lawful* and so is *subject to reversal on appeal*".

   Three degrees of formal bindingness are singled out:

---

[9] See MacCormick and Summers (1997), p. vii.

[10] See *Appendix: Final Version of the Common Questions, Comparative Legal Precedent Study, September 1994*, in MacCormick and Summers (1997), pp. 554–555; the account is given a wider scope in the essay of Peczenik (1997), pp. 461–479.

(1a) *Strictly binding precedents*: precedents are *strictly binding*, if, and only if, they are subject *neither* to *overruling*, *nor* to any *exception* whatsoever;
(1b) *Defeasibly binding precedents*: precedents are *defeasibly binding*, if, and only if, they are *not* subject to *overruling*, *but* they are subject to (a well-defined or not-well-defined set of) *exceptions*;
(1c) *Softly binding precedents*: precedents are *softly binding*, if, and only if, they are subject *both* to overruling or modification, *and* to exceptions.

2. De facto *persuasive force* = Df. "a judgment not respecting a precedent's force, though lawful, is subject to criticism on this ground, and may be subject to reversal on this ground".

   Two varieties of *de facto* persuasive force are singled out, apparently not mutually exclusive:

(2a) *Defeasible persuasive precedents*: precedents are *defeasible persuasive*, if, and only if, they "should be applied unless exceptions come into play (exceptions may or may not be well defined)";
(2b) *Outweighable persuasive precedents*: precedents are *outweighable persuasive*, if, and only if, they "should be applied unless countervailing reasons apply".[11]

3. *Complementary justificatory force* = Df. precedents have *complementary justificatory force*, if, but only if, the subsequent decisions where they are *not mentioned*, though lawful and justified, are not "as well justified" as they would be if the precedents were invoked.[12]
4. *Mere illustrative force or other like value* = Df. precedents have the force of a *mere example*, if, and only if, the subsequent decisions, where they are not even mentioned, are lawful and well justified as well.

I see two major drawbacks in the *Bielefelder Kreis*'s account of the practical relevance of precedents-*ratio* in our legal culture and experience.

The first and, to my view, more serious drawback concerns the way the *de facto* persuasive force of precedents has been characterized. Here, an unduly normative language has been used: one that is appropriate only when accounting for the formal, or *de iure*, relevance of precedents. It is claimed, as we have seen, that "a judgment not respecting a precedent's force, though lawful, is subject to criticism on this ground, and *may be subject to reversal on this ground*", where the verb "may" seems to mirror the idea of a norm authorizing reversal; it is claimed, furthermore, that a precedent has persuasive force when it "*should* be applied unless countervailing reasons apply". The normative terminology employed suggests that, perhaps, the distinction between formal bindingness and *de facto* persuasive force is not watertight. It does not point, as in my previous remarks (Sect. 9.5.1 above), to two

[11] *Appendix: Final Version of the Common Questions, Comparative Legal Precedent Study, September 1994*, 555.

[12] *Appendix: Final Version of the Common Questions, Comparative Legal Precedent Study, September 1994*, 555.

neatly distinguished dimensions of the practical relevance of precedents: the *normative* dimension, depending on positive legal norms, on the one hand; and the *factual* dimension, depending on legal culture and tradition, on the other.

The second drawback of the *Bielefelder Kreis*'s account concerns the way of characterizing the three different forms of formal bindingness of precedents. Here, a more articulated picture seems preferable, one capable of coping with two different kinds of defeasibility, and working as a tool for furthering both our grasp of reality and our classificatory capacities.

9.5.3 Eight Ideal-Typical Systems

Concerning the *formal* or *de iure* relevance of precedents—or, more precisely: of the *ratio decidendi* of precedent-judgments—eight ideal-typical systems may be singled out, basically by way of a thought experiment. These are:

1. Forbidden-relevance systems;
2. Very weak argumentative relevance systems;
3. Weak argumentative relevance systems;
4. Strong argumentative relevance systems;
5. Weak binding force systems;
6. Strong binding force systems;
7. Very strong binding force systems;
8. Discretionary-relevance systems.

(1) Forbidden-Relevance Systems The systems of this kind characterize for forbidding any practical relevance whatsoever to judicial precedents. On an ideal graph, they represent the zero degree of precedents' practical relevance. How can such an outcome be accomplished? Let's distinguish between the practical relevance *outside* of the individual lawsuits where the judgments are pronounced (external practical relevance) and *inside* of them (internal practical relevance).

As to external practical relevance, this may be prevented by a strict regulation that:

(a) rules out in principle any form of precedents' authoritativeness, even of a persuasive, *de facto*, form, by prohibiting any reference to judicial precedents in judicial opinions; and
(b) to make the ruling out effective, forbids the publication, report, annotation, comment, etc., in whatever ways, of judicial decisions.

This means, notice, that precedent-judgments would be doomed to a secret life in jealously guarded judicial archives. In this way, each judge having to decide a case would be able to draw no support at all from the previous decisions of other judges: each judge would be alone in front of a case at hand, provided only with her law-books (codes, regulations, and, perhaps, abstract juristic writings). What about a judge asking for advice and chatting with her colleagues, in the same judicial seat or elsewhere, about the cases they decided? On a very strict forbidden-relevance system, even such contacts among judges would be forbidden.

Coming to internal practical relevance, this may be prevented by a regulation according to which the appeal judge ought to act under a thick veil of ignorance about the way the case was decided by the lower court. In this way, each trial, though on appeal, becomes a totally new trial on the same issue.

Forbidden-relevance systems appear utterly weird to contemporary sensibilities. They seem, all things-considered, deeply irrational, unworkable, legal systems.

On the one hand, the strict prohibition of precedents' external relevance is doomed to result in a heavily impoverished legal culture. Case law is, to begin with, the privileged place where statutes, customs and other regulations may be tested as to their meaning, scope and determinacy on the bench of the real facts of the cases; case law is, furthermore, one of the major agency of law's development, of its constant adaptation to the "needs" and "requests" coming from "society"; case law provides, finally, a further forum of principle, besides the political arena, where new solutions, and new rights, may be worked out by the cooperation of judges, jurists and lawyers. All this would be lost in a rigorous forbidden-relevance system.

On the other hand, the strict prohibition of precedents' internal relevance is doomed to result in the total arbitrariness of judicial decision-making: due to the principle of the veil of ignorance, each judge, at each of the several degrees of a trial, may decide the case simply by flipping a coin. Of course, the legislator may impose to the judges a duty of justification, and make judicial opinions secret, to be read by a review court only, say, in trials for bribery or gross judicial negligence. But the whole machinery looks utterly foolish.

(2) Very Weak Argumentative Relevance Systems In this kind of systems, the positive law doctrine of (the external relevance of) precedent contains two basic prescriptions:

(2a) Judges would do better to retrieve, and mention in their opinions, any relevant precedent;
(2b) Judges would do better to follow the relevant precedents, in order to promote the values of certainty, predictability, and the protection of people's expectations.

The two prescriptions are given, however, by way of mere *recommendations* for good judicial practice. Nothing unpleasant follows from failing to follow them. From a formal perspective, a judgment where these recommendations are not met, is perfectly lawful and valid, both as to its *content* (substance), and as to the formal adequacy of its *motivation* (argument), though the latter would have been a better piece of opinion, had the recommendations been followed. Thus, we may regard these systems as characterized by a formal relevance that is, at once, *argumentative* and *very weak*.

(3) Weak Argumentative Relevance Systems In this kind of systems, the positive law doctrine of (the external relevance of) precedent includes again two basic prescriptions:

(3a) Judges ought to retrieve, and mention in their opinions, any relevant precedent;
(3b) Judges would do better to follow the relevant precedents, in order to promote the values of certainty, predictability, and the protection of people's expectations.

In this case, the doctrine of precedent contains, by hypothesis, two heterogeneous ingredients: one *duty-imposing norm* and one *recommendation*. The violation of the duty affects the validity of a judgment: it may be appealed, and reversed, on that point. Once that duty has been fulfilled, however, the judgment is lawful and valid, even though the recommendation is not followed—and the judge, for instance, simply decide otherwise, without any argument, after having quoted the relevant precedents.

Systems like these are characterized by a *formal* or *de iure* relevance that is, at once, *argumentative* and *weak*. The presence of a relevant precedent, even one pointing to a different outcome from the one actually reached by the present judge, ought to be marked out; but the judge has no duty of providing arguments supporting her departure from it. Unaccounted for distinguishing and overruling are perfectly lawful.

(4) Strong Argumentative Relevance Systems A system grants judicial precedents a *strong argumentative formal* or *de iure* relevance, whenever its doctrine of (the external relevance of) precedent contains the following prescriptions:

(4a) Judges ought to retrieve, and mention in their opinions, any relevant precedent;
(4b) Judges ought to follow the relevant precedents, unless they can provide "good", "serious", "stronger", "prevailing", "overwhelming" reasons for departing from them or overruling them.

In this system, the doctrine of precedent contains, by hypothesis, two *duties*. The violation of each one of them affects the validity of judgments, which may be appealed, and reversed, on both counts. In the terms of the *Bielefelder Kreis*, this system would be, roughly, a system characterized by *softly binding precedents* (or, perhaps, by *outweighable persuasive force*). I prefer to conceptualize this ideal-type in terms of a *formal* or *de iure strong argumentative* force of precedents. Precedents impose on judges who want to get rid of them (overrule them, depart from them) a burden of argumentation: they have to find reasons for presenting a different *ratio decidendi* as better, stronger, (more) correct than the old one.

(5) Weak Binding Force Systems A system grants judicial precedents a *weak binding force*, or an *open-defeasibility*, relevance, whenever its doctrine of (the outside relevance of) precedent contains the following prescriptions:

(5a) Judges ought to retrieve, and mention in their opinions, any relevant precedent;
(5b) Judges ought to follow the relevant precedents, even though they could provide "good", "serious", "stronger", "prevailing", "overwhelming" reasons for departing from them or overruling them;
(5c) Judges may nonetheless abstain from following the relevant precedents, if, and only if, the case at hand falls within an exception belonging to an open list, the judge of the case may herself contribute to fill up (for, say, the list contains vaguely worded paradigmatic cases, open to analogical and *a fortiori* extensions).

In the *Bielefelder Kreis*'s account, as we have seen (Sect. 9.5.2 above), two situations are distinguished—*defeasibly binding* precedents and *defeasibly persuasive* precedents—sharing the common feature of the precedent-*ratio* being subject to *exceptions*, *either* of a well-defined *or* of a not well-defined sort. However, in an adequate analytical account of the several kinds, and systems, of *formal* or *de iure* relevance of judicial precedents, the situations where a precedent-*ratio* is subject to "well-defined exceptions" should be carefully kept apart from the situations where a precedent-*ratio* may be subject, instead, to "not-well-defined exceptions". To make things easier (but of course, the model could be made more complex and articulated, to be more realistic), I will assume the following: exceptions to a precedent-*ratio* are *well-defined* if, and only if, they are a closed set of precisely worded items. By contrast, exceptions to a precedent-*ratio* are *not-well-defined* if, and only if, they are an open set or the items are vaguely worded.

Argumentative relevance goes along with the possibility of overruling (even without providing any justification for it, where it is very weak or weak; mandatorily justified, where it is strong). Contrariwise, binding force, which exists where overruling is formally precluded (e.g., by a positive norm like 5*b*), goes along, nonetheless, with distinguishing (defeasibility-distinguishing, internal distinguishing, exception-distinguishing).

Now, to any practical purpose, there is in fact a difference between strong argumentative relevance and, as we shall see, strong and very strong binding force. The difference however appears to be quite dim, when strong argumentative relevance is compared with weak binding force. This is so, because, either by adding some exception of her own invention, or by precisifying in the desired way a vaguely worded exception, a judge may get to the same result she cannot get to by means of overruling.

(6) Strong Binding Force Systems A system grants judicial precedents a *strong binding force*, or a *closed-defeasibility*, relevance, whenever its doctrine of (the external relevance of) precedent contains the following prescriptions:

(6a) Judges ought to retrieve, and mention in their opinions, any relevant precedent;

(6b) Judges ought to follow the relevant precedents, even though they could provide "good", "serious", "stronger", "prevailing", "overwhelming" reasons for departing from them or overruling them;
(6c) Judges may nonetheless abstain from following the relevant precedents, if, and only if, the case at hand falls within an exception belonging to a closed set of precisely worded exceptions.

The binding force of precedents, in systems of this kind, is stronger than in the previous case, for judges may defeat the precedent-*ratio* if, but only if, an exception of a *given* set holds: i.e., an exception which, by hypothesis, they cannot themselves create or modify—but within the unavoidable fringes of vagueness coming along with every ordinary language expression.

(7) Very Strong Binding Force Systems A system grants judicial precedents a *very strong binding force*, or an *absolute binding force*, whenever its doctrine of (the external relevance of) precedent contains the following prescriptions:

(7a) Judges ought to retrieve, and mention in their opinions, any relevant precedent;
(7b) Judges ought to follow the relevant precedents, even though they could provide "good", "serious", "stronger", "prevailing", "overwhelming" reasons for departing from them or overruling them;
(7c) Judges ought to regard, and treat, the relevant precedents as subject to *no exception* whatsoever.

(8) Discretionary-Relevance Systems Finally, a system grants judicial precedents a *discretionary-relevance*, whenever its doctrine of (the external relevance of) precedent contains the following prescription:

(8a) Judges may take towards precedents whatever position they think proper, from case to case—i.e., they may feel absolutely bound by some precedent, or consider it as endowed with a strong or weak binding force, or regard it as endowed with a strong, weak or very weak argumentative force, or even think precedents ought not to be given any relevance whatsoever as to the decision of subsequent cases.

I do not know if any historical legal system is, or ever was, like this. There are, however, legal experiences the judicial practice of which, from an external, sociological viewpoint, can be described as informed by something like a principle of discretionary-relevance, for judges seem to assume it, as a formal or *de iure* doctrine, in their decision-making.[13]

To conclude, I wish to make three remarks.

[13] In the Italian legal experience, for instance, judges seem to adopt a principle of discretionary-relevance that allows them to oscillate between considering precedents as endowed with (very) weak argumentative relevance and considering them as endowed with strong argumentative relevance.

1. The present theory of ideal-typical systems can be made even more complex by considering also the horizontal and vertical dimensions of the formal relevance of judicial precedents (see Sect. 9.5.1 above).
2. The eight systems are *ideal-types*. Their explanatory and classificatory power always depend on adjustments to be made in the light of the legal experience that is being investigated.
3. Positive law regulations of judicial precedents, strict and demanding as they may be on paper (if there is any), are always to be taken, so to speak, *salva interpretatione*: i.e., always keeping in mind the interpretive techniques jurists and judges can use, in a legal system, both for interpreting the "rules on precedent", and for identifying, and coping with, the *rationes decidendi* having precedential value.

Chapter 10
Defeasibility and Legal Indeterminacy

it is usually not possible to define a legal concept such as "trespass" or "contract" by specifying the necessary and sufficient conditions for its application. For any set of conditions may be adequate in some cases but not in others, and such concepts can only be explained with the aid of a list of exceptions or negative examples showing where the concept may not be applied or may only be applied in a weakened form

—H.L.A. Hart (1948–1949)

10.1 The Problem

The present chapter will be devoted to defeasibility and legal indeterminacy. I will proceed by a three-stages argument. In the first stage, I will provide a very sketchy analysis of "legal indeterminacy", aiming at pointing out a few basic, and, so far as possible, clearly stated notions (Sect. 10.2 below). In the second stage, roughly the same job will be done as to "defeasibility" (Sect. 10.3 below). In the third, and final, stage, I will match the outcomes of the inquiries from the two previous stages (Sects. 10.4–10.7 below). My way of proceeding has the unmistakable whiff of old-style, analytic philosophy, conceptual analysis. It is a well-known fact, however, that "legal indeterminacy" and "defeasibility" dwell as elusory butterflies in the meadow of jurisprudence. That is why something like an entomologist's approach—incommodious as it may appear—seems nonetheless to be of some use.

10.2 Legal Indeterminacy

At the dawn of the twentieth century, path-breaking situation-sensible jurists on both sides of the Atlantic denounced indeterminacy—under a variety of headings ("interpretation", "gaps", "discretion", "judicial law-making", etc.)—as an intrinsic

P. Chiassoni, *Interpretation without Truth*, Law and Philosophy Library 128,
https://doi.org/10.1007/978-3-030-15590-2_10

structural feature of (Western) legal systems. They wished to free legal thinking from the spell of "formalism". They turned indeterminacy into a basic issue on the jurisprudential agenda, and a notorious matter of concern for the science of legislation and the theory of the Rule of Law.

I assume a (useful) theory of legal indeterminacy to be a methodologically aware discourse,[1] purporting to cast light on its matter by inquiring issues like the *objects* of indeterminacy, the *sources* of indeterminacy, the *notions* and *forms* of indeterminacy, the *problems* indeterminacy rises for both legal theory and legal politics (for both expository and censorial jurisprudence, to recall a well-known Benthamite distinction).

This frame I will take into account in the following, tentative, analysis of legal indeterminacy. I will deal, first, with the objects and sources of indeterminacy: i.e., with what in the law is, or may be, apt for being "indeterminate" and the factor(s) explaining why that something is, in some sense, indeterminate (Sect. 10.2.1). Then, I will define a few notions (Sect. 10.2.2).

10.2.1 Indeterminacy in Law and Its Sources

When legal philosophers claim that "the law is indeterminate", or deal with "law's indeterminacy", their statements apparently refer to a variety of puzzling situations. These consist, e.g. in: (1) indeterminate legal *solutions* (answers, normative consequences) to (real or hypothetical) cases at hand; (2) indeterminate *legal provisions* (*legal provisions, legal sources*); (3) indeterminate legal *norms* (rules, commands, standards, principles, etc.); (4) indeterminate legal *concept-words*; (5) indeterminate legal *concepts*; (6) indeterminate *methodological rules* (canons, techniques, methods, directives, codes, etc. for textual or meta-textual interpretation[2]); (7) indeterminate legal *systems*.

As we shall see in a moment, some of these indeterminacy situations are—or may be regarded as—*original* (independent, freestanding); while others, by contrast, are—or may be regarded as—*derivative*, i.e., dependent on other indeterminacy situations.

[1] Methodological awareness shows itself, for instance, in the following dispositions: avoiding any confusion between theory and ideology, being aware of the different levels of discourse, having a theory of definition (where lexicographic definitions and stipulative definitions are carefully kept separate), distinguishing between theory and definition, subject-of-enquiry and method of enquiry, conceptual frameworks and "the world", etc. And, of course, endorsing the principles and tools of analytical investigations I rehearsed at the outset: see Chap. 1, Sects. 1.2 and 1.3 above.

[2] On these notions, see Chap. 2, Sect. 2.2, above.

10.2.1.1 Indeterminate Legal Solutions

When a lawyer maintains that, as to a certain—real or imaginary—case (situation, behaviour, relationship) at hand, “the law is indeterminate”, she often means that “the solution (the answer, the normative consequence) the law provides for that case is *indeterminate*”. Now, such a sentence can be understood in three different ways (to say the least).

First, it may be understood as claiming that the law *does* provide *a complete (gapless) set of abstract alternative solutions* to the case at hand, but it is indeterminate as to *which one* is to be applied.

Second, it may be understood as claiming that the law provides *two or more competing solutions* to the case at hand, without specifying which one ought to be preferred.

Third, it may be understood as claiming that the law *does not* provide *any solution at all* to the case at hand.

If the lawyer is a judge, and at some point in her dealing with a case she finds herself in one of the three situations above, we may say that the judge is in a situation of *adjudicative indeterminacy.*

10.2.1.2 Mutually Exclusive Answers

Adjudicative indeterminacy obtains, to begin with, when the law *does* provide *a complete (gapless) set of abstract alternative solutions* to the case at hand, but it is indeterminate *which one* is to be applied. It is adjudicative indeterminacy by *mutually exclusive answers.*

Consider the following example. Provided the case at hand, *a* (say, the entering by John Doe into the City Park on a skate-board), may be *either* C (entering into the City Park *on a vehicle*), *or* not-C (not entering into the City Park *on a vehicle*), the judge has identified a complete normative (micro) system made of two norms: N_1 “(x) (Cx –> Sx)” (“Whoever enters into the City Park on a vehicle ought to pay a 5 € fine”); and N_2 “(x) (¬Cx –> ¬Sx)” (“Whoever enters into the City Park on a not-vehicle ought not to pay a 5 £ fine”). If *a* is C (C*a*), it has the normative consequence S (S*a*). Contrariwise, if *a* is ¬C (¬C*a*), it has the normative consequence ¬S (¬S*a*). The two norms, however, prove indeterminate as to the descriptive term that identifies the conditioning facts (in our example “vehicle”).

In such situations, judges face a *gap of recognition.*[3] Gaps of recognition obtain whenever the meaning of some of the descriptive terms in the norms (“valid contract”, “sacrilegious contract”, “vehicle”, “park”, “living will”, “trespass”, etc.)

[3] See Alchourrón and Bulygin (1971), ch. 1. What about a situation where the judge has identified *one* legal norm as relevant (say, through the textual interpretation of a given legal provision), but this norm proves, in turn, ambiguous? I consider such a case to be tantamount to a situation of *plurality of competing answers*, and will deal with it in a moment, under the heading of ambiguous *legal provisions.*

comes out to be vague in front of the facts of the case. On the basis of the extant semantic rules concerning the scope of the descriptive terms at stake, those facts might be included, as well as not included, within the scope of the norms. Since, by hypothesis, the guidance offered by semantic rules has run out, there is only one way to cure this form of indeterminacy, if it is to be cured at all (as it ought to be in modern legal systems forbidding *non liquet* judgments). The way consists in stipulating a new (piece of a) semantic rule, seeing to that specific event.[4]

We are now in a position to see more clearly *what is* indeterminate, and *why*, whenever a judge faces a gap of recognition—or, in my terminology, a situation of mutually exclusive answers adjudicative indeterminacy.

Any such situation depends, at least *prima facie*, on the indeterminacy of some *legal concept*, or of the corresponding *concept-word* (predicate term), in the sentence expressing the norm.[5]

The indeterminacy of a legal concept (concept-word), however, is *derivative*: it can be regarded as depending, in turn, on *interpretive rules*. Indeed, one and the same legal concept (one and the same concept-word) may prove vague, say, according to its up-to-date literal meaning (according to conventional semantic rules), while, at the same time, it may prove determinate according to the meaning suggested for it, say, by legislative history, the "proper" institutional goal of the norm or its background reasons. This suggests that the original source of the situations of adjudicative indeterminacy due to mutually exclusive answers is to be placed, ultimately, with interpretive rules. It is *their* "indeterminacy" that usually reverberates upon legal sources (in the present case: upon the concept-words contained in legal provisions), and, from there, upon the corresponding legal norms and the legal answers they provide for a case.

At this point, however, we face a further need for analysis. "Indeterminacy of interpretive rules"—in the present case: of rules concerning textual interpretation—is a tricky phrase. It may refer, to say the least, to two different properties of interpretive rules.

On the one hand, by "indeterminacy of interpretive rules" one may refer to their *content indeterminacy*: i.e., to the fact that (many, if not all) interpretive rules, as they are handed down by the methodological tradition and juristic literature, usually provide a poor—partial, defective, indeterminate—guidance to judges and other interpreters, one that is a far cry from the requirements of rational legal reasoning.[6]

[4] For instance, by stipulating that any deal made on Saturday is a "sacrilegious contract"; that any trained dolphin, to be used by a child for riding in the park's pond, is a "vehicle"; that any post-card expressing ever-lasting love to a city or other place on earth is a (piece of a) "living will"; that any street like Park Avenue is a "park", etc.

[5] Here, as in the whole book, I assume norms to be linguistic entities, and, frequently, the meanings of legal provisions (legal provisions). See Chap. 2, Sect. 2.2.1.1, Chap. 5, Sect. 5.2, above.

[6] From the viewpoint I have adopted in the text, the existence of gaps of recognition, as defined by Alchourrón and Bulygin, precisely depends on the partial defective guidance offered by the single translation rule assumed to be paramount: "Let words be read according to their conventional semantic rules". On translation rules, see Chap. 2, Sect. 2.2.1.1, Chap. 3, Sect. 3.4, above.

On the other hand, by "indeterminacy of interpretive rules" one may refer to their *systemic indeterminacy*: i.e., to the fact that the set of interpretive rules judges may or ought to apply to (identify and) justify their interpretive outcomes is both *open* (new items may be included and old ones may be discarded, revised, modified, qualified, etc.) and *un-ordered* (there is no fixed *ex ante* hierarchy among the rules or their respective outcomes).

As a consequence, within the constraints provided by the legal culture or society at large, each judge is ultimately responsible for the interpretive code—the discrete set of interpretive rules—she chooses to apply to decide any single case at hand.[7] Such a choice usually depends, in turn, on the judge's normative vision about the law (legal ideology).

10.2.1.3 Plurality of Competing Answers

Adjudicative indeterminacy obtains, furthermore, when the law provides *two or more competing solutions* to the case at hand, without specifying which one ought to be preferred. It is adjudicative indeterminacy by *plurality of competing answers*. Five puzzling situations are to be considered here: ambiguous legal provisions, generic norms, normative conflicts, explicit gaps, and, finally, the plurality of alternative reconstructions of a normative set (legal system).

1. Ambiguous Legal Provisions To begin with, the plurality of competing answers may be the effect of the ambiguity of a single, relevant, legal provision. The judge assumes that the legal norm for an individual case C_i at hand ought to be derived from the legal provision LP_0. LP_0, however, is capable of being read in several alternative ways, leading to a set of alternative (explicit) norms:

$$\text{Int.}(LP_0) = [N_1 \vee N_2 \vee N_1 \,\&\, N_3 \vee \ldots N_n].$$

Ambiguity may stem from the syntactic structure of the legal provision (*syntactic ambiguity*) or from the conventional linguistic meaning of its descriptive terms (*semantic ambiguity*).

These forms of ambiguity, however, are paramount, if, and only if, the interpreter adopts a simple interpretive code, containing a linguistic meaning translation rule.[8] Indeed, as soon as we look at the interpretation of legal provisions from the vantage point of interpretive rules and interpretive codes, and as soon as we take into account the plurality of such rules and the variety of interpretive resources, we must acknowledge that the basic form of ambiguity affecting legal provisions is neither syntactic,

[7] On interpretive rules and interpretive codes see Chap. 2, Sect. 2.2.1.1, Chap. 3, Sects. 3.4 and 3.6, Chap. 5, Sect. 5.2, and Chap. 6, Sects. 6.2 and 6.3, above.

[8] See Chap. 3, Sect. 3.4, above.

nor semantic, but, rather, *pragmatic*: i.e., it is an ambiguity that depends on interpreters' legal ideologies and methodological choices.[9]

2. Generic Norms A plurality of competing answers may also show up in the following situation. The judge has identified a norm—usually, a (general, fundamental, basic) *principle*—as the relevant (explicit or implicit) norm to be used to adjudicate a claim. The norm, however, is (eminently) generic ("Let right be done", "First, do no harm", "No person may profit from her own wrongdoing", "Every person is entitled to the blessings of liberty", etc.). As a consequence, it allows for a plurality of competing specifications in the face of real (or imaginary) cases. Several alternative, more specific, rules (rules of detail, *Konkretisierungen*) may be derived out of it, according, again, to the interpreters' ideology and methodological choices.

3. Normative Conflicts A plurality of competing answers may also be the effect of a situation where: (it is assumed that) there is a normative conflict; the conflict is (perceived as) a *real* conflict: it cannot be settled by resorting to one ordered set of criteria established by the "authoritative" or "conventional" code obtaining in the legal culture of the moment. Notice that the identification of normative conflicts depends on interpretive rules.[10] Accordingly, even in a situation of normative conflict, the original source of adjudicative indeterminacy is to be placed, ultimately, with such rules—and with the individual and collective ideologies that govern their precisification, selection and use.

4. Explicit Gaps Adjudicative indeterminacy due to the presence of a plurality of competing answers may also be the effect of a situation where: (a) there is an explicit gap, i.e., it is assumed that available legal provisions, however interpreted, cannot provide any explicit norm for a case at hand[11]; (b) there are several alternative ways of filling up the gap, several integration rules, leading to different outcomes (e.g., by analogical reasoning, *a contrario* reasoning, concretization of fundamental principles, reasoning from the Nature of things, etc.); (c) according to the "authoritative" or "conventional" integration code obtaining in the legal culture of the moment, there is no settled, binding, hierarchy among the integration rules available. Here again, as in the two previous puzzling situations, the ultimate factors responsible for this kind of adjudicative indeterminacy stay with interpretive and integration rules, their systemic indeterminacy, and the interpreters' ideological allegiances.

5. Alternative Reconstructions of a Legal System It may also happen that the content of a legal system is indeterminate. It is not clear *which* norms it is made of, since alternative reconstructions are available. This may be the case, for instance, whenever in a legal system: a norm N_1 has been derogated; N_1, however, may also be logically derived from a combination of two other norms of the system, say, N_2

[9] See Chaps. 2–6 above.

[10] On this point, see Chap. 2, Sect. 2.2.2, Chap. 6, Sect. 6.5.5, above.

[11] On explicit gaps see Chap. 7, Sect. 7.2 above.

and N_3; the derogating norm, however, does not say anything about whether N_2, or N_3, or both have been also derogated; consequently, the system is indeterminate as to the norms making it up, for it may be regarded as containing, alternatively, N_2, but not N_3, or *vice versa.*[12] Upon consideration, this situation of indeterminacy depends on a gap in the system: i.e., on the fact that a suitable derogating norm is missing. Accordingly, it boils down to the indeterminacy situation considered at point 4 above.

10.2.1.4 No-Answer

Adjudicative indeterminacy obtains, finally, when the law *does not* provide *any solution at all* to the case at hand. It is *no-answer* adjudicative indeterminacy. We are here at the extreme borders of a legal order. By hypothesis, no possible combination of legal sources and interpretive or integration rules provides the judge with some, explicit or implicit, norm, suitable to the case at hand. Given the complexity of legal sources in modern legal systems, and, above all, the varieties of combinations and uses of interpretive and integration rules, such an event appears mostly academic.

10.2.2 Five Notions of Legal Indeterminacy

If we take stock of the preceding analysis and pay attention to the objects of indeterminacy (what, in law, is apt to be indeterminate), five notions of legal indeterminacy are worthwhile considering. These are: adjudicative indeterminacy, textual indeterminacy, normative indeterminacy, methodological indeterminacy and ideological indeterminacy.

1. Adjudicative Indeterminacy obtains whenever the law, from the standpoint of adjudication, does not provide *one determinate solution* (answer, normative consequence) for an individual case at hand.

2. Textual Indeterminacy (Legal Provisions Indeterminacy, Sources Indeterminacy) obtains whenever a *legal provision* proves ambiguous. The ambiguity of a legal provision can be *syntactic*, *semantic* or *pragmatic*. *Pragmatic ambiguity* can be, in turn, *methodological* or *ideological*: i.e., it can depend either on the existence of a plurality of alternative interpretive methods, or on the existence of a plurality of alternative ideological outlooks, leading to alternative meanings. Here and now, as we have seen, *all* legal provisions are methodologically ambiguous (universal methodological ambiguity); contrariwise, legal provisions are only potentially ambiguous from an ideological standpoint, since different ideologies

---

[12] For such an indeterminacy situation, see Bulygin (1981), p. 42 ff.

may nonetheless overlap, pointing to one and the same meaning as to a legal provision at hand (potential ideological ambiguity).[13]

3. Normative Indeterminacy obtains in three situations: (a) the relevant *norm*—be it an explicit or an implicit norm—is ambiguous, vague or generic in relation to a case at hand, and competing alternative ways out are available; (b) there is a normative gap, and competing alternative ways of filling it up are available; (c) there is a normative conflict, and competing alternative ways of overcoming it are available.

4. Methodological Indeterminacy obtains in two different, often concomitant, situations. First, the tools (rules, directives, methods, techniques, canons) that may be used in order to justify some piece of textual interpretation, norm-qualification, norm-concretization, gaps filling, etc., make up an *open* and *un-ordered set* (*systemic indeterminacy*). Second, the tools (rules, directives, methods, techniques, canons) that may be used in order to justify some piece of textual interpretation, norm-qualification, norm-concretization, gaps filling, etc., prove, in themselves, indeterminate (*content indeterminacy*).

5. Ideological Indeterminacy obtains, finally, whenever, due to ideological pluralism, competing alternative ways of reading legal provisions, reading norms, precisifying norms, concretizing norms, filling up gaps and solving normative conflicts are available.

Apparently, the key causal factors bearing on adjudicative, textual and normative indeterminacy are the factors behind pragmatic indeterminacy: namely, methodological indeterminacy and ideological indeterminacy, which is in turn the effect of ideological pluralism.

A legal order characterizes for *radical indeterminacy*, if, and only if, *every* legal provision *and every* legal norm is *indeterminate*, from the standpoint of adjudication, as an effect of the interplay between methodological indeterminacy and ideological pluralism.

Contrariwise, a legal order characterizes for *moderate indeterminacy*, if, and only if, the interplay of methodological indeterminacy and ideological pluralism allows for areas of textual and normative *determinacy*: from the standpoint of adjudication, *not every* provision, *nor every* norm, is indeterminate. The more it is so, the more moderate the legal order's indeterminacy is.

[13] See Chap. 5, Sect. 5.2, above.

10.3 Defeasibility in Law

Though it always enjoyed an undercover presence in (Western) legal thinking, mainly under the heading of the rule-exception issue,[14] the term and subject of "defeasibility" is a relatively new entry in the jurisprudential realm. After a first appearance in the late 1940s, due to Herbert Hart's essay *The Ascription of Responsibility and Rights,*[15] defeasibility disappeared for almost 40 years from legal philosophical writings, to gain a new currency, along with studies in deontic logic and artificial intelligence and the law, from the late 1980s to early 1990s onwards.[16]

While some legal philosophers take a sceptical view about it,[17] it seems, nonetheless, that it would be a mistake to dismiss defeasibility simply as a fashionable label for well-known, unsurprising, corners of the legal maze. Indeed, defeasibility features as the main character in critical lines of inquiry pointing at deeply rooted conceptions about crucial issues in law.

A tentative list of the targets of the defeasibility turn in legal thinking would include, in my view, not less than eight different views.

1. The objectivist conception of the rule-exception relationships. This view sees norms and "their" exceptions as given, objective, entities in the legal domain. It is tantamount to metaphysical realism in law and represents an enduring, though perhaps unconscious, heritage of the age of formalism.
2. Epistemological realism as to the science of the law. This view regards knowledge in the legal domain as direct, objective, apprehension of fully-fledged norms and exceptions, together with legal rights, duties, responsibilities, etc., *out there*; it represents the epistemic counterpart of the objectivist conception of the rule-exception relationships.
3. The conditional conception of the logical form of legal norms. This view maintains that legal norms are properly represented as conditional, or hypothetical, normative sentences, where a certain legal consequence (say, the duty to do q: Oq) follows from, or is ascribed to, the set of *sufficient* conditions specified in the antecedent ("p –> Oq"; "(*x*) (A*x* –> OB*x*)").
4. The Aristotelian conception of the definition of legal concepts. According to this view, a (proper) definition of a legal concept requires the identification of a set of necessary and sufficient defining properties. This view, however, is a piece of old-time, pre-Benthamite, conceptualism, owing its present survival to the sup-

[14] See, e.g., Bentham (1791), p. 112 ff.; Larenz (1979), pp. 252–253, 257 ff.; Schauer (1991b), p. 871 ff.

[15] Hart (1948–1949), pp. 145–166.

[16] Among the forerunners of the "defeasibility turn" in deontic logic, in the late 1960s, Hansson (1969), pp. 373–398—as reported by Alchourrón (1993), pp. 43–84. Another major contribution, in the early nineteen seventies, is Åqvist (1973).

[17] See, e.g., Rodríguez and Sucar (1998), p. 103 ff., 143.

port from—to quote Hart's words—"philosophers'" truth-functional theory of meaning.[18]

5. *Naïf* norm-universalism. This view amounts, very roughly speaking, to the confident belief that *general* legal norms can actually and thoroughly control people's behaviours, as opposed to the (more modest) perspectives represented, on the one hand, by *critical* norm-universalism (being content with a net of interlocking, reasonably effective, general norms), and, on the other hand, by outright normative particularism.
6. The deductive, or monotonic, conception of the logical relationships between legal norms. This is the view considering norms as linguistic entities apt for the law of the strengthening of the antecedent and *modus ponens*.
7. The linear conception of legal reasoning. This is the cognitive, psychological, model that represents legal reasoning—and notably, interpretive reasoning—as a simple, linear, forward-going, process, from a fixed set of starting points (inputs, data) to a set of conclusions (outputs). It represents the cognitive counterpart of the deductive conception of the relationships between norms.
8. The so-called separation thesis. This is the view according to which there is no necessary connection between law and morals, so that it makes perfect sense to distinguish between the law as it is and the law as it ought to be.

Some of the views above, (surely, the separation thesis, the conditional conception of the logical form of legal norms, and the monotonic conception of normative logic, but also some of the other ones, at least in some nuanced version and from a loose, common-sense, perspective) are usually considered as pieces of that influential theory of law which goes under the name of "legal positivism", or, on the Continent, "normativism" ("normativistic legal positivism").

Thus, the defeasibility turn in legal theory, with its several strands, may be viewed—from a unifying perspective—as the revolutionary attempt to open the way for a new theoretical paradigm in legal thinking: as an intellectual venture fostering a (supposedly) advanced form of *critical, defeasibility-centred, normativism*, that should replace what, by present standards, should be regarded, instead, as the *naïf normativism* dominating such a large part of twentieth century jurisprudence.[19]

As I did while dealing with legal indeterminacy (Sect. 10.2 above), I will assume—as a regulative ideal to my present, very tentative, inquiry—that a useful theory of legal defeasibility (defeasibility in law) would be a methodologically-aware discourse, purporting to cast light on its subject matter, by dealing with issues like the *objects* of defeasibility, the *sources* of defeasibility, the *notions*, and *forms*, of defeasibility, the *problems* defeasibility makes for both legal theory and legal politics.

[18] As is well known, this is the line of criticism that Hart set forth since his earliest jurisprudential essays: Hart (1948–1949); Hart (1954), pp. 21–48.

[19] It goes without saying, of course, that the very same, supposedly "*naïf*" normativism of the present days is, in its turn, an advanced, sophisticated, form of "critical" normativism, if compared to the "*naïf*" normativism characterizing jurisprudence in the nineteenth and twentieth centuries.

This frame I will take into account in the following, tentative, analysis of defeasibility in law. I will deal, first, with the objects and sources of defeasibility (Sect. 10.3.1); then, I will define a few notions (Sect. 10.4).

10.3.1 Objects and Sources

In the scholarly literature, many different things are qualified as "defeasible", though sometimes the very logical possibility of such qualification is contested.

A tentative survey suggests that while dealing with "defeasibility in law", or "law's defeasibility", legal philosophers deal with one or more of the following 11 objects: (1) defeasible *facts*; (2) defeasible *beliefs*; (3) defeasible legal *concepts*; (4) defeasible *legal provisions* or *legal texts*; (5) defeasible legal *interpretations*, or defeasible *meanings*, of legal provisions; (6) defeasible legal *norms*, rules, principles, standards, etc. (norm-defeasibility); (7) defeasible legal *reasoning*; (8) defeasible legal *positions*, jural relations, legal entitlements, etc. (status defeasibility); (9) defeasible legal *arrangements*, like contracts, wills, etc. (arrangement defeasibility); (10) defeasible legal *claims*; (11) defeasible legal *conclusions*. A theory of defeasibility should make clear which objects—out of the tentative list above—on a closer inspection can be conveniently regarded as defeasible, and why. Accordingly, in what follows I will briefly consider in turn each one of them, in order to see: first, what their "defeasibility" consists in; second, whether, and why, they can, or cannot, be suitably considered as "defeasible"; third, which are the factors making them defeasible—i.e. what is, or may safely be regarded as being, the source or sources of their defeasibility. The inquiry is meant to pave the way for the identification of a few, more precise, notions of defeasibility: a few *explicata* out of the bubbling cauldron of intuitive "defeasibility" *explicanda*.

10.3.1.1 Defeasible Facts

According to Jaap Hage, a first class of defeasibility-apt things consists in the (relevant) *facts* of the lawsuits:

> A contract that has come into existence after an offer and an acceptance can be invalidated if one of the parties involved invokes a defeating condition, such as fraudulent misrepresentation, or undue influence. Since this case of defeasibility *concerns the (retro-active) change of the facts*, and *not* our *beliefs* about the facts, we may call it *ontological defeasibility*.[20]

[20] Hage (2004), p. 1, italics added; Hage (2003), p. 221 ff. See also Sartor (2006), p. 10, for a similar idea of an "ontic defeasibility": "there are *facts* [...] that are normally sufficient to determine certain legal or moral outcomes, but can be made irrelevant (undercut) or can be outweighed (rebutted) by further facts [...] when seen from the ontic perspective, defeasibility does not pertain to conclusions or rules, but rather to facts, in the sense of *relevant* aspects of the situation at issue, and it concerns their ability to constitute normative (legal or moral) qualifications and effects".

Facts, however, are what they are—and, brain-in-a-vat scepticism apart, we do know that pretty well since we always, sometimes painfully, run into them. They cannot properly be "defeasible", i.e. subject to *retro-active change*, as is suggested by Hage. Unless, of course, we own a serviceable machine through which we, the lucky travellers, may go back in time and fix things up as we like (school grades, marriages, payments, job-opportunities, land-occupations, auction offers, treasure-troves, etc.). Accordingly, the only way to make sense of Hage's idea of ontological defeasibility is to look at it as a metaphor. The very words Hage employs suggest this way out: what he is really talking about in the quoted passage above are, in fact, two different, opposing *descriptions* of the factual grounds of a lawsuit. Plaintiff says: there was offer and acceptance, and no fraudulent misrepresentation or undue influence occurred. Defendant replies: yes, there was offer and acceptance, but fraudulent misrepresentation and undue influence occurred. Eventually, ontological defeasibility boils down to the *revisability* of the parties' *descriptions* concerning the relevant facts of a lawsuit, in front of new evidence.

10.3.1.2 Defeasible Beliefs

According to several legal philosophers (J. Hage, J. Rodríguez, G. Sartor, etc.[21]), *beliefs* would make for another, theoretically relevant, class of defeasibility-apt things.

The beliefs they have in mind may be about several different aspects of any legal experience: the normative status of an action, the norms making up a given legal system, the proper justification for some legal conclusion and/or its premises, the proper interpretation of a given legal provision, etc. Such beliefs are "defeasible" in the sense that, like the facts-descriptions above, they too would be liable or open to revision: to be modified, specified or utterly discarded, in view of further information which may emerge in the course of the enquiry.

Clearly, beliefs-defeasibility, whatever the subject-matter of the beliefs, is *second-order* "legal" defeasibility. It is not, properly speaking, defeasibility *of* any *legal* item whatsoever, meaning by that things *belonging to*, *being part of*, or anyway *within*, the law. Furthermore, at least in some cases, it seems to be a typical form of *derivative* defeasibility: our beliefs (opinions, views, normative propositions) about some aspects of a legal order are liable to change, for the legal items which they refer to are themselves "defeasible", in the generic sense of being subject to, liable to, open to, revision and change. But, of course, beliefs-defeasibility might also be altogether dependent on our own epistemic limitations: something in

However, there is no *relevance* at all without some (presupposed) *criterion of relevance*: i.e., some standards according to which certain facts are to be deemed relevant (important, worthwhile considering, etc.) in view of regulating a situation.

[21] Hage (2004), p. 2; Hage (2003), p. 221 ff.; Sartor (2006), p. 11, where "cognitive defeasibility" is defined as the defeasibility of the beliefs concerning ontic reasons (facts) and legal conclusions; Rodríguez and Sucar (1998), p. 119 ff.

the law might be perfectly indefeasible, while we have only tentatively sound beliefs about it.

10.3.1.3 Defeasible Concepts

The claim that legal concepts—or at least, many or the most interesting of them—are defeasible is a well-known contribution Herbert Hart made to contemporary jurisprudence.[22] There are several ways of reading Hart, but, to the present purpose, philological issues will be put aside. In view of sharpening concepts for juristic use, the thesis of the defeasibility of legal concepts may be accounted for as including the following tenets.

1. Legal concepts are not suitable objects for definitions purporting to fix a closed list of necessary and, in Hart's words, "always" sufficient properties.[23]
2. On the contrary, their defining properties are better conceived of as an *open list*, where paradigmatic properties in paradigmatic cases provide the flexible criterion for analogical extension to further properties in further cases. Accordingly, the logical form of a proper definition of a legal concept should be characterized by the presence of an "etcetera" clause.[24]
3. Furthermore, two different groups of properties should be considered, and kept apart, in any proper definition of a legal concept, namely: *positive* properties (pointing to positive conditions of application) and *negative* properties (pointing to negative conditions of application).

Positive properties are to be regarded as stating the necessary and *normally* sufficient conditions for a concept to be applied to an individual case (a given set of facts) at hand. This means, more precisely, that they jointly establish a *sufficient* condition for applying the concept to a case, *if*, and *only if—once* they have been duly identified (also by saturating the "etcetera clause", if any) *and* considered as satisfied—*some further conditions* are *not* satisfied instead, for the presence of these negative properties would *defeat* the positive properties, i.e., would make the concept not anymore applicable to those very facts. Accordingly, the logical form of any proper definition of a legal concept should also be characterized by the presence of an "unless" clause.[25]

---

[22] See, e.g., Hart (1948–1949); Hart (1954), Baker (1977), pp. 26–57; MacCormick (1995), pp. 99–117; Hage (2004), p. 2; Hage (2003), p. 221 ff.; Sartor (2005), p. 78.

[23] Hart (1948–1949), pp. 148, 149 footnote 1.

[24] Hart (1948–1949), p. 147.

[25] See Hart (1948–1949), p. 147, 148, 150. To quote a key passage: "it is usually not possible to define a legal concept such as "trespass" or "contract" by *specifying the necessary and sufficient conditions* for its application. For *any* set of conditions may be adequate in some cases but not in others, and such concepts can only be explained with the aid of *a list of exceptions or negative examples* showing where the concept may not be applied or may only be applied in a weakened form" (p. 148, italics added). In a later essay, the conditions after the unless-clause are classified under two basic headings: *excusing* conditions and *invalidating* conditions: see Hart (1958b), p. 96.

We are now in a position, following Hart, to identify four basic logical forms for the definition of a defeasible legal concept of the sort Hart had in mind:

$$(x)(\mathrm{A}x \,\&\, \mathrm{B}x) \,\&\, \neg(\mathrm{D}x \vee \mathrm{E}x \vee \mathrm{F}x) \text{->} \mathrm{T}x \tag{10.1}$$

$$(x)(\mathrm{A}x \,\&\, \mathrm{B}x) \,\&\, \neg(\mathrm{D}x \vee \mathrm{E}x \vee \mathrm{F}x \vee \ldots) \text{->} \mathrm{T}x \tag{10.2}$$

$$(x)(\mathrm{A}x \,\&\, \mathrm{B}x \,\&\, \ldots) \,\&\, \neg(\mathrm{D}x \vee \mathrm{E}x \vee \mathrm{F}x) \text{->} \mathrm{T}x \tag{10.3}$$

$$(x)(\mathrm{A}x \,\&\, \mathrm{B}x \,\&\, \ldots) \,\&\, \neg(\mathrm{D}x \vee \mathrm{E}x \vee \mathrm{F}x \vee \ldots) \text{->} \mathrm{T}x. \tag{10.4}$$

Form (10.1) reads: "For any *x*, *if x* is A and B, and *unless x* is D, or E, or F, *then x* is T".

Form (10.4) reads: "For any *x*, *if x* is A, and B, *etc.*, and *unless x* is D, or E, or F, or *etc.*, *then x* is T".

Form (10.3) reads: "For any *x*, *if x* is A, and B, *etc.*, and *unless x* is D, or E, or F, *then x* is T".

Form (10.2) reads: "For any *x*, *if x* is A and B, and *unless x* is D, or E, or F, or *etc.*, *then x* is T".

Forms (10.1) and (10.3) concern *closed-defeasible* concepts: the set of negative, or defeating, conditions is, by hypothesis, a closed set—no "etc." ("and so on") clause holds for these conditions.

Forms (10.2) and (10.4) concern, instead, *open-defeasible* concepts: the set of negative, defeating, conditions is, by hypothesis, an open one, as indicated by the "etc." clause.

Leaving aside, at least for the moment, the issue whether, and in which sense, legal concepts (which ones?) are—or should be regarded as—"necessarily" defeasible, the four logical forms above may be considered as useful presentation tools for the definition of any legal concept whatsoever that, in a process of actual or hypothetical decision-making, proves, at some stage of the process, defeasible: i.e. provided with a set of negative, or defeating, defining conditions. The normal situation being apparently, from this perspective, the following: an (assumed) open-defeasible legal concept gets saturated, as to its open defeasibility conditions and in view of its application to a case at hand, in such a way as to be transformed into a (*pro tanto*) closed-defeasible concept.

What makes legal concepts defeasible? There seems to be a simple answer for such a question. Once we reject Jhering's conceptualist Heaven, legal concepts are just tools worked out by jurists, and continuously re-arranged and sharpened by them, to do things in the legal domain. By "their very nature", they are neither open-defeasible, nor closed-defeasible, nor indefeasible. Convenience, juristic theories, and interpretive and definitional attitudes make them what they are.

10.3.1.4 Defeasible Provisions

Sometimes, legal philosophers seem to identify *legal provisions*—legislative formulations, enacted statutes—as defeasibility-apt things:

> any *reasonable approach* to *systemic interpretation* of enacted statutes – claims, for instance, Neil MacCormick[26] – will also *treat legislative formulations as effectively defeasible* since *only providing presumptively sufficient or necessary conditions* as to whatever is enacted.

However, in the very light of their words (e.g., of MacCormick's words), the idea of a defeasible legal provision appears, at best, misleading. In fact, it rests on confusion between two kinds of entities that should be kept separate. On the one hand there are legal provisions; on the other hand there are norms. *Legal provisions* are *syntactic entities*: they are token sentences, belonging to the discourse of a certain legal source, and considered apart from any interpretation whatsoever. They are, indeed, the starting point for processes of legal interpretation: they are the sentences which interpreters, by means of some code of textual interpretation and some set of interpretive resources, translate into one or more explicit norms. *Norms*, from this viewpoint, are instead *semantic entities*: they are the *meanings* of legal provisions, or, more precisely, what may be presented, and argued for, as the "correct" ("reasonable", "true", "proper", etc.) meaning of a given legal provision, according to an interpretive code and a set of interpretive resources (historical data, pieces of scientific information, basic moral values, fundamental legal principles, juristic theories, etc.).[27]

Now, from a conceptual point of view, only semantic entities (in the broad sense I am using the term here)—namely, sentences that *are*, or are assumed *to be*, *norms*—may be *treated* as providing "presumptively sufficient or necessary conditions" for some legal consequence. No such treatment is available, contrariwise, for syntactic entities.[28] As a consequence, the idea of a defeasible legal provision is not to be taken at face value, if it is to make any sense. Two different, related, readings may be considered.

On a first reading, the claim that "legal provisions are defeasible" may be understood as tantamount to the claim that *literal norms are defeasible*. On this reading, it is a claim concerning the defeasibility of those norms that, by hypothesis, represent the literal meaning of legal provisions—being, usually, perfectly isomorphic to the latter. So, literal norms—the norms resulting from a literal interpretation of legal provisions—would be defeasible: would only provide presumptively sufficient, or merely necessary but not necessarily sufficient, conditions for some legal conse-

[26] MacCormick (1995), p. 115, italics added.

[27] See Chap. 2, Sect. 2.2.1, Chap. 3, Sects. 3.4 and 3.6, above.

[28] As we have seen (see, e.g., Chap. 5, Sects. 5.2 and 5.4, above) there are indeed two kinds of norms from this perspective: *explicit* norms and *implicit* norms. Implicit norms are sentences representing norms that, by hypothesis, are not the meaning of any legal provision, being rather identified by means of certain argumentative processes from one or more explicit and/or implicit norms (e.g. by analogical or *a contrario* reasoning).

quence. Notice that this claim—as the passage from MacCormick suggests—apparently belongs to a purportedly "reasonable approach to systemic interpretation of enacted statutes": it belongs, in other words, to a specific *prescriptive* methodology of statutory construction. And it is the very endorsement of such a "reasonable" methodological outlook (along with its theoretical background) that ultimately accounts for the defeasibility of the literal norms in a legal order—for their being liable to negative conditions of application imposed, in MacCormick's view, by other norms of the system.

It is worthwhile noticing, by the way, that modifications to literal norms, which consist in adding negative conditions for the application of the legal consequence they state, may take, in general, two different forms. On the one hand, these modifications may be presented, and argued for, as corresponding, say, to an *intentional* or *teleological* reading of the legal provision itself: in such a case, the literal (*explicit*) norm is being replaced by a different, intentional or teleological, (*explicit*) norm, that is the outcome of a re-interpretation of the relevant legal provision according either to the (actual, presumed, counterfactual) "intention" of the lawgiver, or to the "underlying reasons" of the norm/legal provision itself.[29] On the other hand, the modifications to the literal norm may also be presented, and argued for, as the outcome of taking into account *other* relevant *norms* of the same legal system: in such a case, the literal (*explicit*) norm is being replaced by an *implicit* norm, resulting from the combination of the literal norm with (pieces and/or consequences of) other norms of the system (I will return to this point later). In the former case, we may speak of an *internal-interpretive defeasibility* of literal norms; in the latter case, of their *external-* or *systemic-interpretive defeasibility*. The latter case seems to correspond to what MacCormick had in mind in the passage I quoted above.

On a second reading, the claim that "legal provisions are defeasible" may be understood as expressing a general interpretive disposition *towards* legal provisions. Namely, the disposition, which interpreters may choose to adopt, to interpreting legal provisions as sentences expressing defeasible norms of the two varieties above: i.e., internally or externally defeasible norms. From this point of view, we may even talk of legal provisions as "having the dispositional property" of being interpreted as expressing defeasible norms. Provided we always remember that such a property is, ultimately, in the eye of interpreters.

[29] See Alchourrón (1996b), p. 341 ff., where he outlines a "dispositional approach" for the interpretive identification of the negative conditions that may be regarded either as "implicit exceptions", or as "implicit non-exceptions", or even as "indeterminate as exceptions", from the point of the (counterfactual) dispositions of the lawgiver. See, also, Ferrer Beltrán and Ratti (2008), where, from an interpretive approach perspective (one dealing, I would say, with the "sources" of defeating conditions), they distinguish between "teleological" (background reasons), "authoritative" (lawgiver's actual intention), and "dispositional" (lawgiver's counterfactual intention) defeasibility.

10.3.1.5 Defeasible Interpretations

Some legal philosophers claim—by way of a theoretical statement belonging to descriptive jurisprudence, and, notably, to analytical and sociological methodology—that "interpretations are defeasible".[30] This claim points, apparently, at two essential features of interpretive practices, as they in fact are here and now. On the one hand, the *process* of legal interpretation (*interpretation-activity*) is, from the viewpoint of its structure, "defeasible": starting from a legal provision and a certain set of interpretive rules and interpretive resources, interpreters identify the (*pro tanto*) all-things-considered correct interpretation (interpretive outcome) of the provision for a case at hand, as the result of a process where they go through intermediate, tentative, interpretive outcomes, liable to be changed in the light of further information (other interpretive rules, other interpretive resources, etc.). We may also talk of a *retro-active* or *feed-back* structure, for it is, up to a certain point, a continuous going back-and-forth from the legal provision to some norm tentatively identified as one of its meanings. This feature of interpretive *reasoning*—as a cognitive or psychological process—is common to other kinds of reasoning in law, and accounts for their being qualified as "defeasible", as we shall see in a moment. On the other hand, the *outcomes* of the process of legal interpretation (*interpretation-products*) are, in turn, defeasible: they are liable to be changed—revised, modified, discarded—as further information is added, until the interpreter reaches what she regards as an equilibrium point; for instance, when time has run out and a reasonable amount of "information" has been "processed". At that point, she stays with a certain interpretive outcome as the final one for the case at hand.

The idea of defeasible interpretations (defeasible interpretive outcomes) is usually conveyed through a language borrowed from cognitive science, centred on the ideas of revisability of beliefs in connection with the constant revisability of the theories (information, inputs) on which such beliefs depend. This way of looking at legal interpretation is not objectionable in itself. Provided, however, that it is not taken to suggest the misleading conclusion according to which interpretation would be a matter of gathering, and neutrally processing, information showing up in a piecemeal, never-ending, way. Indeed, which "information" shows up, and when, and how to "process" it, is to a large extent a value-laden, ideologically compromised, discretional undertaking by law's interpreters.

[30] See, e.g., Bayón (1997), pp. 184–185; Rodríguez (1997), p. 97 ff.; Rodríguez and Sucar (1998), p. 116. The very same idea is conveyed by at least two further theories of legal interpretation (two further psychological, or cognitive, models of the process of legal interpretation), where, however, the term "defeasibility" does not (still) show up. On the one hand, there is the hermeneutic model, centred on the idea of hermeneutic circles. See, e.g., Alexy (1993), p. 416 ff. On the other hand, there is the feedback or retroactive model, centred on the distinction between a "first interpretation" and the several, following "re-interpretations" of the same legal provision. See, e.g., Chiassoni (1990), p. 121 ff. and Chiassoni (2011), ch. 2. See also Chap. 3 above.

10.3.1.6 Defeasible Reasoning

Quite often, legal philosophers state that legal reasoning is defeasible. There are, however, at least two different ways of understanding such a statement, corresponding to two quite different theoretical perspectives.

To begin with, the statement "legal reasoning is defeasible" may be advanced as a psychological, cognitive science descriptive proposition concerning a purportedly essential feature of the mental process of reasoning with legal, or legally relevant, data, to get to legal conclusions. From this perspective, legal reasoning is defeasible, not for its being "legal", i.e. due to some peculiarity of the law-world, but, simply, for its being a form of human "reasoning". Indeed, from a cognitive point of view, every reasoning, as a mental process, is defeasible: it is typically a proceeding through tentative outcomes, liable to be changed, revised, or altogether abandoned, in a further stage of the process, in the light of new pieces of information.[31] As is the case, as we saw above, with interpretive reasoning.

The statement "legal reasoning is defeasible", however, may also be waged as a claim from a logical point of view: namely, as a claim concerning a purportedly essential feature of the inferences between legal norms, and between legal norms and other premises and conclusions of legal reasoning—considered, here, not as mental processes, but as pieces of justificatory discourses. Those who make such a claim—like, for instance, Jaap Hage—purport to suggest that classical monotonic logic (centred on the law of the strengthening of the antecedent and *modus ponens*) is not suited to account for legal reasoning, and should be replaced by some form of non-monotonic logic.[32] Other legal philosophers however—notably Carlos E. Alchourrón—maintain that what apparently would make "legal reasoning" defeasible are its basic ingredients—the *legal norms*—and claim, consequently, that there is no need to get rid of monotonic logic to account for normative inferences, provided the logical form of legal norms is suitably changed to accommodate to their defeasible character.[33]

On its first, cognitive science, version, the claim about the defeasibility of legal reasoning is true, but trivial: a useful way of conveying what has been clear to many theorists of legal reasoning, well before the rising of the defeasibility turn in legal thinking.[34] On its second, logical, version, it is a contested claim pointing to what seems to be the gist of the whole matter: the (alleged) defeasibility of legal norms. Before getting to it, however, a few other allegedly defeasible legal items have to be briefly considered.

---

[31] According, e.g., to Sartor (2006), p. 11: "Defeasible reasoning [is] a structured process of enquiry, based upon drawing *pro-tanto* conclusions, looking for their defeaters, for defeaters of defeaters, and so on, until stable results can be obtained"; see also Sartor (2005), p. 79; MacCormick (2005), pp. 252–253, where reasoning in law is presented as "arguing defeasibly"; Prakken and Sartor (2004), p. 118 ff.

[32] See, e.g., Hage (1997), p. 4 ff.

[33] See e.g. Alchourrón (1995), Alchourrón (1996a), pp. 5–18.

[34] On this point, see also Bayón (2001), pp. 334–335.

10.3.1.7 Defeasible Conclusions

Some legal philosophers claim that what should be regarded as really "defeasible", within the legal domain, are "legal conclusions". Legal conclusions—according to Henry Prakken and Giovanni Sartor—are typically defeasible due to the working of three factors: first, the non-monotonic structure of legal inferences, which mirrors in turn the defeasible character of the mental process of reasoning in law ("inference-based defeasibility")[35]; second, the procedural rules concerning evidence ("process-based defeasibility")[36]; third, the choices and evaluations that affect the selection and changes of the "theories" from which legal conclusions are derived ("theory-based defeasibility").[37] This claim can be considered as parasitic upon the claim concerning the defeasibility of legal reasoning—though it adds some information about the working, and influence, of procedural rules. It seems we are still dwelling, here, at the margins of the defeasibility issue.

10.3.1.8 Defeasible Arrangements, Positions, Claims

We also quite often run into claims to the effect that "legal arrangements (e.g., contracts, wills, etc.) are defeasible", "legal rights (duties, privileges, powers, immunities, etc.) are defeasible", "legal claims are defeasible", and so on. Saying that "legal arrangements are defeasible" is apparently tantamount to saying that they "can be upset or set aside despite an *initial appearance of validity and durability*".[38] Legal arrangements, however, are instruments ascribing bundles of legal positions to certain persons. Accordingly, saying that arrangements are defeasible is tantamount to saying that—some, or all, of—the legal positions they purported to grant are liable to be considered invalid, null, void, unenforceable, etc. Why is that so? Apparently, the following explanation may be provided. Arrangements—and the depending rights, duties, liabilities, etc.—derive whichever validity (legal force) they have from some set of legal norms that regulates them. Unfortunately, these

[35] Prakken and Sartor (2004), p. 118: "legal *conclusions*, though correctly supported by certain pieces of information, cannot be inferred when the theory including this information is *expanded* with further pieces of information (we use the term "theory" to mean in general any set of premises intended to provide an account of a legal domain)".

[36] See Sartor (2006), p. 12: "*procedural* defeasibility" is characterized as "the defeasibility of the outcomes of legal proceedings, depending to [on] the distribution of the burden of proof between the parties".

[37] Prakken and Sartor (2004), pp. 130, 131, 133: "[*theory-based defeasibility*] results from the evaluation and choice of theories which explain and systematize the available input information [...] different theories of the same legal domain are possible, we need ways of comparing those theories and [...] selecting the most appropriate one [...] the parties in a case, given a shared legal background, develop alternative legal theories, and victory goes to the party who develops the better theory [...] theory-based argumentation, the idea that legal debates consist of the dialectical exchange of competing theories, supporting opposing legal conclusions in the issue at stake [and where] the weaker (less coherent) theory is defeated by the stronger one".

[38] MacCormick (1995), p. 99, italics added.

norms—leaving aside their explicit derogation (and any mistake by the parties or their legal counsels)—may work as Hartian open-defeasible concepts: they may (be supposed to) have a loose end, through which new negative conditions can be added, which were not considered at the time the arrangement was made, nor could have been so. Consequently, arrangements—and their accompanying rights, duties, etc.—are *defeasible* (in the sense of being *liable to supervening invalidity*, i.e., to be later considered invalid, void, etc.), because the norms on which they depend are *defeasible* (in the different sense of being *liable to be saturated with new negative conditions* for the application of their legal consequence). The defeasibility of arrangements, rights, duties, etc., is, thus, a *derivative* and, more precisely, a *norm-dependent* phenomenon. The same conclusion—perhaps with some qualifications—also holds for those rights, duties, etc., that are, at least *prima facie*, directly ascribed to persons by legal norms (e.g. by constitutional norms, legislative norms, etc.). And, apparently, it would also hold, to conclude, regarding the defeasibility of "claims": i.e., as to the liability of people's requests for judicial protection of their (alleged) entitlements to be overridden and rejected.

Neil MacCormick, however, takes a different view on the matter:

> Is it *rules* that are defeasible, or *certain formulations of them*, or *claims* made on the basis of such *formulations*, including *legal-doctrinal statements* based on the text of legal 'sources' such as the statute-book or the law reports? [...]
>
> As with rights, so with rules, it is not the statute nor the precedent that is defeasible in the light of exceptional circumstances relevant to legal principles, when we deal with implicit defeasibility. *It is the claim* based on a particular formulation or interpretation of the rule that is *defeated* in the light of the principle. Thereafter, more cautious formulations of the rule, or doctrinal expositions that draw attention to *exceptions established by case law*, will be called for.[39]

The passage contains many ideas—and, to my mind, also some confusion—very useful to deal with the widespread claim concerning the defeasibility of legal norms. It is to this topic, so far delayed, that I now turn.

10.3.1.9 Defeasible Norms

The standard theory going along the claim that "legal norms are defeasible" can be presented, by way of a rational reconstruction, as including the following tenets.

1. Defeasible Norms in Action As a matter of fact, legal norms, like the legal concepts showing up in their formulations, usually work as defeasible conditionals: they are usually treated by judges and jurists as conditionals the normative consequences of which are subject to "exceptions", i.e., to *negative conditions* of applica-

[39] MacCormick (2005), p. 252.

tion.[40] Negative or defeating conditions may be (considered and treated), in turn, either as a closed-set or as an open-set.[41]

2. Closed-Defeasible Norms When its defeating conditions are a closed-set, a norm is a *closed defeasible norm*. Lawyers (judges, jurists, attorneys, etc.) assume it is possible to identify, at any given moment, the *whole set* of its negative conditions of application. This means that, starting from any *prima facie* norm (say, any norm in its standard form, corresponding, for instance, to the literal reading of a legal provision), like for instance:

$$\text{PFN}': (x)(\text{A}x \,\&\, \text{B}x \text{->} \text{OR}x)$$

it is assumed to be possible to identify an *all-things-considered* norm, which contains by hypothesis *all* the negative conditions of application of its normative consequence (in our case: "OR*x*"), if any:

$$\text{ATCN}': (x)(\text{A}x \,\&\, \text{B}x) \,\&\, \neg(\text{D}x \vee \text{E}x \vee \text{F}x) \text{->} \text{OR}x.$$

This set of negative conditions, furthermore, would be liable to be identified *beforehand*: that is to say, (presumably) by way of abstract interpretation and previous to any application of the norm to any individual case.[42]

Notice that the task of identifying, and exhaustively stating, the negative conditions of application of a norm—or, more precisely, of its normative consequence (like, e.g., "OR*x*")—is an *interpretive* task. Norms do not grow on trees. Accordingly, such a process would usually require two steps: first, the identification of some set of legal sources (legal provisions), according to some criterion of validity and legal provisions selection (both operations belonging to, though not exhausting, *meta-textual interpretation*); second, the interpretation of the identified set of legal provisions according to a selected interpretive code and a selected set of interpretive resources, so as to get a set ("system") of explicit and implicit norms out of it (where textual and meta-textual interpretation activities combine).[43] Such a process has a defeasible structure (see Sect. 10.3.1.5, "Defeasible interpretations", above), and is

[40] Sometimes, legal theorists seem to claim, not that legal norms *usually* are, or are *treated as*, defeasible by jurists, judges, etc. (see, e.g., Alchourrón 1996b, p. 341), but that they are *necessarily* so. Consider, for instance, the following passage from Atria 2002 (quoted critically by MacCormick 2005, p. 252): "Hence the rules formulated by legal agencies are always defeasible *for the sake of better pursuing these aims and values* through an appropriately nuanced interpretation of them, and with a regulated discretion in applying them [...] Defeasibility of rules *is built into* the kind of activity that regulative institutions define through these rules" (italics added). For a sceptical stance on the issue see, e.g., Schauer (1998), pp. 223–240.

[41] This claim, as we have seen, is also made in relation to judicial precedent (see Chap. 9, Sects. 9.5.2 and 9.5.3 above).

[42] On abstract interpretation, see Chap. 4, Sect. 4.2.1, and Chap. 6, Sect. 6.2 footnote 3, above.

[43] On textual and meta-textual interpretation, see Chap. 2, Sect. 2.2.1, above.

typically value-laden, discretionary, and sensible to juristic theories and methodological outlooks.

The closed-set of the negative conditions of application of a norm is liable to change, both across interpreters and over time. This is the effect of two basic factors: on the one hand, a change in the interpretive code and/or in the relevant interpretive resources, leading to different interpretations of the *same* set of legal sources (the same set of legal provisions); on the other hand, a change in the set of legal sources, due, for instance, to the adding, by normative authorities, of a new legal provision that may be interpreted as expressing some further negative condition of application for some previously existing norm. Thus, any change in the closed set of the negative conditions of application of a norm (normative consequence) depends either on methodological indeterminacy and ideological pluralism, allowing for a plurality of alternative interpretive codes and interpretive outputs (see Sect. 10.2.2 above), or on the dynamic character of legal orders (change of legal sources)—the first of the two factors being in any case paramount, due to the fact that ideologies, operating through interpretive techniques, can be able to neutralize the working of new pieces of ("unpalatable") enacted law.

In the light of the preceding remarks, the standard, commonsense notion of a *closed-defeasible norm*, as a norm the negative conditions of application thereof may be identified *exhaustively* and *beforehand*, if it is to make any sense, has to be re-defined (subject to rational reconstruction), so as to take expressly into account, and bring to the fore, the fact that closed defeasible norms are *interpretation-dependent entities*. This may be done, for instance, along the following lines.

Closed-Defeasible Norm A norm is a *closed-defeasible norm*, if, and only if, relative to *whichever* set of *interpretive inputs* interpreters may select and use in a moment t_o, it contains an *exhaustive* set of negative conditions of application.

A set of *interpretive inputs* includes: (*a*) an interpretive *code* containing rules for textual and meta-textual interpretation; (*b*) a set of interpretive *resources*; and (*c*) a set of *legal provisions*.

Assuming the set of legal provisions to be constant, two different kinds of closed-defeasible norms may be singled out. On the one hand, there are those norms that are liable to *one* and the *same* exhaustive set of negative conditions of applications. In such, very unlikely situations, a norm may be regarded as a *simple closed-defeasible norm*.

Simple Closed-Defeasible Norm A norm is a *simple closed-defeasible norm*, if, and only if, relative to *whichever* set of *interpretive inputs* interpreters may select and use in a moment t_o, it contains *one* and the *same exhaustive* set of negative conditions of application.

Thus, whichever available set of interpretive inputs (*Ii*) (interpretive code plus interpretive resources) is being chosen and used in t_o, the outcome would be the same:

$$N = f(Ii_1 \ldots Ii_n / t_o) = (x)(Ax \,\&\, Bx) \,\&\, \neg(Dx \vee Ex \vee Fx) \rightarrow ORx.$$

On the other hand, however, there are also those norms that are liable to *different, alternative*, exhaustive sets of negative conditions of applications, according to different sets of interpretive inputs (i.e., to different interpretive codes plus interpretive resources). In such, very likely situations, a norm may be regarded as a *complex, alternative, closed-defeasible norm.*

Complex Closed-Defeasible Norm A norm is a *complex closed-defeasible norm*, if, and only if, relative to the sets of *interpretive inputs* interpreters may select and use in a moment t_o, it contains a plurality of *different alternative exhaustive* sets of negative conditions of application.

Thus, given the available sets of interpretive inputs, the outcome would be a norm like the following:

$$N = f(Ii_1 \ldots Ii_n / t_o) = (x)(Ax \& Bx) \& \neg[(Dx \vee Ex \vee Fx) \vee (Dx \vee Ex \vee Gx) \vee (Ex \vee Hx \vee Lx)] \rightarrow ORx.$$

The notion of closed-defeasibility is troublesome. How do we *know* that the set of negative conditions of application of a norm at time t_o is *closed*? That it is *exhaustive*? We do not know, and, in fact, we cannot know. Indeed, given the fact that closed-defeasible norms are interpretive entities, the closed or open nature of a defeasible norm is a matter of decision (calling, of course, for adequate justification). It can happen, accordingly, that one and the same norm be considered, and treated, as closed-defeasible by some interpreters, while others regard, and treat it, as open-defeasible.

3. Open-Defeasible Norms A norm is an *open-defeasible norm* whenever the set of its negative conditions of application has a loose end: its members—legal philosophers would say—*cannot* be identified *exhaustively beforehand*.[44] This does not mean, of course, that when the norm is to be applied to a case, application is being frustrated by its (assumed) open-endedness. It means, rather, that: (a) the law-applying agencies are (considered to be) *authorized* to determine the norm's set of negative conditions of application, at least for the time being, in front of an individual case to be adjudicated; (b) the content of their decisions—i.e., the way they are going to tie up the loose ends of a norm's negative conditions of application—is, by hypothesis, not foreseeable. Juan Carlos Bayón has expressed this point in clear terms:

> A *genuine defeasible norm* [i.e., an open-defeasible norm] leaves the law *indeterminate* as to the very cases *included* in its conditioning facts, so that the judgment about any of those

[44] According to Bayón, for instance, defeasible norms are norms with "open-ended character", i.e. "they are subject to implied exceptions which cannot be exhaustively specified in advance" (Bayón 2001, p. 338). The logical form of such a norm would be, for instance, something like the following: "(*x*) (A*x* & B*x*) & ¬(D*x* v E*x* v ...) –> OR*x*". From this perspective, notice, closed-defeasible norms are not "really" defeasible norms. I will come back to this issue soon in the text.

cases *always* requires a *discretional decision among open alternatives* by the law-applying agency.[45]

Adjudication turns open-defeasible norms into *pro tanto* closed-defeasible norms. Now, this *pro tanto* closing is likely to occur according to juristic advice, and, above all, due to rational justification requirements, in a principled way: that is to say, any "new" (so far not yet identified in a judicial decision) negative condition is being added, if, and only if, "good reasons" can be provided for, having to do with the "proper" interpretation of the "norm" in itself, or with its "proper" standing within a legal system. However, if law-applying agencies have such a duty of justification, as it is the case in most existing legal orders, then any "new" negative condition of application of a norm—by hypothesis, *not* included in the *standard formulation* of the norm which a law-applying agency takes as the starting point of its reasoning—is tantamount, from a methodological point of view, to a negative condition that is identified, and justified, on the basis of a *new* set of interpretive inputs, one that is different from the one(s) on which the standard formulation of the norm, with its negative conditions, depends.

The commonsense notion of an open-defeasible norm I mentioned above also includes the idea, as we have seen, that the new negative condition cannot be "anticipated" ("specified in advance"). Accordingly, a tentative re-definition of the notion—again, by way of a rational reconstruction—may run, roughly, as follows:

Open-Defeasible Norm A norm, containing a set of negative conditions of application NC_i at the moment t_o, is an *open-defeasible norm*, if, and only if:

(a) some *new* negative condition of application (i.e., different from the ones already in the set NC_i and not logically derivable from them without further premises) can be added to the set of negative conditions NC_i, in a subsequent moment t_1, on the basis of some new set of interpretive inputs;
(b) the *new* negative condition of application and the accompanying set of interpretive inputs cannot be anticipated at moment t_o.

From the viewpoint of sociological methodology, the claim that "norms are open defeasible" is a true descriptive normative proposition, as to a given legal order at a certain time, whenever, due to methodological indeterminacy (loose interpretive codes and the possibility for interpreters to shift from one code to another), any norm whatsoever, in its present standard formulation can be, and is in fact, regarded as open to a set of exceptions that cannot be stated exhaustively in advance. For, say, the genius of some interpreter, triggered by new situations, intellectual progress, or compelling material or spiritual interests, may combine or revisit current sets of interpretive inputs in such a form as to justify the adding (the "making explicit" of) a new negative condition.

The claim "norms are open defeasible", however, may also be a piece of a *prescriptive methodology* addressed to (fellow) jurists and judges working in a given legal system. In such a case, it is tantamount to a second-order interpretive rule,

[45] Bayón (1997), p. 188.

running roughly as follows: "You may always regard norms as open defeasible prescriptions, and re-interpret them accordingly, provided the new exceptions you add to them can be justified according to a reasonable set of interpretive inputs".[46] Such a prescriptive methodology's claim has its counterpart in an opposite methodological option, in favor of the closed-defeasibility of norms, running, for instance, as follows: "You ought to regard norms as simple closed-defeasible prescriptions, according to the right interpretive code IC_i".

Sometimes, it is suggested that closed-defeasible norms are not *really* defeasible, being rather *indefeasible* norms. Indeed, so the argument goes, if *every* condition—both positive and negative—has been duly identified and stated, then what we get is a full-fledged, indefeasible, norm. Such a conclusion, however, is a matter of conceptual preference: it depends on a different notion of "norm-defeasibility", one that considers the open-endedness of negative conditions of application to be a *defining property* of the very concept of a "defeasible norm". Such a conclusion would not hold, however, if we use a different concept of a "defeasible norm": for instance, as along the lines above, meaning by it simply that a norm is *liable to negative conditions* of application.

Only the Supreme Deities of theoretical and practical expediency can adjudicate the issue. Nonetheless, though open-end defeasibility is surely a theoretically more exciting phenomenon, there seems to be no reason, from a conceptual point of view, for wiping out from the domain of "defeasibility" the other—not so-innocent—phenomenon of closed-end defeasibility.

---

[46] For instance, Richard Tur claims apparently that legal norms *ought to* be considered, and treated, as open-defeasible norms basically on two counts. First, because of tradition's sake: they have been treated as open-defeasible standards all the time (at least, in a legal system such as the English common law). Second, because of the superior rationality of such an option: in fact, treating legal norms as undefeasible prescriptions would amount to endorsing a "flatly formalistic approach to law application" (Tur 2001, pp. 355–368). He also develops a descriptive side, grounded on the following points: Law is best *represented*, most clearly *understood*, and most effectively *taught* as defeasible. Law's defeasibility depends on the *open-ended defeasibility* of legal norms. Legal norms, as open-ended defeasible norms, are better represented and understood—taking stock of Kelsen's, Hart's, and Critical Legal Studies' inquiries—as normative conditional propositions, where the normative consequence is subject to a double set of *open-ended defeating (negative) alternative* conditions: on the one hand, "operative" *exceptions*, that may be either pre-established (explicit, specified), or *yet to be established* (implicit, unspecified); on the other hand, *overrides* ("overriding considerations"), i.e., defeating considerations of equity or justice, policy, purpose, mercy, rights, and "any other 'damn good reason' and 'compelling objection'" (p. 368). Accordingly, the proper logical form for a legal norm would be something like the following: "if A, then ought to be B, unless *either* (1) *operative specified or yet-to-be-specified exceptions* ($e_1 \ldots e_n$) *or* (2) *overriding considerations* from the legal system's basic standards/values (*inner morality*) ($oc_1 \ldots oc_n$)". See also MacCormick (1995), p. 115; MacCormick (2005), p. 241.

10.4 Explicit v. Implicit Norm-Defeasibility

A distinction is sometimes drawn between *explicit defeasibility* and *implicit defeasibility*. Neil MacCormick, for instance, argues as follows:

1. Rules-defeasibility may be either "express", or "implicit";
2. A rule is *expressly defeasible* whenever it has been formulated in such a way as to contain both its positive conditions of (internal) application (say: C_1, C_2, C_3), and some negative condition of application ("exception" or "proviso": E_1, for example).
3. The most interesting cases of rules-defeasibility, however, are those where rules are *implicitly defeasible*. This situation obtains whenever *express rules* "may be subjected to a *fresh interpretation* in the light of some *significant legal principle* in some relatively *unusual circumstances*". Whenever, in other words, they may be "*trumped* by recourse to some *unstated condition* that is deemed to be *implicitly overriding, given the principles and/or values at stake*".
4. The two properties are not mutually exclusive: "Even in cases of *express defeasibility*, there may be possibilities of *implicit defeasibility* over and above the explicit conditions of defeasance".[47]

The distinction between closed-defeasible and open-defeasible norms, on the one hand, and explicit and implicit defeasibility, on the other, are logically independent.

The distinction between *closed-defeasible* and *open-defeasible* norms concerns their liability to a closed or an open set of negative conditions of application—always keeping in mind, however, that the identification of any such set is an *interpretative* activity, depending on *methodological options*, and typically rife with leeways and the possibility of reaching different outcomes, both synchronically and diachronically.

The distinction between *explicit* and *implicit* norm-defeasibility, on the contrary, depends on a key distinction from the *general theory of legal norms*: namely, the distinction between explicit norms, i.e., the meaning-contents of authoritative legal provisions, and implicit norms, that are identified by means of logic and/or argumentative techniques from explicit or (other previously identified) implicit norms. From this perspective, *explicit norm-defeasibility* concerns explicit norms, and is tantamount to their liability to the negative conditions of application that may be read "into" their legal provision, by means of suitable techniques of textual interpretation. Contrariwise, *implicit norm-defeasibility* points at the possibility that, given a certain *explicit* norm EN_1 ("$A \& \neg EC_1 \rightarrow OB$"), with its explicit negative conditions of application ("$\neg EC_1$"), *further* negative conditions for the application of the legal consequence stated by EN_1 ("OB") can be identified, that *cannot be read* into its legal provision (say: "IC_1" and "IC_2").[48] This means that the norm EN_1 has to be

[47] MacCormick (2005), p. 240 ff., italics added.

[48] The same remarks apply to judge-made and other unwritten law norms, in their standard, established form.

supplemented with these further implicit conditions: namely, that it has to be transformed into a derivative implicit norm IN_1: "A & ¬(ENC_1 v INC_1 v INC_2) –> OB".

Notice that the liability of explicit norms to implicit exceptions, in the way just considered, is *not* tantamount to their being liable to an *open* set of negative conditions. These norms may in fact be *implicitly* defeasible, while at the same time being *closed*-defeasible: provided the implicit negative conditions are (considered to be) a closed set, relative to the sets of interpretive inputs interpreters may select and use in a moment t_0.

10.5 Norm-Defeasibility and Axiological Gaps

Some legal philosopher has maintained that there are tight connections between norm-defeasibility and another honourable widget in the toolbox of (Continental) jurisprudence: namely, so-called *axiological gaps*.[49] It has been suggested that defeasibility and axiological gaps are in fact nothing but "two sides of the same coin".[50] Clearly, this is a metaphoric form of speech. Metaphors are double-edged swords, fatally covering with haze whatever wisdom they may convey. So it seems worthwhile dedicating a few words on de-metaphorizing the metaphor.

Axiological gaps obtain whenever a norm may be considered either as *over-inclusive*, or as *over-reaching*, in the light of some other norm, assumed to represent the benchmark for its appropriateness (appropriateness standard). A norm (usually, a simple, explicit, literal norm) is *over-inclusive*, if, and only if, in virtue of a certain expression (descriptive term) contained in its formulation, it connects a certain legal consequence *also* to a class of situations that, by the appropriateness standard, ought to be regulated *differently*. In this situation, the axiological gap is represented by the *presence* of a (sub-optimal) not-discriminating norm *and* the *absence* of the (optimal) discriminating norm.[51] Contrariwise, a norm (usually, a complex, explicit, literal norm, or a complex norm resulting from an exclusionary *a contrario* reading of a legal provision) is *over-reaching*, if, and only if, in its *negative component*, it *denies* to a class of situations the *same* legal consequence it provides instead, in its *positive component*, for the opposite class—whereas, according to the appropriateness standard, the two classes of situations ought to have the *same* legal conse-

---

[49] On axiological gaps, the seminal contribution is Alchourrón and Bulygin (1971). See also above, Chap. 7, Sect. 7.2.2.

[50] See, e.g., Guastini (2008), p. 97 ff.

[51] Consider the following legal provision at the entrance of a fine arts museum: "Couples allowed". In its literal reading it may express, from the viewpoint of some appropriateness standard, an *over-inclusive* norm for, apparently, it allows into the museum *any* sort of couple whatsoever—married heterosexual couples, unmarried heterosexual couples, married homosexual couples, unmarried homosexual couples, inter-species couples, couples of friends, couples of fine-arts-freak cyber-dogs, etc.

quence.[52] In this situation, which is the exact reverse of the former, the axiological gap consists in the *presence* of a (sub-optimal) discriminating norm *and* the *absence* of the (optimal) not-discriminating norm that is required by the appropriateness standard.

Norm-defeasibility may be used as a tool for providing remedy to the first of the two situations of axiological gap above.[53] First, it is assumed that the over-inclusive norm is defeasible: namely, subject to negative conditions that may not appear at a literal reading of the corresponding legal provision.[54] Second, the legal provision is re-interpreted in a narrowing-down way, so as to make it express a norm that is not anymore over-inclusive. This means that, by means of a defeasibility driven re-interpretation of the legal provision, a normative gap proper is created within the system. Third, by means of some gaps-filling technique, the normative gap proper is cured, setting forth a new norm in tune with the appropriateness standard.[55]

Defeasibility and axiological gaps (due to the presence of over-inclusive norms) are indeed related objects. However, they should not be confused: indeed, the disease (axiological gaps, as a disguised form of normative conflict) should never be confused with the therapy (defeasibility and the defeasibility technique of restrictive re-interpretation).

10.6 A Tentative Reconstruction

Leaving aside defeasible facts and defeasible beliefs, the cases of defeasible reasonings, defeasible conclusions, defeasible claims, defeasible legal positions, and defeasible arrangements all point to trivial, or contested, or, in most cases, derivative situations of "defeasibility". Indeed, from the viewpoint of the defeasibility and legal indeterminacy issue, the pivotal cases seem to be those of defeasible legal provisions, defeasible interpretations, and, last but of course not least, defeasible norms.

---

[52] Consider the following legal provision at the entrance of a fine arts museum: "Married couples only". In its literal reading, it expresses what I am calling a *complex* literal norm. Indeed, the legal provision expresses *two* norms jointly: one positive norm, or positive component of the complex norm ("Married couples allowed"), and one negative norm, or negative component of the complex norm (say, "Unmarried couples and singles not allowed"). The same outcome may have been obtained by way of an *a contrario* exclusionary interpretation of the following legal provision at the entrance of the fine arts museum: "Married couples". In both cases, from the viewpoint of some appropriateness standards (say, one consisting in a certain principle of human equality or human dignity), the negative component of the norm might appear sub-optimal, and the complex norm over-reaching.

[53] On defeasibility and axiological gaps, see also Chap. 8, Sect. 8.4 above.

[54] The same remarks would hold, of course, for any "standard" norm: i.e. for any norm, e.g. a judge-made norm, circulating in a standard formulation.

[55] See Chiassoni (2011), ch. 3, § 8.

I hope I have made clear why, to my mind, the claim that "legal provisions are defeasible" cannot be taken at face value. Suggesting, as you may recall, two alternative readings, both of which share the idea that *norms*—as semantic entities—are the properly defeasible objects; while legal provisions, as syntactic entities, may be defeasible, so to speak, only in a metonymical way: i.e., by way of a semantic transfer between the linguistic-form and "its" meaning-content.

Furthermore, I have suggested that the claim that "interpretations are defeasible" is tantamount to claiming that *explicit legal norms* are (or may be) defeasible: for "interpretations", as this word was used above, is tantamount to the outcome of some interpretive process concerning some legal provision—an outcome that represents, by hypothesis, a *norm* expressed by that legal provision.

Consequently, at least for the present purpose, the notion of a defeasible norm seems to be the most relevant, and interesting, to cope with. Now, I think it may be worthwhile adopting, as the starting point for a conceptual reconstruction, a basic, generic, (so far as possible) neutral, notion of a defeasible norm. This notion may be something like the following:

Df. 1 *Defeasible norm*: a norm is *defeasible*, if, and only if, the normative consequence it states is liable (i.e., may be subject) to a set of negative conditions of application ("exceptions", "defeaters", "defeating conditions").

Taking this notion into account, four, more specific, notions may be defined, arranged into two logically independent couples: namely, explicitly-defeasible norm, implicitly-defeasible norm, closed-defeasible norm (with the two varieties I considered before), and open-defeasible norm. These seven notions, together, should provide an elementary conceptual framework for fishing in the river of commonsense.

Df. 2 *Explicitly-defeasible norm*: an explicit norm is *explicitly-defeasible*, if, and only if, its normative consequence is liable to a set of negative conditions of application that may be read into its legal provision by means of suitable techniques of textual interpretation.[56]

Df. 3 *Implicitly-defeasible norm*: an explicit norm is *implicitly-defeasible,* if, and only if, its normative consequence is liable to a set of negative conditions of application that cannot be read into its legal provision, but derive from other norms of the same legal system.

Df. 4 *Closed-defeasible norm*: A norm is a *closed-defeasible norm*, if, and only if, relative to *whichever* set of *interpretive inputs* interpreters may select and use in the moment t_0, it contains an *exhaustive* set of negative conditions of application.

Df. 5 *Simple closed-defeasible norm*: A norm is a *simple closed-defeasible norm*, if, and only if, relative to *whichever* set of *interpretive inputs* interpreters

[56] A similar notion may be defined concerning judge-made norms, and other unwritten law norms, in their standard formulations, as objects of interpretation techniques allowing their "internal" re-interpretation. See Chap. 9, Sect. 9.4 above.

may select and use in the moment t_o, it contains *one and the same exhaustive* set of negative conditions of application.

Df. 6 *Complex closed-defeasible norm*: A norm is a *complex closed-defeasible norm,* if, and only if, relative to the sets of *interpretive inputs* interpreters may select and use in the moment t_o, it contains a plurality of *different alternative exhaustive* sets of negative conditions of application.

Df. 7 *Open-defeasible norm*: A norm, containing a set of negative conditions of application NC_i at the moment t_o, is an *open-defeasible norm*, if, and only if:

(a) some *new* negative condition of application (i.e., different from the ones already in the set NC_i and not logically derivable from them without further premises) can be added to the set of negative conditions NC_i, in a subsequent moment t_1, on the basis of some new set of interpretive inputs;
(b) the *new* negative condition of application and the accompanying set of interpretive inputs cannot be anticipated at moment t_o.

If we look at the *sources* of norm-defeasibility—i.e. at what makes legal norms liable to explicit or implicit exceptions—the basic factors seem to belong to the realm of interpretation (legal methodology) and juristic normative theories (ideologies) about the proper way to regard "the law" and act accordingly.[57]

While dealing with "defeasible legal provisions", we have seen that *explicit norm-defeasibility* may be regarded, as to its source, as depending on norm's *internal-interpretive defeasibility*. The liability of explicit norms to exceptions that may be read into their legal provisions depends on juristic (normative) theories about the nature of enacted law and the "proper" ways to interpret it. These theories usually hold: (a) that enacted law is a *teleological entity*, i.e., something with background reasons that ought to be taken into account while interpreting it—which is an enduring homage to the principle of sufficient reason, as an identifying tract of our notions of reason and rationality; (b) that enacted law is an *intentional entity*, i.e., something provided with an author "meaning something by it" (wishing to communicate something by it), whose (actual, presumed, counter-factual) intention is accordingly to be given pride of place in its interpretation. Explicit norms, however, are also treated as implicitly defeasible. As we saw before, *implicit norm-defeasibility* may be regarded, as to its source, as depending on norm's *external-* or *systemic-interpretive* defeasibility. Juristic theories support this view by well-known ideas: (a) legal norms never "walk alone": they are, contrariwise, (to be regarded as) components of ordered (consistent, coherent, and gapless), dynamic, normative sets; (b) accordingly, they are always to be interpreted and re-interpreted taking into

[57] Several legal philosophers make this claim, though for different reasons. One of the most original positions is set forth in Bayón (1997), p. 182 ff. There, Bayón explains norm-defeasibility (what I would call, roughly, their open- and implicit- defeasibility) by resorting to the idea of a "closure rule as to relevance", presented as an "interpretative convention" according to which norms ought to be regarded as liable to explicit exceptions *only*. As a consequence, norms are "defeasible" (in Bayón's sense), when such an interpretive principle is *not* part of what I would call the "authoritative" or "conventional" interpretive code of a given legal order.

account the systemic nature of the law, i.e. by means of the varied set of techniques of systemic interpretation; (c) any diachronic modification, by normative authorities, in the set of legal provisions (Alchourrón's "Master Book") will always affect the normative system (or rather: the several "Master Systems", again in Alchourrón's words[58]) through the services of an indispensable middleman: interpretation.

10.7 Defeasibility and Legal Indeterminacy

The relationship between defeasibility and legal indeterminacy can be conceived either as one of *equivalence* (defeasibility is tantamount to indeterminacy), or as one of *difference* (defeasibility is not tantamount to indeterminacy). In the latter case, they can be either mutually *related* or *unrelated* items. Three sorts of relationships can be hypothesized: defeasibility *depends on* indeterminacy (*defeasibility as a dependent variable*); indeterminacy *depends on* defeasibility (*indeterminacy as a dependent variable*); defeasibility and indeterminacy are *independent* properties in the legal domain (*independency*).

Some legal philosophers seem to take something like the equivalence view. They maintain that defeasibility is really not (meaningfully) distinguishable from indeterminacy. The two concepts would refer roughly to the same wide array of well-known puzzling situations. And—so the argument goes—since the concept of indeterminacy and other related concepts are better established in legal thinking, there seems to be no need to resort to the new entry defeasibility. Consequently, "defeasibility" can be dispensed with altogether, without any inconvenience either to legal thinking or to legal practice.[59]

Other legal philosophers, contrariwise, maintain defeasibility and indeterminacy to be notions that refer to different phenomena in the legal domain. They suggest, furthermore, that indeterminacy is to be regarded as a dependent variable of defeasibility.[60]

It goes without saying that any meaningful statement about the relationships between such theory-laden things as defeasibility and indeterminacy depends on a clear and reasoned statement of the conceptual framework one is going to use. In what follows, I will bring to the fore a few connections between defeasibility and

---

[58] See Alchourrón (1996b), p. 331 ff.

[59] See, e.g., Rodríguez and Sucar (1998), pp. 116–118, 143: "it is possible to account for the different problems that may suggest using the notion of defeasibility in relation to legal norms *without making use of that idea*".

[60] See, e.g., Alchourrón (1996b), p. 341 ff.: "Usually *our understanding of the rule* will allow us to give a list of implicit exceptions as well as a list of circumstances which are not mentioned because they are rejected as exceptions. *But the relativity of the notion of normality makes many situations ambiguous from the interpreter's point of view* [...] Unless the exceptions are made explicit the conceptual content of the normative expression is left undetermined [...] Defeasibility, more than simple ambiguity, makes the identification of the norms of a legal system very difficult"; Bayón (1997).

legal indeterminacy, taking into account the several notions I have identified in the preceding sections.

Leaving aside adjudicative indeterminacy, that is a derivative form of legal indeterminacy, and focussing instead on textual indeterminacy, normative indeterminacy, methodological indeterminacy and ideological indeterminacy (see Sect. 10.2.2 above), three theses can be set forth as to the relationships between defeasibility and indeterminacy: the indirect dependence of textual indeterminacy on norm-defeasibility, the direct dependence of normative indeterminacy on norm-defeasibility, the direct dependence of norm-defeasibility on methodological and ideological indeterminacy.

1. Indirect Dependence of Textual Indeterminacy on Norm-Defeasibility Norm-defeasibility is a property of *norms*. It concerns norms, not legal provisions. The idea that norms are defeasible (that they are liable to negative conditions of application beyond what is contained in their standard form), however, can have an indirect bearing on the ambiguity of legal provisions, so far as explicit norms are considered. In a legal culture where norms are considered, and can be treated, as defeasible, legal provisions are likely to suffer from the (pragmatic) ambiguity consisting in their being assumed as capable of expressing, alternatively, a literal meaning that may contain no negative condition of application, or, rather, a teleological meaning containing a closed set of negative conditions of application, or, else, a teleological meaning containing an open set of negative condition of application, etc.

2. Direct Dependence of Normative Indeterminacy on Norm-Defeasibility The idea of norm-defeasibility, when accepted and put to work inside of a legal culture, can have the effect of producing situations of normative indeterminacy. Out of the five cases of normative indeterminacy I considered (see Sect. 10.2.2. above)—ambiguity, vagueness, generality, gaps, and normative conflicts—, however, only ambiguity, gaps and normative conflicts can be the effect of norm-defeasibility. First, as soon as interpreters (decide to) consider a norm, in its standard formulation, as defeasible, the norm may prove ambiguous if two or more alternative sets of negative conditions of application can be argued for. Second, a normative gap proper can be the output of norm-defeasibility. As we have seen while dealing with axiological gaps and defeasibility (see Sect. 10.5 above), this occurs whenever a normative gap proper is *created* in order to remedy to a (purported) axiological gap. In such situations, as you may recall, a (presumed) over-inclusive norm is eliminated by re-interpreting the corresponding legal provision so as to express *not* an over-inclusive norm *anymore*, but a norm containing a negative condition of application and leaving some class of cases unregulated. Third, a normative conflict can be the output of *not* considering norms as defeasible. The idea and technique of norm-defeasibility can be used, in fact, to re-interpret a legal provision or an implicit norm at hand, in such a way as to make a *prima facie* normative conflict disappear, by "making explicit", and adding, some negative condition of application.

3. Direct Dependence of Norm-Defeasibility on Methodological and Ideological Indeterminacy Norm-defeasibility can be seen as a dependent variable of methodological and ideological indeterminacy. The more a legal culture provides interpreters with a wide set of indeterminate and un-ordered tools for interpretation and integration, and the more it is characterized by ideological pluralism, the more it is likely that norms will be considered and treated as open-defeasible, and subject to both explicit and implicit defeasibility.

Chapter 11
Legislation

Here, then, in the very cradle of legislative empire grew up another power, in words the instrument of the former, in reality continually its censor and not infrequently its successful rival
—J. Bentham (1977)

The conscientious, intelligent judge will consider government a sort of orchestra, in which, in symphonies authorized by the people, the courts and the legislature each play their parts
—J. Frank (1949a)

11.1 The New Science of Legislation

The turn of the century has seen the rise of theories which, taking up one of the key concerns of juridical Enlightenment,[1] claim a new deal for legislation in the realms of jurisprudence and practical philosophy.

Jeremy Waldron set to the task of working out a "jurisprudence of legislation" capable of rescuing the respectability of lawmaking through (democratically elected) parliamentary assemblies in the related domains of political philosophy and analytical jurisprudence.[2] In the same line of Waldron, Luc Wintgens and others started campaigning for "legisprudence": "a new theory of legislation" the business

[1] See, e.g, Bentham (1789); Filangieri (1780–1785). On juridical Enlightenment, see e.g. Tarello (1976), Comanducci (1978), pp. 7–24; Postema (1986), parts II and III; Lieberman (1989), chs. 2, 13.

[2] Waldron (1999b), at 1, 2, we read: "legislation and legislatures have a bad name in legal and political philosophy, a name sufficiently disreputable to cast doubt on their credentials as respectable sources of law [...] I want us to see the process of legislation – at its best – as something like the following: the representatives of the community come together to settle solemnly and explicitly on common schemes and measures that can stand in the name of them all, and they do so in a way that openly acknowledges and respects [...] the inevitable differences of opinion and principle among them"; Waldron (1999a), part I.

P. Chiassoni, *Interpretation without Truth*, Law and Philosophy Library 128,
https://doi.org/10.1007/978-3-030-15590-2_11

of which is identifying ("detect") and explaining "the principles of legislation" that "underlie the activity of the legislator" in view of promoting rational lawmaking.[3]

In a 1950 essay where the term "legisprudence" was apparently coined, Julius Cohen complained legal realists did not pay due attention to legislation, though it was undeniably "one of the prime sources of policy-making", and advocated, along with "Realism in jurisprudence", i.e., as to adjudication and case-law, the need for "Realism in legisprudence": the promotion of "a working arrangement" between social and natural sciences and legislation, as a means for "the pursuit of reason as the *sine qua non* of the democratic way of life".[4]

American legal realists, as Cohen rightly emphasizes, were indeed primarily concerned with judicial lawmaking, and, consequently, did not pursue the project of making legislation a rational, scientifically reputable, enterprise along the lines he fosters. Nonetheless, it would be too hasty to conclude, from such a premise, that legal realism does not have a theory of legislation. In fact, it does have one. In this final chapter, I purport to argue for three claims:

1. So far as jurisprudence is concerned, the responsibility for legislation's disrepute is to be ascribed, largely though not entirely, to legal realism;
2. Legal realism's theory of legislation, with its cynical critique of the rosy picture heralded by *Gesetzespositivismus* and like views, is, on the whole, sound;
3. Any vindication of the dignity of legislation as regards to other legal sources (like, e.g., case-law), as well as any advocacy of the rational study of legislation against jurisprudential neglect, must either take the realistic theory seriously, or be doomed to idle utopianism.[5]

The first claim points to legal realism as one of the sources of legislation's *theoretical* disrepute. It aims at suggesting the present jurisprudential focus on adjudication, which Waldron finds a so disappointing "fixation", to be due not only (i) to the ideological orientation in favor of judges, and against legislatures, that we may find

[3] See, e.g.: Wintgens (2002), including essays by L. Wintgens, L. D. Eriksson, K. Pietilä, S. Eng, C. Dahlman, H. Tolonen, K. Tuori, A. Verhoeven, W. Voermans, and H. Winter; Wintgens (2006), pp. 1–25; Wintgens (2012), p. 7: "Current legal theory is premised on the central role of the judge in contemporary legal systems. Although this evolution has contributed much to a vibrant understanding of law, it has also left the role of the legislator largely ignored and under-theorised. Legal theory routinely takes the law as 'just there', and limits its theoretical undertakings to law as a 'given'. Law, it claims, is the result of political decision-making. But once law comes into force, it can be somehow miraculously separated from politics. And the realm of politics is impure – unlike law's 'neutral' and 'objective' methods of reasoning and decision-making". It goes without saying that legisprudence *à la* Wintgens is a normative enterprise: starting from the Kantian premise of individuals' moral autonomy and freedom, it purports to establish the right principles of legislation and, on the basis thereof, the duties legislatures ought to fulfil to be legitimate.

[4] Cohen (1949–1950), pp. 886–897. According to the *Black's Law Dictionary*, 7th ed., "Legisprudence" is "The systematic analysis of statutes within the framework of jurisprudential philosophies about the role and nature of law".

[5] Waldron and Wintgens seem to be aware of legal realism, so far as statutory interpretation is concerned. See e.g. Waldron (1999b), p. 10; Wintgens (2006), p. 21 ss. However, as we will see later on (Sect. 11.4 below), Waldron apparently resists to a full endorsing of realism.

in the legal culture of constitutional states, or (ii) to a legalistic "worry" for preserving the imagery of law's "neutrality" and "distance from politics", or even (iii) to a snobbish distaste for parliamentary assemblies,[6] as surely it may also be the case, but mainly (iv) to a widespread awareness about the structural limits of legislation (even of sophisticated forms of legislation), which represents one of the main contributions of the realistic theory to contemporary legal culture. I will not argue anymore for this claim here, being content with its apparent reasonableness from the vantage point of jurisprudential history. The third claim gets whatever force it might have from the plausibility of the second claim. In support of this latter claim, I will try to present the realistic theory of legislation in its best light.

11.2 Legal Realism

The phrase "legal realism" is notoriously ripe with indeterminacy. A few distinctions will help clearing the way.

1. "Legal realism" can be used from either an historical or a philosophical perspective. In the first case, it stands for a category in the eye of legal historians, pointing to specific tokens in contemporary legal thinking and legal culture. In the latter case, it stands for one of the rarefied, abstract pigeonholes in the philosophy of law, along with such things as "natural law theory", "legal positivism", "legal formalism", "interpretivism", etc.
2. Legal realism as a historical category—*historical legal realism*—refers to well-known movements in Western legal culture: American Realism, Scandinavian Realism, and, more recently, even Italian Realism.
3. Contrariwise, legal realism as a philosophical category—*philosophical legal realism*—refers to a bunch of claims and attitudes which are usually, but not necessarily, associated with historical realism. Philosophical realism reaches beyond the borders of historical realism: Jeremy Bentham and Hans Kelsen, for instance, may be considered as many representatives of philosophical realism, though they do not belong to the circles of legal philosophers within historical realism.
4. Philosophical realism is a set of epistemological, theoretical and normative claims and attitudes about the law.
5. From the standpoint of epistemology, philosophical realism characterises as an empiricist outlook: scientific knowledge of the law is viable, provided it is about what, and how, the law is *in fact*; it must be grounded on experience; it must get rid of any idea of a "metaphysical" law and "metaphysical" ways of thinking about it.
6. As a general theory of law, philosophical realism is the outcome of a thoroughly empiricist-driven consideration of the phenomena making up "positive law". Its

[6] See Waldron (1999b), ch. 2.

central point is the critique ("denial") of "the objectivity of law": i.e., of the idea according to which the law, any positive "legal system", is an ordered collection of rules "out there", waiting to be discovered and applied to real or fancied situations. Theoretical realism regards the objectivity of law as a myth: a piece of metaphysical thinking, consciously or unconsciously entertained to ideological purposes, and needing to be dispelled. This is to be done by bringing to the fore how the law really is and works. For instance, by pointing out the following truths. There are no general rules as full-fledged, ready-to-go legal prescriptions applying to individual cases (rule-scepticism). Legal rules have no true meaning interpretation can simply discover (interpretive-scepticism). Legal concepts do not have true meanings deriving from the very nature of law and legal institutes (concept-scepticism). Positive legal orders are not, in and by themselves, consistent and gapless normative systems (system-scepticism). Legal facts are not hard-and-fast items out there for judicial discovery (fact-scepticism). Legal reasoning does not work as a discovery-device, but, rather, as a justification-device, i.e., as a tool for *ex post* rationalizations (reasoning-scepticism, window-dressing theory). Adjudication is not, and cannot be, tantamount to a sheer combination of logic plus objective knowledge, as it is suggested by mechanical jurisprudence and judges-as-slot-machines theory (adjudication-scepticism). The traditional doctrinal study of law is not, properly speaking, "legal science": it is legal policy, usually in disguise (legal science-scepticism).

7. As a normative outlook, finally, philosophical realism amounts to the juristic deontology taking side for the dominion, the "rule", of reason upon positive law. Positive legal orders ought to be, as far as possible, rational concerns: inspired and driven by the tenets of formal and means-to-end rationality.[7]

11.3 Legal Realism and Legislation

"Legislation" suffers from process-product ambiguity. Legislation-process is the set of operations, performed by people acting as the "legislative" organs of a legal order, the outcome of which consists in "enacting" or "passing" things that are usually known as "laws", "statutes", or "acts". Legislation-product is the discrete set of laws, statutes or acts representing the output of a legislation-process.[8]

---

[7] See, e.g., Holmes (1897), p. 457 ff.; Frank (1930), Llewellyn (1930, 1931), Kelsen (1945), p. 123 ff.; Ross (1946, 1958), Tarello (1962), Castignone (1974), Olivecrona (1971), Twining (1985), Leiter (2007), Part I; Millard (2008), pp. 177–189; Guastini (2011b), pp. 138–161; Llewellyn (2011). On philosophical legal realism, see also Chap. 1, Sect. 1.1, above.

[8] In its more encompassing meaning, "legislation" refers to the whole domain of the so-called written law (*ius scriptum*), i.e., the law provided with an authoritative, fixed, formulation, as opposed to unwritten law (*ius non scriptum*), like background implicit principles and the *rationes decidendi* making up the reservoir of judicial precedents (on which, see Chap. 9, Sect. 9.3, above). Here, I will leave this larger meaning aside, focussing instead on the stricter meaning considered in the text.

Theories of legislation may be descriptive or normative.

Normative theories of legislation are about what, and how, legislation ought to be. They apply the principles of some previously selected normative ethics (theory of justice, theory of the state, etc.) to establish the proper way of instituting legitimate legislative organs, the proper rules and forms of legislative process, the proper way of gathering "the facts" and getting "witnesses", the proper forms of legislative drafting, the proper contents for legislative acts, etc. Normative theories of legislation belong to (Bentham's) censorial jurisprudence and political philosophy. They may concern legislation in general, or be limited to legislation as a source of law in a given variety of legal-political arrangement.

Descriptive theories of legislation, in turn, may be causal-explanatory, doctrinal or jurisprudential. Very roughly speaking: causal-explanatory theories purport to account for the causes and effects of pieces of legislation in one or more legal orders; doctrinal theories of legislation purport to account for the rules and principles that, in fact, govern legislation in one or more legal orders; jurisprudential theories purport to account for the structural and functional features of legislation in general, usually within a general theory of legal sources including case-law (precedent), customs, executive orders, etc. Jurisprudential theories are usually build upon the outputs of causal-explanatory and doctrinal descriptive enquiries.

Philosophical realism copes with legislation in two different ways. On the one hand, as descriptive realism, purports to provide a realistic jurisprudential theory of legislation. On the other hand, as normative realism, it is a normative ethics concerning the way legislation ought to be.

Leaving normative realism aside, in the next section I will provide an outline of (what I take to be) the theory of legislation of descriptive realism. In so doing, as anticipated, I will argue for the second and third claims I made at the outset (see Sect. 11.1 above).

11.4 The Realistic Theory of Legislation

Since the eighteenth century, it is commonplace considering central jurisprudential problems about legislation to encompass the following: To the purpose of clear and exact legal thinking, what are statutes? In which sense, if any, may statutes be regarded as the outcomes of acts-of-will by a legislature? In which sense, if any, does legislation "make" law? Properly speaking, is legislation "law", or, rather, a "source of law"? How can, and do, statutes work in fact? Is the actual working of statutes really affected by legislative intent? Which is the actual role of legislation (legislature) *vis à vis* adjudication (judges)? Which is the actual position of statutes *vis à vis* case-law? Which role does statutory interpretation play, if any, in the legislature/judges, legislation/adjudication, statutes/case-law relationships? Where is the distinction between legislation (law-making) and adjudication (law-applying) to be properly drawn?

To these momentous and delicate issues, the realistic theory of legislation answers by upholding five inter-locked thesis: the will-of-the-text thesis, the norm-formulations thesis, the no one-to-one correspondence thesis, the structural indeterminacy thesis, and, finally, the structural mercy thesis.[9]

1. The Will-of-the-Text Thesis Surely, statutes are the outcomes of acts-of-will by the components of a legislative body or legislature (legislators). Statutes may, and usually do, presuppose knowledge and reasoning on the part of the lawmakers. Nonetheless, the condition *sine qua non* for there being a statute may safely be located with the idea of legislators exercising their faculty of volition: no will, no statute. This view about legislation is, in turn, an instance of the old and widespread view on law in general called "voluntarism".

Provided it is the case that statutes are related to acts-of-will, it is worthwhile asking *what* precisely is being, or can be, willed by a legislature whenever it passes a statute. According to an influential view dating from modern natural law theory, but also endorsed by eminent "legal positivists" like, e.g., John Austin, the matter of legislators' acts of will would consist in some normative meaning-content of the enacted statutes. Legislators, so the picture goes, first entertain some normative meaning-content in their mind, and then look for the most suitable linguistic formulation thereof.

Now, the realistic theory of legislation claims that picture is unworkable to any theoretical purpose, and must consequently be abandoned.

The traditional voluntarist view may seem sound whenever monocratic legislatures—like absolute kings and unbound tyrants directly exercising their powers—are concerned. Even in such cases, however, there seems to be no use for the idea of a meaning-content "poured into the statute" by the legislator, unless we can know for sure what it is.[10] Legislators might be dead; if they are not, asking to living legislators would simply elicit a new exercise of their absolute lawmaking power. Indeed, how can we *know* that what the legislator tells us *now* to be the meaning-content she meant to attach to her statute is in fact so? Nay, what we would really get out of our inquiry would be just a *new* piece of legislation, endowed with *ex post facto* binding force and, perhaps, needing in turn of a "clarifying" legislative act.

[9] For the present reconstruction of the realistic theory of legislation I considered the following works: Bentham (2010), p. 161ff., 169ff., 174ff., 227 ff.; Bentham (1977), p. 89 ff., 137 ff.; Austin (1885), p. 525 ff., 620 ff., 989 ff., 1028 ff.; Gray (1909), p. 145 ff.; Frank (1930), p. 186 ff., 310–311; Radin (1930), p. 863 ff.; Cohen (1933), p. 230 ff.; Kelsen (1941), p. 271 ff.; Kelsen (1945), p. 134 ff.; Frank (1949b), pp. 290–291, 292 ff.; Ross (1958), chs. III and IV; Kelsen (1960), chs. V and VIII; Llewellyn (1960), p. 521 ff.; Tarello (1980), chs. II and VIII; Troper (2003), pp. 98–112; Dworkin (1986), ch. 1–3, 9; Eskridge and Frickey (1998), p. 240 ff., 569 ff.; Chiassoni (1999a), p. 21 ff.; Chiassoni (2011), ch. 2; Dworkin (2011), Part II; Llewellyn (2011), p. 119 ff.; Guastini (2011a), Parts I and V. See also Chaps. 3, 4, and 5 above.

[10] Autocratic legislators in fact can make known their mind about the "proper" meaning of their statutes by means, say, of declarations accompanying the enacted text, or released through other channels of institutional communication.

The traditional voluntarist view, by contrast, looses any plausibility whatsoever since the very start, whenever legislatures are collective bodies. Here, the idea of the legislature willing a given meaning-content for its statutes is sheer fiction. The legislation process involves many actors (in contemporary democracies, up to several hundreds people); some, though voting for it, may have conflicting views about the meaning and purpose of a statute; some, having no view at all, may cast their vote out of party's discipline or for some other reason wholly unrelated to the statutes' content; some may even not know the text they are approving (for instance, they have been very busy with their far-away constituency and jumped into the House to say "aye" directly after a sleepy night on the plane). In such a situation, whichever claim about the proper "location" of the will-of-the-content of statutes is fated to belong to normative theory of legislation: it cannot but express and mirror some ideology about how legislation *ought to* be conceived and acted-upon. Even where, by hypothesis, we may presume the several individuals making up the legislature did converge upon some meaning-content for the statutes they enacted, this may be difficult to ascertain and the outcome may be dubious (remember the "ask-to-the-legislature" predicament we mentioned above). Furthermore, the practical relevance of the will-of-the-content of statutes, provided there is one and it can be known for sure, is by no means a matter of course. Far from being an issue enjoying of a self-evident, "natural", solution, this will necessarily depend on the adoption of some normative theory of legislation, granting overcoming practical value to legislature's convergent will-of-the-content.

All the previous considerations lead legal realism to the following conclusion. Whenever a statute is passed by a legislature, there can be only one sure object of volition to any theoretical purpose: the statute's *text*. Any richer claim, any claim going beyond the text, really is *theoretically* unwarranted.[11]

In a careful examination of the legislative intent issue, Jeremy Waldron seems to get to a different conclusion:

> Beyond the meaning embodied conventionally in the text of the statute that has been put before the House and voted upon, there is no state or condition corresponding to "the intention of the legislature" to which anything else – such as what particular members or groups of members said or thought or wrote or did – could possibly provide a clue.[12]

Apparently, according to Waldron, what legislators will when they pass a statute is not simply the text of the statute, it is also the *meaning conventionally embodied* in it. Surely, Waldron's claim appears a matter of course, fully in tune with our current "intuitions" and habitual modes of thinking. Indeed, when we, in our ordinary conversations, do use sentences in a natural language, we are obviously willing they shall be meant according to their conventional meaning. Why legislators, who are people like us, should behave differently?

The argument, however, is too simple to be good. To begin with, we cannot grant that, in ordinary conversations, the will of the users of a natural language always is

---

[11] See Chap. 5, Sects. 5.2 and 5.4 above.

[12] Waldron (1999b), p. 27.

to that effect. Indeed, conversations can be very sophisticated games where conventional meanings happen to be deliberately bypassed and consciously abused.[13] Furthermore, we must pause to reflect upon what the ascription to legislators of (the will-of-the-text plus) the will-of-the-text's-conventional-meaning does amount to. Now, from a lawyer's perspective such a will amounts to a will concerning the "proper", "correct", "right" reading of the statutory text. It is, in other words, a will concerning the proper way of *interpreting* statutes. If that is the case, however, the existence of such a will, far from being a matter of course, raises the same problems we considered while dealing with the will-of-the-content claim. May we assuredly claim such a will to be present in any case in which a statute is being passed? How do we (and Waldron) *know* that? Is not, perhaps, the case that such a confident claim about legislators' will-of-the-text's-conventional-meaning is really a piece of wishful thinking? Is not, after all, such a confident claim suspiciously in tune with the Enlightenment, rationalist ideology about how legislation *should* work and *ought to* be conceived and acted upon? For all these reasons, Waldron's seemingly plausible claim is to be rejected as deprived of any sound *theoretical* foundation, as a piece of legislative ideology (in disguise).

2. The Norm-Formulations Thesis According to common sense, legislatures do make "laws": indeed, what else should a "legislature" do? Such a claim, in turn, is usually deemed to be equivalent to saying, perhaps in a more precise language, that legislatures enact statutory norms, that they "produce" bundles of statutory norms.

Though it is grounded on what appears as flat evidence, such a view—realism claims—is likely to be misleading. Indeed, what legislatures do actually and undoubtedly produce are, as we have just seen, statutory *texts*. A statutory text is a set of authoritatively fixed strings of words, composed according to the lexicon and the grammar of a natural language. So, properly speaking, what legislatures do produce are *norm-formulations* (*legal provisions*): sentences (assumed to be) working as official linguistic expressions of statutory norms. Consequently, the statement "legislatures produce statutory norms" is true if, but only if, "norms" is being used as synonymous with "norm-formulations".[14]

Those who usually make that statement, however, would not be content with the realist's way of putting things. They would refuse to accept realism's ostensive argument ("Look, here is the 'Prevention of Terrorism Act'. What do you see beyond signs having all the appearances of strings of words in the language of modern English?"). They would insist that legislatures do actually produce not just norm-formulations, but, as they say, *norms*. They would charge legal realism with providing an unduly impoverished view of legislation: one dictated, perhaps, by their notorious keen on the judiciary. These objections bring us to the third thesis of the realistic theory of legislation.

[13] On the Gricean picture of ordinary conversation see Chap. 3, Sect. 3.5 above.

[14] See the complementary remarks below. See also Chap. 5, Sects. 5.2 and 5.4 above.

3. The No One-to-One Correspondence Thesis We have seen that the ostensive argument, by itself, is likely not to win the day. Realists however would keep on claiming that what legislatures really "produce", strictly theoretically speaking, are not norms, but norm-formulations (legal provisions), adding further reasons. These include, as we shall see in a moment, the no one-to-one correspondence thesis. Here you are the way a realist might argue.

From a strictly theoretical standpoint, statutory *norms* are the meaning-contents of statutory norm-formulations. Being meaning-contents, their identification depends on the *interpretation* of norm-formulations. Norm-formulations do not interpret themselves: they are not self-interpreting entities. Interpreters—like judges, lawyers, jurists, or people-at-large—are always needed to do the job. Norm-formulations do not apply themselves to individual or generic cases. On the contrary, their application always requires, ultimately, some law-applying agency, usually a judge. Claiming the contrary would amount to incurring into the *ex opere operato* fallacy: it would be wrongly presuming statutes can work by themselves, as if automatically, upon the social realities they concern. As a matter of fact, due to the working of several conspiring factors, including methodological indeterminacy and ideological pluralism, there is no one-to-one correspondence between norm-formulations and norms. Rather, to each norm-formulation there corresponds *a frame of alternative norms*: i.e., each norm-formulation can be translated in alternative ways, each one corresponding to a different norm.[15]

In the light of the preceding remarks, the statement "legislatures produce statutory norms" may be safely asserted, if, and only if, one makes clear: first, that the immediate, direct, outputs of legislation are norm-formulations; second, that to each norm-formulation does not correspond one, and only one, norm, but a frame of alternative norms; third, that the identification of the frame of norms corresponding to each norm-formulation is a matter of interpretation.

One may claim, accordingly, that legislatures produce norm-formulations *and* the corresponding frames of norms. The latter, however, can be regarded as an output of legislature's own work only indirectly: through the necessary meddling of interpreters. Any different picture is likely to be misleading.

4. The Structural Indeterminacy Thesis The no one-to-one correspondence thesis suggests, as we have seen, that we are safer considering that legislatures, properly speaking, do not produce statutory norms, but, rather, statutory norm-formulations (provisions) needing (judicial) interpretation in order to be applied.

This is a very far flight from the idea(l) of legislatures' juridical omnipotence. It is, nonetheless, a claim lying at the very heart of the realistic theory of legislation. Realists believe to have watertight reasons for it. The no one-to-one correspondence thesis depends on the general indeterminacy thesis, which is in turn, as we shall see, a corollary of (what I call) the structural indeterminacy thesis. The general indeterminacy thesis claims indeterminacy to be general all over legislation (-product): it

---

[15] See Chap. 5, Sect. 5.2, and Chap. 10, Sect. 10.2.2, above.

asserts, within the terms which will be made clear in a moment, that every statutory norm-formulation is, prior to its application, indeterminate.[16] Why would statutory law be generally indeterminate? Indeterminacy's measuring rods are manifold and uncertain. So far as statutes are concerned, several different notions of indeterminacy may be singled out. To the present purpose, it seems worthwhile considering three of them that, apparently, roughly correspond to the ones most discussed in legal theory: radical indeterminacy, contingent indeterminacy, and structural indeterminacy. They are all, it must be emphasized, notions of indeterminacy from the standpoint of statutory interpretation.[17]

The *radical indeterminacy thesis* claims statutes to be *radically indeterminate*: statutory norm-formulations do not have, properly speaking, any meaning whatsoever *prior* to interpretation. Interpreters *create* the meaning of statutory provisions. This is notably the case with judicial interpretation: due to the combinations of factors like the dynamic structure of legal orders, the uncertainties of statutory language as a piece of a natural language, the traditional tools of statutory interpretation (like, e.g., the letter/spirit distinction), judges may ascribe whatever meaning they wish to statutory norm-formulations, even a meaning *outside* of the set (in Kelsenian terms: "the frame") of the previously recorded or conjecturable ones, and this meaning will be the ground of valid individual norms until its eventual repeal by a higher court, if any.

The *contingent indeterminacy thesis* claims statutes to be *contingently* indeterminate. Being made of sentences in a natural language, they share in the fate of these linguistic entities. Accordingly, statutory norm-formulations may happen to have a clear and determinate meaning as to the cases at hand, which depends on ongoing social and juristic conventions about legislative language. These conventions, however, may run out and, where this happens, the meaning of statutory provisions becomes indeterminate. In the former cases, statutes are determinate: they do have a clear and determinate meaning *prior* to (judicial) interpretation; this clear and determinate meaning can be *discovered* by interpreters; therefore, one can claim legislatures do not simply produce norm-formulations, but also the norms these express according to established social and juristic conventions. In the latter cases, on the contrary, statutes are indeterminate: they do not have a clear and determinate meaning *prior* to (judicial) interpretation and liable to discovery; their meaning must instead be *created* by (judicial) interpretation. In such cases, it appears legislatures have produced norm-formulations but, properly speaking, no statutory norm (where the law is indeterminate, there is no law). Indeterminacy besets statutory norm-formulations as a dispositional property that may show up according to the circumstances.

Finally, the *structural indeterminacy thesis* claims statutes to be always liable to a plurality of alternative interpretations. It is not the case, properly speaking, that

[16] By the way, the thesis is in turn a specification of the more sweeping thesis about the general indeterminacy, in Kelsenian terms, of any 'superior norm' whatsoever. See, e.g., Kelsen (1960), ch. VIII.

[17] On legal indeterminacy, see also Chap. 10, Sect. 10.2 above.

statutes do not have any meaning prior to interpretation. It is the case, rather, that they may always be read in several different ways, on a scale ranging from a narrower to a larger meaning. In any case, the identification of the meaning, which will be ascribed to a statutory norm-formulation in view of its application, will not be (just) a matter of discovery, but a matter of (usually reasoned) choice. From the standpoint of structural indeterminacy, the radical indeterminacy thesis fails because statutes *do* have meaning before interpretation; the contingent indeterminacy thesis fails too, however, because the meaning, by which a statutory provision is applied to cases, also in so-called "clear" or "easy" cases, is *never* a matter of sheer discovery, but always of (reasoned) decision. The following features of statutory language and statutory interpretation support the structural indeterminacy thesis:

a. the natural, "unintentional", indeterminacy of texts in a natural language, which are typically affected by vagueness and ambiguity;
b. the fatal indeterminacy of legislative intent, if any (see point 1. above, concerning the will-of-the-text claim), which also depends on the impossibility, even for the most careful and willing legislature, both to have a clear idea of the situations presently falling within the scope of a statute, and to forecast future situations to which the statute may apply;
c. the "intentional" indeterminacy resulting from the legislature's use of expressions (interpretable as) referring to vague standards ("fair amount", "just compensation", "due process of laws", "good behaviour", "in restraint of trade or commerce", etc.);
d. the traditional canons of statutory interpretation, forming a disordered set of indeterminate interpretive tools interpreters are called to select, make determinate and put in order, on the basis of their own views about the 'proper' interpretive code to be used, either in general, or on an *ad hoc* basis (methodological indeterminacy);
e. juristic constructions, like theories about contracts, torts, property rights, criminal liability, trespass, etc., usually making a set of competing, alternative views;
f. juristic ideologies about law, legal sources, legal norms, justice, democracy, the constitution and constitutional state, etc., which are usually a set of competing, alternative views, deeply affect the methodological choice of the "proper" interpretive code to be used, and determine the basic normative attitude of each interpreter *vis à vis* legislation, on a scale ranging between full, unconditioned, active cooperation, on the one hand, and full, relentless, sabotage, on the other (ideological pluralism).

The structural indeterminacy thesis—it is worthwhile emphasizing—insists that norm-formulations always are ambiguous, liable to more than one interpretation, from the standpoint of juristic methodology and theories of interpretation (universal methodological ambiguity[18]). This does not rule out that norm-formulations may be applied, in a given time-range, in one and the same enduring meaning. Certainty and easy cases, however, are the outcomes, according to the circumstances, of moral

[18] See Chap. 5, Sect. 5.2, above.

persuasion, wilful cooperation, conformism, opportunism, prudence and even cowardice.

The realistic theory of legislation is liable to be regarded as oscillating between the radical indeterminacy and the structural indeterminacy thesis, both of which point to the general indeterminacy of statutory texts.

From a meta-theoretical vantage point, the structural indeterminacy thesis seems preferable. It has the advantage of being more in tune with established and useful ways of thinking, while preserving at the same time a full "anti-formalist" orientation. On the one hand, unlike the radical indeterminacy thesis, it avoids the queerness of denying statutes to have meaning *prior* to interpretation; it preserves, furthermore, the conceptual distinction between "law-interpretation proper" (any ascription of meaning to a norm-formulation, justifiable on the basis of ongoing interpretive tools and theories of interpretation) and "law-creation" (any ascription of meaning to a norm-formulation, not so justifiable, or by pure fiat). On the other hand, unlike the contingent indeterminacy thesis, it maintains that statutory interpretation can never be (just) an act of knowledge, discovering the clear and determinate conventional meaning of norm-formulations. Indeed, so the realistic argument goes, such a presumed "discovery" really depends on, and presupposes, a previous methodological *decision*: i.e., the decision of considering the clear and determinate conventional meaning of norm-formulations as their legally correct meaning to all practical purpose. The contingent indeterminacy thesis, its theoretical pretence notwithstanding, does actually dwell on a deep normative commitment in favour of conventional meanings.

5. The Structural Mercy Thesis All the previous four thesis anticipate, and prelude to, what may be regarded as the last, momentous, piece of the realistic theory of legislation: the structural mercy thesis. According to it, statutes, far from being controlling over their judicial applications, far from providing society with hard-and-fast rules ready to be complied with and applied, are at the mercy of their authoritative interpreters, like judges and other law-applying officials. The thesis, it must be noted, insists that statutes are in a condition of *structural* mercy: a situation of dependence resulting from the way statutes are and cannot but be; a situation of dependence resulting, as we have seen, from their being not-self-interpreting, not-self-applying, structurally indeterminate, strings of words. This feature does not necessarily result, and in fact rarely results, in judicial (and officials') anarchy. As we all (should) know, however, whatever influence statutes may have in a society cannot depend but on practical factors, ranging from right to might.

References

Aarnio A (1981) On the truth and validity of interpretative statements in legal dogmatics. Rechtstheorie 12:423–448
Aarnio A (1987) The rational as reasonable. A treatise on legal justification. Reidel, Dordrecht
Alchourrón CE (1993) Philosophical foundations of deontic logic and the logic of defeasible conditionals. In: Meyer J, Wieringa R (eds) Deontic logic in computer science: normative system specification. Wiley & Sons, London, pp 43–84
Alchourrón CE (1995) Para una Lógica de las Razones Prima Facie, unpublished manuscript
Alchourrón CE (1996a) Detachment and Defeasibility in deontic logic. Studia Logica 57:5–18
Alchourrón CE (1996b) On law and logic. Ratio Juris 9:331–348
Alchourrón CE, Bulygin E (1971) Normative systems. Springer, Wien
Alchourrón CE, Bulygin E (1975) Introducción a la metodología de las ciencias jurídicas y sociales. Buenos Aires, Astrea [the book represents a revised and enlarged translation of Alchourrón, C.E., Bulygin, E. (1971)]
Alchourrón CE, Bulygin E (1989 [1991]) Los límites de la lógica y el razonamiento jurídico. In: Alchourrón CE, Bulygin E (eds) Análisis lógico y derecho. Centro de Estudios Constitucionales, Madrid, pp 303–328 [also published as: Limits of logic and legal reasoning. In: Martino A (ed) Expert systems in law. North-Holland, Amsterdam, 1992, pp 9–27]
Alexy R (1978 [1989]) Theorie der juristische Argumentation: Der Theorie des rationalen Diskurses als Theorie der juristischen Begründung (A theory of legal argumentation. The theory of rational discourse as theory of legal justification). Clarendon Press, Oxford
Alexy R (1993) Rechtsinterpretation, it. tr., Interpretazione giuridica. In: Enciclopedia delle scienze sociali. Istituto dell'Enciclopedia Italiana, Roma, 7:416–423
Alexy R (2002) A theory of constitutional rights. Oxford University Press, Oxford
Åqvist L (1973) Modal logic with subjunctive conditionals and dispositional predicates. J Philos Log 2(1):1–76
Atienza M (2013) Curso de argumentación jurídica. Trotta, Madrid
Atria F (2002) On law and legal reasoning. Hart, Oxford
Austin J (1885) Lectures on jurisprudence or the philosophy of positive law, 5th edn. Murray, London
Austin JL (1950 [1961]) Truth. In: Austin JL (ed) Philosophical papers. Clarendon Press, Oxford, pp 85–101
Austin JL (1956–1957 [1961]) A plea for excuses. In: Austin JL (ed) Philosophical papers. Clarendon Press, Oxford, pp 123–152
Austin JL (1962) How to do things with words, 2nd edn. Harvard University Press, Cambridge, Mass
Ayer AJ (1952) Language, truth and logic, 2nd edn. Dover, New York

P. Chiassoni, *Interpretation without Truth*, Law and Philosophy Library 128,
https://doi.org/10.1007/978-3-030-15590-2

Baker GP (1978 [1977]) Defeasibility and meaning. In: Hacker PMS, Raz J (eds) Law, morality and society. Essays in honour of H.L.A. Hart. Clarendon Press, Oxford, pp 26–57
Barberis M (2014) Introduzione allo studio del diritto. Giappichelli, Torino
Barberis M (2016) For a truly realistic theory of law. Revus J Const Theory Philos Law 29:7–14
Bayón JC (1997 [2003]) Derrotabilidad, indeterminación del derecho y positivismo jurídico. In: Bayón JC, Ródriguez (ed) Relevancia normativa en la justificación de las decisiones judiciales. El debate Bayón-Rodríguez sobre la derrotabilidad de las normas jurídicas. Gaido P, Sánchez R, Seleme HO (eds) Externado, Bogotá, pp 157–208
Bayón JC (2001) Why is legal reasoning defeasible? In: Soeteman A (ed) Pluralism in law. Kluwer, Dordrecht, pp 327–346
Bentham J (1789) Introduction to the principles of morals and legislation. In: Burns JH, Hart HLA (eds) University of London/The Athlone Press, London, 1970
Bentham J (1791) Of laws in general. In: Hart HLA (ed) The Athlone Press, London, 1970
Bentham J (1977) A comment on the commentaries. In: Burns JH, Hart HLA (eds) A comment on the commentaries and a fragment on government. University of London/The Athlone Press, London
Bentham J (2010) In: Schofield P (ed) Of the limits of the Penal Branch of jurisprudence. Clarendon Press, Oxford
Bianchi C (1998) Il contestualismo. SIFA National Conference, Bologna, September 23–26, 1998 (http://sifa.unige.it/2eve/ab98/bia.htm)
Bianchi C (2001) La dipendenza contestuale. Per una teoria pragmatica del significato. ESI, Napoli
Bianchi C (2002) Contestualismo radicale. In: Penco C (ed) La svolta contestuale. McGraw-Hill, Milano, pp 253–265
Bianchi C (2005) Pragmatica del linguaggio, 2nd edn. Laterza, Roma-Bari
Bianchi C (2009) Pragmatica cognitiva. Laterza, Roma-Bari
Bix B (1993) Law, language, and legal determinacy. Oxford University Press, Oxford
Bix B (2003) Can theories of meaning and reference solve the problem of legal determinacy? Ratio Juris 16(3):281–295
Bix B (2007) Joseph Raz and conceptual analysis. APA Newsl 6(2):1–7
Bix B (2009) Global error and legal truth. Oxf J Leg Stud 29(3):535–547
Bix B (2010) Will versus reason. Truth in natural law, positive law, and legal theory. In: Pritzl K (ed) Truth. Studies of a Robust presence. The Catholic University of America, Washington, DC, pp 208–231
Black T (2005) Contextualism in epistemology. In: The Internet Encyclopedia of Philosophy, 2005 (http://www.iep.utm.edu/c/contextu.htm)
Bobbio N (1950 [1976]) Scienza del diritto e analisi del linguaggio. In: Scarpelli U (ed) Diritto e analisi del linguaggio. Milano, Comunità, pp 287–324
Bobbio N (1963 [1994]) Lacune del diritto. In: Bobbio N (ed) Contributi ad un dizionario giuridico. Giappichelli, Torino, pp 89–102
Bobbio N (1971) Le bon législateur. Logique et analyse 53–54:243–249
Bohman J, Rehg W (2014) Jürgen Habermas, The Stanford Encyclopedia of Philosophy (Fall 2014 Edition), Edward N. Zalta (ed) https://plato.stanford.edu/archives/fall2014/entries/habermas
Borges JL (1964 [1969]) El instante. In: Borges JL (ed) Elogio de la sombra. Emece, Buenos Aires, 1996
Brandom RB (1994) Making it explicit. Reasoning, representing, and discursive commitment. Harvard University Press, Cambridge
Brown JR, Fehige Y (2011) Thought experiments. In: Stanford Encyclopedia of philosophy, First published Sat Dec 28, 1996; substantive revision Fri Jul 29, 2011 (http://plato.stanford.edu/entries/thought-experiment/)
Bulygin E (1966 [2015]) Judicial decisions and the creation of law. In: Bulygin E (2015) Essays in legal philosophy. Bernal C, Huerta C, Mazzarese T, Moreso JJ, Navarro PE, Paulson SL (eds). Oxford University Press, Oxford, pp 75–87.

Bulygin E (1981 [1995]) Teoria e tecnica della legislazione. In: Bulygin E (ed) Norme, validità, sistemi normativi. Giappichelli, Torino, pp 29–49
Bulygin E (1986 [2015]) Legal dogmatics and the systematization of law. In: Bulygin E (2015). Essays in legal philosophy. Bernal C, Huerta C, Mazzarese T, Moreso JJ, Navarro PE, Paulson SL (eds). Oxford University Press, Oxford, pp 220–234
Bulygin E (1991 [1994]) On Legal Interpretation. In: Koch H-J, Neumann U (eds) Praktische Vernunft und Rechtsanwendung / Legal system and practical reason, ARSP-Beiheft 53. Franz Steiner, Stuttgart, pp 11–22
Bulygin E (1995a) Cognition and interpretation of law. In: Gianformaggio L, Paulson SL (eds) Cognition and interpretation of law. Giappichelli, Torino, pp 11–35
Bulygin E (1995b) Some replies to critics. In: Gianformaggio L, Paulson SL (eds) Cognition and interpretation of law. Giappichelli, Torino, pp 305–313
Bulygin E (1995c) Prefazione. In: Bulygin E (ed) Norme, validità, sistemi normativi. Giappichelli, Torino, pp vii–xiii
Bulygin E (1999) True or false statements in normative discourse. In: Egidi R (ed) In search of a new humanism. The philosophy of Georg Henrik von Wright. Kluwer, Dordrecht, pp 183–191
Bulygin E (2004) On legal gaps. In: Comanducci P, Guastini R (eds) Analisi e diritto 2002–2003. Ricerche di giursprudenza analitica. Giappichelli, Torino, pp 21–28
Bulygin E (2006) El positivismo jurídico. Fontamara, Cátedra Ernesto Garzón Valdés, México
Bulygin E (2009) Mi vision de la filosofia del derecho. Doxa. Cuadernos de Filosofía del Derecho 32:85–90
Burgess AG, Burgess JP (2011) Truth. Princeton University Press, Princeton
Bustamante T, Bernal Pulido C (2012a) Introduction. In: Bustamante T, Bernal Pulido C (eds) On the philosophy of Precedent. Proceedings of the 24th World Congress of the International Association for Philosophy of Law and social Philosophy, Beijing, 2009. Vol III, ARSP Beiheft 133. Franz Steiner Verlag, Stuttgart, pp 7–10
Bustamante T, Bernal Pulido C (eds) (2012b) On the Philosophy of Precedent. Proceedings of the 24th World Congress of the International Association for Philosophy of law and social philosophy, Beijing, 2009. Vol III. ARSP Beiheft 133. Franz Steiner Verlag, Stuttgart
Buzzoni M (2004) Esperimento ed esperimento mentale. Franco Angeli, Milano
Caffi C (2008) Sei lezioni di pragmatica linguistica. Name, Genova
Cappelen H, Lepore E (2005) Insensitive semantics. A defense of semantic minimalism and speech act pluralism. Blackwell, Oxford
Caracciolo R (1988) El sistema jurídico. Problemas actuales. Centro de Estudios Constitucionales, Madrid
Carnap R (1936 [1949]) Truth and confirmation. In: Feigl H, Sellars W (eds) Readings in philosophical analysis. Appleton-Century-Crofts, New York, pp 119–127
Carnap R (1950 [1956]) Empiricism, semantics, and ontology. In: Carnap R (ed) Meaning and necessity. A study in semantics and modal logic, Enlarged edn. The University of Chicago Press, Chicago, pp 205–221
Carnap R (1963) Intellectual autobiography. In: Schilpp PA (ed) The philosophy of Rudolf Carnap, La Salle, Ill. Cambridge University Press, Open Court / London, pp 1–84
Carrió GR (1965) Notas sobre derecho y lenguaje. Abeledo-Perrot, Buenos Aires
Castignone S (1974) La macchina del diritto. Il realismo giuridico in Svezia. Comunità, Milano
Celano B (2016) Pre-conventions. A fragment of the background. Revus 1:2–16
Chiassoni P (1990) L'interpretazione della legge: normativismo semiotico, scetticismo, giochi interpretative. In: AA.VV. Studi in memoria di Giovanni Tarello, Vol II. Giuffrè, Milano, pp 121–161
Chiassoni P (1998) L'interpretazione dei documenti normativi: Giustiniano e i Glossatori. In: Gianformaggio L, Jori M (eds) Scritti per Uberto Scarpelli. Giuffrè, Milano, pp 199–223
Chiassoni P (1999a) L'ineluttabile scetticismo della "scuola genovese". In: Comanducci P, Guastini R (eds) Analisi e diritto 1998. Ricerche di giurisprudenza analitica. Giappichelli, Torino, pp 21–76

Chiassoni P (1999b) La giurisprudenza civile. Metodi d'interpretazione e tecniche argomentative. Giuffrè, Milano

Chiassoni P (2000a) Significato letterale: giuristi e linguisti a confronto (Another View of the Cathedral). In: Velluzzi V (ed) Significato letterale e interpretazione del diritto. Giappichelli, Torino, pp 1–63

Chiassoni P (2000b) Interpretive games: statutory construction through Gricean Eyes. In: Comanducci P, Guastini R (eds) Analisi e diritto 1999. Ricerche di giurisprudenza analitica. Giappichelli, Torino, pp 79–99

Chiassoni P (2001) Archimede o Eraclito? Sul primato teorico dello scetticismo. Materiali per una storia della cultura giuridica XXXI:365–375

Chiassoni P (2002) Finzioni giudiziali. Progetto di voce per un vademecum giuridico. In: Brunetta d'Usseaux F (ed) Le finzioni del diritto. Giuffrè, Milano, pp 59–87

Chiassoni P (2004) Codici interpretativi. Progetto di voce per un Vademecum giuridico. In: Comanducci P, Guastini R (eds) Analisi e diritto 2002–2003. Ricerche di giurisprudenza analitica. Giappichelli, Torino, pp 55–124

Chiassoni P (2005a) L'utopia della ragione analitica. Origini, oggetti e metodi della filosofia del diritto positivo. Giappichelli, Torino

Chiassoni P (2005b) Il precedente giudiziale: tre esercizi di disincanto. In: Comanducci P, Guastini R (eds) Analisi e diritto 2004. Ricerche di giurisprudenza analitica. Giappichelli, Torino, pp 75–101

Chiassoni P (2006) A nice derangement of literal-meaning freaks: linguistic contextualism and the theory of legal interpretation. In: Comanducci P, Guastini R (eds) Analisi e diritto 2005. Ricerche di giurisprudenza analitica. Giappichelli, Torino, pp 115–126

Chiassoni P (2008) On the wrong track: Andrei Marmor on legal positivism, interpretation, and easy cases. Ratio Juris 21(2):248–267

Chiassoni P (2009) L'indirizzo analítico nella filosofía del diritto. I. Da Bentham a Kelsen. Giappichelli, Torino

Chiassoni P (2011) Técnicas de interpretación jurídica. Breviario para juristas. Marcial Pons, Madrid-Barcelona-Buenos Aires

Chiassoni P (2012) The model of ordinary analysis. In: Duarte d'Almeida L, Edwards J, Dolcetti A (eds) Reading H. L. A. Hart's the concept of law. Hart, Oxford, pp 247–267

Chiassoni P (2013) Wiener realism. In: Duarte d'Almeida L, Gardner J, Green L (eds) Kelsen revisited. Hart, Oxford, pp 131–162

Chiassoni P (2016a) Da Bentham a Kelsen. Sei capitoli per una storia della filosofia analitica del diritto. Giappichelli, Torino

Chiassoni P (2016b) Supporting the force of law: a few complementary arguments against essentialist jurisprudence. In: Bezemek C, Ladavac N (eds) The force of law reaffirmed. Frederick Schauer meets the critics. Springer, Switzerland, pp 61–71

Chiassoni P (2016c) Legal interpretation without truth. Revus J Const Theory Philos Law 29:93–118

Chiassoni P (2016d) The heritage of the 19th century: the age of interpretive cognitivism. In: Pattaro E, Roversi C (eds) Legal philosophy in the twentieth century: the civil law world, Tome 2: main orientations and topics. Springer, The Netherlands, pp 565–600

Chiassoni P (2016e) The age of discontent: the revolt against interpretive cognitivism. In: Pattaro E, Roversi C (eds) Legal philosophy in the twentieth century: the civil law world, Tome 2: main orientations and topics. Springer, The Netherlands, pp 608–618

Cohen FS (1933 [1959]) Ethical systems and legal ideals. An essay on the foundations of legal criticism. Cornell University Press, Ithaca

Cohen J (1949–1950) Towards realism in legisprudence. Yale Law J 59:886–897

Coleman J, Leiter B (1995) Determinacy, objectivity, and authority. In: Marmor A (ed) Law and interpretation. Essays in legal philosophy. Clarendon Press, Oxford, pp 203–278

Comanducci P (1978) L'illuminismo giuridico. Il Mulino, Bologna

Conte AG (1957) Ricerche in tema d'interpretazione analogica. In: Conte AG (1997) Filosofia dell'ordinamento normativo. Studi 1957–1968. Giappichelli, Torino, pp 1–62
Conte AG (1962) Saggio sulla completezza degli ordinamenti giuridici. Giappichelli, Torino
Conte AG (1968 [1985]) Completezza e chiusura. In: Conte AG (ed) Nove studi sul linguaggio normativo. Giappichelli, Torino, pp 15–37
Cross R (1977) Precedent in English law, 3rd edn. Clarendon Press, Oxford
Dagan H (2013) Reconstructing American legal realism and rethinking private law theory. Oxford University Press, Oxford
Dagan H (2017) Contemporary legal realism. In: Sellers M, Kirste S (eds) Encyclopedia of the philosophy of law and social philosophy. Springer Science and Business Media B.V
Dagan H (2018) The real legacy of American legal realism. Oxf J Legal Stud 38(1):123–146
Dascal M, Wróblewski J (1988) Transparency and doubt: understanding and interpretation in pragmatics and in law. Law Philos 7:203–224
Davidson D (2005) Truth and predication. The Belknap Press of Harvard University Press, Cambridge
Del Mar M (2015a) Introducing fictions: examples, functions, definitions, and evaluations. In: Del Mar M, Twining W (eds) Legal fictions in theory and practice. Springer, Heidelberg, pp ix–xxix
Del Mar M (2015b) Legal fiction and legal change in the common law tradition. In: Del Mar M, Twining W (eds) Legal fictions in theory and practice. Springer, Heidelberg, pp 225–254
Del Mar M, Twining W (eds) (2015) Legal fictions in theory and practice. Springer, Heidelberg
Dembski WA (1994) The Fallacy of contextualism. The Princeton Theological Review (also published at http://www.arn.org/docs/dembski/wd_contexism.htm)
Diciotti E (1999) Verità e certezza nell'interpretazione della legge. Giappichelli, Torino
Diciotti E (2003) L'ambigua alternativa tra cognitivismo e scetticismo interpretativo, Siena, Università degli Studi di Siena, Dipartimento di Scienze Storiche, Giuridiche, Politiche e Sociali, Working Paper 45
Diciotti E (2007) Regola di riconoscimento e concezione retorica del diritto. Diritto & Questioni Pubbliche 7:9–42
Diciotti E (2013) Norme espresse e norme inespresse. Sulla teoria dell'interpretazione di Riccardo Guastini. Rivista di filosofia del diritto/J Legal Philos 1:103–123
Diciotti E (2014) Il realismo giuridico e l'interpretazione della legge. Analisi e Diritto:57–71
Domaneschi F (2014) Introduzione alla pragmatica. Carocci, Roma
Dorsey D (2006) A Coherence theory of truth in ethics. Philos Stud 127:493–523
Duarte d'Almeida L, Gardner J, Green L (eds) (2013) Kelsen visited. New essays on the pure theory of law. Hart, Oxford
Dworkin R (1967 [1977]) The model of rules I. In: Dworkin R (ed) Taking rights seriously. Harvard University Press, Cambridge, pp 14–45
Dworkin R (1975 [1977]) Hard cases. In: Dworkin R (ed) Taking rights seriously. Harvard University Press, Cambridge, pp 81–130
Dworkin R (1977) No right answer? In: Hacker PMS, Raz J (eds) Law, morality and society. Essays in honour of H.L.A. Hart. Clarendon Press, Oxford, pp 58–84
Dworkin R (1986) Law's empire. Harvard University Press, Cambridge
Dworkin R (1989) La complétude du droit. In: Amselek P (ed) Controverses autour de l'ontologie du droit. Presses Universitaires de France, Paris, pp 127–135
Dworkin R (2006) Justice in Robes. The Belknap Press of Harvard University Press, Cambridge
Dworkin R (2011) Justice for Hedgehogs. The Belknap Press of Harvard University Press, Cambridge
Dyzenhaus D (2004) The genealogy of legal positivism. Oxf J Legal Stud 24:39–67
Eco U (1979) Lector in Fabula. La cooperazione interpretativa nei testi narrativi. Bompiani, Milano
Eco U (1990) I limiti dell'interpretazione. Bompiani, Milano
Eco U (1992) Interpretation and overinterpretation. Cambridge University Press, Cambridge
Eco U (2012) Dire quasi la stessa cosa. Esperienze di traduzione. Bompiani, Milano
Endicott T (1994) Putting interpretation in its place. Law Philos 13:451–479

Endicott T (2001) Raz sulle lacune: una tesi sorprendente. Ars Interpretandi 6:367–393
Endicott T (2002) Law and language. Stanford Encyclopedia of Philosophy, First published Thu Dec 5, 2002; substantive revision Fri Apr 15, 2016
Eskridge W, Frickey P (1998) Cases and materials on legislation. Statutes and the creation of public policy. West, St. Paul
Feigl H (1949) Logical empiricism. In: Feigl H, Sellars W (eds) Readings in philosophical analysis. Appleton - Century – Crofts, New York
Ferrajoli L (1989) Diritto e ragione. Teoria del garantismo penale. Laterza, Roma-Bari
Ferrajoli L (2012 [2014]) El constitucionalismo entre principios y reglas. In: Ferrajoli L, Ruiz Manero J (eds) Un debate sobre principios constitucionales. Palestra, Lima, pp 173–234
Ferrer Beltrán J, Ratti GB (2008) Validità, defettibilità, e criteri di riconoscimento, unpublished manuscript
Ferrer J, Ratti GB (eds) (2010) El realismo jurídico genovés, Madrid-Barcelona-Buenos Aires, 2011
Filangieri G (1780–1785) La scienza della legislazione. Grimaldi, Napoli, p 2003
Foriers P (1974) Présomptions et fictions. In: Foriers P, Perelman C (eds) Les présomptions et les fictions en droit. Bruylant, Bruxelles, pp 7–26
Frank J (1930) Law and the modern mind. Stevens & Sons, VI Printing, London, p 1949
Frank J (1949a) Courts on trial. Myth and reality in American justice. Princeton University Press, Princeton
Frank J (1949b [1930]) Notes on fictions. In: Frank J (ed) Law and the modern mind, Sixth Printing. Stevens, London, pp 312–322
Fuller LL (1967) Legal fictions. Stanford University Press, Stanford
Fuller LL (1969) The morality of law, Revised edn. Yale University Press, New Haven
Gardner J (1988) Concerning permissive sources and gaps. Oxf J Leg Stud 8(3):457–461
Gardner J (2012) Law as leap of faith. Essays on law in general. Oxford University Press, Oxford
Gianformaggio L (1983 [2008]) Modelli di ragionamento giuridico. Modello deduttivo, modello induttivo, modello retorico. In: Gianformaggio L (ed) Filosofia del diritto e ragionamento giuridico. Giappichelli, Torino, pp 89–107
Golding MP, Edmunson WA (eds) (2005) The Blackwell Guide to the philosophy of law and legal theory. Blackwell, Oxford
Gottlieb G (1968) The logic of choice. An investigation of the concepts of rule and rationality. Allen & Unwin, London
Gray JC (1909) The nature and sources of law. Columbia University Press, New York
Greenberg M (2011) Legislation as communication? Legal interpretation and the study of linguistic communication. In: Marmor A, Soames S (eds) Philosophical foundations of language in the law. Oxford University Press, Oxford, pp 217–256
Grice PH (1967 [1989]) Logic and conversation. In: Grice PH (ed) Studies in the Way of Words. Harvard University Press, Cambridge, pp 22–40
Guastini R (1985) Produzione di norme a mezzo di norme. Informatica e diritto 11:7–31
Guastini R (1992) Dalle fonti alle norme, 2nd edn. Giappichelli, Torino
Guastini R (1995) Interprétation et description de norms. In: Amselek P (ed) Interprétation et Droit. Bruylant, Presses Universitaires D'Aix-Marseille, Bruxelles, pp 89–101
Guastini R (1996) Distinguendo. Studi di teoria e metateoria del diritto. Giappichelli, Torino
Guastini R (1998) Teoria e dogmatica delle fonti. Giuffrè, Milano
Guastini R (2004) L'interpretazione dei documenti normative. Giuffrè, Milano
Guastini R (2006) Il diritto come linguaggio, 2nd edn. Giappichelli, Torino
Guastini R (2008) Nuovi studi sull'interpretazione. Aracne, Roma
Guastini R (2010) Nuevos estudios sobre la interpretación. Externado de Colombia, Bogotá
Guastini R (2011a) Interpretare e argomentare. Giuffrè, Milano
Guastini R (2011b) Rule-Scepticism restated. In: Green L, Leiter B (eds) Oxford studies in philosophy of law. Oxford University Press, Oxford, pp 138–161
Guastini R (2013) Replica. Rivista di filosofia del diritto/J Leg Philos 1:125–136

Guastini R (2015) A realistic view on law and legal cognition. Revus J Const Theory Philos Law 27:45–54
Haas W (1962 [1968]) The theory of translation. In: Parkinson GHR (ed) The theory of meaning. Oxford University Press, Oxford, pp 86–108
Habermas J (1999) Wahrheit und Rechtsfertigung. Sp. tr., Verdad y Justificación. Trotta, Madrid, 2002
Hage J (1997) Reasoning with rules. An essay on legal reasoning and its underlying logic. Kluwer, Dordrecht
Hage J (2003) Law and defeasibility. Artif Intell Law 11(2–3):221–243
Hage J (2004) Law and defeasibility. IVR – Encyclopaedia Jurisprud Leg Theory Philos Law
Hansson B (1969) An analysis of some deontic logics. Nous 3:373–398
Hare RM (1949 [1971]) Imperative sentences. In: Hare RM (ed) Practical inferences. Macmillan, London, pp 1–21
Hare RM (1952) The language of morals. Clarendon Press, Oxford
Hart HLA (1948–1949 [1951]) The ascription of responsibility and rights. In: Flew AGN (ed) Logic and language. First series. Blackwell, Oxford, pp 145–166
Hart HLA (1954 [1983]) Definition and theory in jurisprudence. In: Hart HLA (ed) Essays in jurisprudence and philosophy. Clarendon Press, Oxford, pp 21–48
Hart HLA (1956 [2013]) Discretion. Harv Law Rev 127(2):652–665
Hart HLA (1958a [1983]) Positivism and the separation of law and morals. In: Hart HLA (ed) Essays in jurisprudence and philosophy. Clarendon Press, Oxford, pp 49–87
Hart HLA (1958b [1968]) Legal responsibility and excuses. In: Hart HLA (ed) Punishment and responsibility. Essays in the philosophy of law. Clarendon Press, Oxford, pp 28–53
Hart HLA (1961) The concept of law. Third edition, with a Postscript edited by PA Bulloch and J Raz, And with an introduction and notes by L. Green. Oxford University Press, Oxford, 2013
Hart HLA (1967 [1983]) Problems of the philosophy of law. In: Hart HLA (ed) Essays in jurisprudence and philosophy. Clarendon Press, Oxford, pp 88–119
Hart HLA (1977 [1983]) American jurisprudence through English Eyes: the Nightmare and the Noble Dream. In: Hart HLA (ed) Essays in jurisprudence and philosophy. Clarendon Press, Oxford, pp 123–143
Hart HLA (1983a) Introduction. In: Hart HLA (ed) Essays in jurisprudence and philosophy. Clarendon Press, Oxford, pp 1–18
Hart HLA (1983b) Essays in jurisprudence and philosophy. Clarendon Press, Oxford
Himma KE (2007) Reconsidering a Dogma: conceptual analysis, the naturalistic turn, and legal philosophy. In: Freeman MDA, Harrison R (eds) Law and philosophy. Oxford University Press, Oxford, pp 1–23
Himma KE (2015) Conceptual jurisprudence. An introduction to conceptual analysis and methodology in legal theory. "Revus" 26:65–92
Holmes OW Jr (1897) The path of the law. Harv Law Rev 10:457–478
Hospers J (1967) An introduction to philosophical analysis, Revised edn. Routledge and Kegan Paul, London
Iglesias Vila M (1999) El Problema de la discreción judicial. Una aproximación al conocimiento jurídico. Centro de Estudios Políticos y Constitucionales, Madrid
Jackson F (1998) From metaphysics to ethics: a defence of conceptual analysis. Clarendon Press, Oxford
Jori M (2016) Pragmatica giuridica. Mucchi, Modena
Kahneman D (2011) Thinking, fast and slow. Penguin, London
Kalinowski G (1978) Lógica de las Normas y Lógica Deóntica. Posibilidad y relaciones. Fontamara, México, 2003
Kant I (1787) Kritik der reinen Vernunft (Critique of pure reason) (trans: Guyer P, Wood AW) Cambridge University Press, Cambridge, 1998

Kelsen H (1919 [2015]) On the theory of juridic fictions. With Special Consideration of Vaihinger's Philosophy of As-If. In: Del Mar M, Twining W (eds) Legal fictions in theory and practice. Springer, Heidelberg, pp 3–22
Kelsen H (1934) On the theory of legal interpretation. Legal Stud 10(1990):127–135
Kelsen H (1941 [1957a]) The pure theory of law and analytical jurisprudence. In: Kelsen H (ed) What is justice? Justice, law, and politics in the mirror of science. University of California Press, Berkeley, pp 266–286
Kelsen H (1945) General theory of law and state. Harvard University Press, Cambridge
Kelsen H (1957) What is justice? In: Kelsen H (ed) What is Justice? Justice, law, and politics in the mirror of science. University of California Press, Berkeley, pp 1–25
Kelsen H (1960) Reine Rechtslehre, 2nd edn. Deuticke Wien [eng. tr. The pure theory of law. The University of California Press, Berkeley, and Los Angeles, 1967]
Korta K, Perry J (2015) Pragmatics. In: Zalta EN (ed.) Stanford Encyclopedia of Philosophy, First published Tue Nov 8, 2006; substantive revision Thu Apr 2, 2015
Kosko B (1994) Fuzzy thinking. The new science of fuzzy logic. Flamingo, London
Lacey N (2004) A life of H. L. A. Hart. The nightmare and the noble dream. Oxford University Press, Oxford
Laporta F (2007) El imperio de la ley. Una visión actual. Trotta, Madrid
Larenz K (1979) Methodenlehre der Rechtswissenschaft. Sp. tr. Metodología de la ciencia del derecho. Ariel, Barcelona, 1994
Lecaldano E (1996) Etica. Utet, Torino
Leibniz GW (1667) Nova methodus discendae docendaque jurisprudentiae. It. Tr. Il nuovo metodo di apprendere ed insegnare la giurisprudenza. Giuffrè, Milano, 2012
Leiter B (1995) Legal indeterminacy. Legal Theory 1:481–492
Leiter B (2007) Naturalizing jurisprudence. Essays on American legal realism and naturalism in legal philosophy. Oxford University Press, Oxford
Leiter B (2008) Naturalizing Jurisprudence: Three Approaches. The University of Chicago Law School, Public Law and Legal Theory Working Paper n. 246, http://www.law.uchicago.edu/academics/publiclaw/index.html
Leiter B (2012) Naturalism in Legal Philosophy. Stanford Encyclopedia of Philosophy, https://plato.stanford.edu/entries/lawphil-naturalism/
Leiter B (2013) Legal realisms, old and new. Valparaiso Univ Law Rev 47:949–963
Lieberman D (1989) The province of legislation determined. Legal theory in eighteenth-century Britain. Cambridge University Press, Cambridge
Lifante Vidal I (1989) Dos conceptos de discrecionalidad jurídica. Doxa. Cuadernos de Filosofía del Derecho, 25, Alicante, Departamento de Filosofia del Derecho, pp 181–198
Lifante Vidal I (2018a) Argumentación e interpretación jurídica. Escepticismo, intencionalismo y constructivismo. Tirant lo Blanch, Valencia
Lifante Vidal I (2018b) Representación y responsabilidad. Fontamara, México
Lind D (2015) The pragmatic value of legal fictions. In: Del Mar M, Twining W (eds) Legal fictions in theory and practice. Springer, Heidelberg, pp 83–109
Llewellyn KN (1930) A realistic jurisprudence – the next step. Columbia Law Rev 30:431–467
Llewellyn KN (1931) Some realism about realism – responding to Dean Pound. Harv Law Rev 44:1222–1264
Llewellyn KN (1960) The common law tradition. Deciding appeals. Little, Brown & C, Boston-Toronto
Llewellyn KN (2011) The theory of rules. Edited and with an introduction by F. Schauer. The University of Chicago Press, Chicago
Lucy W (2002) Adjudication. In: Coleman J, Shapiro S (eds) The Oxford handbook of jurisprudence and philosophy of law. Oxford University Press, Oxford, pp 206–267
Lynch MP (2001) A functionalist theory of truth. In: Lynch MP (ed) The nature of truth. Classic and contemporary perspectives. The MIT Press, Boston, pp 723–749
Lynch MP (2009) Truth as one and many. Clarendon Press, Oxford

MacCormick N (1995) Defeasibility in law and logic. In: Bankowski Z, White I, Hahn U (eds) Informatics and the foundations of legal reasoning. Kluwer, Dordrecht, pp 99–117
MacCormick N (2005) Rhetoric and the rule of law. A theory of legal reasoning. Oxford University Press, Oxford
MacCormick N, Bankowski Z (1991) Statutory interpretation in the United Kingdom. In: MacCormick ND, Summers RS (eds) Interpreting statutes. A comparative study. Dartmouth, Aldershot
MacCormick N, Summers RS (eds) (1997) Interpreting Precedents. A comparative study. Ashgate, Aldershot
MacFarlane J (2003) Future contingents and relative truth. Philos Q 53:321–336
Maine HS (1861 [1887]) Ancient law. Its connection with the early history of society, and its relation to modern ideas. Third American-From Fifth London Edition. Holt & C, New York
Makkonen K (1965) Zur Problematik der juridischen Entscheidung. Eine strukturanalytische Studie. Turun Yliopisto, Turku
Marconi D (2007) Per la verità. Relativismo e filosofia. Einaudi, Torino
Marmor A (2005) Interpretation and legal theory, 2nd edn. Hart, Oxford
Marmor A (2008) The pragmatics of legal language. Ratio Juris 21:423–452
Marmor A (2011a) Philosophy of law. Princeton University Press, Princeton
Marmor A (2011b) Truth in law. University of Southern California Law School, Los Angeles, CA 90089-0071, USC Legal Studies Research Paper No. 11-3, 1-28
Marmor A (2012) Farewell to conceptual analysis (in Jurisprudence). University of Southern California Law School, Los Angeles, CA 90089-0071, USC Legal Studies Research Paper No. 12-2, 1-26
Marmor A (2014) The language of law. Oxford University Press, Oxford
Marshall G (1996) Trentatré cose che si possono fare con i precedenti. Un dizionario di common law. Ragion Pratica 6:29–39
Mazzarese T (1998) La interpretación como traducción. Esclarecimientos de una analogía común. Isonomía 9:73–102
McCann M (2016) Preface to the new legal realism volumes I and II. In: Mertz E, Macaulay S, Mitchell TW (eds) The new legal realism. Volume I. Translating law-and-society for today's legal practice. Cambridge University Press, New York, pp xiii–xxi
Mendonca D (2003) Estudio preliminar. In: Mendonca D, Schmill U (eds) Ficciones Jurídicas. Kelsen, Fuller, Ross. Fontamara, México, pp 7–22
Mertz E (2016) Introduction. New legal realism: law and social science in the New Millennium. In: Mertz E, Macaulay S, Mitchell TW (eds) The new legal realism. Volume I. Translating law-and-society for today's legal practice. Cambridge University Press, New York, pp 1–25
Millard E (2008) Positivisme logique et réalisme juridique. Analisi e Diritto:177–189
Moore M (2003) The plain truth about legal truth. Harv J Law Public Policy 26:23–47
Moreso JJ (1997a) La indeterminación del derecho y la interpretación de la Constitución. Centro de Estudios Políticos y Constitucionales, Madrid [Eng. Tr. Legal indeterminacy and constitutional interpretation. Kluwer, Dordrecht, 1998]
Moreso JJ (1997b) Significado, interpretación y proposiciones normativas. Apunte para un debate. Unpublished presentation at the "Jurisprudence Workshop", Dipartimento di Cultura Giuridica "Giovanni Tarello" (Genoa, December 15, 1997)
Moreso JJ (1999) De nuevo sobre la Vigilia. A modo de réplica a mis críticos italianos. Unpublished presentation at the "Jurisprudence Workshop", Dipartimento di Cultura Giuridica "Giovanni Tarello" (Genoa, May 20, 1999)
Moreso JJ, Navarro P, Redondo C (2000 [2002]) Gaps and conclusive reasons. Sp. tr. In: Moreso JJ, Navarro P, Redondo C (eds) Conocimiento jurídico y determinación normative. Fontamara, México
Olivecrona K (1971) Law as fact, 2nd edn. Stevens & Sons, London
Patterson D (1996) Law and truth. Oxford University Press, New York

Peczenik A (1997) The binding force of precedent. In: MacCormick N, Summers RS (eds) Interpreting precedents. A comparative study. Ashgate, Aldershot, pp 461–479
Peczenik A, Wróblewski J (1985) Fuzziness and transformation: towards explaining legal reasoning. Theoria 51:24–44
Pedersen N, Wright CD (2012) Pluralist Theories of Truth. Stanford Encyclopedia of Philosophy, March 5, 2012 (http://plato.stanford.edu/entries/truth-pluralist/)
Pedersen N, Wright CD (2013 [2013b]) Truth, pluralism, monism, correspondence. In: Pedersen N, Wright CD (eds) Truth pluralism: current debates. Oxford University Press, Oxford
Penco C (2002a [2002b]) Le ragioni di una svolta. In: Penco C (ed) La svolta contestuale. McGraw-Hill, Milano, pp xiii–xxxv
Penco C (ed) (2002b) La svolta contestuale. McGraw-Hill, Milano
Penco C, Domaneschi F (eds) (2013) What is said and what is not. The semantics/pragmatics interface. CSLI Publications, Stanford
Perelman Ch (1974 [2012]) Présomptions et fictions en droit. In: Perelman Ch (ed) Ethique et droit. Editions de l'Université de Bruxelles, Bruxelles, pp 717–729
Perelman C (1979) Logique juridique. Dalloz, Paris
Perelman Ch (1982 [2012]) Droit et rhétorique. In: Perelman Ch (ed) Ethique et droit. Editions de l'Université de Bruxelles, Bruxelles, pp 661–667
Perry J (2002a) Contesti. De Ferrari, Genova
Perry J (2002b) Indicali, contesti e costituenti inarticolati. In: Penco (ed) pp 241–252
Pino G (2013) Interpretazione cognitiva, interpretazione decisoria, interpretazione creative. Rivista di filosofia del diritto/J Leg Philos 1:77–101
Pintore A (1996) Il diritto senza verità. Giappichelli, Torino
Poggi F (2011) Law and conversational implicatures. Int J Semiot Law–Revue international de Sémiotique juridique 24(1):21–40
Poggi F (2013) The myth of literal meaning in legal interpretation. Analisi e Diritto 2013:313–335
Poggi F (2016) Grice, the law and the linguistic special case thesis. In: Capone A, Poggi F (eds) Pragmatics and law: philosophical perspectives. Springer, Switzerland, pp 231–248
Postema GJ (1986) Bentham and the common law tradition. Clarendon Press, Oxford
Prakken H, Sartor G (2004) The three faces of defeasibility in law. Ratio Juris 17(1):118–139
Quine WVO (1960) Word and object. The M.I.T. Press, Cambridge
Quine WVO (1969) Ontological relativity and other essays. Columbia University Press, New York
Quine WVO (1975 [1981]) Five milestones of empiricism. In: Quine WV (ed) Theories and things. The Belknap Press of Harvard University Press, Cambridge, pp 67–72
Quine WVO (1978 [1981]) On the nature of moral value. In: Quine WV (ed) Theories and things. The Belknap Press of Harvard University Press, Cambridge, pp 55–66
Quine WVO (1986) Philosophy of logic, 2nd edn. Harvard University Press, Cambridge
Quine WVO (1987) Truth. In: Quine WVO (ed) Quiddities. An intermittent philosophical dictionary. The Belknap Press of Harvard University Press, Cambridge, pp 212–219
Quine WVO (1992) Pursuit of truth, Revised edn. Harvard University Press, Cambridge
Radin R (1930) Statutory interpretation. Harv Law Rev 43:863–885
Raz J (1979 [1979b]) Legal reasons, sources and gaps. In: Raz J (ed) The authority of law. Essays on law and morality. Clarendon Press, Oxford, pp 33–77
Raz J (2009) Between authority and interpretation. On the theory of law and practical reason. Oxford University Press, Oxford
Recanati F (2003) Literalism and contextualism: some varieties, https://jeannicod.ccsd.cnrs.fr/ijn_00000371
Recanati F (2004) Literal meaning. Cambridge University Press, Cambridge
Recanati F (2008) Philosophie du langage (et de l'esprit). Gallimard, Paris
Recanati F (2010) Truth-conditional pragmatics. Clarendon Press, Oxford
Redondo R (1997) Teorías del derecho e indeterminación normativa. Doxa 20:177–196
Rodríguez JL (1997) La derrotabilidad de las normas jurídicas. In Bayón JC, Ródriguez (2003) Relevancia normativa en la justificación de las decisiones judiciales. El debate Bayón-

Rodríguez sobre la derrotabilidad de las normas jurídicas, Gaido P, Sánchez R, Seleme HO (eds) Externado, Bogotá, pp 67–101
Rodríguez JL (2002) Lógica de los sistemas normativos. Centro de Estudios Constitucionales, Madrid
Rodríguez JL, Sucar G (1998 [2003]) Las trampas de la derrotabilidad. Niveles de análisis de la indeterminación del derecho. In: Bayón JC, Ródriguez, Relevancia normativa en la justificación de las decisiones judiciales. El debate Bayón-Rodríguez sobre la derrotabilidad de las normas jurídicas, Gaido P, Sánchez R, Seleme HO (eds) Externado, Bogotá, pp 103–155
Ross A (1946) Towards a realistic jurisprudence. A criticism of the dualism in law. Munksgaard, Copenhagen
Ross A (1958) On law and justice. Stevens & Sons, London
Ross A (1969) Legal fictions. In: Hughes G (ed) Law, reason, and justice. Essays in legal philosophy. New York University Press/University of London Press, New York/London, pp 217–234
Ruiz Manero J (1990) Jurisdicción y normas. Dos estudios sobre función jurisdiccional y teoría del derecho. Centro de Estudios Constitucionales, Madrid
Russell B (1912) The problems of philosophy, 2nd edn. Oxford University Press, Oxford
Russell B (1940) An inquiry into meaning and truth. Allen and Unwin, London
Sartor G (2005) Legal reasoning. A cognitive approach to the law. Springer, Dordrecht
Sartor G (2006) Syllogism and Defeasibility: A Comment on Neil MacCormick's Rhetoric and the Rule of Law, Florence, European University Institute, EUI Working Paper Law No. 2006/23
Scarpelli U (1959) Contributo alla semantica del linguaggio normative. Nuova edizione. Giuffrè, Milano, 1985
Schauer F (1984) Easy cases. South Calif Law Rev 58:399–440
Schauer F (1991a) Playing by the rules. A philosophical examination of rule-based decision-making in law and in life. Clarendon Press, Oxford
Schauer F (1991b) Exceptions. Univ Chicago Law Rev 58:871–899
Schauer F (1998) On the supposed defeasibility of legal rules. Curr Legal Probl 51:223–240
Schauer F (2008) Why precedent in law (and elsewhere) is not totally (or even substantially) about analogy. Perspect Psychol Sci 3:454–460
Schauer F (2009) Thinking like a lawyer. A new introduction to legal reasoning. Harvard University Press, Cambridge
Schauer F (2013) Legal realism untamed. Tex Law Rev 82:749–780
Schauer F (2015) Legal fictions revisited. In: Del Mar M, Twining W (eds) Legal fictions in theory and practice. Springer, Heidelberg, pp 113–131
Schauer F (2018) American legal realism. In: Sellers M, Kirste S (eds) Encyclopedia of the philosophy of law and social philosophy. Springer Science and Business Media B.V
Searle JR (1974–1975 [1979]) The logical status of fictional discourse. In: Searle JR (ed) Expression and meaning. Studies in the theory of speech acts. Cambridge University Press, Cambridge, pp 58–75
Searle JR (1978) Literal meaning. In: Searle JR (1979) Expression and meaning: studies in the theory of speech acts. Cambridge University Press, Cambridge, pp 117–136
Searle JR (1980) The background of meaning. In: Searle JRU, Kiefer F, Bierwish M (eds) Speech acts theory and pragmatics. Reidel, Dordrecht, pp 221–232
Smith Churchland P (2013) Foreword. In: Quine WVO (ed) Word and object, New Edition. The MIT Press, Boston, pp xi–xiv
Soames S (2007) Interpreting legal texts: what is, and what is not, special about the law. Paper presented at "An International Conference on Law, Language, and Interpretation", University of Akureyri, Akureyri, Iceland, April 1–2, 2007
Soames S (2011) Toward a theory of legal interpretation. In: Soames S (ed) Analytic philosophy in America: and other historical and contemporary essays. Princeton University Press, Princeton
Soames S (2014) Deferentialism, living originalism, and the constitution. USC School of Philosophy, Draft June 2014
Soler S (1962) La interpretación de la ley. Ariel, Barcelona

Solum LB (1996 [2010]) Indeterminacy. In: Patterson D (ed) A companion to philosophy of law and legal theory, 2nd edn. Blackwell, Oxford, pp 479–492
Spaak T (2015) Realism about the nature of law. Ratio Juris 30:75–104
Stalnaker R (2014) Context. Oxford University Press, Oxford
Stavropoulos N (1996) Objectivity in law. Oxford University Press, Oxford
Stavropoulos N (2014) Legal Interpretivism. In: Zalta EN (ed.) Stanford Encyclopedia of Philosophy, First published Tue Oct 14, 2003; substantive revision Tue Apr 29, 2014
Strawson PF (1959) Individuals. An essay in descriptive metaphysics. Routledge, London
Strawson PF (1962) Analyse, Science et Métaphysique. In: La philosophie analytique. Les Éditions de Minuit, Paris", pp 105–118
Strawson PF (1985) Analyse et Métaphysique. Vrin, Paris
Sucar G (2008) Concepciones del derecho y de la verdad jurídica. Marcial Pons, Madrid
Sucar G, Cerdio Herrán J (2017) Introducción. Problemas iusfilosóficos contemporáneos en torno a las relaciones entre derecho y verdad. Una cartografía de cuestiones y tentativas de solución. In: Sucar G, Cerdio Herrán J (eds) (2017b) Derecho y Verdad IV. Problemas. Tirant lo Blanch, Valencia, pp 9–594
Summers RS (1991) Statutory interpretation in the United States. In: MacCormick ND, Summers RS (eds) Interpreting statutes. A comparative study. Dartmouth, Aldershot
Tarello G (1962) Il realismo giuridico Americano. Giuffrè, Milano
Tarello G (1968 [1974]) La semantica del neustico. Osservazioni sulla «parte descrittiva» degli enunciati precettivi. In: Tarello G (ed) Diritto, enunciati, usi. Studi di teoria e metateoria del diritto. Il Mulino, Bologna, pp 329–361
Tarello G (1976) Storia della cultura giuridica moderna. I. Assolutismo e codificazione del diritto. Il Mulino, Bologna
Tarello G (1980) L'interpretazione della legge. Giuffrè, Milano
Tarski A (1944 [2001]) The semantic conception of truth and the foundations of semantics. In: Lynch MP (ed) The nature of truth. Classic and contemporary perspectives. The MIT Press, Boston, pp 332–363
Tarski A (1969) Truth and proof. Scientific American, June, 63–77
Troper M (2001 [2011b]) Une théorie réaliste de l'interprétation. In: Troper M (ed) La théorie du droit, le droit, l'état. Presses Universitaires de France, Paris, pp 69–84
Troper M (2003) La philosophie du droit. Presses Universitaires de France, Paris
Tur RHS (2001) Defeasibilism. Oxf J Leg Stud 21(2):355–368
Tuzet G (2011) Una teoria coerentista delle finzioni. Ragion Pratica 37:529–551
Tuzet G (2015) Finzioni. In: Ricciardi M, Rossetti A, Velluzzi V (eds) Filosofia del diritto. Norme, concetti, argomenti. Carocci, Roma, pp 269–284
Twining W (1985) Karl Llewellyn and the Realist Movement. Reprinted with Postscript. Weidenfeld and Nicolson, London
Urmsom JO (1962 [1992]) The history of philosophical analysis. In: Rorty RM (ed) The linguistic turn. Essays on philosophical method. With two retrospective essays. The University of Chicago Press, Chicago, pp 294–301
Varzi A (2005) Ontologia. Laterza, Roma-Bari
Vassallo N (2002) Conoscenza e natura. De Ferrari, Genova
Velluzzi V (ed) (2000) Significato letterale e interpretazione del diritto. Giappichelli, Torino
Velluzzi V (2013a) Introduzione. Rivista di filosofia del diritto/J Legal Philos 1:73–76
Velluzzi V (ed) (2013b) Interpretazione e costruzione del diritto. Riflessioni su Interpretare e argomentare di Riccardo Guastini. Rivista di filosofia del diritto/J Legal Philos 1:73–136
Villa V (2012) Una teoria pragmaticamente orientata dell'interpretazione giuridica. Giappichelli, Torino
von Wright GH (1951) A treatise on induction and probability. Routledge and Kegan Paul, London
von Wright GH (1963) Norm and action: a logical enquiry. Routledge & Kegan Paul, London
von Wright GH (1984a) Truth, knowledge, and modality. Philosophical Papers Vol III. Blackwell, Oxford

von Wright GH (1984b) Determinism and future truth. In: von Wright GH (ed) Truth, knowledge, and modality. Philosophical Papers Vol III. Blackwell, Oxford, pp 1–13
Waismann F (1951) Verifiability. In: Flew AGN (ed) Logic and language. First Series. Blackwell, Oxford, pp 117–144
Waldron J (1999a) Law and disagreement. Oxford University Press, Oxford
Waldron J (1999b) The dignity of legislation. Cambridge University Press, Cambridge
Wilson D, Sperber D (2012a) Meaning and relevance. Cambridge University Press, Cambridge
Wilson D, Sperber D (2012b [2012a]) Introduction: pragmatics. In: Wilson D, Sperber D (eds) Meaning and relevance. Cambridge University Press, Cambridge, pp 1–27
Wilson D, Sperber D (2012c [2012a]) Mood and the analysis of non-declarative sentences. In: Wilson D, Sperber D (eds) Meaning and relevance. Cambridge University Press, Cambridge, pp 210–229
Wilson D, Sperber D (2012d [2012a]) Explaining irony. In: Wilson D, Sperber D (eds) Meaning and relevance. Cambridge University Press, Cambridge, pp 123–145
Wintgens LJ (ed) (2002) Legisprudence: a new theoretical approach to legislation. Proceedings of the fourth Benelux-Scandinavian symposium on legal theory. Hart, Portland and Oxford
Wintgens LJ (2006) Legisprudence as a new theory of legislation. Ratio Juris 19(1):1–25
Wintgens LJ (2012) Legisprudence: practical reason in legislation. Ashgate, Aldershot
Wittgenstein L (1953 [1958]) Philosophical investigations, 2nd edn. Blackwell, Oxford
Wittgenstein L (1958) Preliminary studies for the "philosophical investigations" generally known as the blue and brown books. Harper Torchbooks, New York
Wright C (2001) Minimalism, deflationism, pragmatism, pluralism. In: Lynch MP (ed) The nature of truth. Classic and contemporary perspectives. The MIT Press, Boston, pp 751–787
Wright C (2013) A pluralism of pluralisms. In: Pedersen NJLL, Wright CD (eds) Truth pluralism: current debates. Oxford University Press, Oxford. Chap. 7
Wróblewski J (1969) Legal reasoning in legal interpretation. Logique et analyse 14:409–419
Wróblewski J (1971) Legal decision and its justification. Logique et analyse 12:2–31
Wróblewski J (1983) Fuzziness of legal system. In: Kangas U (ed) Essays in legal theory in honor of Kaarle Makkonen. Oikeustiede, 16:311–330
Wróblewski J (1985) Constitución y teoría general de la interpretación jurídica. Civitas, Madrid
Wróblewski J (1992) In: Bankowski Z, MacCormick N (eds) The judicial application of law. Kluwer, Dordrecht
Young JO (2008) The coherence theory of truth. In: Stanford Encyclopedia of Philosophy. September 9, 2008 (http://plato.stanford.edu/entries/truth-coherence/)

MIX
Papier aus verantwortungsvollen Quellen
Paper from responsible sources
FSC® C105338

If you have any concerns about our products,
you can contact us on
ProductSafety@springernature.com

In case Publisher is established outside the EU,
the EU authorized representative is:
Springer Nature Customer Service Center GmbH
Europaplatz 3, 69115 Heidelberg, Germany

Printed by Libri Plureos GmbH
in Hamburg, Germany